The National Kitchen & Bath Association

Kitchen Basics

A Training Primer for Kitchen Specialists

By Patrick J. Galvin
with Ellen Cheever, CKD, CBD, ASID

*The creation of this industry resource was made possible by a grant from
The Center for Kitchen & Bathroom Education & Research through special funding
provided by Wilsonart International, manufacturers of WILSONART® Brand
laminates and Gibraltar solid surfacing materials.*

• Information about this book and other Association programs and publications may be obtained from the National Kitchen and Bath Association, 687 Willow Grove Street, Hackettstown NJ 07840, Phone (908) 852-0033, Fax (908) 852-1695. Contact NKBA by e-mail at: educate@nkba.org, or visit web site at www.nkba.org.

• ISBN Number 1-887127-13-5.

• Director of Education and Product Development, Nick Geragi, CKD, CBD.

• This book was produced by:
Galvin Publications
118 Bennington Dr.
E. Windsor NJ 08520

• Illustrations by Annette DePaepe, CKD, CBD, ASID.

• Fourth Edition graphic illustrations by Design Services Unlimited, Syracuse NY 13206.

• Cover kitchen designed by Alan Asarnow, CKD, CBD, Ulrich, Inc.

• Photo by Maura McEvoy.

Acknowledgements

The following companies have participated in the production of NKBA's KITCHEN BASICS Manual.

Amana Refrigeration, Inc.
American Standard, Inc.
Aristokraft, Inc.
Dupont Corian
Elkay Manufacturing Co.
Eljer Plumbingware
Formica Corporation
GE Appliances
Heritage Custom Kitchens, Inc.
Jenn-Air Company
KitchenAid, Inc.
Kohler Company
KraftMaid Cabinetry, Inc.
KWC Faucets
Maytag Company
Merillat Industries, Inc.
Nevamar Corporation
Quaker Maid/WCI Cabinet, Inc.
Rutt Custom Kitchens
St. Charles Companies
Whirlpool Corporation
WILSONART
Wood-Mode Cabinetry

Kitchen Basics

A Training Primer for Kitchen Specialists

Contents

1 Welcome to the Kitchen Industry
—This is What It's All About; an Overview

When anyone thinks of the movie business the connotation is glamor and big money. We visualize millions of people lining up to pay $8 or more to buy tickets to the newest or biggest attraction. In a typical year consumers will spend about $7 billion going to the movies.

The kitchen industry is bigger.

That's right. Consumers will spend $27 billion on kitchen remodeling in a good year. Add a million-plus kitchens in new house construction and you get an idea of the wide horizons of your chosen industry.

It is a large industry, and it also is complicated. The function of other rooms in a house are defined by the room's furnishings, and those furnishings can be moved at will. Thus a living room can be changed to a dining room at any time, or a den to a home office, simply by moving the furnishings. The kitchen differs in that it must be both designed and installed. It is permanent, with permanent plumbing and wiring that must be fitted to it precisely.

Remodeling a kitchen, therefore, demands special entry-level training for the designer/salesperson who must combine many skills and several trades to merge the needs and budget of a client with the products and capabilities of the employer and the physical limitations of the space available.

This manual and the school that goes with it have been developed by the National Kitchen & Bath Association to provide that training.

Fig. 1.1. The kitchen industry is vast, with an ever-widening range of products to furnish a room that serves multiple purposes.

What you will learn

This manual will present basic information to enable the student to begin working as a designer/salesperson in any of the various forms of retailing in the industry, or in the sales force of a cabinet distributor or manufacturer. The training will include:

- How to sell, plan and design kitchens;
- Layout techniques;
- Lighting, venting, plumbing, electrical and construction basics;
- Cabinets and countertops, what they're made of, how and where to use them;
- Appliances, fixtures and fittings, types and design factors;
- How to control the job and relate to the customer as a true professional.

Cabinets lead the product parade

Cabinets are the most important product to the kitchen specialist for two reasons:

1. Because of sheer mass they set the style and dominant color of the room.

2. Because they come in many sizes or are made to order, they provide the flexibility that enables the designer to fit a kitchen to customer needs and to room space.

Basically, there are three types of cabinet manufacturer: Custom, stock, and specialty. A combination of stock cabinets with some custom features is known as semi-custom.

The *custom* cabinet manufacturer makes cabinets in a factory, but the cabinets are not made until a specialist has designed and sold a kitchen. Thus the cabinets are made to fit the design. These usually are sold to independent or factory kitchen specialists who in turn sell to the public. In many cases they also are sold to home builders for upscale new homes, either direct or through the same dealer network.

The *stock* cabinet manufacturer makes cabinets in preset sizes and styles, in quantity, to be stocked in manufacturer or distributor warehouses. Stock cabinets are sold mainly to distributors and to builders. Distributors sell to

Fig. 1.2. Stock and custom cabinet manufacturers produce in similar plants, but the choices differ.

builders, to kitchen specialists and also to other outlets that sell cabinets, such as building supply stores and lumber yards. Often a home center chain will buy in sufficient quantity to qualify as a distributor, and will buy stock cabinets direct from the manufacturer. Home centers sometimes have separate, identifiable kitchen departments with separate designer/salespersons, and in such cases they also may handle custom cabinets.

Specialty cabinet manufacturers are those that set up to supply specific housing tracts where hundreds of houses might have only three or four kitchen floorplans, and make cabinets only to fit those floorplans. For example, the specialty manufacturer might make 100 identical single cabinets to fit a wall 96" (244 cm) wide that would be the same in 100 houses. A similar wall with stock or custom cabinets would have combinations of cabinets in different sizes.

Semi-custom cabinets are stock cabinets, basically, but many have added options in sizes, wood species and interior fittings or accessories. Semi-custom might be offered by either stock or custom manufacturers.

Stock and custom cabinets are made in the same 3" (7.6 cm) modules in similar plants with similar machinery. Custom offers many more choices, special shapes, special sizes and, usually, better joinery and finishes.

Some cabinet manufacturers also make countertops. Some started as manufacturers of tops surfaced with high-pressure decorative laminate and expanded into laminate-surfaced cabinets because they use the same materials and the same specialized machinery. The advent of prelaminated melamine board led many others into laminated cabinets.

(For more on cabinets, see Appendix B)

Countertop methods and materials

Kitchen counter surfaces might be decorative high-pressure laminate (HPL), or ceramic tile, or a man-made solid material, or marble or granite. Other materials such as solid wood, stainless steel or tempered glass often are used as counter inserts to provide specialized work space (mixing, cutting, chopping) or landing space on a counter for hot pots off the cooktop. HPL is the standard. All of the others are upgrades.

HPL tops usually are made to order by a local "plastic fabricator." They also are available from various outlets as "blanks." Blanks are straight sections 4', 6', 8', 10' or 12' long, (122 cm, 183 cm, 244 cm, 305 cm or 366 cm, respectively) with 4" (10 cm) or 5" (13 cm) backsplash. Blanks will be postformed or self-edged. A postformed top uses a single sheet of melamine laminate 1/16" (1.6 mm) thick that is formed over a substrate, from the bottom of the front apron up over the front edge, back and then up over the backsplash and back to meet the wall. A self-edged top (also known as square-edge) has separate strips of matching laminate applied to the edges. Most HPL top are joined with precision miters in corners.

A postformed top, being all one piece, makes a smoother, cleaner surface with no joints to catch food particles or other soil. But it cannot be curved because the material, already curved once in the forming, is not capable of compound curves. Self-edged tops have no such limitation, so designers often prefer them for islands and peninsulas or other effects.

(For more on HPL tops, see Appendix C.)

Tops of ceramic tile or a solid surface material often require the services of another contractor. The kitchen specialist might *design* a tile counter (or backsplash or wall), but setting tile is a skilled trade. And it takes special training to shape, cut and handle solid surfaces. *(See Appendix C.)*

Appliances, fittings and fixtures

The other elements that go into kitchen planning and design are the major appliances and the sink and its accessories. While cabinets and tops usually dominate a kitchen visually, their function is to support work centers that are designed around major appliances and the sink, as will be detailed in Chapter 3.

Appliances can be built in or free standing. Free-standing appliances generally are lower priced, although full-featured deluxe models are also available. Built-ins are sized to fit flush with kitchen cabinets and, with decorator panels, the dishwasher, compactor and refrigerator can blend into the design, matching or harmonizing with cabinets, tops or other surfaces.

Notes

Built-ins generally are preferred by kitchen professionals because the design can be better integrated and can be more flexible. An example of bad design integration might be a free-standing refrigerator which, being large, can stand out as a design monstrosity. Even when partially integrated with decorator panels, it will protrude as much as 7" (18 cm) beyond the base cabinets. Built-in models, however, are 24" (61 cm) deep to match the depth of standard base cabinets, so they can be truly integrated.

An example of design flexibility can be the built-in cooktop and built-in oven. A cooktop recesses into the countertop and a built-in oven, which nowadays might be seldom used, can be in another wall outside of the work triangle (see Chapter 3), freeing space within the busy work area for needed cabinetry.

A built-in dishwasher is another appliance preferred by professionals. A free-standing (or portable) dishwasher is a continuing problem because it always has to be put somewhere, then wheeled out for use. Building it in under the counter at or near the sink is always preferable. Even when the customer can't or won't buy a built-in dishwasher designers try to place a 24" (61 cm) base cabinet adjacent to the sink cabinet for future dishwasher installation.

Of the major appliances, a trash compactor might be an exception to the built-in preference. It might make sense to locate a free-standing compactor in a utility room or on the route to the trash area outside, especially when kitchen space is limited. Trash separation and collection for recycling has become an important factor, and it demands both space and a fresh approach by the kitchen designer. (More on that in Chapter 3.)

Kitchen fixtures include the sink, faucet, disposer, possibly a water purification unit and whatever accessories there might be, such as a pull-out hose spray or a unit for instant hot water.

(For more on kitchen appliances, fixtures and fittings, see Appendix A.)

How and where kitchens are sold

There are three major marketplaces where kitchens are sold: Remodeling, new home construction, and replacement.

Fig. 1.3. Kitchen distributors serve home builders and home centers. They often act also as factory reps.

New home construction normally is served by kitchen distributors who keep several lines of stock and semi-custom cabinets in their warehouses for builders. Kitchen distributors often will also serve as independent factory representatives for custom cabinet producers. As reps they will act as liaison between a custom manufacturer and both home builders and kitchen specialists in the area.

Kitchen dealers also serve home builders who plan on featuring custom cabinetry in their upscale homes.

Both kitchen distributors and kitchen dealers often set up fine showrooms and offer a professional design service for their builder customers.

The **replacement** market is entirely different from the other two markets in that it seldom includes design. Homeowners or builders buy appliances or cabinets to replace what has worn out or grown old, and price usually is the main consideration. While design is seldom involved, good salesmanship is important to the kitchen specialist who is involved in the replacement business.

This replacement sector also includes **cabinet resurfacing** which often is offered as a service by a kitchen specialist firm. Resurfacing, which sometimes includes purchase of new doors and drawer fronts, is an acceptable way to get a new look in a kitchen, although it might preserve an inadequate design.

The largest market by far is **kitchen remodeling**. It is served in various ways.

A considerable amount of remodeling is by do-it-yourselfers who might really do it themselves or might simply buy and then hire the work out. These customers buy cabinets at home centers, building supply stores or similar outlets which might offer stock cabinets, countertop blanks and a "cutting station" which will cut mitered corners, make sink cutouts and otherwise work the tops. These sales are over-the-counter, with little planning or design involved.

In many cases, however, these outlets will set up separate, identifiable kitchen departments with separate trained personnel, and in such cases they may offer both stock and custom cabinets and a professional design service. At this point they become true kitchen specialists.

Homeowners, interior designers and contractors who want professional planning and design in a new kitchen will go to the showroom headquarters of a kitchen specialist, preferably one who is a member of the National Kitchen & Bath Assn. and with Certified Kitchen Designers (CKDs) on staff. This is where most kitchen remodeling jobs are sold, and **it is at this point that the shopper for a new kitchen stops being a "customer" and becomes a "client."**

Professional planning and design services also can be available from independent designers and architects **if** they have expended the time and effort to qualify as kitchen specialists. It is, after all, a specialized field, and professionalism in it requires specialized knowledge of kitchen products, materials and techniques. Some design or architectural firms set up special kitchen departments where the level of advanced training is maintained.

Fig. 1.4a. Retail home centers are major sources of supply for do-it-yourself kitchen remodeling.

Fig. 1.4b. High-end remodeling normally is done by professionals at a kitchen specialist's dealership.

Fig. 1.4c. The independent kitchen designer is a growing factor in design and product specification. Such designers do not have showrooms, but might take clients around to visit showrooms of other specialists.

Notes:

2 The Process of Selling Kitchens
Methods Vary by Type of Business

Selling a kitchen is far different from other kinds of home improvements.

Compare the selling styles.

Even the good, solid home improvement firms operate on the principle that speed pays. Find the customers fast, do the jobs fast, get rid of the customers fast and move on to the next jobs fast. And there is nothing intrinsically bad about that. Roofing, siding and insulation can be done well on that basis when the mechanics are well trained and the firms are responsible. In the kitchen industry, cabinet resurfacing can be done on that basis and, in fact, when a kitchen specialist firm adds cabinet resurfacing it is a good idea to set it up as a separate profit center and operate it that way. The keys are good training and responsibility.

When a professional sells a kitchen the selling procedure is diametrically opposed to that emphasis on speed. Rather than trying to serve and get rid of the customer quickly, the designer-salesperson must take time to work with the homeowner to identify and solve problems. A typical kitchen sale goes through these steps:

1. First contact with the prospect should be in the showroom (except, possibly, for an inquiring phone call). Here the prospect is greeted and "qualified" to determine whether he or she is really interested in buying or is simply in the shopping stage.

Fig. 2.1. Demonstration in the showroom helps sell prospect on the firm and on designer's expertise.

2. The selling job starts immediately if interest is shown. It is important here to sell the prospect on both the designer's expertise and on the the firm itself. The vehicle for this message is in demonstrating products and ideas in the showroom. (Fig. 2.1.)

3. The concept of a retainer (if used) is introduced. An appointment is made for a visit to the home with all concerned parties present, to identify needs and measure the space.

Fig. 2.2. Measuring the space is an important part of the visit to the home. Family members should be interviewed, a survey form should be filled in and retainer fee (if applicable) should be collected.

4. The designer visits the home, interviews the customer, fills in a Survey Form (see Appendix E), measures the space (Fig. 2.2) and looks for special conditions in the walls, floors or elsewhere that might affect installation. The retainer is collected now if not already in hand.

5. A kitchen design is prepared with floorplan, interpretive drawings and any other art that might be needed to show design features (Fig. 2.3). It is priced out and another meeting is scheduled with the customer in the showroom. Many firms now use computers for this artwork

Fig. 2.3. Back in the office, drawings are executed to show features of the kitchen design.

Fig. 2.4. In many kitchen departments, both plans and pricing now are done by computer.

(Fig. 2.4) which execute the drawings and the pricing. Most computer programs are able to draw floorplans and elevations almost instantly, and some will also do perspectives.

6. **Presentation** is made to the customer in the showroom, including appropriate samples and literature. (Fig. 2.5.)

7. **Contract is signed** now if it is an ideal situation, although sometimes the plan must be revised and further meetings are needed. Initial payment is collected. (Fig. 2.6.)

Even now the professional kitchen designer is not finished. Any or all of the following steps might be required (see Figs. 2.8-2.15):
• Cabinets must be ordered along with proper hardware, moldings and accessories.
• Subcontracts must be arranged.
• The entire project must be planned for proper scheduling of various trades for rough-in and finish work. Subcontractors and the home-owner must be kept apprised of this scheduling.
• Installers must be taken to the jobsite and introduced to the homeowner.
• A pre-installation conference must be set where control forms must be initiated that will follow the project to completion.
• The second payment must be collected on delivery of cabinets or on installation.
• Job progress must be checked periodically and in person.
• The job must be checked with the customer on completion, preferably with installers present for minor corrective work, and final payment must be collected.

Fig. 2.5. Kitchen plan is presented to consumer in the showroom or office, with appropriate samples.

Fig. 2.6. Signing of the contract in the office is the culmination of the process, but it is only a midpoint in the responsibilities of most kitchen professionals.

Fig. 2.7. The NKBA Survey Form provides a basis for the home interview. It provides information about home occupants, eating and social habits, customer desires and construction data. This is cover page. For entire Survey Form, see Appendix E.

Fig. 2.8. All non-stock cabinets and other equipment are ordered promptly after the contract is signed.

Fig. 2.9. The preinstallation conference is of critical importance to success of the project. Its purpose is a smoothly-running job for client satisfaction and profit for the firm.

There are many ways to assure client satisfaction and thus create referral business. One is use of a Job Completion List.

This is a list the designer makes on the last day of installation, walking through the project with the customer to note any minor flaws such as finish scratches, sticky drawers, misaligned cabinet doors or hardware, etc. With installers still present any of these can be corrected easily and on the spot. This leaves no reason at all for the client to resist the final payment (Fig. 2.15).

If there is any problem it must be faced here. There often is a tendency to gloss over a problem, sweep it under the rug or pretend it doesn't exist.

Ron Willingham deals with this in a 2-tape presentation on "The Customer" which is synopsized on the facing page. Willingham's is a simple common-sense formula which requires only that you face up to it and deal with it. Then it can be solved.

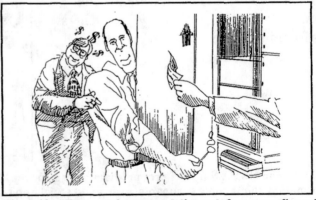

Fig. 2.10. When cabinets are delivered, for many firms it is the time for collecting second payment.

Fig. 2.11. Installation normally takes about a week, and during this time there should be frequent progress checks.

Fig. 2.12. Designer sometimes collects second payment during installation.

Fig. 2.13. Clean-up is an important part of the job, and it should be provided for in the contract.

Fig. 2.14. Make a Completion List of minor flaws to be corrected while the installers are still on the job.

Fig. 2.15. Customer satisfaction is the key to happy collection of the final payment when job is done.

PROBLEM-SOLVING FORMULA
1. Understand the problem.
    a. Get all the facts.
    b. Listen nondefensively.
    c. Repeat back problem as understood.
2. Identify the cause.
    a. What has happened?
    b. What should have happened?
    c. What went wrong?
3. Discuss possible solutions.
    a. Suggest options.
    b. Ask for customer's ideas.
    c. Agree on best course of action.
4. Solve the problem.
    a. Remove the cause, or
    2. Take corrective action.
    c. Ask if customer is satisfied with resolution.

Sales Procedure Variations

Limited service kitchen design firms and home center kitchen departments vary widely in the way they conduct business.. They often will stop their involvement when the contract is signed and then might suggest or recommend other firms to the customer for installation.

Usually the first visit to such a firm results in a kitchen plan, price estimate and a signed order. A visit to the home follows to check measurements. Or the order might be signed in the visit to the home. There might be a third meeting, back at the showroom, to finalize details.

Rule No. 1 here is to know company policy and to follow it. Beyond that:

1. In the design phase, talk to the customer enough to identify needs.

2. Fulfill those needs to the extent your firm's products and the customer's budget will allow.

3. You probably will be working with measurements supplied by the customer. Don't commit to anything until space has been confirmed.

4. Be helpful. Remember, you represent your store and you are the guardian of its reputation.

Full service firms handle all aspects of the project and supply or specify all products to be used.

They may "general" the job, arranging for and supervising installation to ensure customer satisfaction. This follow-up activity is the essence of professionalism, and it is the designer's responsibility to take whatever advanced training that might be needed to do the job right.

The procedure:

1. Visits to the home, as needed.

2. Measurement verification by the designer or a qualified contractor.

3. Physical inspection of kitchen equipment and materials.

4. Supervision of the complete job.

Independent designers often will not have a showroom, so their procedure will consist of a visit to the prospect's home, then one or more visits to showrooms of others to show different cabinet brands and materials. Other meetings are held as needed in the designer's office or client's home.

Notes--How My Firm Operates:

How to plan a kitchen project

The terms "kitchen plan" and "kitchen design" often are used synonymously. But we have to distinguish between planning a kitchen project and designing a kitchen. We'll discuss designing a kitchen in Chapter 3 and laying out a kitchen in Chapter 4, but now let's go into the procedures of planning.

The project might be in a new house which has no existing kitchen, or in a kitchen to be remodeled.

In any case, the first job will be to **measure the space,** always in inches (or centimeters), never in mixtures of feet and inches. No matter how many blueprints or drawings you have, the corners will not be perfectly square and you can not count on the dimensions you see on paper. Remember, if the cabinet run you order is only a quarter-inch (6.3 mm) too long between two walls, it will not fit. Even if the countertop you order is exactly the same size as the space, you won't be able to get it in.

Your **measuring tools** will include:

• A good rule. Specialists usually prefer a 25' (762 cm) metal tape with a 1" (2.5 cm) blade. Some prefer a folding carpenter's rule because of its rigidity. If you use a metal tape it should be stiff and you must be careful to keep it straight.

• A sketch pad with graph paper in 1/4" (6.3 mm) scale, triangle/template to use as a straight edge if you like straight lines, and a pencil with eraser to sketch the room.

First, draw a rough sketch of the room as seen from above. It doesn't have to be to scale. Draw all walls, even if you think your kitchen will use only one or two walls, because you can't be sure at this point that the prospective design won't change and you don't want to have to come back.

When you have drawn the overall room outline, use the proper symbol to draw in the window locations. Draw in the doors, using proper door symbols.

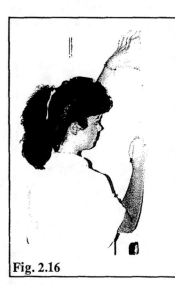

Fig. 2.16

Fig. 2.17

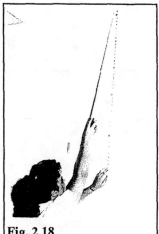

Fig. 2.18

Fig. 2.16. Measuring floor to ceiling is difficult. Many prefer to mark a midpoint on the wall, measure from the ceiling down to the mark, then from the mark to the floor. Fig. 2.17, below left, others go from the ceiling down, pushing the tape down with the knee while holding it flat against the wall. Fig. 2.18, below right, others push the tape up from floor to ceiling.

Start measuring in a corner and proceed around the room at 36" (91 cm) above the floor, which is the countertop elevation.

Measure all elements, such as windows and doors and any obstructions.

Measure to window trim, width of trim, window width and the entire window including trim. Do the same with doors. Then measure the entire wall and make sure this figure is the same as the total of all smaller elements. Trim size can be important because you might have to cut into it or change it to a narrower width. Measure to center line of water supply and gas line, and 220V power lines.

Measure vertically from floor to the bottom of the window stool, from the top of the stool to the top of trim, from top of trim to ceiling, and check the total against the floor-to-ceiling figure.

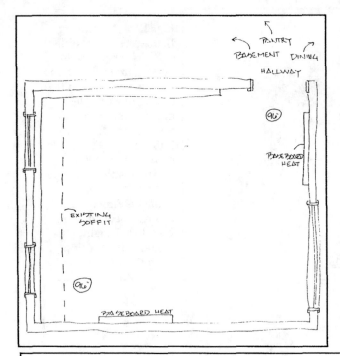

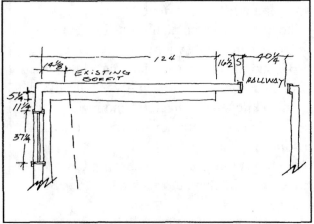

Fig. 2.19. (Left) Start the measuring process by drawing the room outline as closely as possible, using the correct symbols for doors and windows. At this point you will not have any dimensions.

Fig. 2.20. (Above) Next step is to start measuring available wall spaces where you can put cabinets or other equipment.

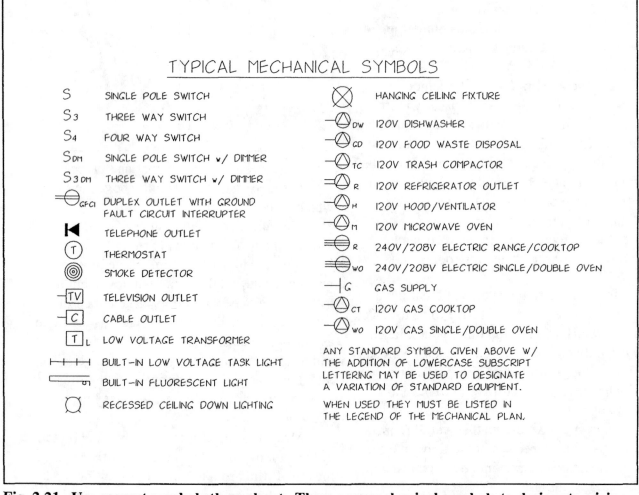

TYPICAL MECHANICAL SYMBOLS

S	SINGLE POLE SWITCH
S_3	THREE WAY SWITCH
S_4	FOUR WAY SWITCH
S_{DM}	SINGLE POLE SWITCH w/ DIMMER
S_{3DM}	THREE WAY SWITCH w/ DIMMER
GFCI	DUPLEX OUTLET WITH GROUND FAULT CIRCUIT INTERRUPTER
	TELEPHONE OUTLET
T	THERMOSTAT
	SMOKE DETECTOR
TV	TELEVISION OUTLET
C	CABLE OUTLET
T_L	LOW VOLTAGE TRANSFORMER
	BUILT-IN LOW VOLTAGE TASK LIGHT
	BUILT-IN FLUORESCENT LIGHT
	RECESSED CEILING DOWN LIGHTING

	HANGING CEILING FIXTURE
DW	120V DISHWASHER
GD	120V FOOD WASTE DISPOSAL
TC	120V TRASH COMPACTOR
R	120V REFRIGERATOR OUTLET
H	120V HOOD/VENTILATOR
M	120V MICROWAVE OVEN
R	240V/208V ELECTRIC RANGE/COOKTOP
WO	240V/208V ELECTRIC SINGLE/DOUBLE OVEN
G	GAS SUPPLY
CT	120V GAS COOKTOP
WO	120V GAS SINGLE/DOUBLE OVEN

ANY STANDARD SYMBOL GIVEN ABOVE W/ THE ADDITION OF LOWERCASE SUBSCRIPT LETTERING MAY BE USED TO DESIGNATE A VARIATION OF STANDARD EQUIPMENT.

WHEN USED THEY MUST BE LISTED IN THE LEGEND OF THE MECHANICAL PLAN.

Fig. 2.21. Use correct symbols throughout. These are mechanical symbols to designate wiring.

Next, label where all the doors go to and inspect each of the adjacent spaces. If a door leads to a utility room, add those walls to your sketch. You must know all of the relationships of adjacent rooms, and if there will be structural changes in the new kitchen you will have to know dimensions of adjacent rooms. Label your sketch to show the direction of north.

On the sketch include plumbing and all electrical outlets.

It seldom happens this way, but in **new construction** the walls should be finished before you measure. The builder's interior trim people can alter dimensions just by the way they install sheetrock. But when you must measure before the interior is finished, measure actual frame dimensions and find out from the builder what the wall and window materials will be. Allow for the thickness, then allow a little extra . You can do this with as little as 1 1/2" (4 cm) of filler or scribes in the cabinet layout.

When construction is incomplete, you should consult with the builder where you see ways to improve economy of space. For example, a builder might not be alert to the fact that locating a door 20" (51 cm) from a wall can deny a run of base cabinets. Base cabinets are 24" (61 cm) deep, the standard counter is 25" (64 cm) deep. In the construction stage it might be easy for the builder to move the door framing a few inches farther from the wall to gain a better kitchen and, quite possibly, a less expensive kitchen. Similarly, to allow a run of wall cabinets, a door would have to be at least 15" (38 cm) from the adjacent wall to allow for depth of cabinets, 12" (31 cm) plus door trim of 3" (8 cm), or whatever the trim width might be.

In a **remodeling** project you never know what is behind the walls that will affect either design or installation or both. Inspect the kitchen itself and check the other sides of the walls. Go to the basement and look for where water, electric and gas supplies go up to the kitchen. All drain piping must be within specific distances from vents (see Chapter 6). If you can't determine vent locations from the basement, go outside and look for small pipes emerging from the roof. Mark all of these locations on your sketch.

From the basement you also might detect other signs of trouble. There might, for example, be an old chimney that has been walled up, or there might be old ductwork in the walls. You might even find old plumbing or electrical services that were abandoned in a previous remodeling and that can be used again.

Also, check thickness of the existing floor and and compare this against the planned flooring material. A 3/4" (19 mm) wood floor or 1/2"-1 1/2" (13-38 mm) tile floor can affect your floor-to-ceiling measurement.

Any of these might affect your new kitchen design and certainly will affect installation costs.

If you are not responsible for field measurement you must make sure that your customer brings you all of this information. Many firms have well-designed how-to-measure brochures for consumers. Stress the need for accuracy and remind the customer to record all dimensions in inches (or centimeters). When a customer brings a plan in, don't start creating a solution until you have verified the dimensions.

NOTE--Page 12 of the NKBA Survey Form (next page) will help in your measuring. The complete Survey appears in Appendix E.)

Fig. 2.22. This is Page 12 from the Survey Form you take with you when you interview the client and measure the space. It shows the dimensions you should take for doors, windows and other obstructions in the room, and how to take them. Follow the same principles if you encounter chimneys, offsets.

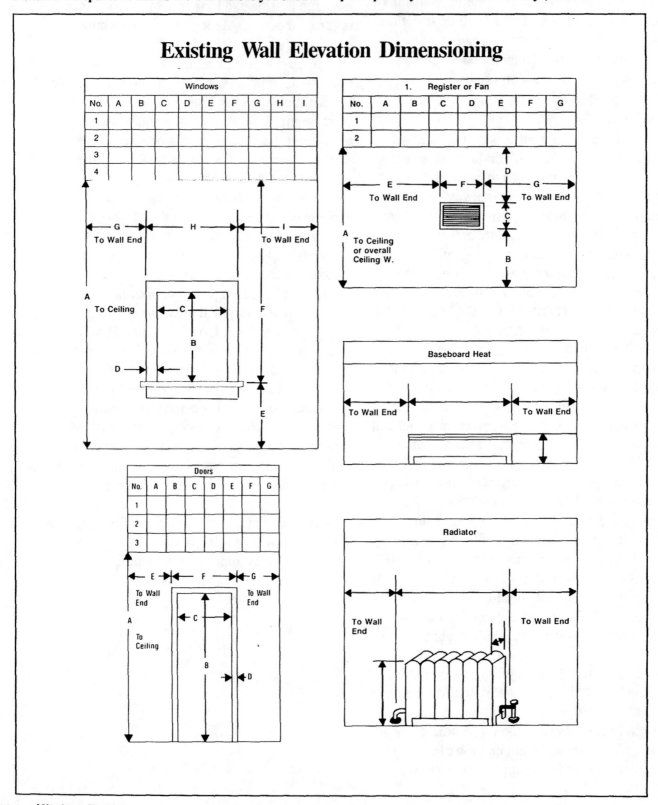

Existing Wall Elevation Dimensioning

Fig. 2.23. Your rough sketch of kitchen space for a remodeling project should look something like this.

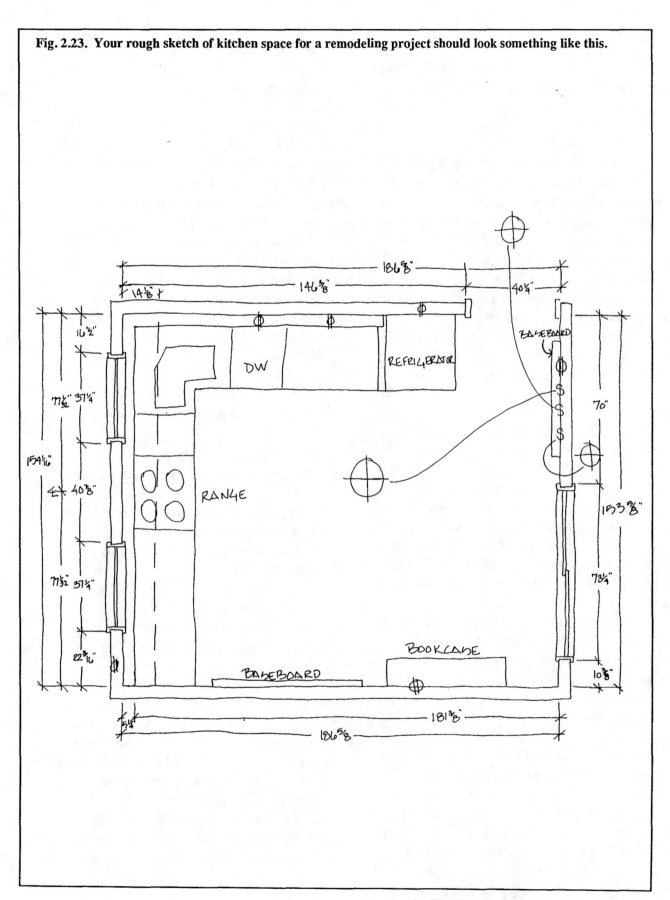

Completing the planning

This chapter is about the process of selling a kitchen and so far we have hardly talked about selling. Obviously selling involves a lot more than the word seems to indicate.

To recap:

1. First we talked about the kitchen industry in general. You have to be familiar with that to operate effectively as a kitchen pro.

2. We looked at and reviewed the Survey forms with which you interview the customer. This is one of the very important factors in selling a kitchen as a real pro, because the real secret of selling kitchens is in solving problems. **We sell solutions to problems.** You have to know a lot about the customers, their desires, their needs, their habits and their houses to identify and solve their problems.

3. We covered measuring, and how important it is to do it right.

Throughout, we've shown you quite a few forms. Paper work. That's how we plan, execute and keep control of the job, and we'll show a lot more forms before we're through.

All of this contributes to selling a kitchen, keeping it sold, and selling the customer on you, on your products and on your firm so that customer's friends, relatives and neighbors will come to you when they need a new kitchen.

All of this is part of the planning, so it also will make the project run smoothly and make it profitable for your firm. Profit is essential. It keeps the firm in business and results in higher income for you.

Once you have done the interview and the measuring, the next steps are:

• to design the best possible kitchen for the customer and the budget (see Chapter 3);

• to present the design and plan to the customer. The presentation must impress the customer with your ability and your professionalism, an impression you should be striving for from your first meeting, through the interview and through the measuring. Any sloppiness in your appearance or in your drawings or in your attention to detail can sabotage your presentation and your selling job.

It is important to realize that **90% of the selling job is accomplished in the first meeting with the customer.** That first meeting is your primary opportunity to impress this prospect with the integrity of your company and with your own knowledge, helpfulness and creativity. If the prospect is sold on you and your company there will be little reason to shop elsewhere. A kitchen is a major purchase, and the prime ingredient in any major purchase by any consumer is confidence. Instill confidence and you have made the sale.

If you work for a professional kitchen firm, throughout the project you may be responsible for initiating and maintaining paperwork controls. Paperwork comes with the territory.

But it has its good side, because it keeps the job under control and prevents costly mistakes.

Without the interview form you can easily forget to ask important questions that affect the design. Without the sketch you can become confused and overlook a wall offset that would throw the entire layout out of whack. Without the finished drawing you could not communicate with the plumbing or electrical contractor.

There are many more forms we'll encounter in this text, including those you will find cataloged in Appendices D and E. Among other things they will help you to know when you scheduled the plumber or electrician for rough-in or finish work. Without them you might have the tile setter coming in before the base cabinets are set and the counter is ready. All have been developed by NKBA to help you sell better, work better and manage better.

So welcome the forms. Before long you may find yourself creating more of them, because they are valuable to company profit, to your income and to customer satisfaction.

Customer Service Means Adding People to the Product

From first contact through final payment, you are intimately involved with the success of a kitchen remodeling project.

If it is a product-only sale, you must sell the features and benefits of the products and be as helpful and constructive as possible in making suggestions for improvement. And you must ask for the order.

In more involved sales where you also plan and design, you must be aware that any facial expression or chance remark can affect the sale. It is important to be totally positive, attentive and helpful.

Don't laugh at the customer's ideas, and don't be pushy about your preferences. If the customer wants an island and you know it won't fit, be sympathetic in explaining. Say "let's try it" and spread some newspapers on the floor to make the point. When going through the Survey form, guide the customer toward what is best for that job. If there is a budget problem, be creative in finding alternatives in the design or choice of products. On the other hand, don't prejudge. A customer often can afford and be willing to spend a lot more

Be scrupulously honest. Remember, you are selling against the bad reputations of fly-by-nighters in the home improvement business. Make it obvious that your firm is a completely different kind of business.

Prepare the customer for the problems of room preparation, tear-out, clean-up. Be there to introduce the installers. Return all phone calls quickly during the project. Make sure a clear, concise "punchlist" is prepared near the end of the job so the tradespeople can fix minor blemishes or hardware alignment, and so you can show the customer you are concerned.

And then remember: A good kitchen remodeling job and a fully satisfied customer results in several more sales in later months. Even this customer may want another kitchen in 10 years.

Tips from the Pros

When measuring a kitchen for remodeling, I always open the existing cabinets to look for hidden obstructions. I sometimes find pipes or a host of things that affect the design.
James Krengel, CKD, St. Paul MN

I have found the framing square useful in checking a corner for squareness as well as measuring around floor molding.
Manny Goldman, E. Windsor NJ.

I don't talk to clients when I measure. To occupy them while I'm in the kitchen I bring along a portfolio of past project and pictures of design ideas found in magazines. I suggest they look through it while I measure the project.
Ellen Cheever, CKD, ASID, New Holland PA

To insure absolute accuracy, "burn an inch." To do this, ignore the first inch on the end of the metal tape measure. Start all dimensioning with the 2" mark, then subtract 1" from any overall dimensions taken.
Leo Kelsey, CKD, Palm Desert CA

If you are going to install a food waste disposer in the new kitchen, measure the existing kitchen drain height. If it is any higher than 20" (51 cm) off the floor where it enters the wall, be sure to add the costs to lower that drain in your estimate.
Bruce Austin, Sacramento CA

Take some Polaroid pictures of the room or use a video camera to film it. This gives you an accurate record of what the room looks like, and is especially good for working with another person who draws your plans.
Gay Fly, CKD, ASID, Houston

When you survey the client, don't just read the questions like a robot. Explain that you are using it so you won't overlook any important question, and use the questions as springboards to be more conversational.
Cameron Snyder, CKD, Taunton MA

How much does a kitchen cost?

That's the tough question, usually the first one, every consumer will ask.

Pricing a kitchen can be fairly easy in a straight product sale when design isn't involved. You add up the prices of the products and add your set charges for any services, and that's it.

But when a complete redesign must be accomplished based on a lengthy interview the question becomes as impossible as it is inevitable. A stammer or a furtive look here can raise doubts and send the customer scurrying off to another source. **That's why it is essential that you prepare yourself for the question by mastering the cost factors that affect price.**

(*Cost* is what you pay for something. *Price* is the amount you charge the customer.)

The factors involved in pricing a kitchen include the following:

1. The products involved. For example, a simple mirror-finish double-compartment sink of 22-gauge stainless steel can go for $75. A deluxe sink with two or three compartments in 18-gauge stainless steel, quartz or other solid material can run $400 to $900. You can buy a simple 2-cycle dishwasher for $250, but the best and quietest runs up to $2500. A 4-element cooktop can be as low as $150 or, with halogen heat or magnetic induction, up to $1500.

For countertops, not installed, 10 lineal feet (305 cm) in decorative laminate can be as low as $250; in ceramic tile $500 to $800, but decorative tiles can be as high as $40 each; in solid surface it can be $1000 to $1500, and in granite or marble it can be $2000 to $2750.

For cabinets, the biggest product purchase, see the accompanying box.

As those figures indicate, prices of products alone can skyrocket the price of a kitchen by as much as 1000%. So in answering the client's price question, think "G-B-B-U," for Good, Better, Best and Ultimate. It is important to know these facts for the products your company offers.

2. Design complication. A look at the "before" plan on the facing page, with two possible solutions, gives you the idea. The first option has no structural changes, using existing space. The second option has major structural changes. Moving the back door can cost up to $1400, plus new door hardware ($70 to $500) and a new screen/storm door ($75-$200).

3. Who does the work. The price of a kitchen can be cut substantially if the customer can do some of the work. For example, the client can save $1000 by doing the painting and papering; $1000 to $1200 by doing the trash removal; $300 to $1000 by removing the old cabinets.

But be very wary of recommending that the customer install cabinets and/or countertops. This calls for skilled labor, for workers who appreciate the importance of plumbing the walls and leveling the floor and who know how to do it right. If a do-it-yourselfer tries to install and ruins an expensive cabinet, you will be blamed. If a wall cabinet is dropped on a counter it can ruin both the cabinet and the countertop.

Cabinet prices and their upcharges

The most inexpensive way to fill 48" (122 cm) of lowerwall space is with a single base cabinet in that width. These figures are for a stock line.

1. Basic box 48" (122 cm) wide. Cost: $400.
    Two roll-out shelves: $100.
    Concealed stepstool in toekick area: $170.
    One drawer with cutlery dividers: $75.
    One drawer to receive stepped spice insert: $50.
Total upcharge: $795.

2. Door style: Framed, raised-panel, cherry in place of plain wood, add 25%: $100.

TOTAL UPGRADED CABINET COST: $895.

NOTE: If that same space were broken down to a 15" (38 cm) 3-drawer unit ($300), a 9" (23 cm) tray storage unit ($200), and a 2-door 24" (61 cm) cabinet ($350), it would total $850 plus three freight and installation surcharges. That would come to $450 more.

Fig. 2.24. "Before" plan. This kitchen had a cramped L-shaped work area with a table in the middle of the room that was used for both breakfast and added work space. Three doors open to garage, back yard and dining room. It needs more storage space and more counter work area.

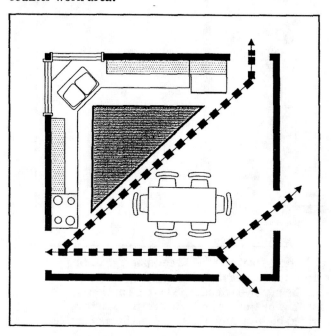

Fig. 2.25. Option #1. The designer avoided structural changes by creating a G kitchen with 20' (610 cm) of base storage, 13' (396 cm) of wall storage and a 30" (76 cm) pantry. One counter combines brunch-desk-entertainment center. A tall étagère ends cabinet run. It has wine rack and built-in refrigerator.

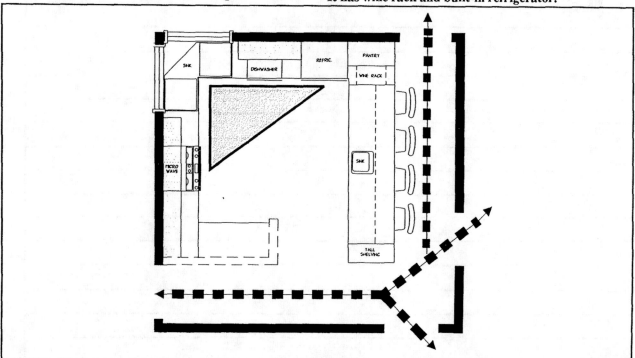

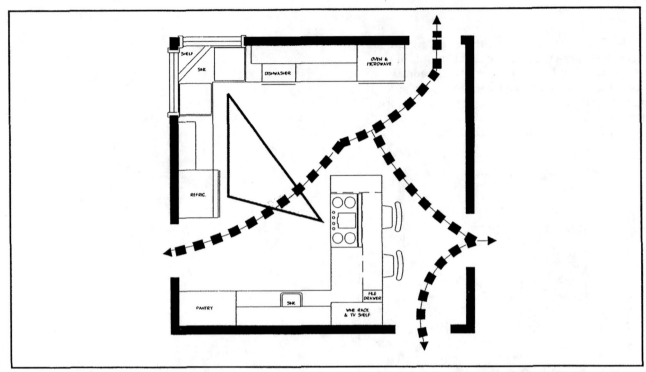

Fig. 2.26. Option #2 includes structural changes that improve space usage dramatically. Back door is moved to provide long wall for a double L. New back door is needed because hinging is switched to refrigerator side. Plan includes 27' (213 cm) of base storage, 18' (549 cm) of wall storage and a 48" (122 cm) pantry. Eating bar and desk are near center of room, second sink serves kitchen helper or bartender. There is spacious work area with wine storage and refrigerator nearby. Separated built-in appliances give freedom of choice.

Notes:

3
How to Design Kitchens
Shapes, Triangles, How to Use Them

As you develop as a designer/salesperson in the kitchen industry you constantly will be talking a new and different but common language with others. That is the language of plans, drawings and symbols. You will find them in detail in the NKBA Graphics and Presentation Standards in Appendix D, but here is a quick overview.

The first point to remember is that **the purpose of all of these drawings is to simplify and make things clear.** There should be no attempts at shortcuts, no assumptions that "they already know that."

The standard drawings involved include, first, the **floorplan,** which is an overhead view, looking down on the room. When the kitchen is designed all cabinets, appliances and other equipment will be in place and labeled with proper nomenclature on the floorplan.

Additional floorplans are made in the form of **overlays** which show wiring, heating, plumbing, venting and cooling. Any of these might be separate overlays. The purpose of these is to provide an easier-to-read plan for any subcontractor who might be doing that work. There are standard symbols to identify such items as different kinds of switches, lights or appliances. A legend of these symbols should appear on a completed floorplan.

A floorplan does not show the customer what the room really looks like from floor level. For this we add interpretive drawings which include elevations and perspective drawings. An elevation shows a wall or section of wall as seen from the front. A perspective drawing shows a section or entire kitchen in perspective, approximately as the eye sees it. Nearer objects appear larger and objects appear to diminish in size as they get farther away. You also might add sketches or other types of drawings to help the customer visualize the kitchen.

You will have to learn to read plans and to create them, but don't let that worry you. This knowledge will grow on you quickly as you work.

Kitchen layouts and their shapes

Because the rooms in a house are square or rectangular and kitchen equipment normally goes against the walls, kitchens tend to fall into definite shapes.

For example, a kitchen fitted onto two adjacent walls is in the shape of an L (Fig. 3.2), so we call it an L kitchen. If it is on three contiguous walls, it is a U kitchen (Fig. 3.4). On four walls it might be a double L (Fig. 3.3). Sometimes we add a fourth leg to that U so we get a G kitchen (Fig. 3.5). If kitchen space is very limited, we might design the kitchen onto only one wall, with everything in line, and get what we call a 1-wall kitchen (Fig. 3.0). When it is on two opposite walls that are fairly close together it is a corridor kitchen (Fig. 3.1). Any of these shapes might be created or modified with the aid of peninsulas or islands (Figs. 3.7, 3.8, 3.9).

In reviewing these we are not trying to fit any formula to squeeze kitchens into specific shapes. There are exotic kitchens installed entirely in circular islands. Some even wrap around outside corners of rooms. This does not mean they are good or bad. It does mean some designer had to cope with particular problems, possibly the taste of a homeowner! The professional will strive to create the finest plan possible to solve space and movement problems efficiently, provide the best products, fit the budget and satisfy the client.Once you have identified the kitchen shapes possible in the room, you should evaluate your choices to determine which provides the best design solution.

Each shape has its pros and cons

Each possibility might have its advantages and/or disadvantages. In Fig. 3.0, for example, we can see that the simple, 1-wall kitchen can be ideal for a small home or condo where very little cooking is done. In fact, it can disappear behind sliding doors if desired. But for a gourmet cook it would be very frustrating because there isn't enough room for food preparation and there isn't enough counter space for putting things down.

In Fig. 3.1 we see how efficient a close grouping of work centers on parallel walls can be. Everything is close at hand and the kitchen does not use up much square footage in the house.

It would be inadequate, however, if two cooks were to try to operate in it, even for such minor functions as fixing snacks for a party, and it also might get a lot of cross-traffic that could be distracting for the cook.

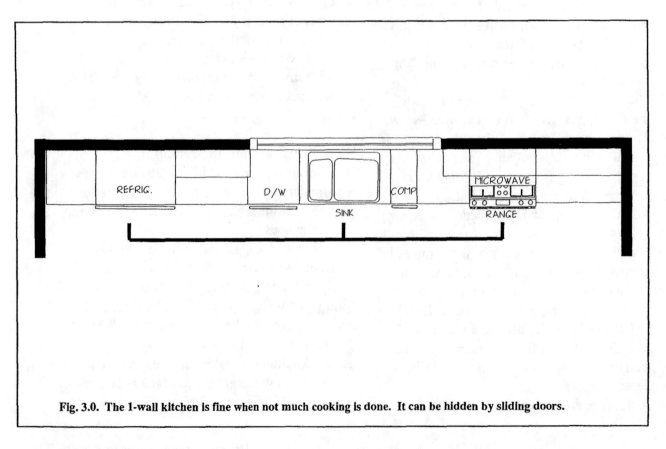

Fig. 3.0. The 1-wall kitchen is fine when not much cooking is done. It can be hidden by sliding doors.

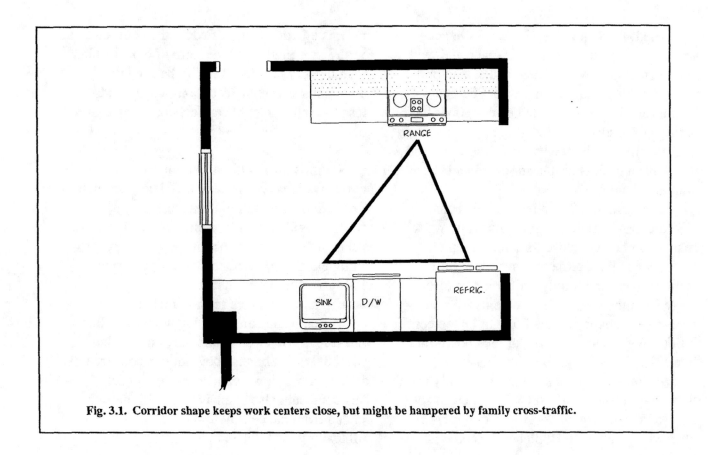

Fig. 3.1. Corridor shape keeps work centers close, but might be hampered by family cross-traffic.

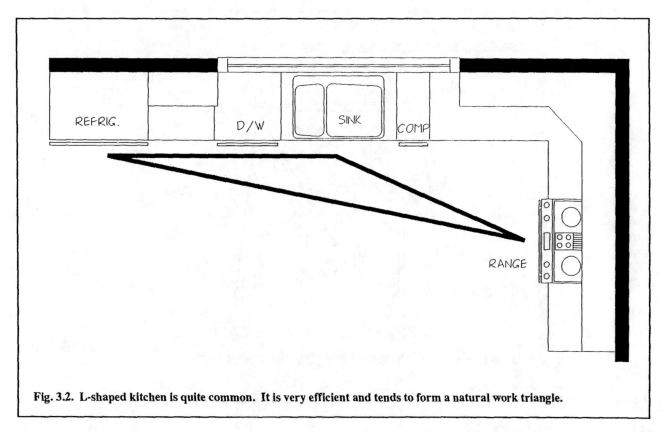

Fig. 3.2. L-shaped kitchen is quite common. It is very efficient and tends to form a natural work triangle.

The L kitchen in Fig. 3.2 can have generous amounts of continuous counter space and, with work centers on two adjacent walls, a natural work triangle is formed that would be bypassed by household traffic. It can be very good if a dining table is to be included in the space. But it might be limited by the length of the walls and thus have a lot less usable space than a U or an L with an island.

The basic U kitchen in Fig. 3.4 is considered the most efficient. Appliances and work spaces can be kept close for a minimum of travel, it can have a maximum of continuous counter space and family traffic can be directed away from the work area. The only disadvantages to a U shape are that it might be too confining for more than one cook, or the cook might like several walkways into the kitchen.

A double L kitchen (Fig. 3.3) usually is one that uses all four walls. It can be a design solution for a room where doorways cut up what otherwise might be a U kitchen. Another shape,

the G, is a U that is modified by the addition of a fourth leg, generally in the form of a peninsula. It can be very efficient and can be used to add counter space when needed, but it also tends to close the space in so it can feel confining to the cook.

Islands and peninsulas can provide creative ways to solve space or efficiency problems. For example, there might not be sufficient wall area to provide enough counter work space. An island can solve that problem (Fig. 3.6) by providing extra work surface, and it can also provide space for one of the work centers such as a cooktop and/or a place for a brunch counter.

A peninsula can add a leg without adding a wall (Fig. 3.8). Even if it is only counter height (without wall cabinets above) it can convert an L kitchen into a U, which can be more efficient. This peninsula also can have wall cabinets suspended from the ceiling for added storage space, still leaving the kitchen open to an adjacent

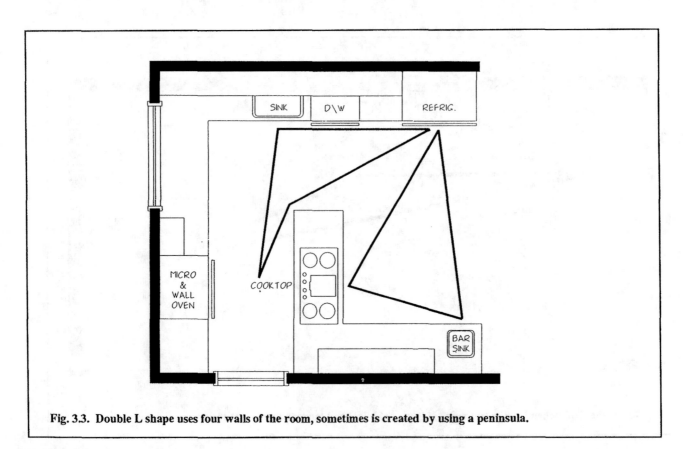

Fig. 3.3. Double L shape uses four walls of the room, sometimes is created by using a peninsula.

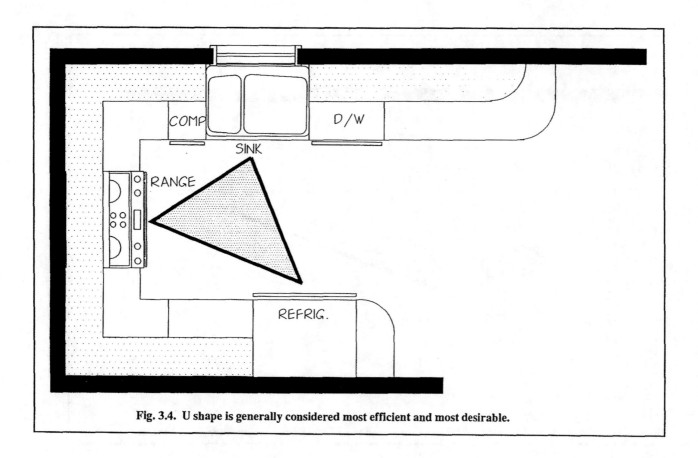

Fig. 3.4. U shape is generally considered most efficient and most desirable.

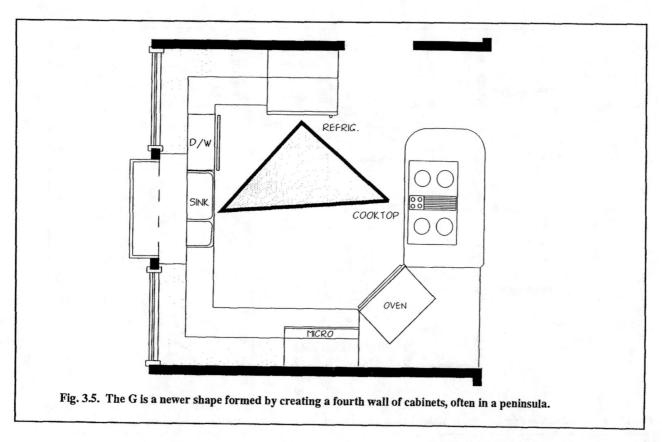

Fig. 3.5. The G is a newer shape formed by creating a fourth wall of cabinets, often in a peninsula.

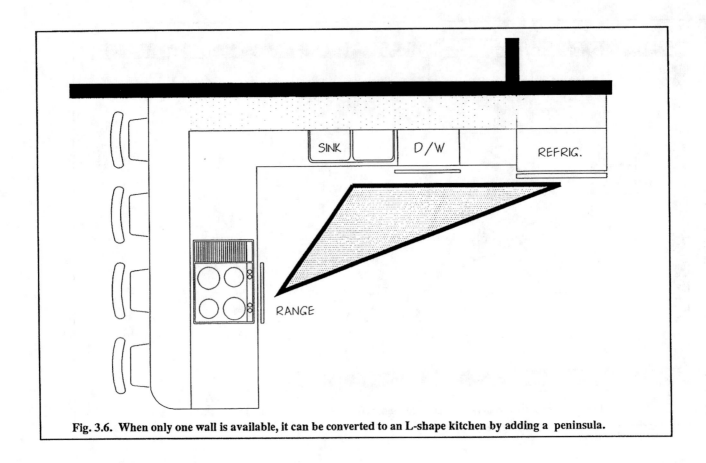

Fig. 3.6. When only one wall is available, it can be converted to an L-shape kitchen by adding a peninsula.

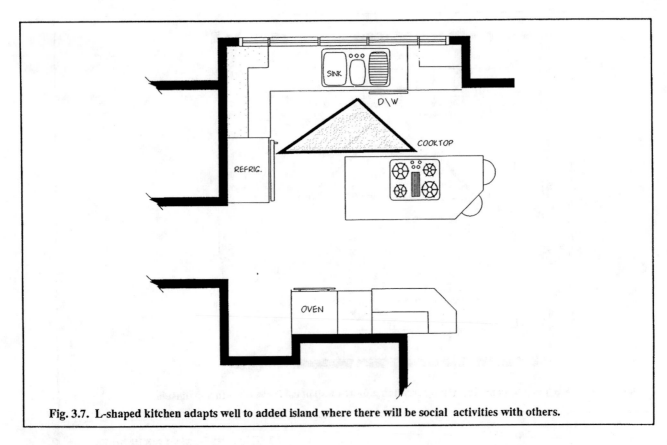

Fig. 3.7. L-shaped kitchen adapts well to added island where there will be social activities with others.

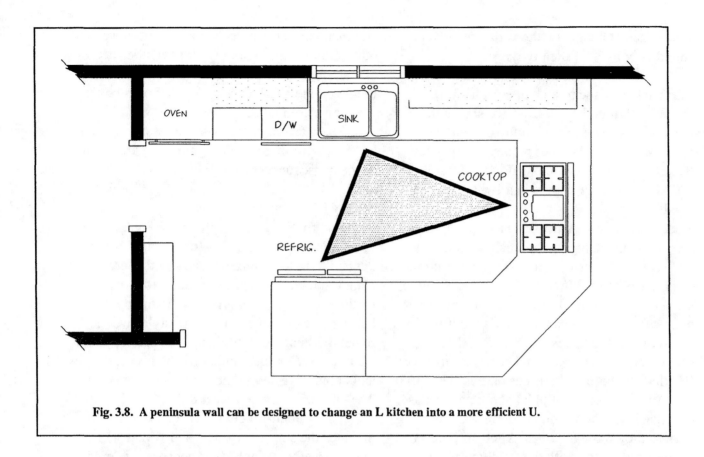

Fig. 3.8. A peninsula wall can be designed to change an L kitchen into a more efficient U.

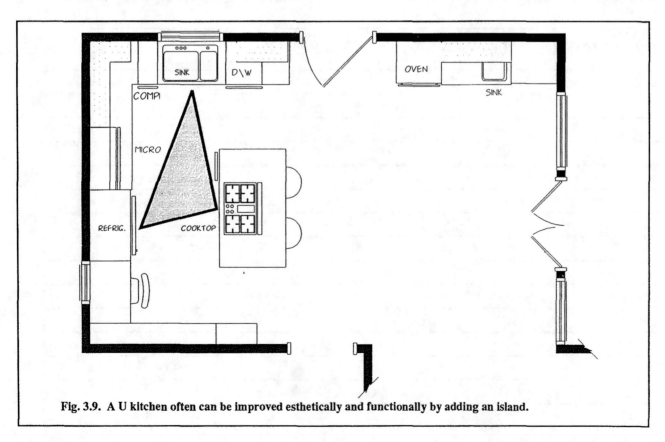

Fig. 3.9. A U kitchen often can be improved esthetically and functionally by adding an island.

living space. Obviously, the variations will be limited only by your creativity.

There can be good reason to change some other kitchen shape to a U, or even to an L. Studies at Purdue University have shown that the same meal prepared for a family of four in kitchens of various shapes required only 450 steps in a U kitchen, compared with 490 steps in an L kitchen and 760 steps in a 1-wall kitchen.

But in planning islands or peninsulas it is important to allow plenty of space. Customers often want an island without realizing the space requirements for using it and getting around it. A good way to handle this without appearing to ridicule the client is to carry some folded boxes in the car. You then can say "let's see if it will fit" and place the boxes on the floor, showing visually how much space and clearance it leaves. (We discuss these space needs on pps. 38- 43.)

Another important point about peninsulas and islands is that customers often want them because they want an "open" kitchen so the cook can be a little more with the family or visitors.

But many regret that decision later, because other family members or visitors can be very distracting, watching football on TV or a noisy movie on the VCR, or playing the boom box or working a computer.

So when customers say they want an open kitchen, grill them to make sure they are aware of the consequences.

Start with work centers, work triangle

The first step in designing the kitchen is to locate the work centers. "Work center" is the kitchen term for centers of activity that are common to all kitchens, or at least to most kitchens. They center around certain appliances, but in our world of changing lifestyles we must remember that they do change. In placing them we must be flexible, guided by the needs, desires and habits revealed in the customer interview. The primary work centers are:

• The **clean-up center** (Fig. 3.10), which includes the sink and dishwasher (Fig. 3.11) and which usually is placed first because it is used

Notes: Work triangle

Notes: Clean-up center

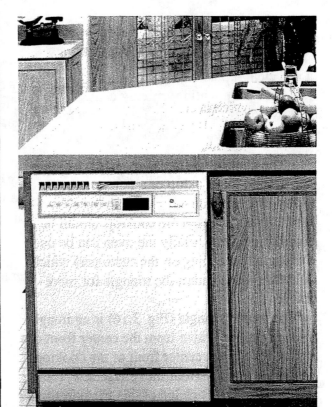

Fig. 3.11. Dishwasher always should be located within close reach of sink for easy loading.

Fig. 3.10. The clean-up center is based on the sink and the dishwasher. Here we also have a compactor, in a logical location when the customer requests it and the design permits.

most and because its placement often depends on plumbing. It should be near the middle of the plan because it is used in food preparation, cooking and clean-up activities.

• The **food preparation/ mixing** center (Fig. 3.12), which is based around the refrigerator (Fig. 3.13). It should be within 4' to 7' (122-213 cm) of the sink.

• The **cooking center** (Fig. 3.14), which is based around the cooktop or range (Fig. 3.15). A cooktop is used much more than an oven, so when built-ins are used the cooktop should be in the work triangle. Usually the oven can be out of the triangle (depending on the customer) which would free space within the triangle for more storage.

The **work triangle** (Fig. 3.16) is an imaginary straight line drawn from the center front of the sink, then to the center front of the cooktop, then to the center front of the refrigerator, then back to the sink. Each leg of this triangle should be between 4' (122 cm) and 9' (274 cm) long. The total of the three legs should be between 12'

(366 cm) and 26' (792 cm). Any less than the lower figure will mean the kitchen is too cramped for comfortable working, and even the lower figure, while workable, will be a little tight. Any more than the larger figure can mean a lot of wasted steps for the cook.

Who says so?

That's a good question, because the University of Illinois Small Homes Council developed the work triangle concept a half-century ago and this is a far different world.

Now, for example, we split the range into cooktop and oven, thus creating a separate center. We sometimes have two sinks, and we often add a bar sink in an entertainment center. We nearly always add a microwave which might be for cooking, for defrosting, for defrosting plus cooking, for popping corn or for just heating a cup of coffee. We have 2-cook kitchens and kosher kitchens and universal kitchens. *(Universal kitchens are those designed so that all features and items are universally usable, regardless of the user's level of ability or disability.)*

Fig. 3.12. The preparation center may be placed next to the refrigerator or across from it. The refrigerator should have a landing space next to the opening side of refrigerator compartment.

Notes: Mixing center

Fig. 3.13. Designers usually allot 36" (91 cm) for a side-by-side refrigerator/freezer unless it is built-in.

NKBA completed a major research project in 1992 which found the work triangle concept still to be valid in at least 90% of the kitchens you design. Where you have added centers, think of the work triangle legs as flexible, even curved. You might have to add a few points so it doesn't look triangular, but **do it with full consideration of the number of steps the cook must take**--not too few, not too many.

In planning kitchens in extra large spaces, designers frequently will use islands or peninsulas to bring the work triangle down to more useful proportions.

Traffic patterns should not intersect any of the legs of the work triangle. A cook holding a big pot of hot soup or measuring out precise grams of spices does not need a child running through to reach the back door or someone wandering through the space for ice cubes (which suggests that a good place for the refrigerator might be at the end of the triangle nearest the entry door or table).

After locating the work centers there are two more important steps. The first is to **assign storage space** (cabinets or shelving). The next is to **check counter space** to make sure there is enough for the jobs to be done in the kitchen.

In determining the amount of cabinet storage space needed in each work center, the first rule is to put things where they are used. Alternatively, think of putting things at the point of first use or last use. For example, dinner dishes are used at the dinner table (the point of first use) so that is the proper place for cabinets to contain them. But if that is impractical, the point of last use would be near the dishwasher.

Similarly, pans usually are stored near the cooktop. But for a lot of food preparation a pan is not used until water is added, and in any event the pans will end up in the dishwasher. It can make sense to provide storage for sauce pans at the sink and for other pans at the cooktop.

So, according to facts revealed in your interview, plan the storage space needed for the work centers. Consider here whether the need is

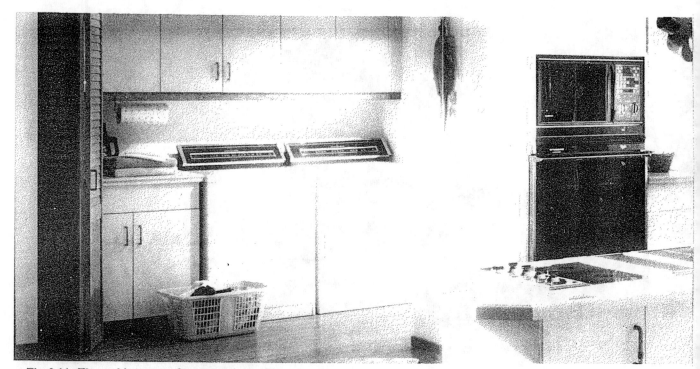

Fig. 3.14. The cooking center focuses on the cooktop or range, which must have landing space on both sides.

Fig. 3.15. When using built-ins, cooktop usually is more important than oven because it is used more.

for drawer space or cabinet shelf space. The "happy medium" cabinet most used has one drawer at the top and then a door covering one or two adjustable shelves plus the cabinet floor. But cabinets are available with two drawers or with all drawers. Shelves can roll out to the cook, rather than remaining stationary.

There are varying philosophies on the advantages of drawer cabinets vs. cabinets with roll-out shelves. Drawers can be opened with one movement, but their placement, sizing and adjustability are limited. Roll-out shelves are behind doors, so access requires two motions:

One to open the doors, another to pull the shelves out. But these offer great placement flexibility and they can be adjustable, so flexible storage is available for the life of the kitchen.

How much storage do your work centers need? A starting point is NKBA's Kitchen Industry Technical Manual #4 on "Kitchen Planning Principles." It contains certain minimums and recommendations for cabinet storage and countertop frontage.

Allocating space for appliances

The space you allot for the sink and appliances is variable and you will have to check

Fig. 3.16. For sufficient but not excessive space, work triangle legs should total 12'-26' (366-792 cm)

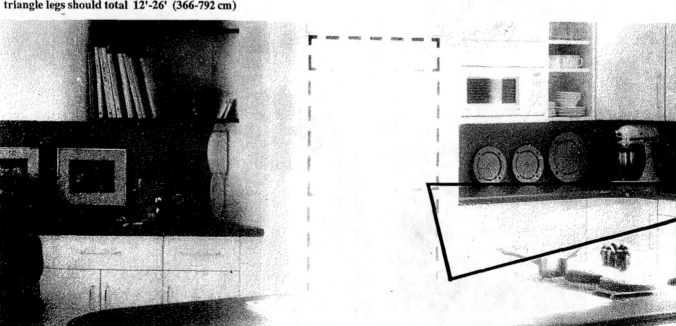

specific models, but here is the range.

• Double bowl sinks may be from 33" to 42" (84-107 cm) wide (Fig. 3.17), although 33" is fairly standard.

• Single bowl sinks may be 24"-30" (61-76 cm), with 24" standard.

• Dishwashers are nearly all 24" (61 cm), but models range from 18"-27" (46-69 cm) (Fig. 3.18.).

• Free-standing refrigerators may be 30"-48" (76-122 cm) for standard models, although most commonly you allot 33" (84 cm) or 36" (91 cm) for regular and 36" (91 cm) or 39" (99 cm) for a side-by-side (Fig. 3.23). Free-standing models are up to 33" (84 cm) deep so they jut out into the space. Add a couple of inches for the handle and they become more of a problem.

Remember this when you design, or you might be stuck with an appliance you can't get in through the door. And include refrigerator depth with handle on the floorplan. Built-in refrigerators are 24" deep (61 cm), so they fit into the kitchen better.

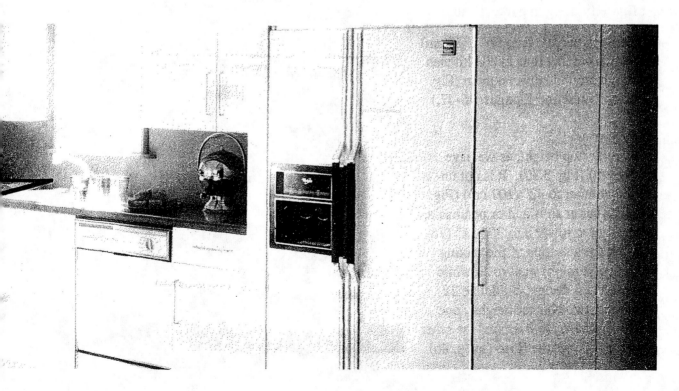

• A cooktop or range may be 20"-48" (51-122 cm), with 30" (76 cm) most common (Fig. 3.19).

• Built-in ovens are from 22"-50" (56-127 cm), but this is very tricky. Built-in ovens have both a cut-out size and an overall size which is the width of the front frame, and almost every model by every manufacturer is different in both dimensions (Fig. 3.20).

• A compactor or under-counter ice maker might be 12"-24" (30-61 cm). Usually a compactor is 12" or 15" (30 or 38 cm) (Fig. 3.22).

• Microwaves (Fig. 3.21) may be full-size or compact, and in either case the sizes vary by brand. For planning, figure full-size at 16"D x 15"-18" H x 24" W (46 x 38-46 x 61 cm), and compact size at 12" x 12" x 22"W (30 x 30 x 56 cm), but always measure before finalizing.

We have accounted for the space for cabinets, appliances and countertops. How about the cook?

The cook needs at least 36" (91 cm) of space between cabinet runs in a walkway and 42" (106cm) of space in a work aisle between centers of kitchen activity. For space to move about with appliance doors open, 48" (122cm) is a good target figure. In designing the kitchen, remember to allow for the appliance door-swings. This means that you need 96" (244 cm) of space for the two cabinet runs in a U kitchen plus space to move around between them (Fig. 3.25). (See Design Guideline 1, pages 46-47.)

How high the counter?

Standard countertop height, as we have noted, is 36" (91 cm) (Fig. 3.30). It is not unusual to raise the counter to 42" (107 cm) (Fig. 3.28) for an eating bar at an island or peninsula. It also is not unusual to lower it to 30"-31" (76-79 cm) (Fig. 3.29) for a section of the mixing center where the cook might want to sit while working. For universal design, Guideline 22 recommends at least two counter heights, one 28"-36" (71-91cm) above the floor and the other 36"-45" (91-114cm) above the floor (see p. 86).

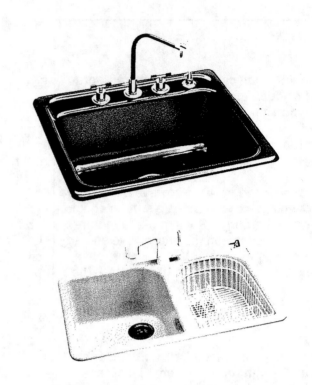

Fig. 3.17. Sinks might be single, double, even triple bowl. Typical size is 33" (84 cm) for double, 24" (61 cm) for single bowl.

Fig. 3.18. There are some smaller and larger dishwashers, but 24" (61 cm) is almost standard.

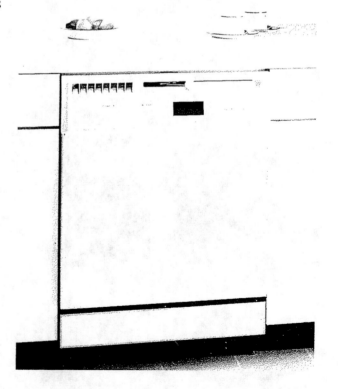

Under-counter appliances such as the dishwasher and compactor are sized to fit under standard counter height, 36" (91 cm), so these sections of counter can't be lowered. However, designers sometimes like to raise the dishwasher 6"-9" (15-23cm) to make it a bit easier to load and unload. That raises the counter, sometimes providing a handy place to locate a microwave.

If the customer has the budget and desire for it, you might want to customize the counter-top heights. For working at the counter while standing, studies have shown the best height would be 2"-3" (5-8 cm) below the flexed elbow or, for a mixing center, 5" (13 cm) below that point.

But check on what the client wants. Always design in terms of the client's needs.

Eating in the kitchen

Nearly every homeowner wants some kind of eating facility in the kitchen, even if it is only to sit down and have a cup of coffee. Usually it is for breakfast and lunch, possibly for dinner.

Fig. 3.20. Built-in wall ovens are single or double. Main oven door should be 3" (7.6 cm) below elbow when open.

Fig. 3.21. Before placing a microwave, remember they are in different sizes. Full-size usually is 16"D x 18"H x 24"W (41 x 46 x 62 cm).

Fig. 3.19. Cooktops and ranges are pretty well standardized at 30" (76 cm) for 4-burner models.

Fig. 3.22. Space-saving compactor is 12" (30 cm) wide, but 15" (38 cm) is more standard.

For an individual alone, a cutting board that pulls out from a base cabinet and a step stool to sit on might be sufficient, but some lines have a table that pulls out from a cabinet run. For more than that we have to consider clearances (Fig. 3.26).

If we place an eating counter on the far side (outside the kitchen) of an island or peninsula, it should be wide enough for elbow room. Allow 24" (61 cm) for each place setting if the eating surface is higher than table height. If the surface is table height, 30" (76cm), the clearance for each diner should be 30" (Fig. 3.27). (see Guideline 33, and note also the requirements for knee space). If the bar is higher than table height, it should be at least 15" (38 cm) deep, but 19" if at table height. (Fig. 3.27).

If you are placing a sink or cooktop in the island or peninsula you must be aware of the possibility of spatter on the diners. You can protect diners with an anti-spatter divider 6" (15 cm) high, or by raising the bar that amount and

Fig. 3.23. Without specific size, allow 33" (84 cm) for regular refrigerator, 36" (91 cm) for side-by-side.

Fig. 3.24. Built-in refrigerator/freezers might be up to 48" (122 cm) wide, but 36" (91 cm) is more common.

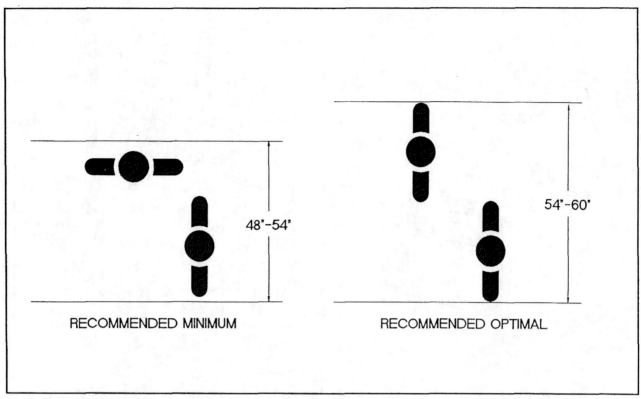

RECOMMENDED MINIMUM   RECOMMENDED OPTIMAL

48"-54"

54"-60"

Fig. 3.25. In planning an island, remember you must make the aisles a little wider when there are several members in the household. There should be at least 48" (122 cm) of passing space between counter and wall.

Fig. 3.26. Several cabinet firms now offer tables that pull out from base cabinets for brunch space.

Fig. 3.27. For eating bars, allow 24" (61 cm) of lateral space for each diner at counter heights of 36" (91cm) or 42" (107cm). If dining surface is table height, 30" (76cm), allow 30" lateral space.

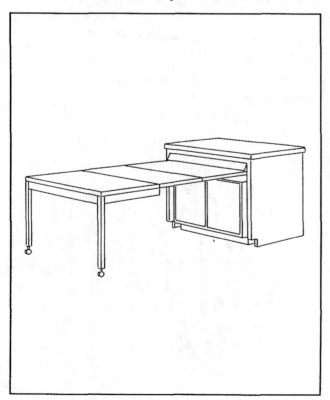

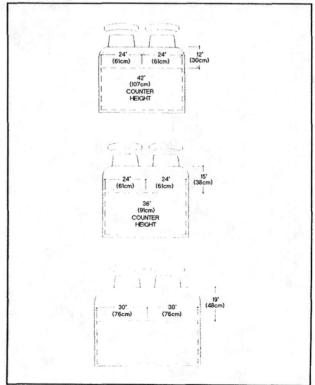

Fig. 3.28. Counters often are raised to 42" (107 cm) for breakfast bars. This requires bar stools for seating.

Fig. 3.29. For mixing centers where the cook will like to sit while working, or for a brunch bar, try 30"-high (76 cm) counters.

Fig. 3.30. Eating counters 36" (91 cm) high lets the surface also serve as a work top.

Fig. 3.31. Eating bars don't have to be routine. You can be creative in shaping them, like this teardrop.

providing higher seats, such as bar stools.

Space between the eating bar and a wall behind it might allow only for persons sitting and eating, or it might be deep enough for movement behind the seats, getting in and out. The minimum here is 36" (66 cm) for diners, but it should be extended to 65" (112 cm) for dining plus space to get in and out freely. (Guideline 5, page 52).

Providing for recycling

Earlier in this chapter we pointed out that the kitchen designer must be aware of ecological concerns and increasing demands to separate waste products and recycle them.

More and more communities are passing laws requiring recycling, and many are even providing containers for pickup.

Everything that is done at the community level puts more demands on the homeowner and on space in the home and in the kitchen or, if there is one, a nearby utility room. It is in the kitchen that we empty cans and bottles and packages, so it is here that we must figure out something to do with them.

Part of the concern is for ordinary garbage. For that we can recommend a food waste disposer, although some homeowners don't want one and others might feel they can't afford one. Some communities don't allow them, fearing they put too much of a strain on their sewerage. Other communities require them by law!

For solid waste we have the compactor. But it isn't reasonable to put in multiple compactors for aluminum, glass, plastics and paper.

Some cabinet manufacturers offer deep drawers to pull out from a base cabinet with two, three or four lift-out bins for separating recyclables. Similar systems are offered by some sink manufacturers. Such systems are convenient and needed, but they also cut into valuable base cabinet space. One result is an increase in the provisions for 12-inch-deep drawers in wall cabinets.

The industry--and you--are on the cutting edge of this issue. How are **you** going to solve the problem when you confront your kitchen customers?

Recycling Ideas:

1. Provide a pass-through to bins on a back porch.

2. Provide a floor chute in the sink base to bins in the basement.

3. Look for alternative locations, such as a nearby utility room.

4. _____

   _____

5. _____

   _____

6. _____

   _____

Notes:

Rules become flexible Guidelines

In 1992, The National Kitchen and Bath Association and the University of Illinois Small Homes Council introduced standards based on extensive research conducted in conjunction with the University of Minnesota.

The rules created at that time became known as the *"31 Rules of Kitchen Design."*

Those rules have now been replaced with the *"40 Guidelines for Kitchen Planning."*

There's good reason for this update. Our society is growing more diverse, and this requires that our guidelines be revised. It requires also that they remain constantly under scrutiny for further changes in our population and the living habits of the various population segments. The current revisions more-fully incorporate universal design as clarified by the Uniform Federal Accessibility Standards (UFAS) and the American National Standard for Accessible and Usable Buildings and Facilities (ANSI A117.1-1992). The dimensions included in these NKBA Guidelines are based in ANSI and UFAS, but they are not intended to replace them.

To date, most single-family residential projects do not fall under any standard for accessibility, but this is changing. If a particular project is subject to local, state or national laws or codes, the designer must comply with those requirements. These guidelines and the space planning provided here are intended to be useful design standards, supplemental to the applicable codes. Not hard-and-fast rules, but Guidelines, they will help you in planning kitchens that are functional and flexible, or universal, to better meet the needs of today's varied lifestyles.

For better and easier understanding, these guidelines are arranged in sections, according to the index at the right.

Index to Kitchen Planning Guidelines:

Section I: TRAFFIC AND WORKFLOW
Guideline 1 to Guideline 5

Section II: CABINETS AND STORAGE
Guideline 6 to Guideline 12

Section III: APPLIANCE PLACEMENT AND USE/ CLEARANCE SPACE
Guideline 13 to Guideline 21

Section IV: COUNTER SURFACE AND LANDING SPACE
Guideline 22 to Guideline 34

Section V: ROOM, APPLIANCE AND EQUIPMENT CONTROLS
Guideline 35 to Guideline 40

NKBA's 40 Guidelines for Kitchen Planning
SECTION 1: Traffic and Workflow—Guideline 1 to Guideline 5

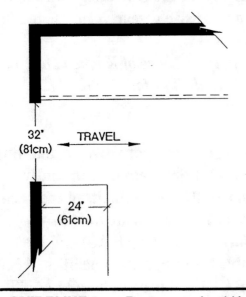

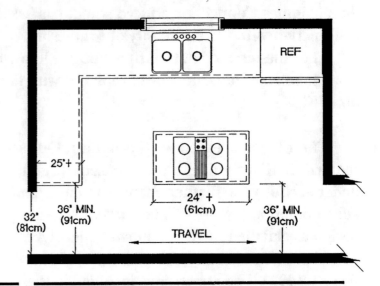

GUIDELINE 1a— Doorways should be at least 32" (81 cm) wide and not more than 24" (61 cm) deep in the direction of travel.

GUIDELINE 1b— Walkways (passages between vertical objects greater than 24" (61 cm) deep in the direction of travel, where not more than one is a work counter or appliance) should be at least 36" (91 cm) wide.

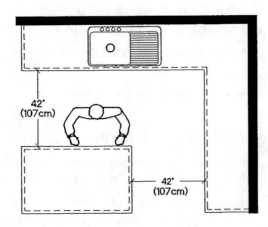

ONE-COOK KITCHEN WORK AISLE

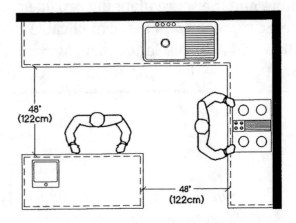

TWO-COOK KITCHEN WORK AISLE

GUIDELINE 1c— Work aisles (passages between vertical objects, both of which are work counters or appliances) should be at least 42" (107 cm) wide in one-cook kitchens, at least 48" (122 cm) wide in multiple-cook kitchens.

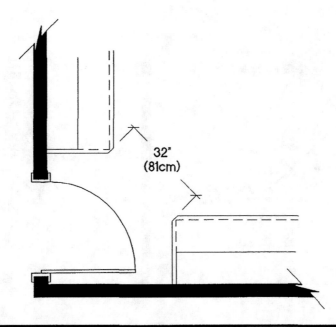

GUIDELINE 1a Clarification—When two counters flank a doorway entry, the minimum 32" (81 cm) wide clearance should be allowed from the point of one counter to the closest point of the opposite counter.

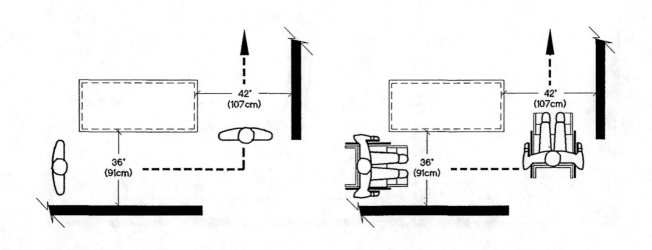

GUIDELINE 1b Clarification— If there are perpendicular walkways, one should be a minimum of 42" (107 cm) wide.

The 36" (91 cm) width of a walkway allows a person using a wheelchair to pass. However, in order to turn when two walkways intersect at right angles, one of the walkways must be a minimum of 42" (107 cm) wide.

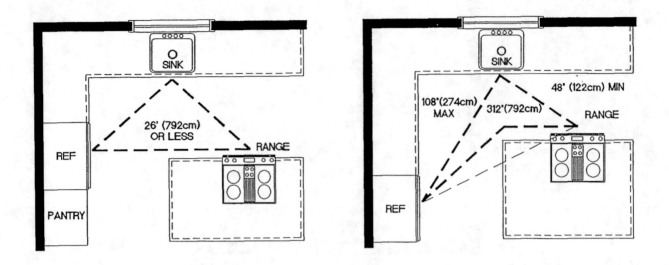

GUIDELINE 2—The work triangle should total 26' (792 cm) or less, with no single leg of the triangle shorter than 4' (122 cm) nor longer than 9' (274 cm). The work triangle should not intersect an island or peninsula by more than 12" (30 cm). (The triangle is the shortest walking distance between the refrigerator, primary food preparation sink and primary cooking surface, measured from the center front of each appliance.)

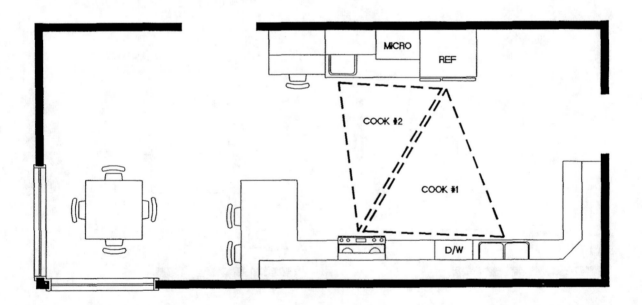

GUIDELINE 2 Clarification— If two or more people cook simultaneously, a work triangle should be placed for each cook. One leg of the primary and secondary triangles may be shared, but the two should not cross one another. Appliances may be shared or separate.

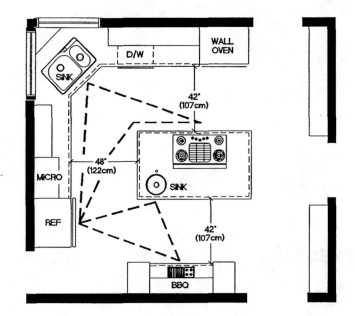

GUIDELINE 2 **Example 1**—A square room can work for two people if a sink is added at the back of an island which also features the primary cook's cooktop. One cook moves from the refrigerator to the island sink, to the BBQ center; the second cook, from the refrigerator to the primary sink to the cooking surface.

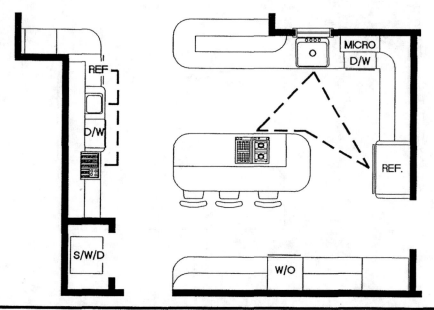

GUIDELINE 2 **Example 2**—In a large, expansive kitchen created for two cooks, two very separate cooking areas are created. There is very little interaction between the cooks unless they are both working at the counter to the left of the sink. The primary cook works from the refrigerator to the sink to the cooktop. Note the microwave placement close to the sink. The secondary cook has access to his own grill, second microwave, sink and under cabinet refrigerator. Two dishwashers complete the separate work environment.

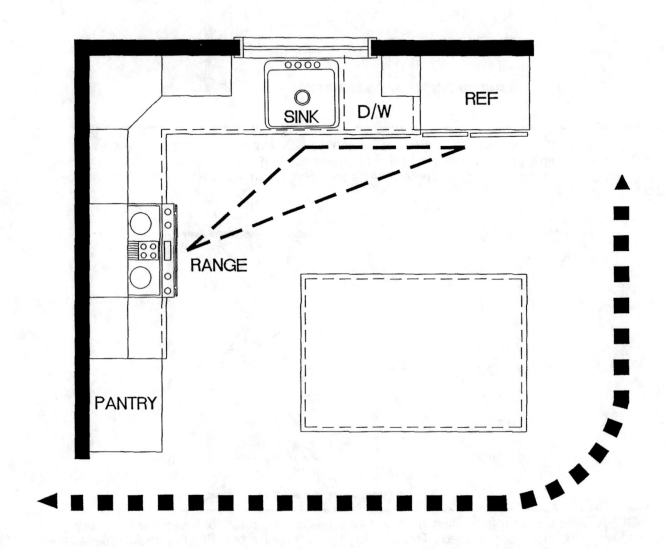

GUIDELINE 3—No major traffic patterns should cross through the work triangle.

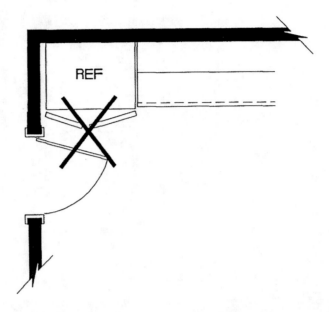

GUIDELINE 4—No entry, appliance or cabinet doors should interfere with one another.

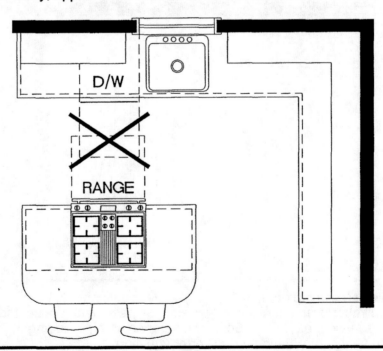

GUIDELINE 4 Example—In an island configuration, an appliance or cabinet door on an island should not conflict with an appliance or cabinet door opposite it.

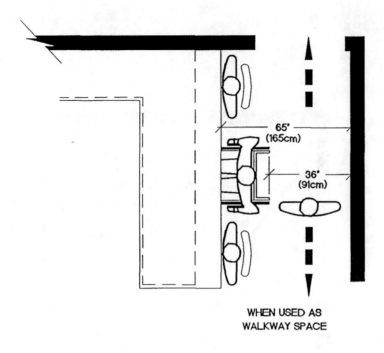

WHEN USED AS
WALKWAY SPACE

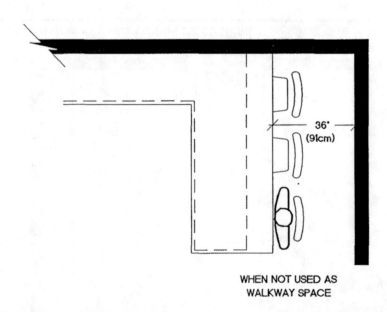

WHEN NOT USED AS
WALKWAY SPACE

GUIDELINE 5—In a seating area, 36" (91cm) of clearance should be allowed from the counter/ table edge to any wall/obstruction behind it if no traffic will pass behind a seated diner. If there is a walkway behind the seating area, 65" (165cm) of clearance, total, including the walkway, should be allowed between the seating area and any wall or obstruction.

The 65" (165 cm) walkway clearance called for behind a seating area allows room for passage by or behind the person using a wheelchair.

Notes

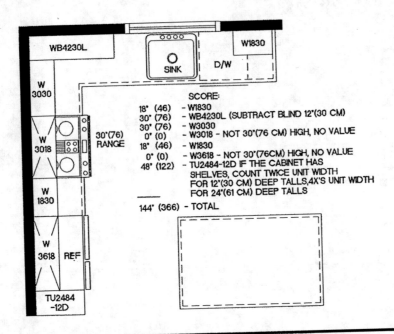

SCORE:

18" (46) - W1830
30" (76) - WB4230L (SUBTRACT BLIND 12"(30 CM)
30" (76) - W3030
0" (0) - W3018 - NOT 30"(76 CM) HIGH, NO VALUE
18" (46) - W1830
0" (0) - W3618 - NOT 30"(76CM) HIGH, NO VALUE
48" (122) - TU2484-12D IF THE CABINET HAS
SHELVES, COUNT TWICE UNIT WIDTH
FOR 12"(30 CM) DEEP TALLS,4X'S UNIT WIDTH
FOR 24"(61 CM) DEEP TALLS

144" (366) - TOTAL

GUIDELINE 6 Wall Cabinet Frontage, Small Kitchens—under 150 sq. ft. (14M²) - allow at least 144" (366cm) of wall cabinet frontage, with cabinets at least 12" (30cm) deep, and a minimum of 30" (76 cm) high (or equivalent) which feature adjustable shelving. Difficult to reach cabinets above the hood, oven or refrigerator do not count unless devices are installed within the case to improve accessibility.

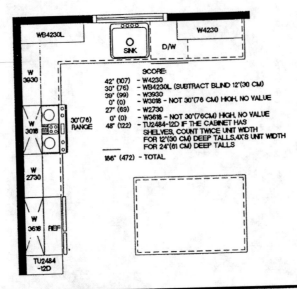

SCORE:

42" (107) - W4230
30" (76) - WB4230L (SUBTRACT BLIND 12"(30 CM)
39" (99) - W3930
0" (0) - W3018 - NOT 30"(76 CM) HIGH, NO VALUE
27" (69) - W2730
0" (0) - W3618 - NOT 30"(76CM) HIGH, NO VALUE
48" (122) - TU2484-12D IF THE CABINET HAS
SHELVES, COUNT TWICE UNIT WIDTH
FOR 12"(30 CM) DEEP TALLS,4X'S UNIT WIDTH
FOR 24"(61 CM) DEEP TALLS

186" (472) - TOTAL

GUIDELINE 6 Wall Cabinet Frontage, Large Kitchens—over 150 sq. ft. (14M²) - allow at least 186" (472cm) of wall cabinet frontage, with cabinets at least 12" (30cm) deep, and a minimum of 30" (76cm) high (or equivalent) which feature adjustable shelving. Difficult to reach cabinets above the hood, oven or refrigerator do not count unless devices are installed within the case to improve accessibility.

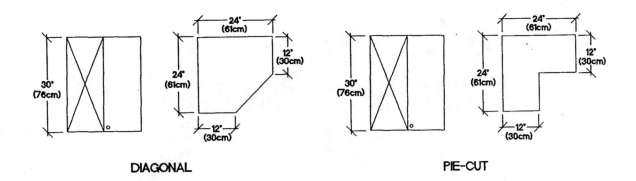

DIAGONAL   PIE-CUT

WALL CABINETS

GUIDELINE 6 Clarification—In Small and Large Kitchens, diagonal or pie cut wall cabinets count as a total of 24" (61 cm).

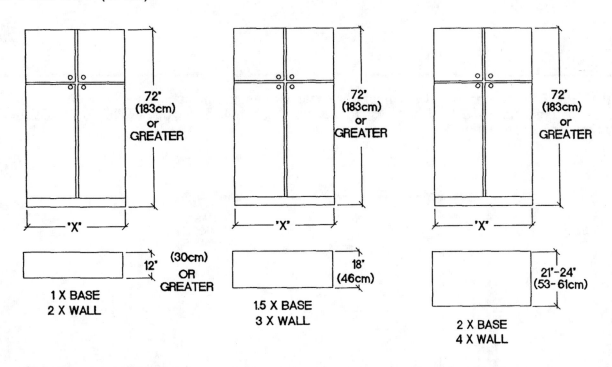

72"
(183cm)
or
GREATER

72"
(183cm)
or
GREATER

72"
(183cm)
or
GREATER

"X"   "X"   "X"

12" (30cm)
OR
GREATER

18"
(46cm)

21"-24"
(53- 61cm)

1 X BASE
2 X WALL

1.5 X BASE
3 X WALL

2 X BASE
4 X WALL

GUIDELINE 6 Clarification—Tall cabinets 72" (183cm) or taller can count as either base or wall cabinet storage, but not both.

The calculation is as follows:
   12" (30cm) deep tall units = 1 x the base lineal footage, 2 x the wall lineal footage.
   18" (46cm) deep tall units = 1.5 x the base lineal footage, 3 x the wall lineal footage.
   21" to 24" (53cm-61cm) deep tall units = 2 x the base lineal footage, 4 x the wall lineal footage.

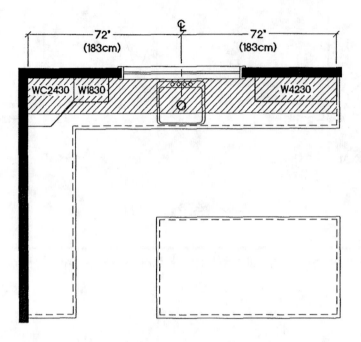

GUIDELINE 7—At least 60" (152cm) of wall cabinet frontage, with cabinets at least 12" (30cm) deep, a minimum of 30" (76 cm) high (or equivalent), should be included within 72" (183cm) of the primary sink centerline.

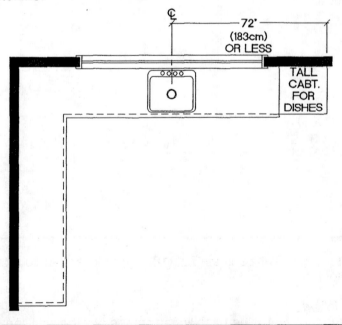

GUIDELINE 7 Clarification—A tall cabinet can be substituted for the required wall cabinets if it is placed within 72" (183cm) of the sink centerline.

Notes:

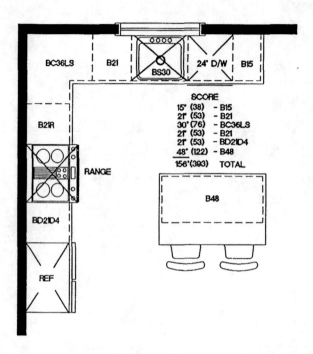

GUIDELINE 8 Base Cabinet Frontage, Small Kitchens—under 150 sq. ft. (14 M²), allow at least 156" (393cm) of base cabinet frontage, with cabinets at least 21" (53cm) deep (or equivalent). The blind portion of a blind corner box does not count.

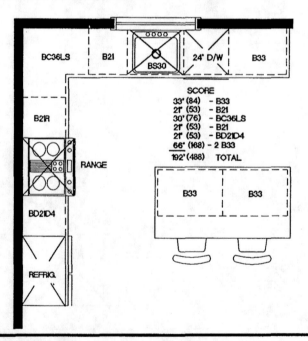

GUIDELINE 8 Base Cabinet Frontage, Large kitchens—over 150 sq. ft. (14 M²) - require at least 192" (488cm) of base cabinet frontage, with cabinets at least 21" (53cm) deep (or equivalent). The blind portion of a blind corner box does not count.

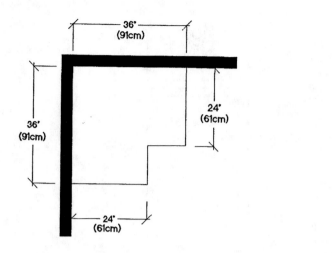
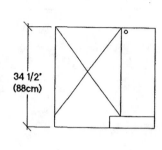

PIE-CUT/LAZY SUSAN BASE CABINET

GUIDELINE 8 Clarification—In both Small and Large kitchens, pie cut/lazy susan base cabinets count as a total of 30" (76 cm) .

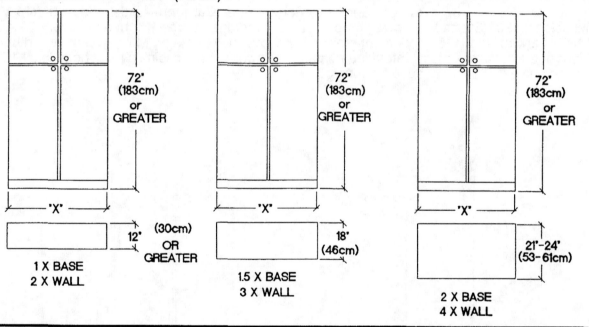

GUIDELINE 8 Clarification—Tall cabinets 72" (183cm) or taller can count as either base or wall cabinet storage, but not both.

The calculation is as follows:
   12" (30cm) deep tall units = 1 x the base lineal footage, 2 x the wall lineal footage.
   18" (46cm) deep tall units = 1.5 x the base lineal footage, 3 x the wall lineal footage.
   21" (53cm) to 24" (61cm) deep tall units = 2 x the base lineal footage, 4 x the wall lineal footage.

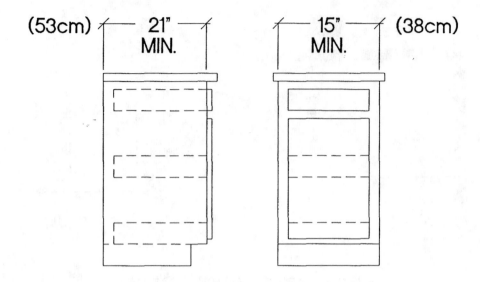

GUIDELINE 9 Drawer/Roll-out Shelf Frontage, Small Kitchens—under 150 sq. ft. (14 M²) - allow at least 120" (305cm) of drawer or roll-out shelf frontage. **Large Kitchens**— over 150 sq. ft. (14 M²) - allow at least 165" (419cm) of drawer or roll-out shelf frontage. Multiply cabinet width by number of drawers/roll-outs to determine frontage. Drawer/roll-out cabinets must be at least 15" (38 cm) wide and 21" (53 cm) deep to be counted.

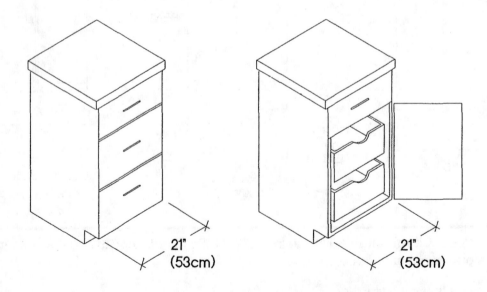

GUIDELINE 9 Example 1—A 21" (53 cm) wide three drawer base would count as 63" (160cm) toward the drawer total. A 21" (53 cm) wide single drawer base with one drawer and two sliding shelves would also count as 63" (160cm) towards the total drawer measurement.

GUIDELINE 9 Example 2—In this example, drawers flank the range.

GUIDELINE 9 Example 3—Drawers can be placed close to the sink so that items used at the sink or stored near the dishwasher are close at hand.

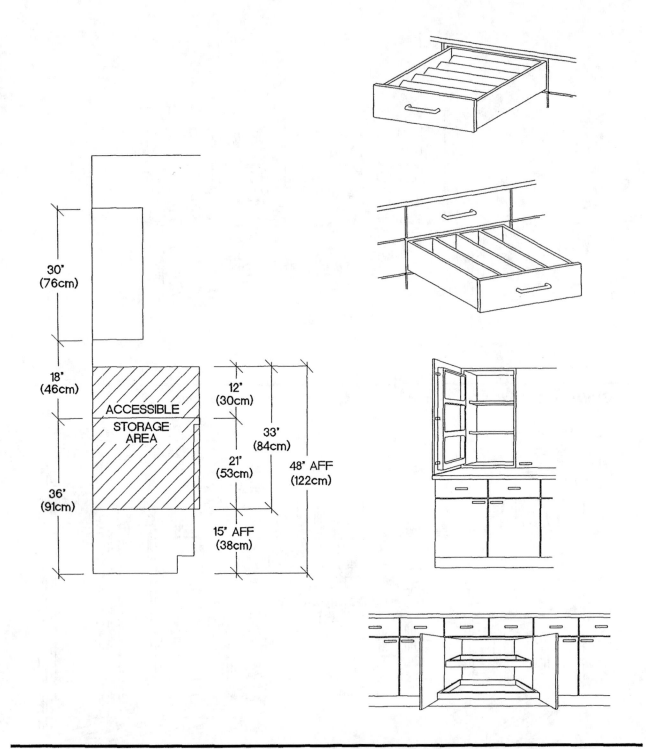

ACCESSIBLE STORAGE AREA

30"
(76cm)

18"
(46cm)

36"
(91cm)

12"
(30cm)

33"
(84cm)

21"
(53cm)

48" AFF
(122cm)

15" AFF
(38cm)

GUIDELINE 10—At least five storage/organizing items, located between 15"-48" (38cm-122cm) above the finished floor (or extending into that area), should be included in the kitchen to improve functionality and accessibility. These items may include, but are not limited to: lowered wall cabinets, raised base cabinets, tall cabinets, appliance garages, bins/racks, swing-out pantries, interior vertical dividers, specialized drawers/shelves, etc. Full-extension drawers/roll-out shelves greater than the 120" (305cm) minimum for small kitchens or 165" (419cm) for larger kitchens, may also be included.

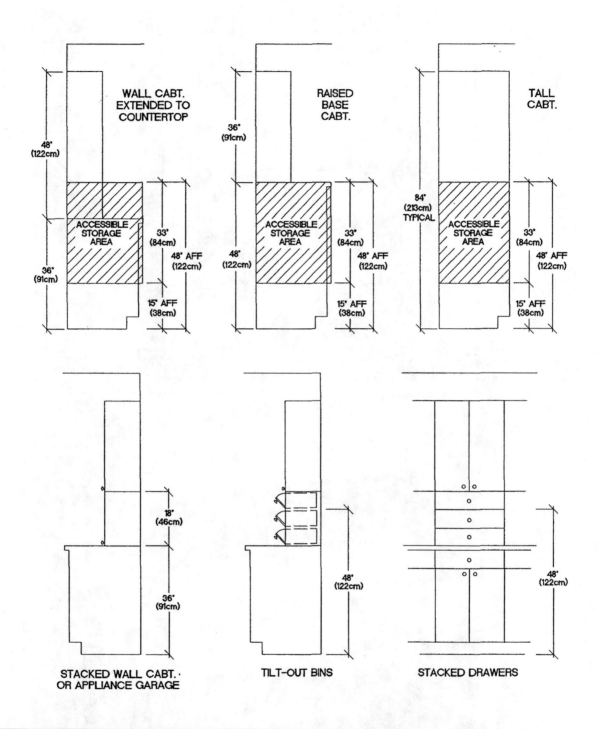

Guideline 10 Examples—Each of these applications puts storage within the 15"-48" (38cm-122cm) range.

GUIDELINE 10 Examples—The goal of this guideline is to increase the amount of accessible storage within the universal range of 15"-48" (38cm-122cm).

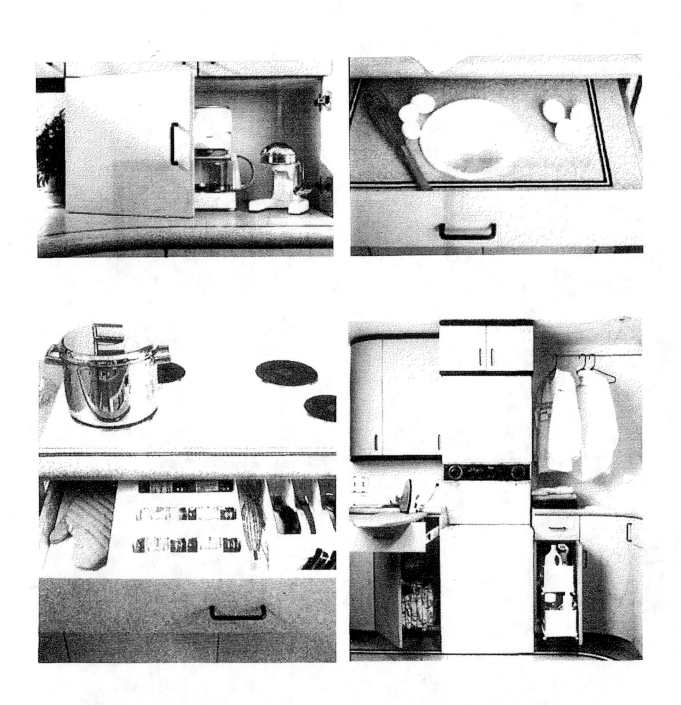

GUIDELINE 10 Examples—The goal of this guideline is to increase the amount of accessible storage within the universal range of 15"-48" (38cm-122cm).

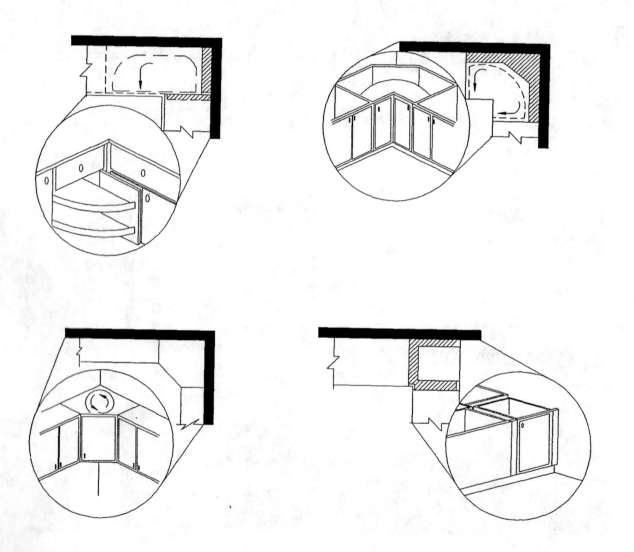

GUIDELINE 11—For a kitchen with usable corner areas in the plan, at least one functional corner storage unit should be included.

Notes:

_____

_____

_____

_____

_____

_____

_____

_____

_____

_____

_____

_____

_____

_____

_____

_____

_____

_____

_____

_____

_____

_____

_____

_____

_____

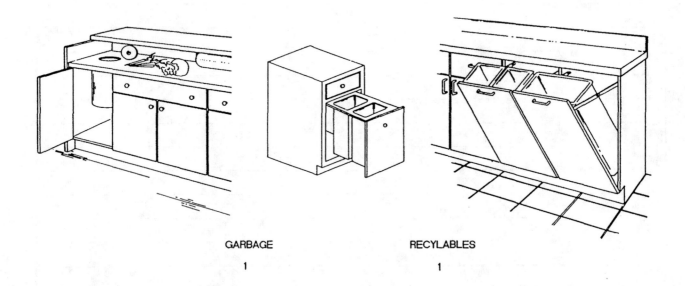

GARBAGE

1

RECYLABLES

1

GUIDELINE 12—At least two waste receptacles should be included in the plan; one for garbage and one for recyclables, or other recycling facilities should be planned.

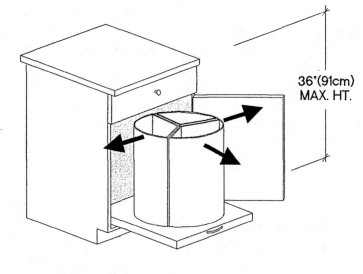

36"(91cm)
MAX. HT.

LATERAL REMOVAL
IS MOST DESIRABLE

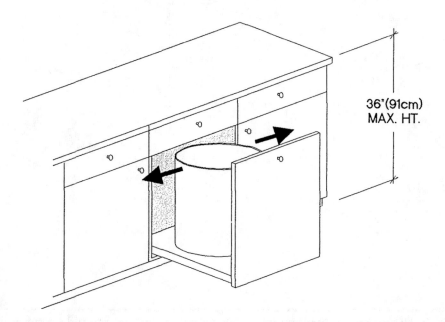

36"(91cm)
MAX. HT.

GUIDELINE 12 Clarification—The top edge of a waste receptacle should be no higher than 36" (91 cm). The receptacle should be easily accessible and should be removable without raising the receptacle bottom higher than the unit's physical height. Lateral removal of the receptacle which does not require lifting is most desirable.

Many recycling and waste receptacles, such as those in deep drawers or tilt-out cabinets require lifting them above the cabinet to empty them. Because this can be difficult for a person of shorter stature or a person with limited strength or mobility, it is more desirable to choose a receptacle that slides out or requires minimum lifting.

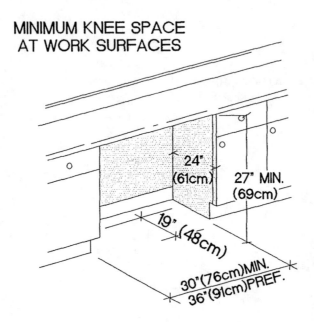

MINIMUM KNEE SPACE
AT WORK SURFACES

GUIDELINE 13—Knee space (which may be open or adaptable) should be planned below or adjacent to sinks, cooktops, ranges, dishwashers, refrigerators and ovens whenever possible. Knee space should be a minimum of 30" (76cm) wide by 27" (69cm) high by 19" (48cm) deep under the counter. The 27" (69cm) height at the front of the knee space may decrease progressively as depth increases.

The actual counter height at a knee space will vary. For a person in a wheelchair, the preferred height is 30" (76cm), but it may be as high as 34" (86cm). For a person with limited endurance or balance, a 36" (91cm) high counter may be comfortable if a stool is provided that is compatible with that counter height. The height of the armrest on a wheelchair or the depth of an appliance also will influence the counter height required for clearance.

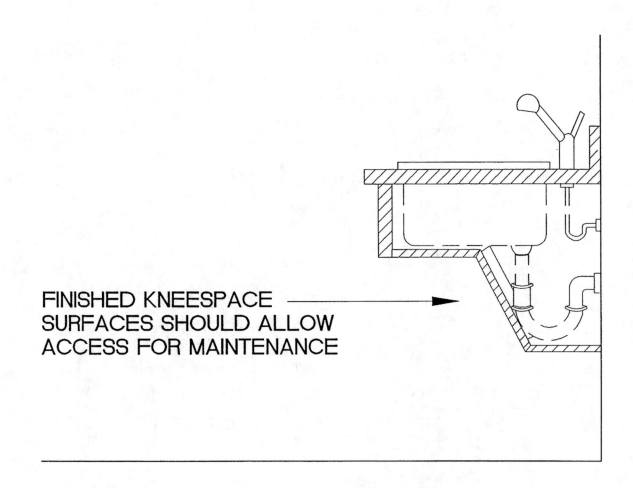

FINISHED KNEESPACE
SURFACES SHOULD ALLOW
ACCESS FOR MAINTENANCE

GUIDELINE 13 Clarification—Surfaces in the knee space area should be finished for safety and aesthetic purposes.

A protective and decorative panel should be part of the design of a knee space. A seated user should be protected from rough surfaces, hot elements, and the working parts of the appliance or fixture. In addition, the appliance, fixture, or plumbing should be protected from repeated impact. Finally, aesthetics dictate the use of a covering to coordinate the look of the space.

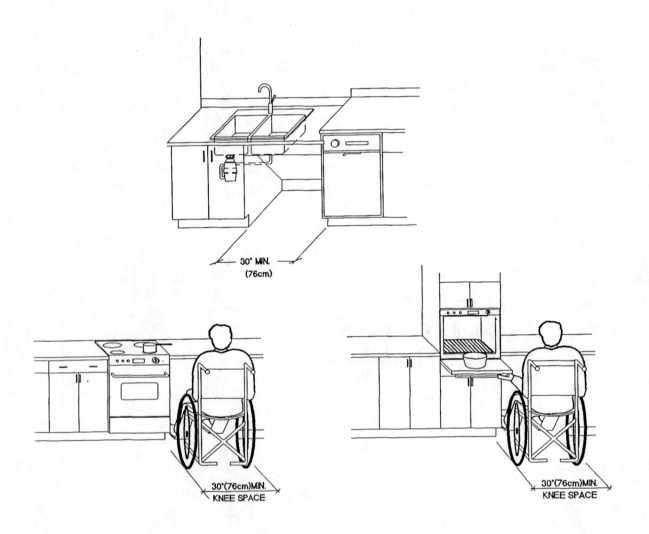

30" MIN.
(76cm)

30"(76cm)MIN.
KNEE SPACE

30"(76cm)MIN.
KNEE SPACE

GUIDELINE 13 Examples—Knee space provided at appliances makes them universally accessible. Surfaces in the knee space area should be finished for safety and aesthetic purposes.

Notes:

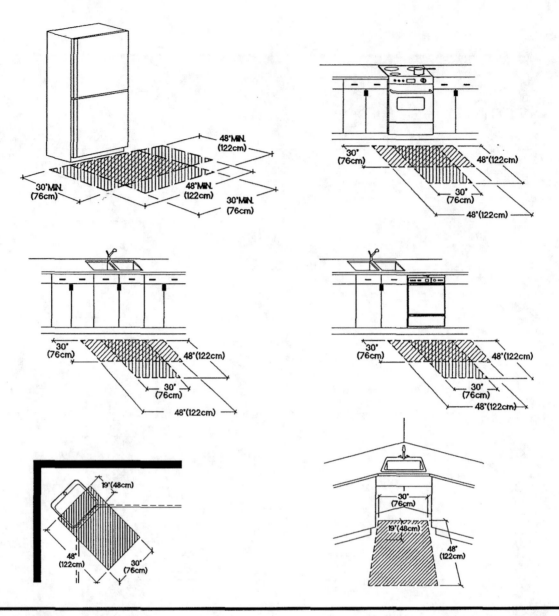

GUIDELINE 14—A clear floor space of 30"x 48" (76x122cm) should be provided at the sink, dishwasher, cooktop, oven and refrigerator. (Measure from face of cabinet or appliance if toekick is less than 9" (23 cm) high.)

If you are working with a standard height toekick, calculate the clear floor space from the face of the cabinetry. If the toekick is raised to 9" (23cm) or higher, you may include the depth of the toekick when figuring clear floor space. The reason is that a 9"-12"(23cm-30cm) toekick allows clearance for the footrest on most wheelchairs.

When a sink or cooktop is designed in an angled corner, there must be the minimum 30"x48" (76cm x 122cm) clear floor space access. Note the corner sink drawing that incorporates knee space where the actual angled countertop edge is less than 30" (76cm), but the distance between the two cabinets is greater. The 30" x 48" (76cm x 122cm) clear floor space may, however, include the knee space below, which begins 19" (48cm) in from the front edge of the counter as measured at the floor.

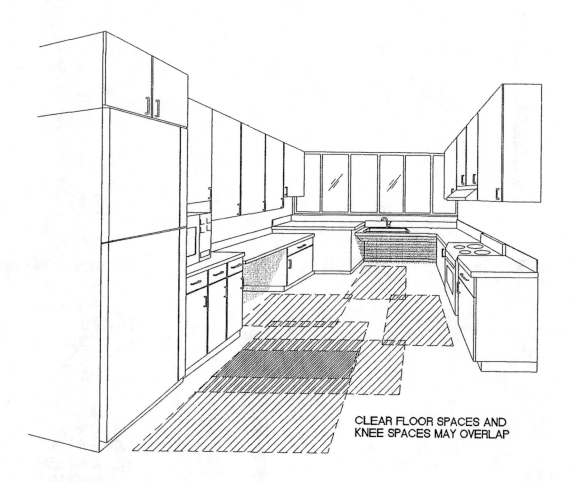

CLEAR FLOOR SPACES AND
KNEE SPACES MAY OVERLAP

GUIDELINE 14 Clarification—These spaces may overlap and up to 19" (48 cm) of knee space (beneath an appliance, counter, cabinet, etc.) may be part of the total 30" (76 cm) and/or 48" (122 cm) dimension.

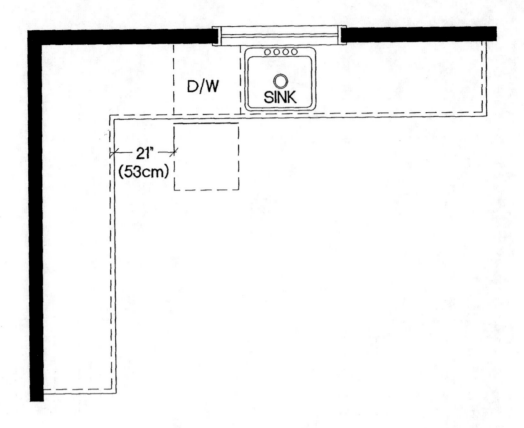

21"
(53cm)

D/W

SINK

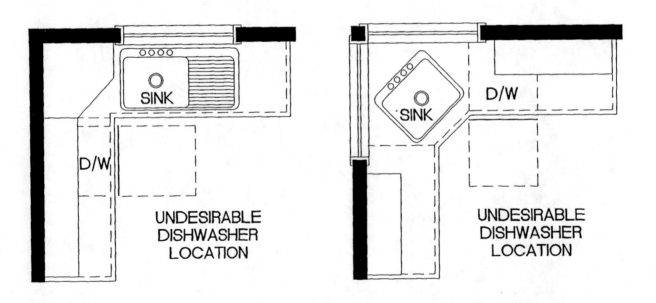

SINK

D/W

UNDESIRABLE
DISHWASHER
LOCATION

SINK

D/W

UNDESIRABLE
DISHWASHER
LOCATION

GUIDELINE 15—A minimum of 21" (53 cm) clear floor space should be allowed between the edge of the dishwasher and counters, appliances and/or cabinets which are placed at a right angle to the dishwasher.

Notes:

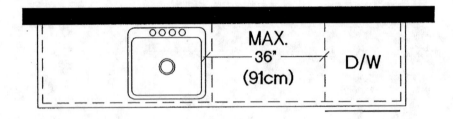

Guideline 16—The edge of the primary dishwasher should be within 36" (91 cm) of the edge of one sink.

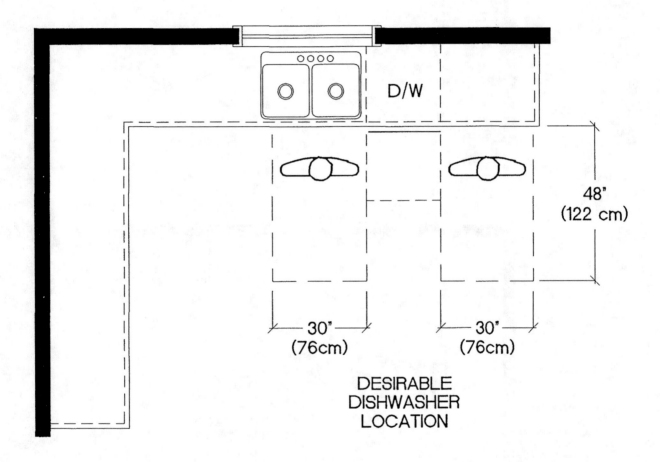

D/W

48"
(122 cm)

30"
(76cm)

30"
(76cm)

DESIRABLE
DISHWASHER
LOCATION

Guideline 16 Clarification—The dishwasher should be reachable by more than one person at a time to accommodate other cooks, kitchen clean-up helpers and/or other family members.

A 30"x48" (76cm x 122cm) clear floor space on both sides of the dishwasher will allow a person access to the dishwasher from either side.

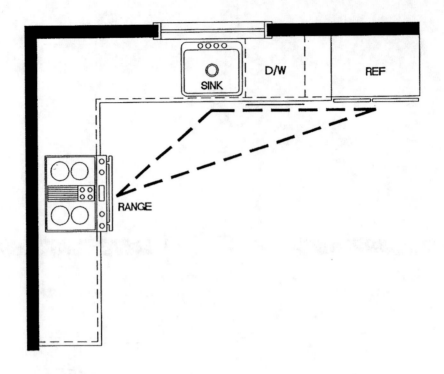

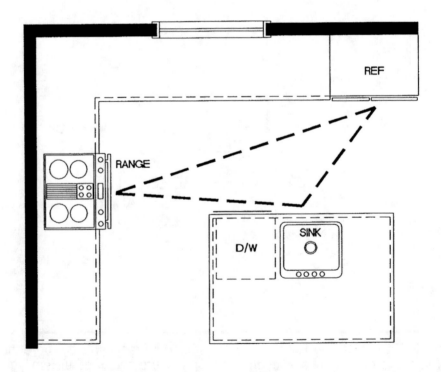

GUIDELINE 17—If the kitchen has only one sink, it should be located between or across from the cooking surface, preparation area or refrigerator.

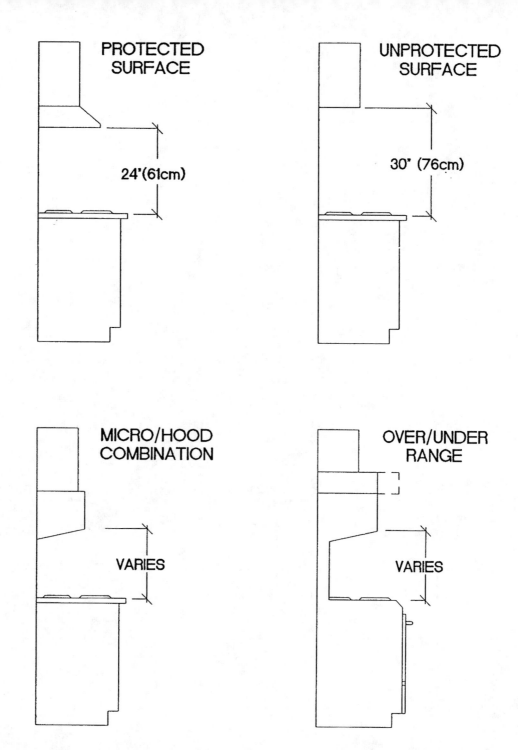

PROTECTED SURFACE

24"(61cm)

UNPROTECTED SURFACE

30" (76cm)

MICRO/HOOD COMBINATION

VARIES

OVER/UNDER RANGE

VARIES

GUIDELINE 18—There should be at least 24" (61 cm) of clearance between the cooking surface and a protected surface above, or at least 30" (76 cm) of clearance between the cooking surface and an unprotected surface above. If the protected surface is a microwave hood combination, manufacturer's specifications may dictate a clearance less than 24" (61 cm).

While manufacturer specifications may call for less clearance with a microwave/ hood or an oven over a cooking surface, safety and access relating to an upper oven or back burners should be considered.

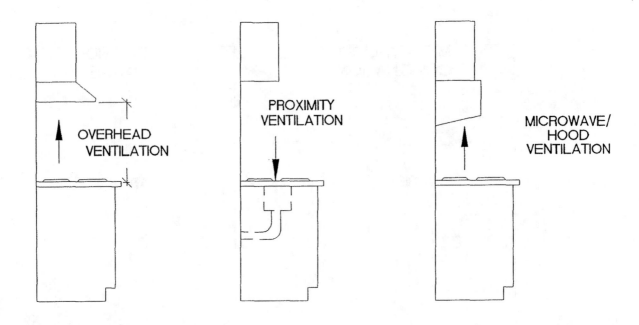

OVERHEAD
VENTILATION

PROXIMITY
VENTILATION

MICROWAVE/
HOOD
VENTILATION

GUIDELINE 19—All major appliances used for surface cooking should have a ventilation system, with a fan rated at 150 CFM minimum.

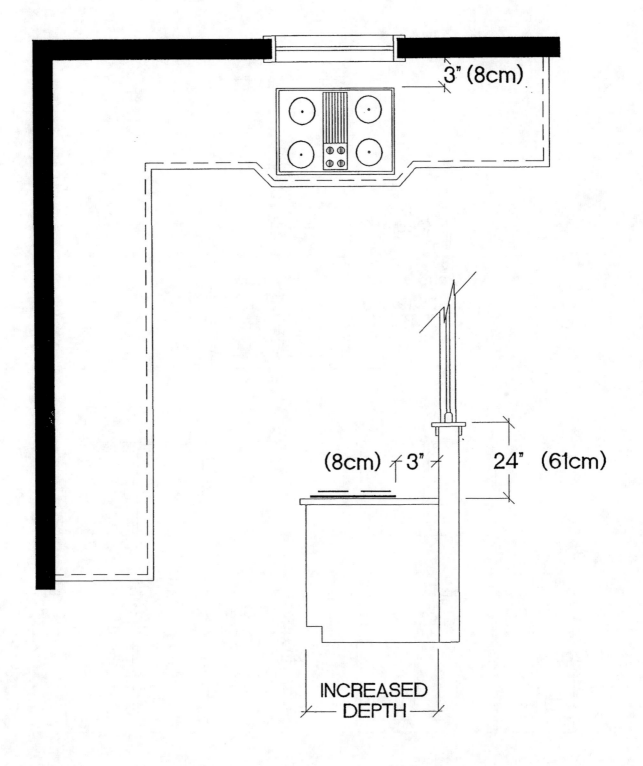

3" (8cm)

(8cm) 3"   24" (61cm)

INCREASED
DEPTH

GUIDELINE 20—The cooking surface should not be placed below an operable window unless the window is 3" (8 cm) or more behind the appliance and more than 24" (61 cm) above it. Windows, operable or inoperable, above a cooking surface should not be dressed with flammable window treatments.

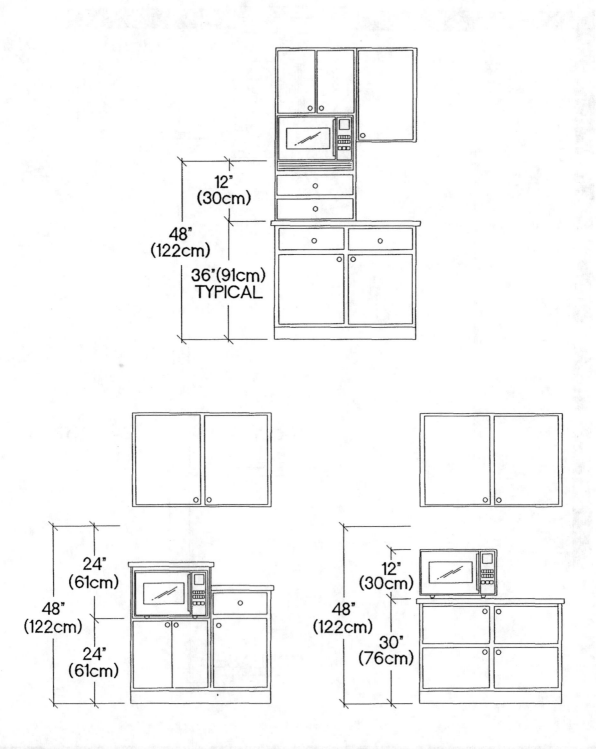

12"
(30cm)

48"
(122cm)

36"(91cm)
TYPICAL

24"
(61cm)

48"
(122cm)

24"
(61cm)

12"
(30cm)

48"
(122cm)

30"
(76cm)

GUIDELINE 21—Microwave ovens should be placed so that the bottom of the appliance is 24" (61 cm) to 48" (122 cm) above the floor.

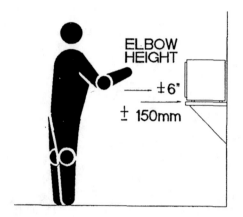

ELBOW
HEIGHT

±6"

± 150mm

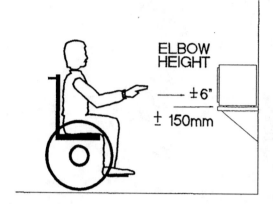

ELBOW
HEIGHT

±6"

± 150mm

CONVENIENT MICROWAVE
HEIGHT

SHOULDER
HEIGHT
-3"

-75mm

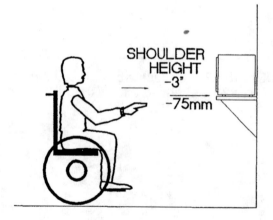

SHOULDER
HEIGHT
-3"

-75mm

SAFE MICROWAVE
HEIGHT

GUIDELINE 21—Clarification - The final placement recommendation should be based on the user's physical abilities, which may require placement outside of the preferred 24" (61 cm) to 48" (122 cm) range.

Appliances designed with a microwave/hood or oven over a range will not meet this guideline but may be a necessary choice. When designing for a seated user, it may be desirable to go below the 24" (61cm) guideline. If this is the case, safety for toddlers becomes an issue and must be addressed.

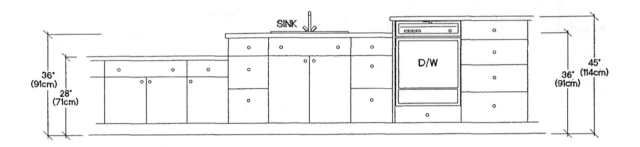

GUIDELINE 22—At least two work-counter heights should be offered in the kitchen, with one 28" - 36" (71cm-91 cm) above the finished floor and the other 36"-45" (91cm-114cm) above the finished floor.

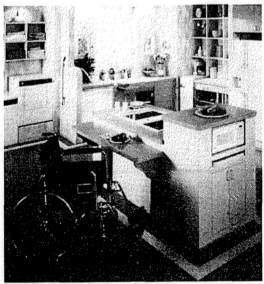

Varying counter heights will create work spaces for various tasks and for cooks of varying stature, including seated cooks.

Notes:

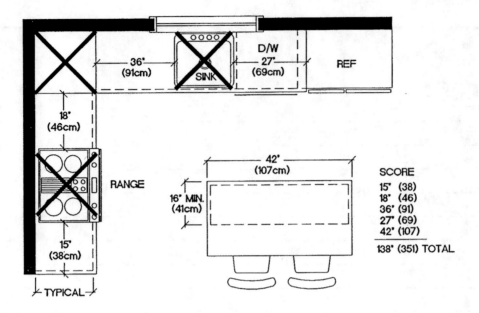

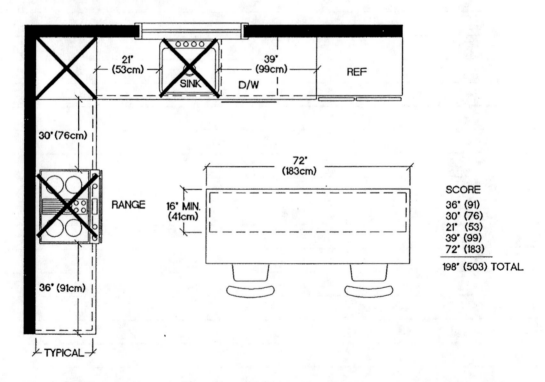

GUIDELINE 23 Countertop Frontage Small Kitchens—under 150 sq. ft. (14 M²) - allow at least 132" (335cm) of usable countertop frontage.

GUIDELINE 23 Countertop Frontage Large Kitchens—over 150 sq. ft. (14 M²) - allow at least 198" of usable countertop frontage.

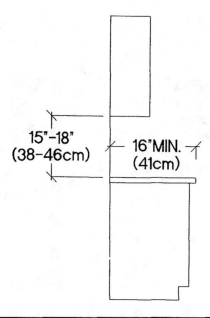

15"-18"
(38-46cm)

16"MIN.
(41cm)

GUIDELINE 23 Countertop Frontage—Counters must be a minimum of 16" (41 cm) deep, and wall cabinets must be at least 15" (38 cm) above their surface for counter to be included in total frontage measurement. (Measure only countertop frontage, do not count corner space.)

The minimum 15" (38cm) of clearance between a work surface and a wall cabinet relates to appliance storage and line of sight. However, there are times when dropping the wall cabinets lower, even onto the counter, will provide needed storage in the universal reach range.

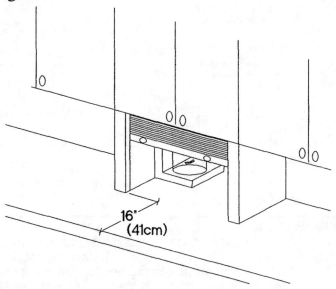

16"
(41cm)

GUIDELINE 23 Clarification—If an appliance garage/storage cabinet extends to the counter, there must be 16" (41 cm) of clear space in front of this cabinet for the area to be counted as usable countertop frontage.

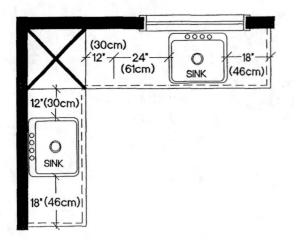

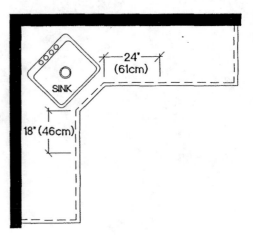

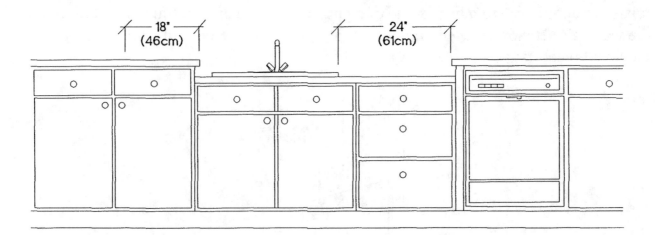

GUIDELINE 24—There should be at least 24" (61 cm) of countertop frontage to one side of the primary sink, and 18" (46 cm) on the other side (including corner sink applications) with the 24" (61 cm) counter frontage at the same counter height as the sink. The countertop frontage may be a continuous surface, or the total of two angled countertop sections. (Measure only countertop frontage, do not count corner space.) *For further instruction on these requirements see Guideline 31.*

Whenever possible, the counter space on both sides of the sink should be at the same height.

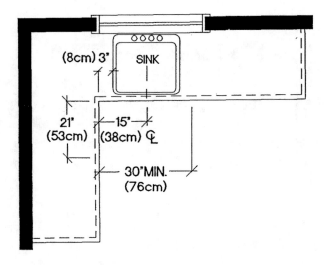

GUIDELINE 24 Clarification—The minimum allowable space from a corner to the edge of the primary sink is 3" (8 cm) ; it should also be a minimum of 15" (38 cm) from that corner to the sink centerline.

The minimum 15" (38cm) to centerline allows 30" x 48" (76cm x 122cm) clear floor space to be planned centered on the sink.

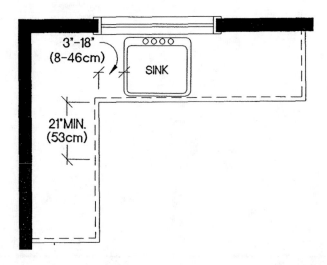

GUIDELINE 24 Clarification—If there is anything less than 18" (46 cm) of frontage from the edge of the primary sink to a corner, 21" (53 cm) of clear counter (measure frontage) should be allowed on the return.

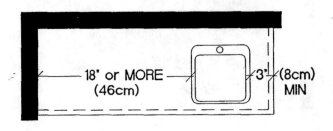

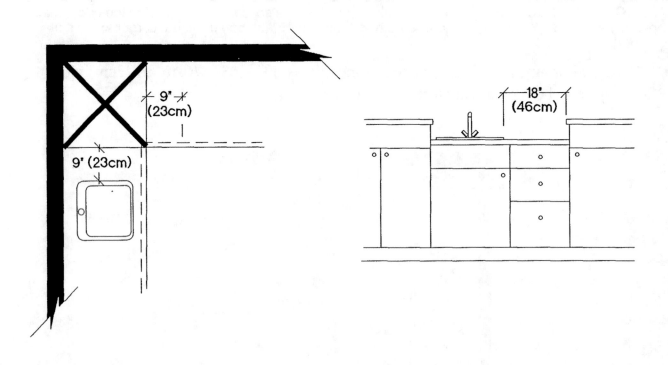

GUIDELINE 25—At least 3" (8 cm) of countertop frontage should be provided on one side of secondary sinks, and 18" (46 cm) on the other side (including corner sink applications) with the 18" (46 cm) counter frontage at the same counter height as the sink. The countertop frontage may be a continuous surface, or the total of two angled countertop sections. (Measure only countertop frontage, do not count corner space.) *For further instruction on these requirements see Guideline 31.*

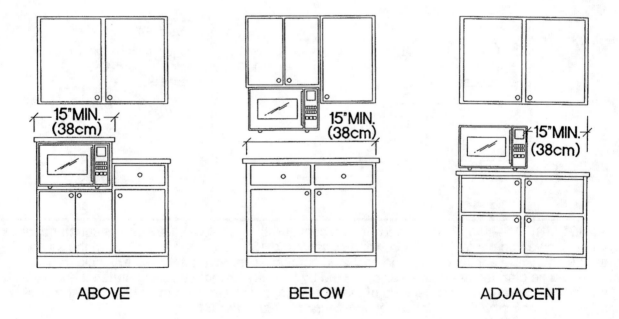

ABOVE   BELOW   ADJACENT

GUIDELINE 26—At least 15" (38 cm) of landing space, a minimum of 16" (41 cm) deep, should be planned above, below or adjacent to a microwave oven. *For further instruction on these requirements see Guideline 31.*

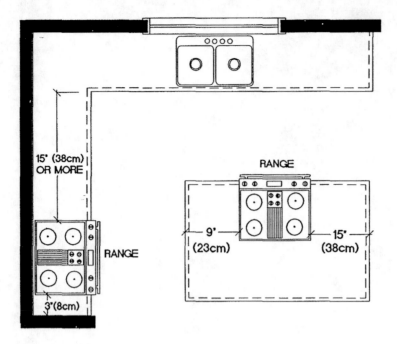

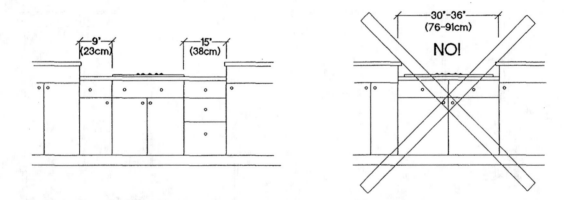

GUIDELINE 27—In an open-ended kitchen configuration, at least 9" (23 cm) of counter space should be allowed on one side of the cooking surface and 15" (38 cm) on the other, at the same counter height as the appliance. For an enclosed configuration, at least 3" (8 cm) of clearance space should be planned at an end wall protected by flame-retardant surfacing material and 15" (38 cm) should be allowed on the other side of the appliance, at the same counter height as the appliance. *For further instruction on these requirements see Guideline 31.*

Maintaining the minimum counter area adjacent to a cooktop at the same height as the cooktop improves safety and accessibility. In case of emergency/fire, the cook should be able to slide a pot right off the burner onto adjacent counter without lifting or lowering. A person with limited strength, grip, or balance will use this technique on a regular basis and in this case, adjacent spaces should be heat-resistant.

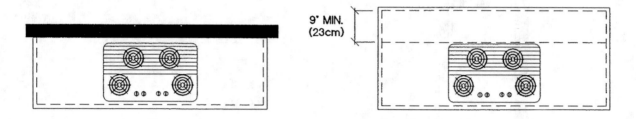

9" MIN.
(23cm)

GUIDELINE 27 Clarification—For safety reasons, countertop should also extend a minimum of 9" (23 cm) behind the cooking surface, at the same counter height as the appliance, in any instance where there is not an abutting wall/backsplash.

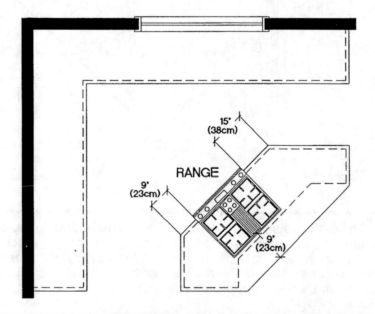

15"
(38cm)

RANGE

9"
(23cm)

9"
(23cm)

GUIDELINE 27 Clarification—In an outside angle installation of cooking surfaces, there should be at least 9" (23 cm) of straight counter space on one side and 15" (38 cm) of straight counter space on the other side, at the same counter height as the appliance.

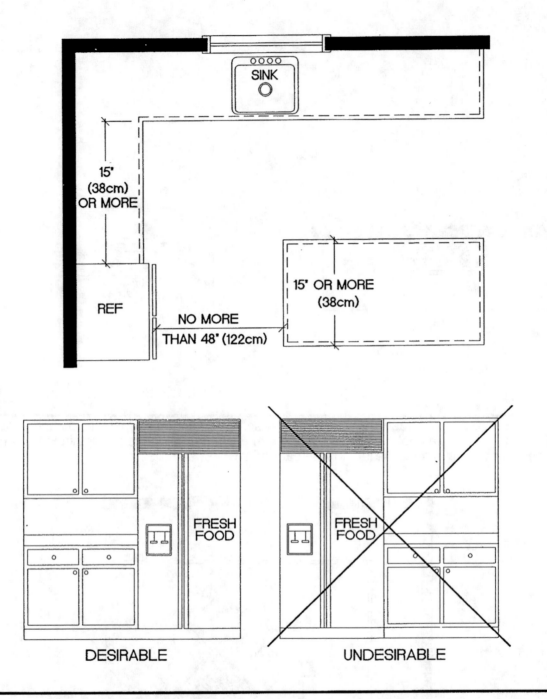

DESIRABLE UNDESIRABLE

GUIDELINE 28—The plan should allow at least 15" (38 cm) of counter space on the handle side of the refrigerator or on either side of a side-by-side refrigerator or, at least 15" (38 cm) of landing space which is no more than 48" (122 cm) across from the refrigerator. (Measure the 48" (122 cm) distance from the center front of the refrigerator to the countertop opposite it.)
For further instruction on these requirements see Guideline 31.

When side-by-side refrigerators are specified, it is preferable to design the space so that countertop can be easily accessed by an individual using the fresh food section.

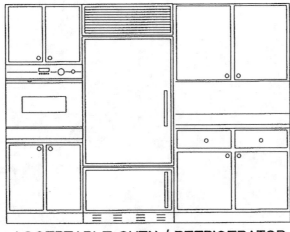

ACCEPTABLE OVEN / REFRIGERATOR
PLACEMENT

GUIDELINE 28 Clarification—Although not ideal, it is acceptable to place an oven adjacent to a refrigerator. For convenience, the refrigerator should be the appliance placed next to available countertop. If there is no safe landing area across from the oven, this arrangement may be reversed.

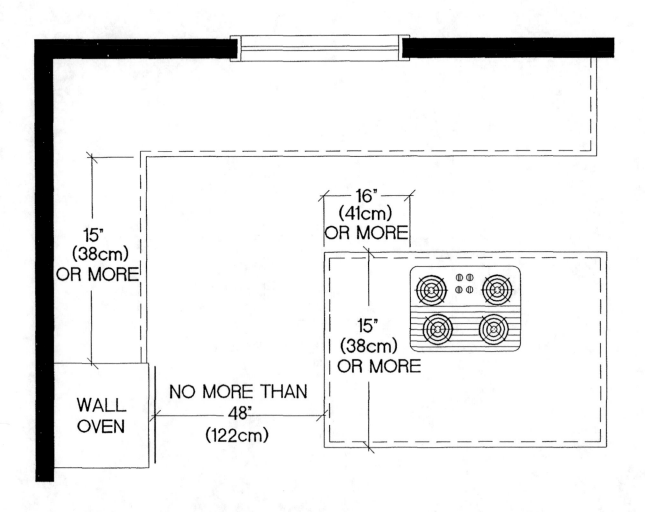

15"
(38cm)
OR MORE

16"
(41cm)
OR MORE

15"
(38cm)
OR MORE

WALL
OVEN

NO MORE THAN
48"
(122cm)

GUIDELINE 29—There should be at least 15" (38 cm) of landing space which is at least 16" (41 cm) deep next to or above the oven if the appliance door opens into a primary traffic pattern. At least 15" (38 cm) x 16" (41 cm) of landing space which is no more than 48" (122 cm) across from the oven is acceptable if the appliance does not open into a traffic area. (Measure the 48" (122 cm) distance from the center front of the oven to the countertop opposite it.) *For further instruction on these requirements see Guideline 31.*

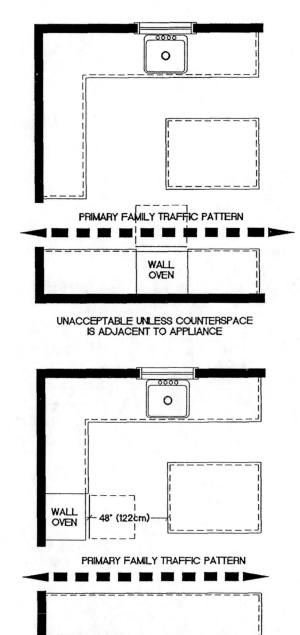

PRIMARY FAMILY TRAFFIC PATTERN

WALL
OVEN

UNACCEPTABLE UNLESS COUNTERSPACE
IS ADJACENT TO APPLIANCE

WALL
OVEN

|← 48" (122cm) →|

PRIMARY FAMILY TRAFFIC PATTERN

ACCEPTABLE TO HAVE LANDING SPACE
ACROSS FROM APPLIANCES

GUIDELINE 29 Examples—In the top example, the oven opens directly into a major traffic pattern leading from the utility area to the family room. This is a dangerous installation which should be avoided unless there is landing space on either side of the oven. In the bottom example, the oven is located within the cook's primary work space, away from the family traffic pattern. Therefore, a landing area can be directly opposite it.

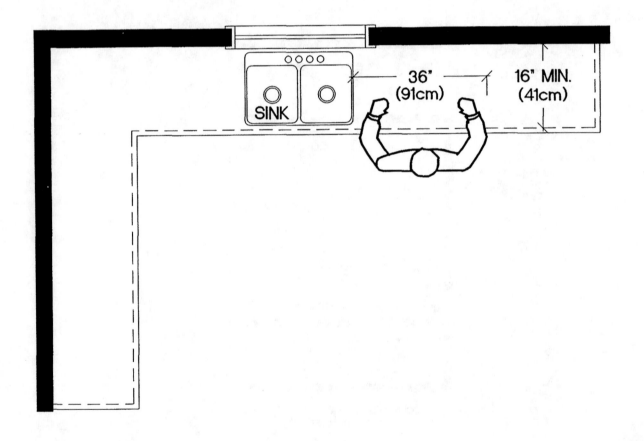

GUIDELINE 30—At least 36" (91 cm) of continuous countertop which is at least 16" (41 cm) deep should be planned for the preparation center. The preparation center should be immediately adjacent to a water source. *For further instruction on these requirements see Guideline 31.*

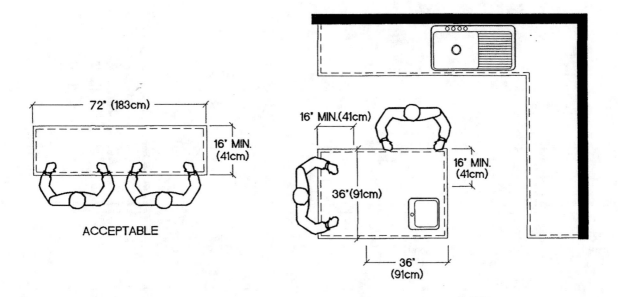

ACCEPTABLE

GUIDELINE 30 Clarification—If two or more people work in the kitchen simultaneously, each will need a minimum 36" (91 cm) wide by 16" (41 cm) deep preparation center of their own. If two people will stand adjacent to one another, a 72" (183 cm) wide by 16" (41 cm) deep space should be planned.

Try to orient the two people so that conversation can be continued during cooking and/or clean up process.

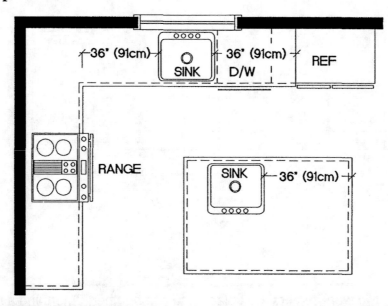

GUIDELINE 30 Clarification—The preparation center can be placed between the primary sink and the cooking surface, between the refrigerator and the primary sink, or adjacent to a secondary sink on an island or other cabinet section.

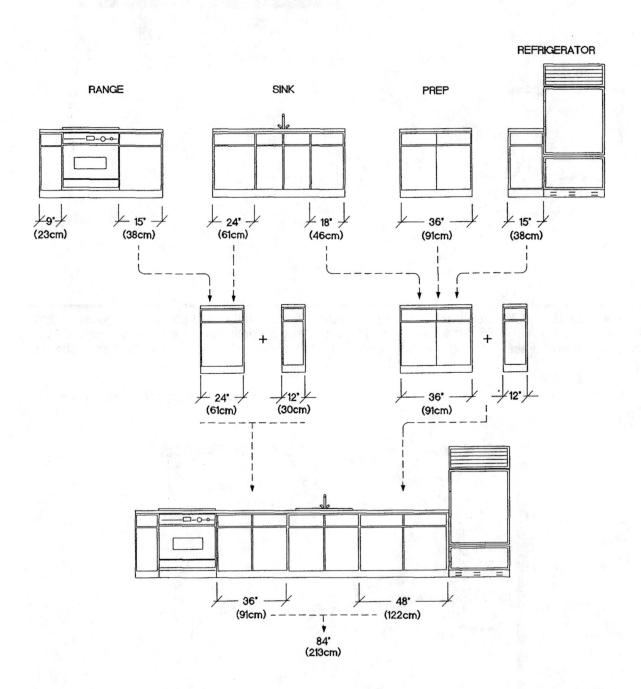

RANGE SINK PREP REFRIGERATOR

9" (23cm) 15" (38cm) 24" (61cm) 18" (46cm) 36" (91cm) 15" (38cm)

24" (61cm) + 12" (30cm) 36" (91cm) + 12"

36" (91cm) 48" (122cm)

84" (213cm)

GUIDELINE 31—If two work centers are adjacent to one another, determine a new minimum counter frontage requirement for the two adjoining spaces by taking the longest of the two required counter lengths and adding 12" (30 cm).

Notes:

_____

_____

_____

_____

_____

_____

_____

_____

_____

_____

_____

_____

_____

_____

_____

_____

_____

_____

_____

_____

_____

_____

_____

_____

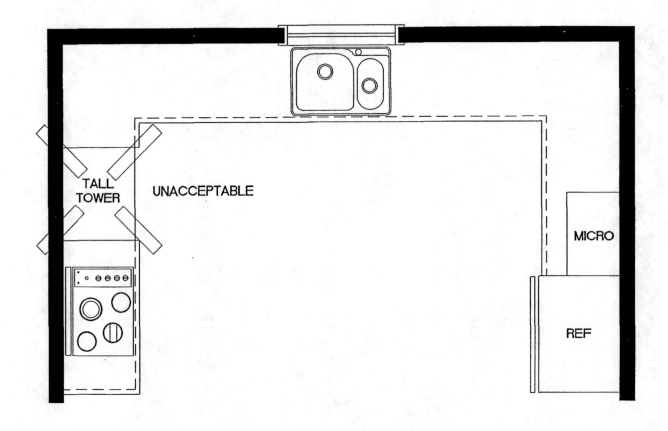

TALL
TOWER

UNACCEPTABLE

MICRO

REF

GUIDELINE 32—No two primary work centers (the primary sink, refrigerator, preparation or cooktop/range center) should be separated by a full-height, full-depth tall tower, such as an oven cabinet, pantry cabinet or refrigerator.

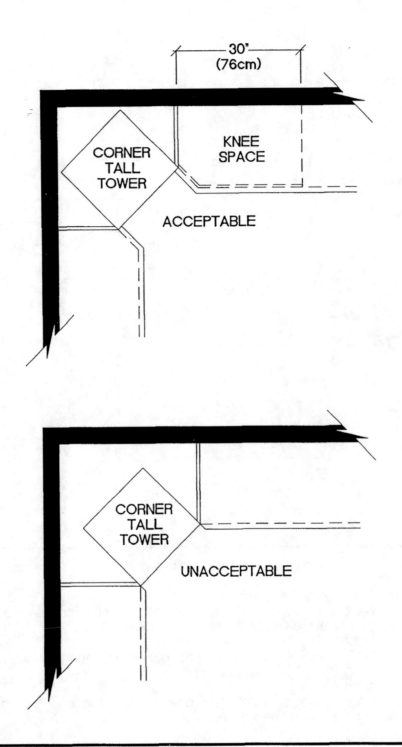

30"
(76cm)

CORNER
TALL
TOWER

KNEE
SPACE

ACCEPTABLE

CORNER
TALL
TOWER

UNACCEPTABLE

GUIDELINE 32 Clarification—A corner-recessed tall tower between primary work centers is acceptable if knee space is planned to one side of the tower.

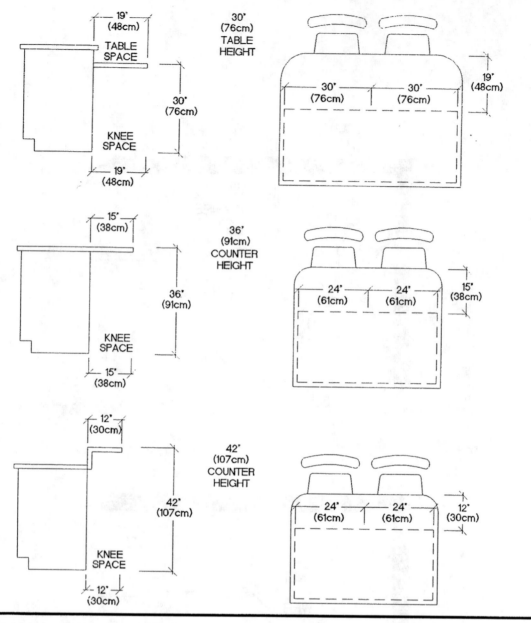

GUIDELINE 33— Kitchen seating areas require the following minimum clearances:

30" (76 cm) high tables/counters:
>allow a 30" (76 cm) wide x 19" (48 cm) deep counter/table space for each seated diner, and at least 19" (23 cm) (48 cm) of clear knee space

36" (91 cm) high counters:
>allow a 24" (61 cm) wide by 15" (38 cm) deep counter space for each seated diner, and at least 15" (38 cm) of clear knee space

42" (107 cm) high counters:
>allow a 24" (61 cm) wide by 12" (30 cm) deep counter space for each seated diner, and 12" (30 cm) of clear knee space

Given that a 30" (76cm) high table or counter will work for a person in a wheelchair, the width of the allowance for each seated diner has been increased to allow for diners using wheelchairs.

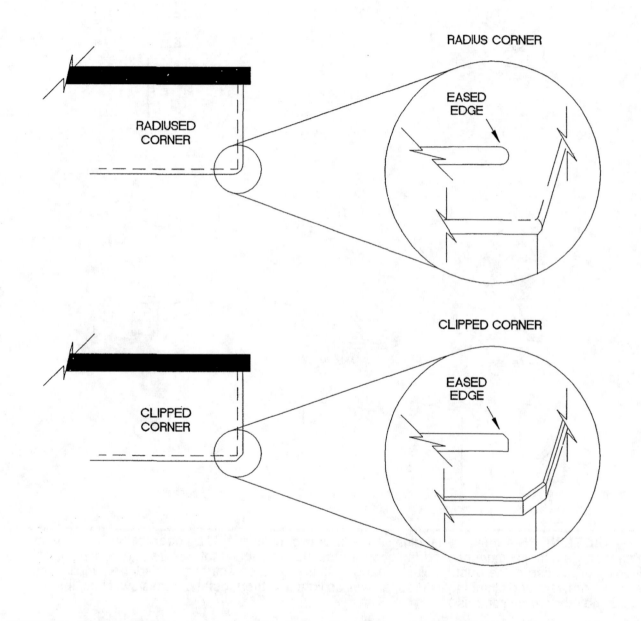

RADIUS CORNER

RADIUSED CORNER

EASED EDGE

CLIPPED CORNER

CLIPPED CORNER

EASED EDGE

GUIDELINE 34—(Open) countertop corners should be clipped or radiused; counter edges should be eased to eliminate sharp edges.

SECTION V: Room, Appliance and Equipment Controls
Guideline 35 to Guideline 40

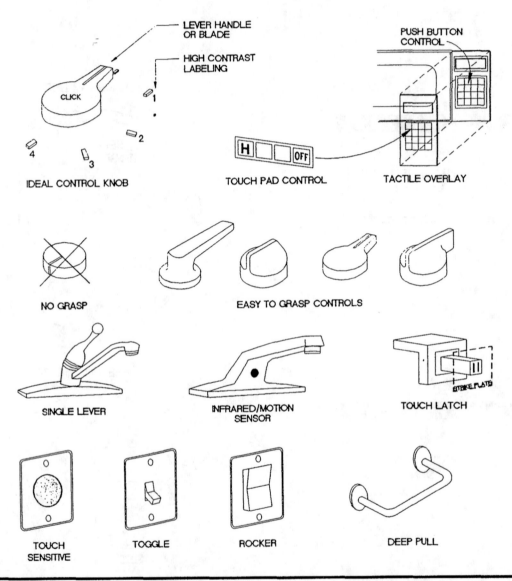

GUIDELINE 35—Controls, handles and door/drawer pulls should be operable with one hand, require only a minimal amount of strength for operation, and should not require tight grasping, pinching or twisting of the wrist. (Includes handles/knobs/pulls on entry and exit doors, appliances, cabinets, drawers and plumbing fixtures, as well as light and thermostat controls/switches, intercoms, and other room controls.)

Controls that meet this guideline expand their use to include people with limited strength, dexterity and grasping abilities. A simple test is to try operating the controls with a closed fist.

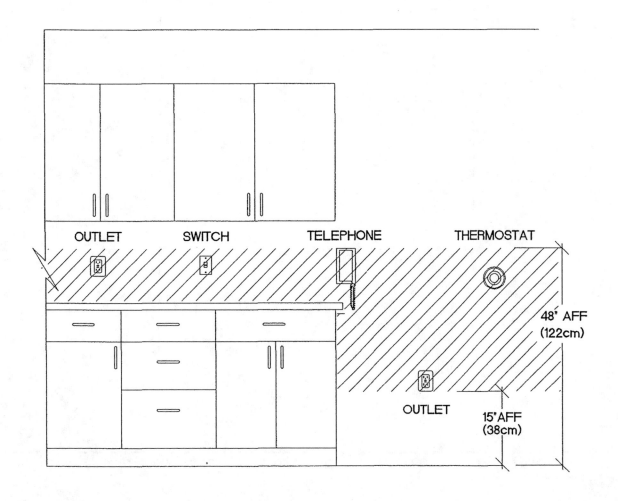

OUTLET   SWITCH   TELEPHONE   THERMOSTAT

48" AFF
(122cm)

OUTLET   15" AFF
(38cm)

GUIDELINE 36—Wall-mounted room controls (ie: wall receptacles, switches, thermostats, telephones, intercoms etc.) should be 15" (38 cm) to 48" (122 cm) above the finished floor. The switch plate can extend beyond that dimension, but the control itself should be within it.

Guideline 37—Ground fault circuit interrupters should be specified on all receptacles within the kitchen.

GFCI are a safety feature throughout the kitchen, including protection when foreign objects are accidentally inserted into an outlet, as well as when an outlet is close to water.

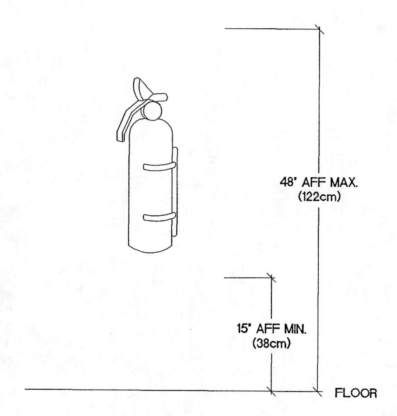

48" AFF MAX.
(122cm)

15" AFF MIN.
(38cm)

FLOOR

Guideline 38—A fire extinguisher should be visibly located in the kitchen, away from cooking equipment and 15" (38 cm) to 48" (122 cm) above the floor. Smoke alarms should be included near the kitchen.

A fire extinguisher that can be seen and reached easily expands access to most people.

GUIDELINE 39—Window/skylight area should equal at least 10% of the total square footage of the separate kitchen, or a total living space which includes a kitchen.

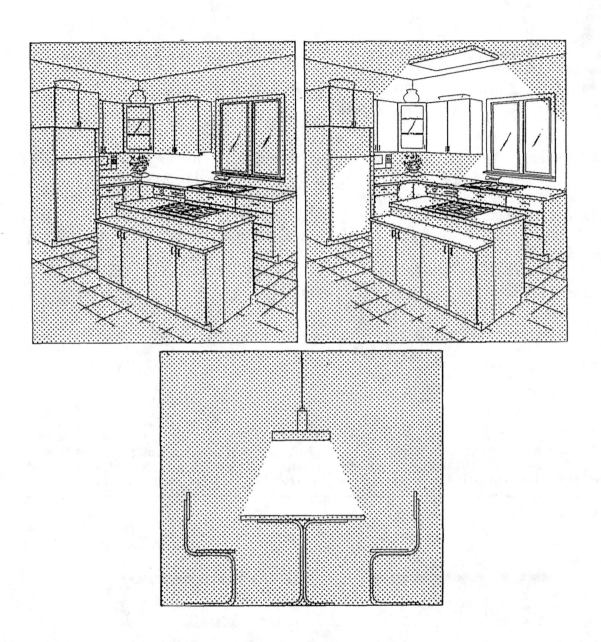

GUIDELINE 40— Every work surface in the kitchen should be well-illuminated by appropriate task and/or general lighting.

4 How to Lay Out the Kitchen
Cabinets, Fillers, Hardware, Accessories

Now let's actually lay out a kitchen. We'll need a good 3H or 4H drawing pencil with eraser, a T-square for a straight edge for horizontal lines and a triangle for vertical lines. NKBA's triangle is handiest because it also is a ruled template.

We'll do a 1-wall kitchen in detail, step by step, and then a U kitchen. In doing it we will use the subtraction method, which is generally known and accepted in the industry.

Before starting you should have any dimensions and information provided by the customer and your own sketch and measurements, plus the cabinet sizes and specifications of the cabinet line you will use. You should familiarize yourself thoroughly with your customer survey.

Fig. 4.0. The first step is to consult our notes and our sketch. Draw the walls of the kitchen and place the window, carefully and accurately, all in inches and not mixing feet and inches. The overall inside dimension is 222 3/4" (565.79cm). There is a window opening that is 40 1/2" wide (102.87cm) including casing. The window C/L (center line) is 120 3/4" (306.71cm) from the right wall and 102" (259.08cm) from the left wall.

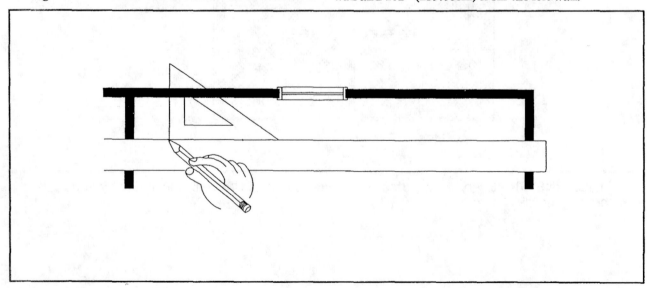

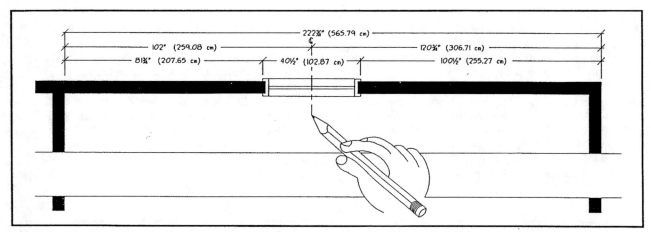

Fig. 4.1. After drawing the walls and the window, take the dimensions from your sketch and put them on your drawing in accord with the Graphics and Presentation Standards (Appendix D). Leave room for C/L dimensions immediately above the walls. On the next line enter the usable space on either side of the window and the window measurement, including trim. There is 81 3/4" (207.65cm) to the left of the window, 100 1/2" (255.27cm) to the right of the window. The window with trim is 40 1/2" (102.87cm). On the next line above that, enter the center line (C/L) of the window, 120 3/4" (306.71cm) from the right wall and 102" (259.08cm) from the left wall. Fill in these figures. Your third line above the drawing will be the total inside length of the wall, 222 3/4" (565.79cm).

Fig. 4.2. Now we are ready to lay out the kitchen. First draw two horizontal lines, one 12" (30.48cm) from the wall and 24" (60.96cm) from the wall. The first shows the depth of the wall cabinets; the second, the depth of the base cabinets, the equipment (appliances) and the tall cabinet we intend to include. The next step is to decide where to put the work centers so the amount of travel is reduced as much as possible. Since the sink/clean-up center is most used, it will be near the center. Most people prefer the sink under the window, so here we center it under the window. We are using a refrigerator hinged at the right, so we put it on the right side so the door will open into the work area. The range, then, should be on the left.

Now we will start putting in the base cabinets. Before putting another line on the paper, do your computations using the subtraction line method of planning to make sure everything will fit properly (see Fig. 4.4). Start at the right of the C/L and figure base cabinets. We have 120 3/4" (306.71cm) to work with. We will figure a 36" (91.44cm) sink base under the window. By centering it we have half, or 18" (45.72cm) to deduct from 120 3/4" (306.71cm), leaving us 102 3/4" (260.99cm). We will place the dishwasher to the right of the sink and deduct 24" (60.96cm) from 102 3/4" (260.99cm), leaving 78 3/4" (200.03cm). (This arrangement is preferred by a left-handed customer.) We need 48" (121.92cm) for the food preparation area between the refrigerator and the sink, so we add a 24" (60.96cm) base cabinet. Since we may want to use a bread box and bulk storage in this area, we will use a drawer base and deduct 24" (60.96cm) from 78 3/4" (200.03cm), leaving 54 3/4" (139.07cm). We are using a 35" (88.90cm) refrigerator and will provide an extra

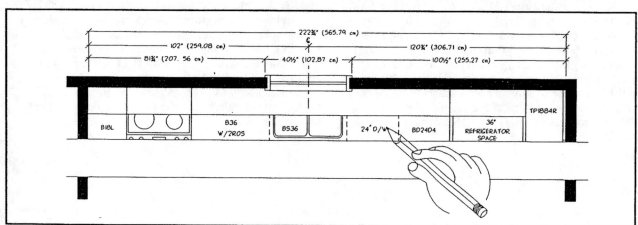

inch (2.54cm) for clearance. Deducting 36" (91.44cm) from 54 3/4" (139.07cm), we have 18 3/4" (47.63cm) left. This is sufficient for a tall storage unit that can be used for staple foods in packages. It would be a unit 18" (45.72cm) wide with door hinged to the right, 24" (60.96cm) deep and 84" (213.36cm) high. To the left of the C/L we have 222 3/4" (565.78cm) less 120 3/4" (306.70cm), or 102" (259.08cm) to work with. Deducting the left side of the sink base, or 18" (45.72cm) from 102" (259.08cm), we have 84" (213.36cm) left. We want a work area on each side of the range.

The range is 30" (76.20 cm) wide and a slide-in. Deducting this from 84" (213.36cm) leaves 54" (137.16cm). We learned previously that we should strive for a desirable 18" (45.72cm) on the far side of the range, so we deduct 18" (45.72cm) from 54" (137.16cm) and we have 36" (91.44cm) left for a 36" (91.44cm) base unit between the range and the sink. We now have our base section. REMEMBER, we are doing all this on scrap paper and will fill in the drawings later.

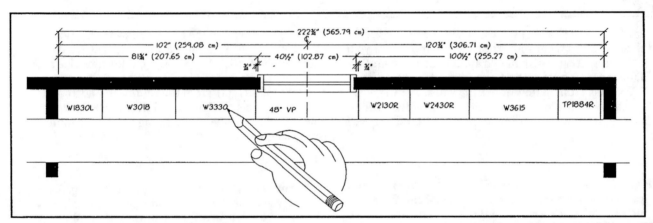

Fig. 4.3. We will now plan the wall cabinets. Wall cabinets usually are sized to line up as nearly as possible with base cabinets. The usable wall space on the right side of the window is 100 1/2" (255.27cm). Our tall cabinet and filler on the extreme right takes 18 3/4" (45.63cm) of that space, leaving 81 3/4" (207.65 cm). To fit the space over the refrigerator we will use a W3615, which is the designation for a wall cabinet 36" (91.44cm) wide and 15" (38.10cm) high. Deducting this from 81 3/4" (207.65cm) we have 45 3/4" (116.21cm) left. We could use a W4530 here but most stock cabinet manufacturers do not make a unit this size. We can use two cabinets, W2130R next to the window and a W2430R over the 24" (60.96cm) base. The W2130R is a wall cabinet 21" (53.34cm) wide and 30" (76.20cm) high, hinged right. The W2430R is a wall cabinet 24" (60.96cm) wide and 30" (76.20cm) high, hinged right. Deducting that total of 45" (114.30cm) from 45 3/4" (116.21cm), we have a 3/4" (1.91cm) reveal between the window casing and the cabinet. To the left of the window we have 81 3/4" (207.65cm) from the wall to the edge of the casing. We will use a W1830L wall cabinet over the B18L base. Deducting

this from 81 3/4" we have 63 3/4" (161.93cm) left. We then use a W3018 cabinet over the range to provide for a ventilating hood under it. Most hoods are about 6" (15.24 cm) high, allowing sufficient clearance over the cooktop when used with a W3018. However, when using extra high and deep hoods it will be necessary to use a W3015. Deducting 30" (76.20cm) from 63 3/4" (161.93cm), we have 33 3/4" (85.73cm) left. Using a W3330L in the remaining space will leave a 3/4" (1.91 cm) reveal between it and the casing, matching the reveal on the other side. Should there be need for a greater amount of reveal on each side of the window, such as for drapery stack-up, the two cabinets on either side of the window could be reduced in size by 3" (7.62 cm). In a kitchen of this small size it may be preferable to provide as much storage space as possible and keep the reveal to a minimum. The cabinets on each side are tied together by using a valance board between them. The valance board is flush with the front face of the cabinets and under the bulkhead or soffit. A standard width valance is 48" (121.92cm). We need only 42" (106.68cm) of valance, so the board would be cut to fit on the job site.

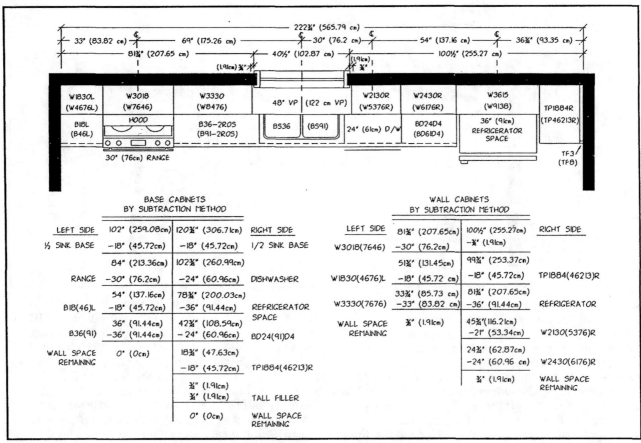

BASE CABINETS BY SUBTRACTION METHOD			
LEFT SIDE	102" (259.08cm)	120¾" (306.7cm)	RIGHT SIDE
½ SINK BASE	−18" (45.72cm)	−18" (45.72cm)	½ SINK BASE
	84" (213.36cm)	102¾" (260.99cm)	
RANGE	−30" (76.2cm)	−24" (60.96cm)	DISHWASHER
	54" (137.16cm)	78¾" (200.03cm)	
B18(46)L	−18" (45.72cm)	−36" (91.44cm)	REFRIGERATOR SPACE
	36" (91.44cm)	42¾" (108.59cm)	
B36(91)	−36" (91.44cm)	−24" (60.96cm)	BD24(91)D4
WALL SPACE REMAINING	0" (0cm)	18¾" (47.63cm)	
		−18" (45.72cm)	TP1884(46213)R
		¾" (1.91cm)	
		¾" (1.91cm)	TALL FILLER
		0" (0cm)	WALL SPACE REMAINING

WALL CABINETS BY SUBTRACTION METHOD			
LEFT SIDE	81¾" (207.65cm)	100½" (255.27cm)	RIGHT SIDE
W3018(7646)	−30" (76.2cm)	−¾" (1.91cm)	
	51¾" (131.45cm)	99¾" (253.37cm)	
W1830(4676)L	−18" (45.72 cm)	−18" (45.72cm)	TP1884(46213)R
	33¾" (85.73 cm)	81¾" (207.65cm)	
W3330(7676)	−33" (83.82 cm)	−36" (91.44cm)	REFRIGERATOR
WALL SPACE REMAINING	¾" (1.91cm)	45¾" (116.21cm)	
		−21" (53.34cm)	W2130(5376)R
		24¾" (62.87cm)	
		−24" (60.96 cm)	W2430(6176)R
		¾" (1.91cm)	WALL SPACE REMAINING

Fig. 4.4, 4.5. Now that we have worked out the cabinet layout we will put in the lines representing the widths of the various units. The lines for the base units will be dotted and extend only to the front line of the wall units. Then draw a solid counter line in front of all base cabinets to indicate the overhang. When you have completed the layout, go over the lines representing the front edges of the wall and base cabinets to strengthen them. Then letter the nomenclature of the cabinets and appliances, using top and bottom guide lines for the letters and numbers to give them a uniform size. Using your template, draw in a sink bowl, refrigerator, range burners and hood to complete the plan. It's good to have a separate listing of appliances and cabinets with your proposal.

To trim the cabinets where they meet the soffit or bulkhead, it is desirable to use a molding. If the bulkhead is deeper than the cabinets, a cove molding should be used under it and against the face of the cabinets above the doors. If the bulkhead is built flush with the face of the cabinets, a batten molding is used to cover the crack between the top of the cabinet and the face board of the bulkhead. Most molding comes in 96" (243.84 cm) lengths. Specify the number of pieces required. In this kitchen, the overall length is 222 3/4" (565.79cm), so three pieces would be required. The molding would be carried across the valance board as well as the cabinets.

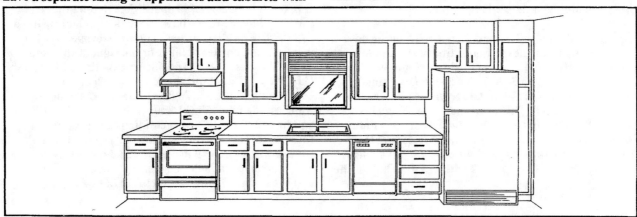

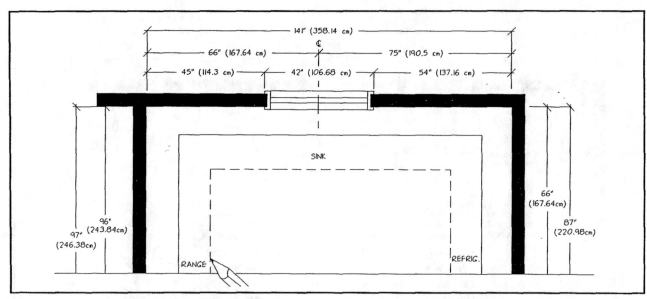

Fig. 4.6. The U kitchen is more complicated in that it has two inside corners. We have a room that is 141"x 208" (358.14 x 528.32 cm). Since we do not intend to develop any storage space initially in the dining room we have not shown it on the drawing. The window wall is 141" (358.14cm) wide. There is a 42" (106.68cm) window including trim, centered 66" (167.64 cm) from the left corner. Usable space to the left of the window is 45" (114.30cm) and 54" (137.16cm) to the right. The left wall next to the dining room is 97" (246.38cm) long. The right wall is 87" (220.98cm) long.

Our first step is to measure out from each wall, 12" (30.48cm) and 24" (60.96cm) respectively, then draw lines around the three sides to indicate the front lines of the wall and base cabinets. You can see that there is sufficient space to develop a U-shaped kitchen. Next we will locate the appliances. We are using a 36"-wide (91.44cm) side-by-side refrigerator and will locate it at the bottom right of our plan because this is adjacent to the entrance door. The sink will be centered under the window and the range will be on the dining room wall to the left of the sink for convenience in serving to either the dining area or dining room.

Fig. 4.7 (next page). The next step is to fit in the base units. We will start at the center line of the window and work to the right. We are using a single-bowl sink 24" x 21" (60.96 x 53.34cm). A self-rimming sink would be one inch (2.54cm) larger in each dimension. We'll provide a 30" (76.20cm) sink base. We have 141" (358.14cm) on this wall. The C/L of the window is 66" (167.64cm) from the left wall, so we deduct this from 141" (358.14cm) to find we have 75" (190.50cm) to the right of the C/L to work with. Deduct half of the

sink cabinet, or 15" (38.10cm), from 75" (190.50cm) and we have 60" (152.40cm) left. We will place a B24R cabinet to the right of the sink. Deduct 24" (60.96cm) from 60" (152.40cm) and we have 36" (91.44cm) left. This is enough space for a corner rotary on this wall, so temporarily we will figure on this unit. To the left of the window C/L we have 66" (167.64cm). We deduct the other half of the sink base, 15" (38.10cm) from 66" (167.64cm) and we have 51" (129.54cm) left. We will figure a blind corner unit on the left wall. This takes 24" (60.96cm) on the window wall, so we take that from 51" (129.54cm) and have 27" (68.58cm) left. We should provide a filler here to permit easy opening of doors and drawers. Since we are on the 3" (7.62cm) module on this wall, we will use a BF3, or 3" base filler. Deducting this from 27" (68.58cm), we have 24" (60.96 cm) left for a dishwasher, which is the correct location for a right-handed person. However, being so close to the corner might not allow easy loading from the dishwasher to the wall cabinets above, so check with the customer.

On the left hand wall we are placing an eye-level free-standing range with an oven above and another below. It takes 30" (76.20cm) of space. We deduct that from the 97" (246.38cm) we have to work with and we have 67" (170.18cm) left for base cabinet storage. We are using a blind corner cabinet to the right of the range and will choose a 42" (106.68cm) base that pulls to 45" (114.30cm). Pull it out the full 3" (7.62cm) to correspond to the 3" (7.62cm) filler on the window wall. We deduct 45" (114.30cm) from 67" (170.18cm) and have 22" (55.88cm) remaining to use to the left of the range. There is no standard 22"-wide cabinet in stock units, so we will use a 21" (53.34cm) drawer base, allowing an extra inch (2.54cm) between the cabinet and the casing. If we wanted to fill the space, which

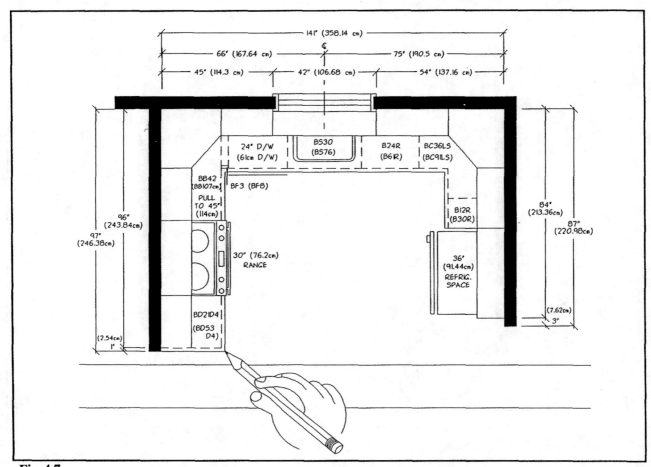

Fig. 4.7

is not necessary, we might pull the corner unit just 1" (2.54cm) and use a BD24 at the end of the range. However, this would give us a problem with wall cabinets later on, so we will go with the first arrangement. On the right hand wall we have 87" (220.98cm). We need 36" (91.44cm) for the refrigerator. It is on the end, so no special clearance problem arises. We choose to leave a 3" reveal to widen the entry walkway. We deduct 3" (7.62cm) from 87" (220.98cm) and have 84" (213.36cm). We deduct 36" (91.44cm) from 84" (213.36cm) and have 48"

(121.92cm) left. Conceivably, we can use a corner rotary in the corner, so we deduct 36" (91.44cm) from 48" (121.92cm) and have 12" (30.48cm) left, enough for a B12R base unit next to the refrigerator. Whether we use an L or R cabinet depends on whether we want access to the cabinet from the refrigerator or the sink area. Normally, all the cabinets should open away from the sink area, so those to the left of the sink would be L cabinets and those to the right, R cabinets where they are single door units. (L indicates left-hinged door as you face the cabinet. R indicates right-hinged.)

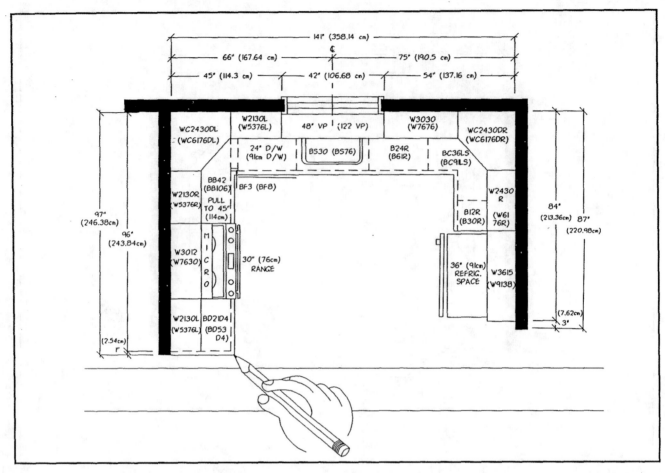

Fig. 4.8. Our next job is to plan the wall cabinets. To the right of the window we show a distance of 54" (137.16cm) from the casing to the wall to be filled with wall cabinets. We will start in the corner with a diagonal corner wall cabinet. It takes up 24" (60.96cm) of space along the wall, so we deduct that from 54" (137.16cm) and have 30" (76.20cm) left, or enough for a W3030. To the left of the window we have 45" (114.30cm). Using a diagonal corner wall cabinet in the left corner, we deduct 24" (60.96cm) from 45" (114.30cm) and have 21" (53.34cm) left, enough for a W2130L.

On the left hand wall we have used 96" (243.84cm) of space for the base units. We have 45"(114.30cm) between the wall and the range. Deducting 24" (60.96 cm) for the other wall area of the diagonal corner wall unit, we have 21" (53.34cm) left for a W2130R. Since this cabinet probably will be used in conjunction with the cooking center, we will use an R cabinet, hinged on the right. Depending on the height of the range unit, we might use a W3015 or W3012 unit over it. If the space is not sufficient for a cabinet, a panel is needed to close the space between the surrounding wall cabinets. A piece cut from plywood shelving or plywood paneling, finished to match, would do the trick if the

manufacturer does not have a piece to fit. Over the BD21 to the left of the range unit we would use a W2130L.

On the right hand wall we probably would use a W3615 over the refrigerator. The height would depend on the height of the refrigerator. The total space used by base units on this wall was 84" (213.36cm). Deducting 36" (91.44cm), we have 48" (121.92cm) left. We have to deduct 24" (60.96cm) for the corner cabinet, and have 24" (60.96cm) left, enough for a W2430. We would then figure a 48" (121.98cm) valance, cut to size, at the window.

In figuring molding, we would measure out from the wall at the left to the front of the wall cabinet, then along the front edge of the wall cabinets to the corner cabinet. Then on the diagonal face of this cabinet, across the wall cabinets on the window wall, including the valance, to the diagonal corner cabinet on the other wall. Then measure across its face and the face of the adjoining cabinets to the end, and back to the wall at the refrigerator cabinet. This adds up to about 283" (718.82cm). Dividing by 96" (243.84cm), the length of a piece of molding, we come out with just a fraction of an inch under three pieces. Since this leaves no margin for error in cutting and fitting, figure an extra length of molding. In fact, when figuring jobs for ordering it is good to have an extra piece of molding in order to save time in case a bad cut is made, or you measured wrong.

We indicate doors on cabinets being hinged so that they open away from the sink area. This is generally good practice, but must be modified in line with the customer requirements and location of work centers. This information should be included on your survey form.

For a perspective view of your kitchen, see Fig. 4.9. For the calculations, see Fig. 4.10, Page 122.

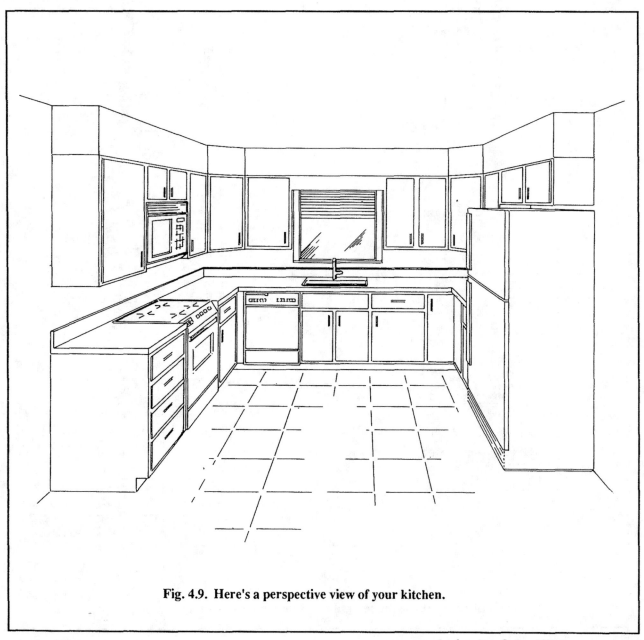

Fig. 4.9. Here's a perspective view of your kitchen.

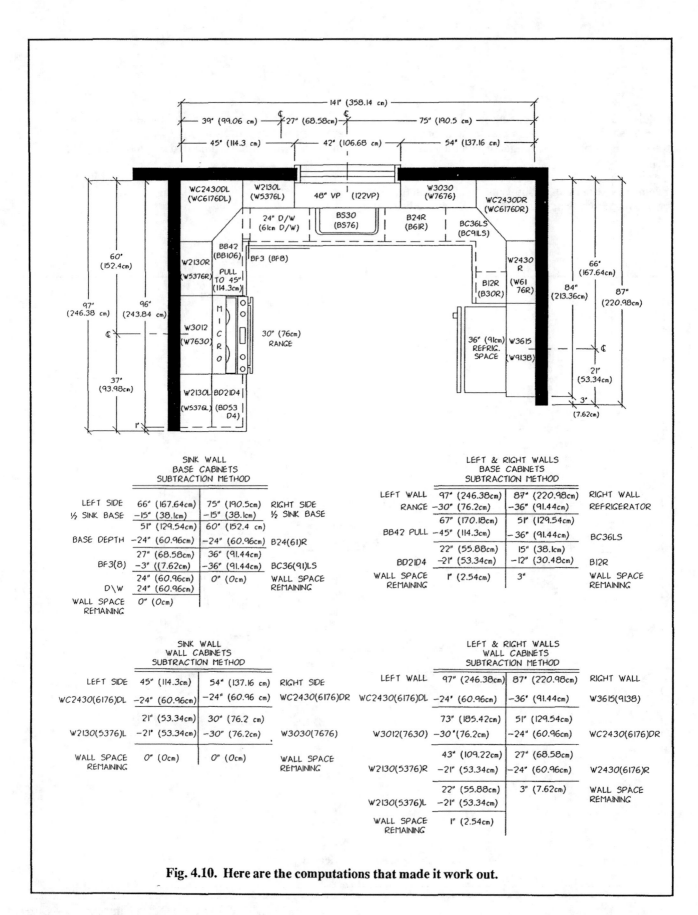

Fig. 4.10. Here are the computations that made it work out.

Fig. 4.11. Without the right fillers in the right places, the kitchen won't fit.

Here a base cabinet is installed against a wall with no filler. If the drawer is pulled out, it hits the window stool. Roll-outs in the cabinet can't be pulled out because the door handle won't permit the door to open more than 90 degrees, which it must for clearance.

When two base cabinets abut at a dead corner, a 2-way corner filler is needed. There's a similar problem with appliances, as seen below.

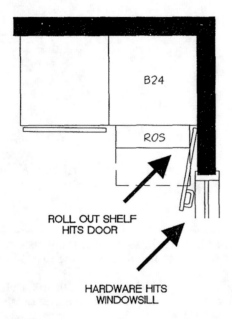

ROLL OUT SHELF
HITS DOOR

HARDWARE HITS
WINDOWSILL

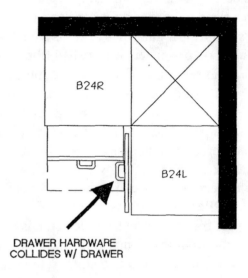

DRAWER HARDWARE
COLLIDES W/ DRAWER

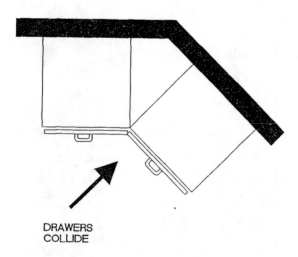

DRAWERS
COLLIDE

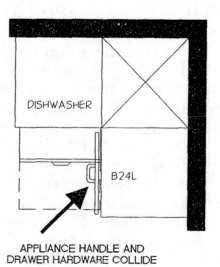

APPLIANCE HANDLE AND
DRAWER HARDWARE COLLIDE

If angled cabinets are not separated by a filler the two drawer heads will collide.

Clearance and the use of Fillers

Laying out a kitchen on paper by subtraction is one thing. On the jobsite we run into realities.

Kitchen cabinets are precision-made. Walls and houses aren't. Cabinets usually are made in 3" (7.6 cm) modules. Houses aren't. To provide clearance for cabinet doors, handles and hinges, for over-sized appliances, for door and window casings and for irregularities in walls we use magical wood or veneer strips called fillers.

We can see some of the potential problems in Fig. 4.11. And we can find these problems mirrored in actual projects around the country.

Fillers supplied by cabinet manufacturers can be ordered to match the cabinet finish or they can be unfinished. They can come as separate pieces or they can be in the form of extended stiles. The stile is a vertical member of the cabinet frame, and an extended stile is a piece of the front frame that is made extra wide so it can be trimmed, or scribed, to fit the wall where the cabinet abuts.

In framed cabinets the filler usually is flush with the front of the cabinet frame, not the door and drawer front (Fig. 4.12). The drawing shows this filler as a separate piece, but it could be an extended stile that only has to be cut to fit.

For frameless cabinets where the entire front is flush, overlaying the cabinet case, the filler would have to be flush with the fronts of the doors and drawers (Fig. 4.13). To hold the filler a cleat can be attached to the case so the filler can be attached to the cleat. The reveal between the filler and the door should match the reveal between doors throughout the kitchen.

For either framed or frameless cabinets the filler might be an unfinished construction piece installed flush with the case. In this case it takes a decorative overlay, such as a veneer or piece of laminate which will match the cabinets. When the filler repeats door detail, it is installed flush with the doors in either framed or frameless cabinets (Fig. 4.14).

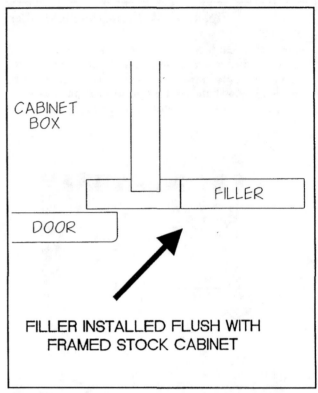

FILLER INSTALLED FLUSH WITH FRAMED STOCK CABINET

Fig. 4.12. In typical stock and semi-custom cabinets, the filler is installed flush with the case.

Fig. 4.13. In frameless cabinets the filler often is installed with a cleat. The filler must be finished on any exposed sides.

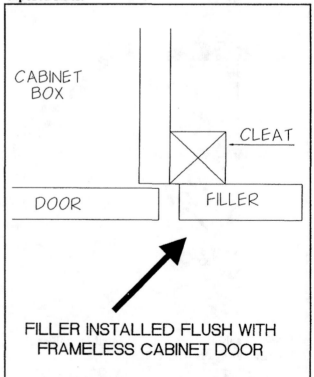

FILLER INSTALLED FLUSH WITH FRAMELESS CABINET DOOR

When corners are not turned with corner cabinets, a filler always is needed where the two cabinet runs abut.

When a blind corner cabinet is used, it is pulled out from the corner so its door and/or drawer will have clearance. But the abutting cabinet will have no clearance without the filler. It needs at least 1" (2.5 cm). However, clearance must be sufficient to clear any door or appliance *handle* plus 1/2" (1 cm) (Fig. 4.15). On frameless cabinets or for framed cabinets with flush overlay doors the filler should be mounted flush with the doors, with a reveal to match the other cabinets. The filler needs a toekick matching other cabinets.

If the two cabinet fronts join leaving a dead space in the corner, the filler will turn the corner with at least 1" (2.5 cm) in each direction.

When a cabinet run abuts direct to a wall (Fig. 4.16) a 1" (2.5 cm) filler is needed, but up to 4" (10 cm) if roll-out shelves must be pulled out past the hinge end of the cabinet door. On a framed cabinet, a scribing filler might suffice.

Wall cabinet fillers must be finished back to

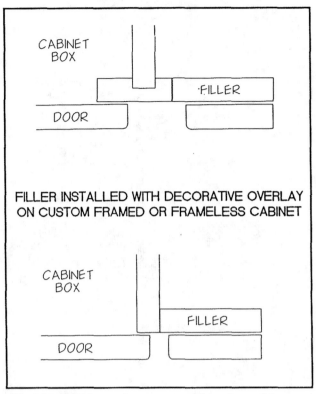

FILLER INSTALLED WITH DECORATIVE OVERLAY ON CUSTOM FRAMED OR FRAMELESS CABINET

Fig. 4.14. Filler may be a construction piece with a decorative overlay to match the cabinets.

the wall, as the bottoms are visible (Fig. 4.17).

Fig. 4.15. Filler must be enough for clearance for handles of doors, drawers or appliances on either side of corner.

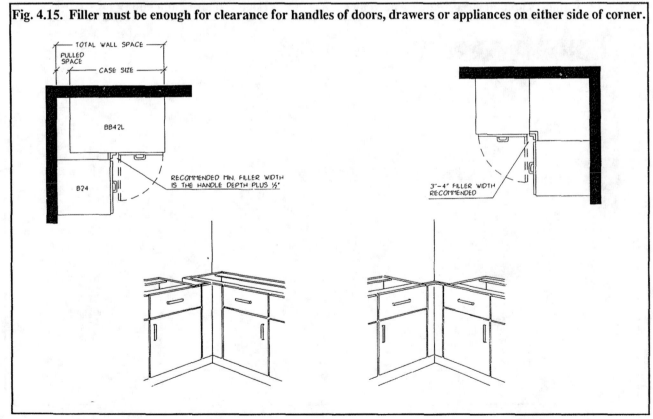

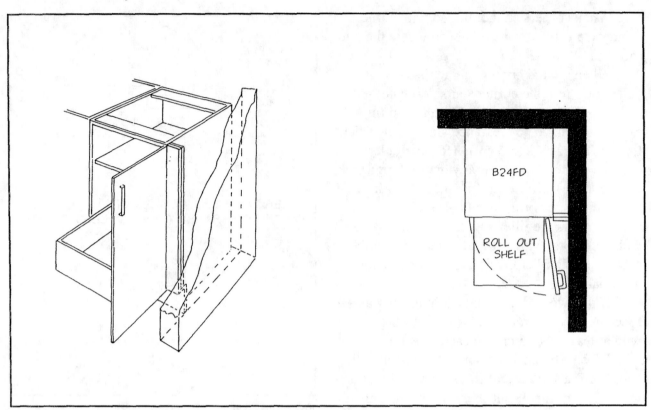

Fig. 4.16. Cabinet run needs 1" (2.5 cm) filler at wall, but more if clearance is needed for roll-out shelves.

Fig. 4.17. Cabinet run that meets blind corner wall cabinet needs filler so door handles don't hit.

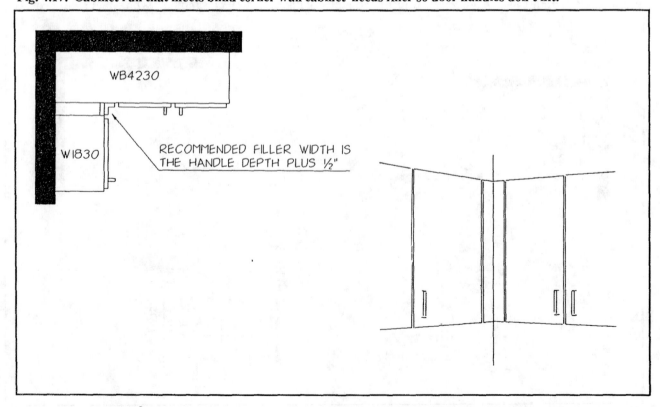

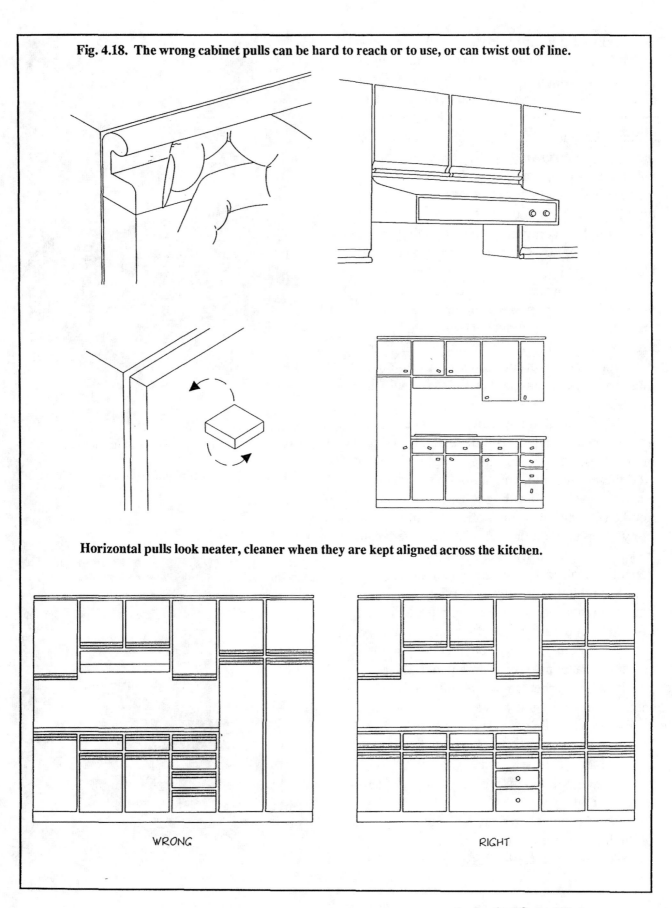

Fig. 4.18. The wrong cabinet pulls can be hard to reach or to use, or can twist out of line.

Horizontal pulls look neater, cleaner when they are kept aligned across the kitchen.

WRONG

RIGHT

Cabinet door and drawer pulls are known collectively as "cabinet hardware." They might be metal, wood, plastic or ceramic. Many mount on the surface, but many are grooved or angled into the doors and drawer fronts. Euro-style cabinets introduced the technique of continuous metal and wood channel pulls. Examples of pulls and problems are shown in Fig. 4.18.

Pulls should have esthetic as well as functional value. They should fit the cabinet style. For example, a continuous channel pull goes with contemporary style, but would be out of place on anything else. Any style might take a round, square or wire pull. The 7 1/2" (19 cm) wire pulls that are popular might not look good on doors of various widths in one kitchen, and if used vertically you would have to match them with a shorter length for drawers. Also, you must be aware of standard drillings for pulls in the cabinets.

As indicated in the drawings, some continuous channels might be a little difficult to figure out by some consumers and should be explained. And these same pulls might not be accessible in a cabinet over a protruding refrigerator or range hood. They also can ruin horizontal line continuity when used on drawers. In this case it can be good to mix the styles and use round knobs beneath the horizontal lines. (Fig. 4.18.)

Round pulls are always good, or are they? On a tambour door a knob could repeatedly bang into the counter and might not be accessible by the cook. Small knobs or other small pulls might be inadequate for a large pantry door. Small squares or rectangles, popular in shiny metals, usually mount with a single screw and easily get out of line.

The important points to remember about cabinet hardware are to make sure it works, make sure it will mount properly and make sure it looks right.

Other cabinet hardware is the basis for most of the interior fittings, or accessories, available for cabinets (Figs. 4.19-4.33).

Fig. 4.19. Roll-out shelves are a popular accessory.

Fig. 4.20. Some pantry cabinets have roll-out shelves.

Cabinet accessories, or interior fittings, are key elements to make a kitchen convenient and modern. They tailor cabinet storage for specific uses. Roll-out shelves (Fig. 4.19) are one of the most popular choices. When only one is installed, the center shelf is most convenient because the space used most in a kitchen is from 20" (51 cm) to 54" (138 cm) off the floor. But some designers prefer to make it the bottom shelf because it is only about 3" (7 cm) off the floor and is most difficult to reach into.

Tall cabinets are the modern version of the old-time pantry. Some have roll-out shelves (Fig. 4.20). Some have fold-out banks of shelves or swing-out shelves (Fig. 4.21), and a simpler version has an assembly of wire baskets or shelves that pull out as a unit (Fig. 4.22).

A simple and useful accessory is the tilt-out panel in front of the sink (Fig. 4.23). It provides a handy place for sponges and pads used at the clean-up center.

Fig. 4.21. Fancier pantries have swing-out shelves.

Fig. 4.22. Pull-out assembly adds pantry convenience.

Fig. 4.23. Sink tilt-out provides place for sponges.

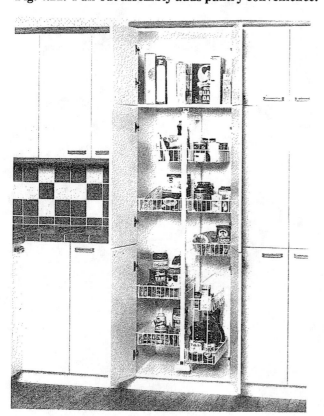

There's a lot of space in a sink cabinet, but the needs of a clean-up center are considerable. A pull-out waste basket is available (not shown), and there is a pull-out wire basket for various cleaning supplies (Fig. 4.24). Every kitchen needs towels, and what better place than close at hand in the form of pull-out towel bars in the sink cabinet (Fig. 4.25).

And one of the newer accessories for these modern times is a recycling bin (Fig. 4.26).

Fig. 4.25. Kitchen always needs a towel bar.

Fig. 4.24. Pull-out wire basket holds cleaning supplies.

Fig. 4.26. Recycling bin is one of newer fittings.

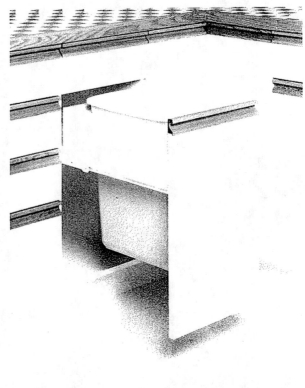

Fig. 4.27. Lazy susan is best base corner treatment.

For turning corners, lazy susan shelving is the most practical answer in a base cabinet (Fig. 4.27). For the wall cabinet run, one answer is a corner wall cabinet with open shelving (Fig. 4.28). But a diagonal corner wall cabinet can also bring the benefits of rotary shelves and the lines can be continued down to the countertop with a diagonal appliance garage (Fig. 4.29). The garage should have a duplex outlet mounted inside, and care must be taken that the outlet not interfere with the movement of a tambour door. Also, be sure the door pull is easily accessible to the cook who might have wet fingers and not be able to use a small knob. This garage also can go in the middle of a cabinet run (Fig. 4.30). Other useful accessories include cutlery compartments in a drawer with cutting board above (Fig. 4.31); a door rack as one of several answers to the problem of storing spices (Fig. 4.32), and tray dividers that go well in awkward space such as the top of a pantry or a cabinet over the refrigerator.

Fig. 4.28. Open shelves go well in corner wall cabinet.

Fig. 4.29. Corner wall cabinet also can have rotary shelves. Appliance garage below needs a duplex outlet.

Fig. 4.30. Appliance garage can go in middle of cabinet run also.

Fig. 4.31. Cutlery compartments, cutting board can augment drawer's usefulness.

Fig. 4.32. Door rack is one of several answers to problem of storing spices.

Fig. 4.33. If you must fill a narrow space, 9" (23 cm) cabinet is a good place for tray dividers.

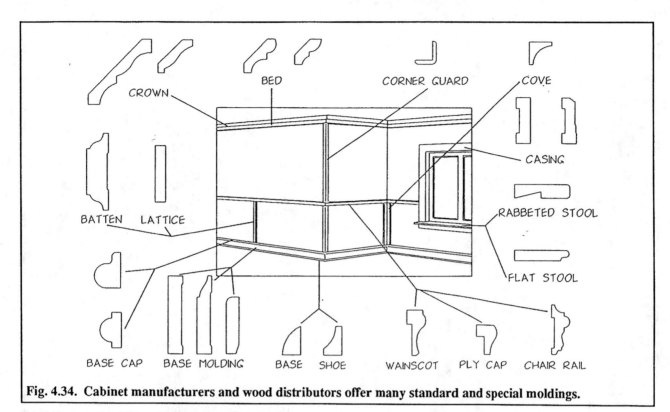

Fig. 4.34. Cabinet manufacturers and wood distributors offer many standard and special moldings.

Moldings, paneling finish the job right

There are some perfectionists who say moldings are used only to cover up mistakes in craftsmanship. But many others are sure they offer the only way to make the job look truly finished.

Wood moldings come in many standard patterns and sizes (Fig. 4.34), but there also are many extra-fancy shapes available. They might be painted or stained, vinyl-wrapped, printed with a wood finish, wood-veneered or unfinished. Many cabinet manufacturers offer standard and special moldings to match their cabinets. Many kitchen designers will combine two or three different moldings for special effects, such as where cabinets or soffits meet (or don't quite reach) the ceiling.

Ready-made moldings usually are sold in 96" (244 cm) lengths. For specifying, remember the thickness always is listed first, then the width, then the length. Both thickness and width always are measured at the widest point.

When designing continuous moldings that wrap around a room and tie in with the cabinet elevations, you must be sure to calculate the heights and forms of kitchen elements that will be affected. For example, baseboard molding should align perfectly with the cabinet toekick. A wainscoting chair rail should tie in with a wood countertop edge, or relate to the top in a way that is visually attractive. It is not unusual for kitchen designers to buy extra cabinet doors to use on walls around a dining area, topped with chair rails or other moldings, and all of these, when within the kitchen, should line up with the cabinet doors and countertops.

Fig. 4.35 (next page). Paneling is used to cover exposed backs of peninsula cabinets, exposed cabinet ends or the under sides of counter overhangs or wall cabinets. Wood paneling is usually 1/4" (6 mm) thick, sometimes 3/4" (19 mm). Wood is generally rotary-cut veneer so woodgrain may not match doors. Melamine and/or laminate panels are generally available in 1/4", 5/8" and 3/4" (6, 16 and 19 mm) thickness. When paneling, always think of how you will finish edges. Thicker panels can be mitered for a furniture look. Butted sheets might be concealed with an inside or outside corner molding.

Fig. 4.35. Exposed edges and joints have to be concealed on a peninsula run.

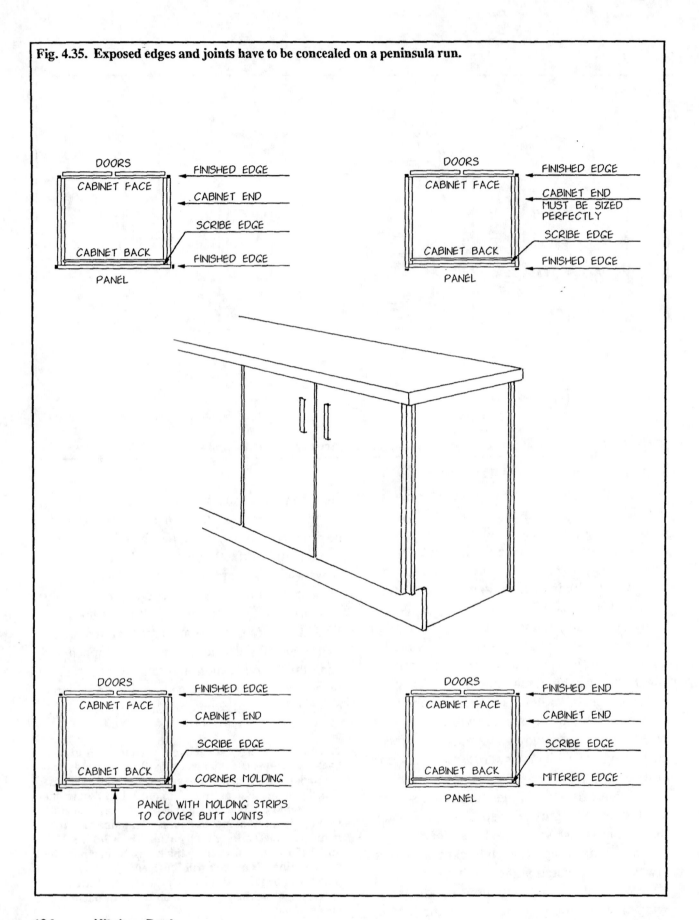

DOORS
CABINET FACE
CABINET BACK
PANEL
→ FINISHED EDGE
← CABINET END
SCRIBE EDGE
← FINISHED EDGE

DOORS
CABINET FACE
CABINET BACK
PANEL
→ FINISHED EDGE
← CABINET END MUST BE SIZED PERFECTLY
SCRIBE EDGE
← FINISHED EDGE

DOORS
CABINET FACE
CABINET BACK
→ FINISHED EDGE
← CABINET END
SCRIBE EDGE
← CORNER MOLDING
PANEL WITH MOLDING STRIPS TO COVER BUTT JOINTS

DOORS
CABINET FACE
CABINET BACK
PANEL
→ FINISHED END
← CABINET END
SCRIBE EDGE
← MITERED EDGE

Turning corners in a kitchen

The way you turn corners in a kitchen is an important part of the design. Basically, there are four ways to turn a base corner and three ways to turn a wall corner.

The simplest, least expensive and least desirable way is to "void" the corner and connect the two cabinet runs, wall or base, with a corner filler. This wastes available storage space.

A pie-cut wall or base corner cabinet is one of several ways to turn a corner (Fig. 4.36). This ordinarily will take reach-in shelving rather than rotary shelves, and a door that will hang from hinges on one side but also will be hinged in the middle so it can turn the square corner. Base corner cabinets 33" and 36" (84 and 91 cm) wide are also available with rotating shelves, commonly called lazy susans. The door may be attached to the susan so it swings inside the cabinet, or it may be hinged so it bifolds away from the user. The wall space requirement is more than the actual cabinet size, therefore the cabinet is pulled away from the wall during installation so that it finishes flush with the adjacent cabinets.

A blind base or wall corner cabinet is designed to pull out from the corner several inches, as specified by the manufacturer. The cabinet run on the adjacent wall must have a filler. This might have half-moon shelves that fit in the cabinet and are attached to the door. Shelves swing out when the door is opened.

Wall blinds generally have simple shelving. Wall space required for these cabinets is more than the actual cabinet size. Make sure both the customer and installer understand this. Always specify how far you want the blind unit pulled, and make sure you match this dimension up with cabinets above.

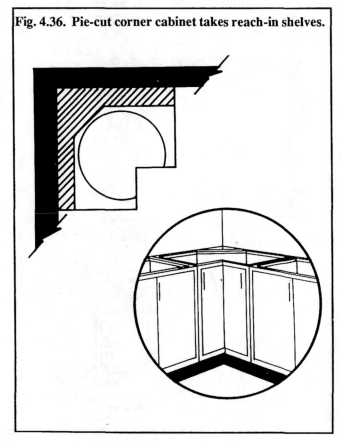

Fig. 4.36. Pie-cut corner cabinet takes reach-in shelves.

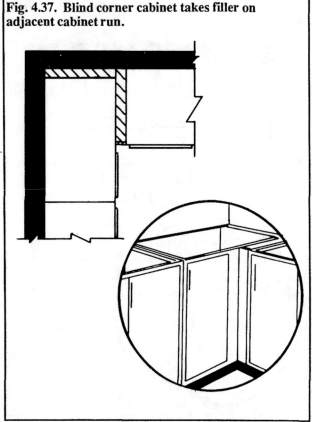

Fig. 4.37. Blind corner cabinet takes filler on adjacent cabinet run.

For a base installation, a reverse peninsula cabinet can be fitted into a peninsula corner, opening into a dining room or other space outside the kitchen. It is useful for occupying dead corner space when there is not enough space in the kitchen for the opening and door of a corner cabinet. If an eating counter will overhang the reverse peninsula cabinet, plan a full door unit because access to a drawer would be blocked. The cabinet always is ordered 3"-6" (8-15 cm) smaller than the 24" (61 cm) available so fillers can be installed on each side. This prevents the back edge of the cabinet from interfering with the toekick on the kitchen side. It also keeps the cabinet away from the return wall on the dining room side.

A popular way to turn a wall corner is with a diagonal unit. It takes 24" (61 cm) on each wall and has a diagonal door connecting the two adjacent cabinet runs. It can feature a rotating shelf system, or have standard shelving.

Fig. 4.38. Reverse peninsula opens into space outside the kitchen.

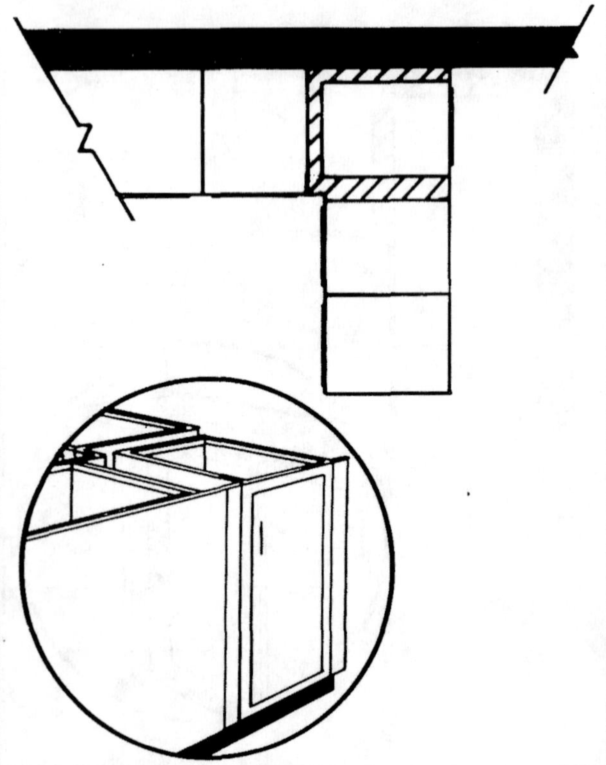

Fig. 4.39. Popular way to turn a wall corner is with a diagonal wall cabinet.

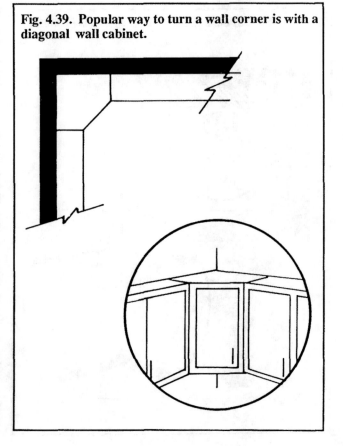

Fig. 4.40. Four ways to make the transition to different wall cabinet heights.

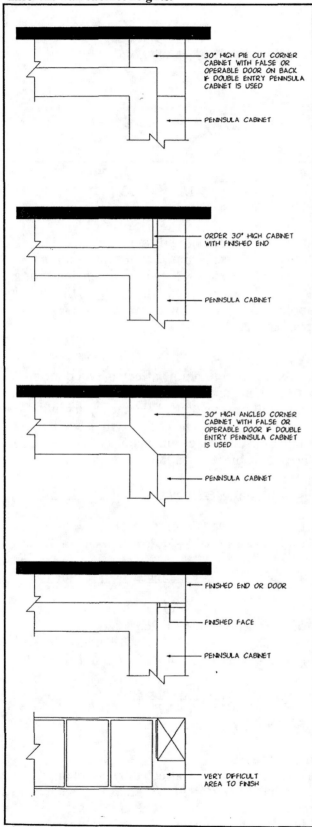

30" HIGH PIE CUT CORNER CABINET WITH FALSE OR OPERABLE DOOR ON BACK IF DOUBLE ENTRY PENINSULA CABINET IS USED

PENINSULA CABINET

ORDER 30" HIGH CABINET WITH FINISHED END

PENINSULA CABINET

30" HIGH ANGLED CORNER CABINET WITH FALSE OR OPERABLE DOOR IF DOUBLE ENTRY PENINSULA CABINET IS USED

PENINSULA CABINET

FINISHED END OR DOOR

FINISHED FACE

PENINSULA CABINET

VERY DIFFICULT AREA TO FINISH

Coping with change: Standard height to peninsula height wall cabinets

Peninsulas often are designed to keep space open from the kitchen to adjacent living quarters such as a den, dining room or living room.

So we seldom put in wall cabinets of standard height. There has to be space below for the open feeling desired and for the cook to talk with those on the other side. So there is going to be a change in cabinet height. It can look great when finished, but how do we get it to look that way?

Fig. 4.40 shows some suggestions. The first is to use a pie-cut corner cabinet that is a standard 30" (76 cm) high with a false door on the back side (the side that faces the other living area). Or, better, order a double-entry peninsula cabinet that has an operable door on the back, so the cabinet can be opened from either side.

Another way is to use shorter peninsula cabinets the entire length of the peninsula, all the way from the wall, but order a finished end on the standard wall cabinet that will be on the kitchen side of the peninsula. Thus the standard cabinet will show, blocked only partially by the peninsula cabinet.

A third way is to order a standard diagonal corner cabinet to end the run in the kitchen and turn the corner of the peninsula, with either a false or operable door on the back side.

You might also extend the run of standard wall cabinets all the way to the far side of the peninsula, ending it with a finished end or a door. Then start the run of peninsula cabinets right from the finished face of the standard cabinet that ends the run.

If you finish the run of standard cabinets just short of the peninsula run, as in the bottom drawing, you end up with a difficult area to finish and an appearance that suggests the work of a do-it-yourselfer.

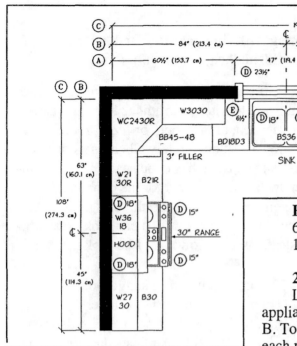

Fig. 4.41. The order check system

Kitchen projects often are stopped during installation because of a dimensional mistake on the plan or an incorrect product on the jobsite. These errors are costly, and can be avoided with a systematic, mathematical approach.

• Original field measurements must be accurate. Check them again at the jobsite after contract signing.

• Check all items ordered against the specs and manufacturer's literature.

• Check each order following a set format. The following system checks appliance sizes, reveal dimensions, center lines and cabinet sizes. It can make cabinet errors disappear.

1. Verify overall wall dimensions

Add up each individual wall section, identified as Dimension String A, and compare it with the overall wall length, identified as Dimension C. Each wall section in Dimension String A designates wall space available or not available for cabinetry. Thus, all window and door dimensions include trim.

Example: Sink run wall:

60 1/2" + 47" + 84 1/2" = 192"
153.7cm + 119.4cm + 214.6cm = 487.7cm

2. Locate and list centerline dimensions

List on the plan the centerline dimensions of all major appliances or plumbing fixtures, listed as Dimension String B. To help determine the exact centerline length, first divide each major appliance, cabinet or window in half, identified as D on the plan above.

3. Verify cabinet sizes

When a cabinet run will not be affected by a door or window, add the cabinet and appliance sizes, then compare them with the overall dimension C. When using a blind corner cabinet, add the total wall space it will use when pulled for installation. Add filler dimensions after you have determined the total cabinet and appliance length.

Example: Sink run base cabinets; wall length 192" (487.7cm)

48" + 18" + 36" + 24" dw + 30" + 36" rf = 192"
121.9cm + 45.7cm + 91.4cm + 61cm + 76.2cm + 91.4cm = 487.6cm

Example: Range run base cabinets; wall length 108" (274.3cm)

24" + 21" + 30" r + 30" = 105"
61cm + 53.3cm + 76.2cm + 76.2cm = 266.7cm
Wall length 108" — 105" = 3" filler
Wall length 274.3cm — 266.7cm = 7.6cm filler

Example: Range run wall cabinets
24" + 21" + 36" h + 27" = 108"
61cm + 53.3cm + 91.4cm + 68.6cm = 274.3cm

4. Determine reveals

When a cabinet run will be affected by doors or windows, determine the reveal, identified as E, by subtracting the cabinets on each individual wall section from the total length of that wall section from Dimension String A. The reveal length on each side of the opening should be equal.

84 1/2" — 78"   = 6 1/2" reveal
214.6cm — 198.1cm = 16.5cm reveal

5. Verify reveal dimensions

To check Step 4, add wall cabinets, reveals and window, then compare your total with the overall wall length, listed as Dimension C.

Example: <u>Sink wall run</u>
24" + 30"   + 6 1/2" + 47"   + 6 1/2" + 42"   + 36"   = 192"
61cm + 76.2cm + 16.5cm + 119.4cm + 16.5cm + 106.7cm + 91.4cm = 487.7cm

6. Verify centerlines

Add cabinets and half of appliance, cabinet or opening (identified as D) for both wall and base runs, then compare your totals with the centerline lengths in Dimension String B.

Example: <u>Left wall to sink/window center = 84" (213.4cm)</u>:
Wall cabinets:
24"   + 30"   + 6 1/2"   + 23 1/2" (half of window) = 84"
61cm + 76.2cm + 16.5cm + 59.7cm (half of window) = 213.4cm

Base cabinets:
48"   + 18"   + 18" (half of sink cab.)   = 84"
121.9cm + 45.7cm + 45.7cm (half of sink cab.) = 213.3cm

Example: <u>Sink center to dishwasher center = 30" (76.2cm)</u>
18" (half of sink cab.)   + 12" (half of dw)   = 30"
45.7cm (half of sink cab.) + 30.5cm (half of dw) = 76.2cm

Example: <u>Dw center to refrigerator center = 60" (152.4 cm)</u>:
12" (half of dw) + 30"   + 18" (half of ref) = 60"
30.5cm (half dw) + 76.2cm + 45.7cm (half ref) = 152.4 cm

Refrigerator center to right wall = 18" (45.7cm)

Example: <u>Top wall to range/hood center = 63" (160 cm)</u>:
Wall cabinets:
24"   + 21"   + 18" (half of hood)   = 63"
61cm + 53.3cm + 45.7cm) (half hood) = 160cm
Base cabinets:
24"   + 3"   + 21"   + 15" (half of range) = 63"
61cm + 7.6cm + 53.3cm + 38.1cm (half range) = 160cm

Example: <u>Center of range/hood to wall end at bottom = 45"(114.3cm)</u>
Wall cabinets: 18" (half of hood)   + 27"   = 45"
45.7cm (half of hood) + 76.2cm = 114.3cm
Base cabinets: 15" (half of range)   + 30"   = 45"
38.1cm (half of range) + 76.2cm = 114.3cm

Notes

(Metric conversions were rounded to the nearest tenth of a centimeter, which results in slight variations when several numbers are added and compared.)

7. Verify appliance/fixture sizes

Compare all appliance and fixture sizes to cabinets and clearances planned. List cutout and overall dimensions of each, as required for installation, on the plan. Also check door clearance requirements at this time.

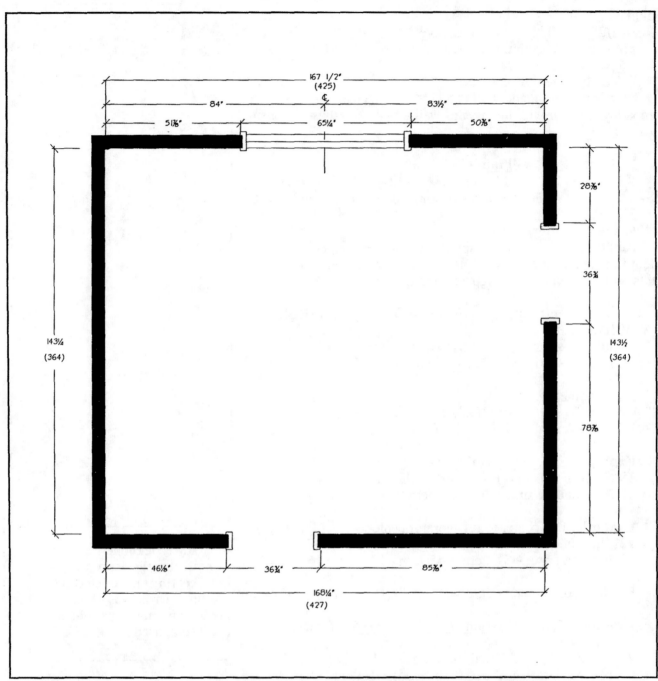

167 1/2" (425)
84"   83½"
51⅞"   65¼"   50⅝"
28⅞"
36¼
143¼ (364)
143½ (364)
78⅞
46⅛"   36¼"   85⅝"
168¼" (427)

After you understand the planning details it's time to put it all together. Here is a typical kitchen that really needs a designer's touch.

Fig. 4.42. A FAMILY OF FOUR with two adults and two children, age 9 and 11, lives in this 12-year-old house. It was damaged by fire, and the husband's Uncle Jake, a building contractor, rebuilt the room. Plumbing is roughed in at the window and a 220V line goes to the wall on the left.

Husband and wife both work. They entertain moderately, using the dining room, but generally they want to eat in the kitchen and keep life simple.

They want a "nice" kitchen but they "don't want to spend a fortune." That rules out any structural changes, although the window can be moved if there is a good reason.

Their budget for the new kitchen is "about $15,000," although they'd like to get by with $12,000 and, if you really impress them, they can stretch it upward a bit.

House styling is nondescript. The house is of frame construction with a brick front. Furnishings do not follow any particular motif. They are nice, but mostly from the "Two Full Rooms for $999" sales.

And they want the whole job done by yesterday!

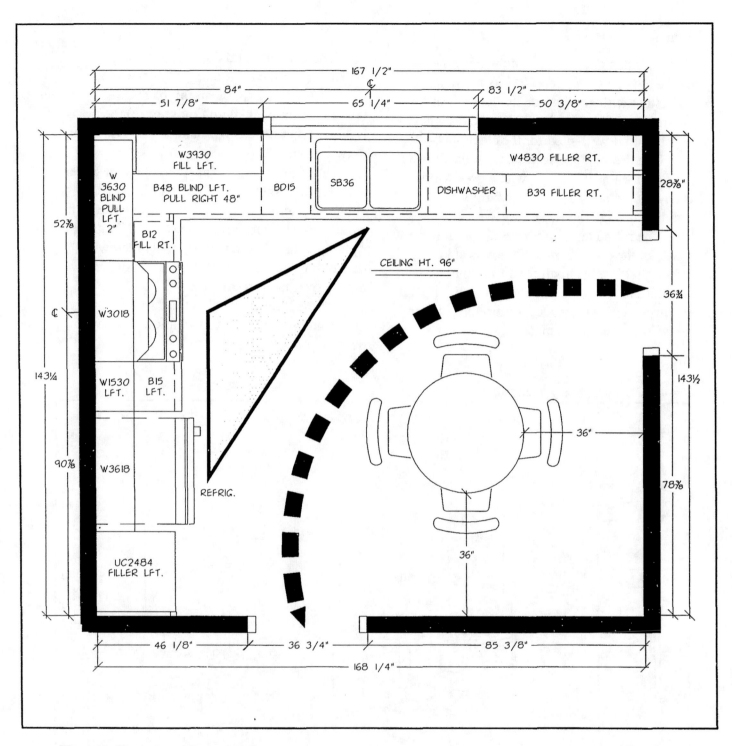

167 1/2"

84"

51 7/8"

65 1/4"

83 1/2"

50 3/8"

W3930
FILL LFT.

W4830 FILLER RT.

W
3630
BLIND
PULL
LFT.
2"

B48 BLIND LFT.
PULL RIGHT 48"

BD15

SB36

DISHWASHER

B39 FILLER RT.

28⅜"

52⅞"

B12
FILL RT.

CEILING HT. 96"

36¾"

W3018

143¼"

C

W1530
LFT.

B15
LFT.

143½"

36"

90⅞"

W3618

36"

78⅞"

REFRIG.

UC2484
FILLER LFT.

36"

46 1/8"

36 3/4"

85 3/8"

168 1/4"

Fig. 4.43. Floorplan, solution No. 1.

Solution No. 1:

This designer respected the customer's desire to keep the price as low as possible, consistent with good products. There was no attempt to move the window, as the designer considered it well-sited for the clean-up center.

The design itself is perfect for the family's needs. It's a neat L shape with a good work triangle that is not affected by family traffic moving through the two doorways.

The round table can be used for all three meals of the day when the family is at home, although it is a bit small for a full dinner. Seats are close to the walls, but this is not significant because there is easy access from the sides and no need for "edging" space.

The Contemporary styling, below, is least expensive for the customer. It has the added advantage of an easy-clean full backsplash.

In Traditional styling (next page) the price is a bit higher because of fancier wood doors and drawer fronts.

In Country styling (next page) the designer added more expensive styling touches. The countertop and backsplash are ceramic tile and a wood strip floor is used. The wall cabinet at the right is replaced with an open plate rack with decorative shelf above, and there is a decorative alcove over the refrigerator.

These three plans give the customer an opportunity to go up or down a few thousand dollars in price.

Fig. 4.44. Contemporary styling solution.

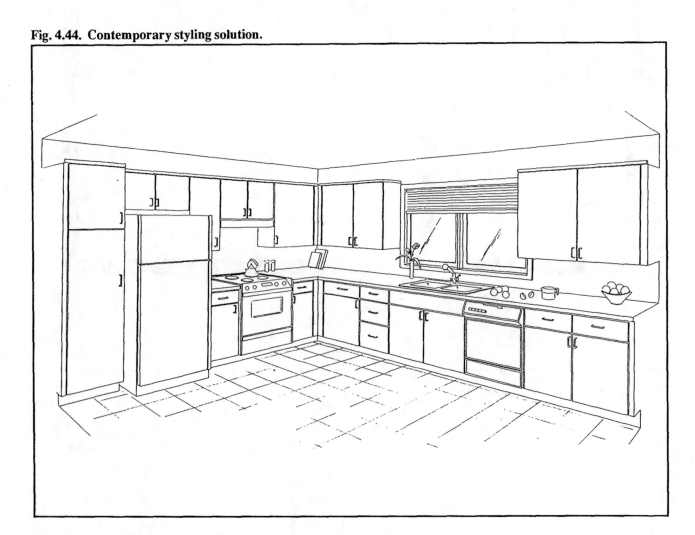

Fig. 4.45. Traditional styling solution.

Fig. 4.46. Country styling solution.

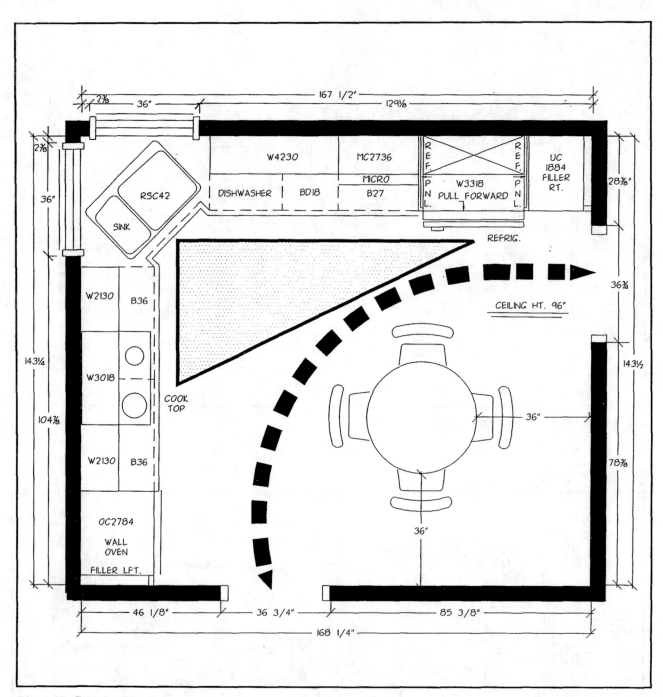

Fig. 4.47. Solution No. 2.

Solution No. 2

This designer decided a corner window would give the kitchen a special touch and a more interesting view outside. It also tends to extend the vista, making the room appear larger. A microwave was added, mounted off the counter beside the refrigerator, a built-in cooktop is placed in the work triangle and a wall oven slightly outside. The L shape makes for a good, efficient work triangle, although the dishwasher door, when open, will crowd a person at the sink. That crowding is helped a little by recessing the diagonal sink front.

As in Solution 1, the eating arrangement is a table and chairs placed clear of the work triangle. Space from table edge to the walls is limited, but again there is access to seating from the sides. Traffic passing through the kitchen does not interfere either with the work triangle or with the diners.

On the next page, the Traditional styling solution uses trim kits to match the cabinetry with panels on the refrigerator and dishwasher.

In the Country styling solution this designer also went to ceramic tile on the countertop and backsplash and to wood strip flooring. The ventilating hood is upgraded to a more stylized model and an open shelf under the cooktop has a decorative treatment. Here we also find a plate rack over the microwave and a decorative open display area over the refrigerator. The wall cabinets are higher and the soffit is replaced by a decorative crown molding at the ceiling.

Fig. 4.48. Contemporary styling solution.

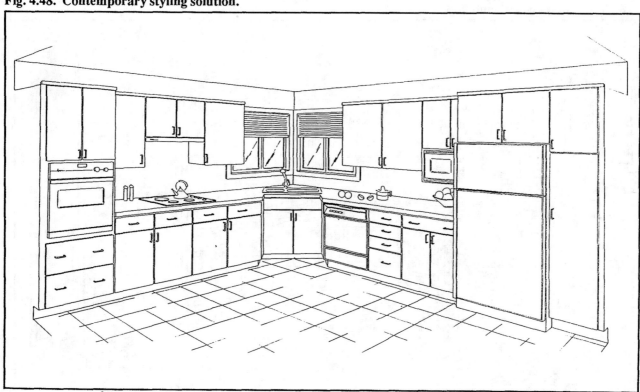

Fig. 4.49. Traditional styling solution.

Fig. 4.50. Country styling solution.

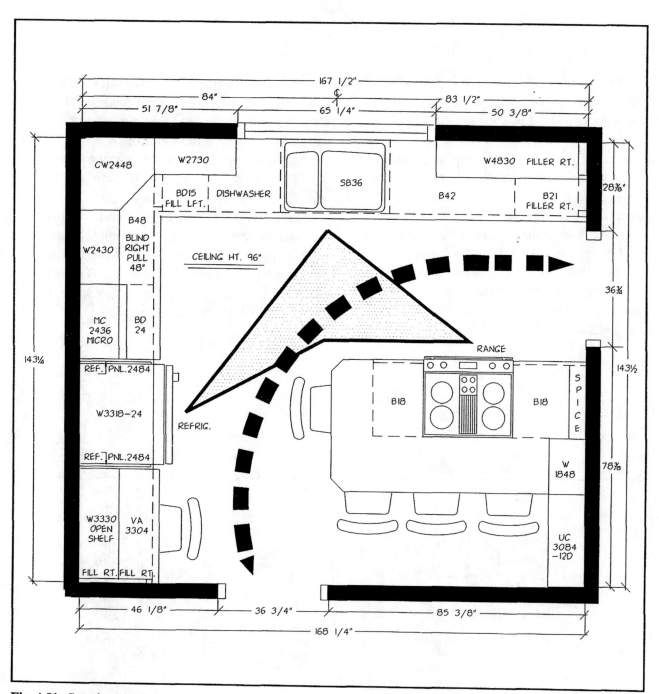

Fig. 4.51. Solution No. 3.

Solution No. 3.

This solution stretches the budget upward with construction of a peninsula in the dining area, with an eating bar 36" (91 cm) high, with high bar stools. A down-draft range is placed in the peninsula. A countertop appliance garage goes in the far corner, under a diagonal corner cabinet, and a home office area is provided to the left of the refrigerator. A microwave is mounted off the counter near the refrigerator.

It is an interesting design solution. However, family traffic intersects two legs of the work triangle, and with family members coming home at about the same time in the evening at meal time, this can be a problem.

The Contemporary and Traditional styling solutions (next page) are about the same, except for cabinet styles and the addition of decorative panels on the refrigerator and dishwasher. But the Country style solution offers some changes.

First, there are the country touches of ceramic tile on counter and backsplash, the plate rack and the wood strip flooring. But adding to the country feel is the set of wall cabinets at the right with glass doors and little drawers below for spices, condiments or whatever. (Go back to the floorplan and you'll see there is a spice rack on the wall beside the range.)

Fig. 4.52. Contemporary styling solution.

Fig. 4.53. Traditional styling solution.

Fig. 4.54. Country styling solution.

Notes

5 Light, Venting & Noise Control
Thoughtful Touches Can Make the Kitchen

Lighting a kitchen entails much more than installing a fixture in the ceiling. A kitchen requires both **general** light and **task** lighting. The first lets you see to get around. The second helps you see to do specific work on the countertops or at the range and sink. What you do with these two kinds of lighting can preserve or spoil a good kitchen design, because the lighting will have a significant effect on how the kitchen will look. Lighting can change "it looks nice" to "wow!" And that creates referrals.

Here are some of the choices you must decide on with your customer:

1. Structural (built-in) lighting or store-bought fixtures;

2. Incandescent bulbs or fluorescent tubes or halogen lights. (In the lighting business these are all referred to as "lamps.")

3. How much intensity (brightness) for general and for task lighting;

4. Fixture types: Luminous ceiling, luminous panels, recessed or surface bullets, tracks, spots, wall brackets, etc.

In considering **structural lighting or commercial fixtures,** we must remember that we are in a business. For an outlet where lighting fixtures are sold, it might pay to promote them (depending on store policy). Many great commercial fixtures are available for the kitchen. However, a full-service kitchen specialty dealership with carpenters on staff will profit more from structural lighting while gaining the advantage of more design freedom. Since structural lighting is built largely on-site, the designer can put any type of light where it is wanted.

Below are a couple of examples of structural lighting.

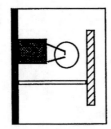 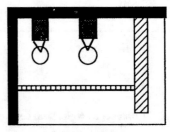

Wall Bracket   **Soffit Lighting**

In the above example (not to scale) of a wall bracket, the edge of the tube and top of the shield should be at least 12" (30 cm) from the ceiling, but otherwise it can go anywhere on the wall. The shield is held by a rod below, so light is directed both upward and downward. In the soffit light, the diffuser at the bottom is 4" (10 cm) below the tubes, and the shield can be from 18" to 24" (46 to 61 cm) from the wall. (For the diffuser, incidentally, choose an acrylic. Other plastics yellow with age.)

The kind of lamps you use can mean a lot in both color rendition and economy.

Fluorescent lamps (tubes) come in many color balances, from Cool White (which strengthens orange, yellow and blue colors in the kitchen) to Natural, or Soft White, which strengthens red and orange. Deluxe Cool White

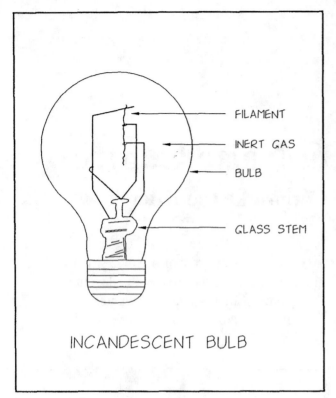

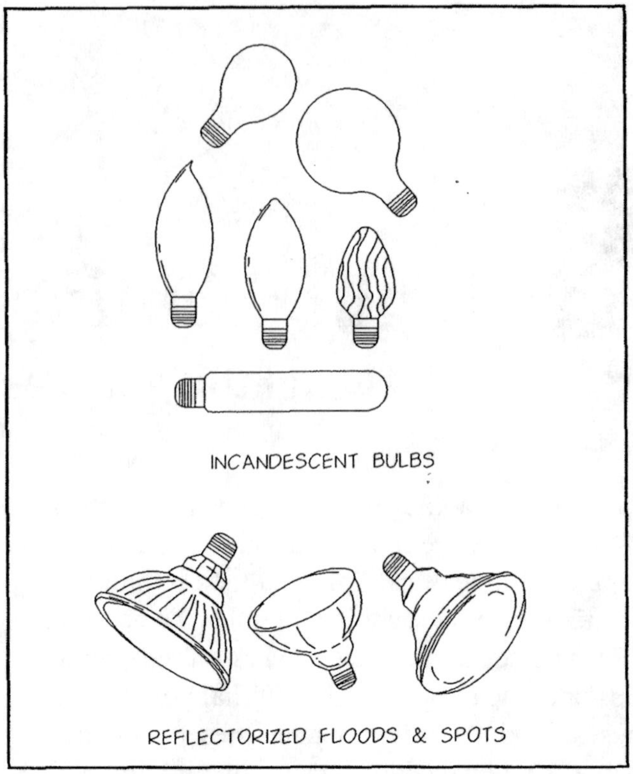

Fig. 5.0. Incandescent light sources.

FILAMENT

INERT GAS

BULB

GLASS STEM

INCANDESCENT BULB

INCANDESCENT BULBS

REFLECTORIZED FLOODS & SPOTS

Fig. 5.1. Incandescent lamps.

Fig. 5.2. Fluorescent light sources and lamps.

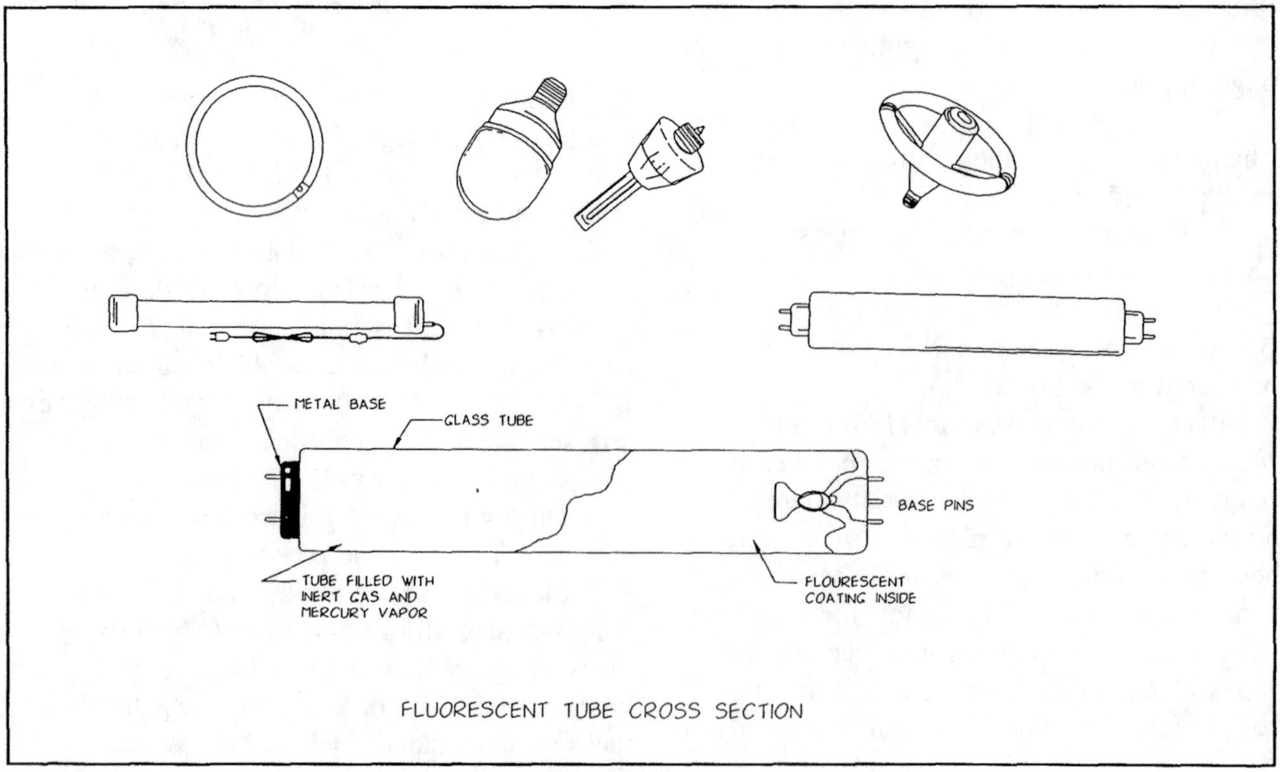

METAL BASE

GLASS TUBE

BASE PINS

TUBE FILLED WITH
INERT GAS AND
MERCURY VAPOR

FLOURESCENT
COATING INSIDE

FLUORESCENT TUBE CROSS SECTION

strengthens all colors nearly equally and gives the best overall color rendition. Daylight tubes strengthen green and blue. Deluxe Warm White simulates incandescent light and is recommended when these two kinds of light are used in the same room. But for colors as the eye sees them there still is no substitute for viewing objects, such as cabinets, under the lights that will be used in the kitchen. New types of fluorescent tubes are being introduced constantly. To keep up with the new light sources, consult with a lighting specialist on a regular basis.

Incandescent lamps are those we always have been familiar with, and perhaps that is why most of us prefer them. They are warm, they strengthen the red side of the spectrum and they are kind to complexions.

But in an energy-conscious age, we must be prepared to tell our customers that incandescence produces only 12 to 21 lumens of light per watt while fluorescence produces 40 to 100 lumens per watt. What this means in practical terms is that if you replace four 75W bulbs in a ceiling fixture with two 40W Soft White fluorescent tubes, at 8 cents per KWH it would save $326.40 in energy cost over the life of the lamps.

Incandescent lamps also generate a lot of heat, adding to the cooling load in summer, but they burn less hot when hanging down. An ordinary 100W bulb upright will reach 446 degrees F (230 C) at the top, 214 degrees (101 C) at the side and 120 degrees (49 C) at the base. The same bulb hanging downward would reach 300 degrees (149 C) at the side, 245 degrees (118 C) at the base and 162 degrees (72 C) at the bottom.

Another kind of lamp is gaining increasing favor in the kitchen, and that is the **low-voltage halogen** lamp. These are tiny bulbs that give out a lot of lumens on 12V to 20V. This actually is a form of incandescence, but the lamp is filled with halogen and the tungsten filament is a different design. It produces as much light as an incandescent bulb 10 times its size, consumes half as much power and lasts up to seven times long- er (2000 hours). They are used in strings hidden in toekicks for general illumination,

under stair steps, in glass-door cabinets to illuminate glassware, on top of wall cabinets and under wall cabinets for task lighting. Each lamp might be only 5W, but if you string 20 of them under a 10' (305 cm) cabinet, that's 100W total of light that is whiter and brighter. One brand of these (Häfele) has 20W lamps that mount 31" apart (80 cm), and each lamp has its own switch. Another (Hettich) looks like a mini can light, is only 3/4" (2 cm) deep so it can recess in a cabinet shelf.

Low-voltage lighting takes a transformer that usually is quite small. It can be hidden in or on top of a cabinet or behind a wall.

General lighting needs in the kitchen vary, as we have suggested, according to reflectance values of light and dark objects in the room. Following are basic guidelines for kitchens in medium to light colors.

General Kitchen Lighting		
Kitchen size	**Incandescent**	**Fluorescent**
75 sq. ft. (7 m²)	150W surface, Two 150W recessed.	60W surface, 80W recessed
75-120 sq. ft. (7-11 m²)	200W surface, Four 100W recessed	60-80W surface 80W recessed
Over 120 sq. ft. (11 m²)	2W per sq. ft. surface, 150W per 40 sq. ft. (3.7 m²) recessed	3/4W per sq. ft. surface, 80-120W per 60 sq. ft. (6 m²) recessed.
(Recessed units with enclosed bottoms at least 12" (30 cm) wide.)		

Task lighting is more specific, putting light where we need it to do some work. This includes the cooktop, sink and countertops. We usually get a socket in the ventilating hood for the cooktop, and this should take a 60W bulb. The requirement for the sink is the same.

For countertops, the best place for task lighting is under the wall cabinets, as near as

What you should know about light and color

A kitchen designer must be able to talk authoritatively to a client about color. Here are some basics.

Hue is the name of a color. *Value* is the lightness or darkness of a hue. *Intensity* is the saturation, or brightness or dullness, of a hue. Adding black to a hue gives a *shade*. Adding white gives a *tint*. Adding gray gives a *tone*. Colors opposite each other on a color wheel are *complementary*. Colors next to each other are *analogous*.

Regular light (*white* light) carries all colors. Objects reflect color selectively. An apple is red because it absorbs all colors except red, which it reflects. Because of this there is another wheel that shows *pigment* colors, slightly different.

Colors are of different wave lengths, so they focus differently in the eye. A red room seems to "advance" and a blue room seems to "retreat" because red focuses behind the retina and blue focuses in front of the retina.

We need color balance in a room because the eye strives for it. If we see two complementary colors in a room they add up to a neutral gray, so the eye is satisfied. The eye doesn't demand equal amounts of these colors. If a room is mostly blue, a single red pitcher on a counter can provide the needed balance, or perhaps the edging on the countertop.

In a kitchen, the fewer hues used, the better, so it is best to keep door and window trim the same color as the walls. Color intensifies in a north room or a small room, so tints might be better except for accents. North light is "cold," so if a room has a north window we should use colors from the warm (reddish) side of the color wheel. Warm hues tend to be cheerful and tend to increase the apparent size of objects in a room, but when used as wall colors they decrease the apparent size of the room itself.

Remember that a lot of dark colors in a room will absorb light and can multiply your need for electric light.

To create a color scheme for your room, a simple formula is to select the dominant hue, then decide where it will go. Then use the color wheel to select complementary colors, then decide where they will go.

possible to the front, not back by the wall. If placed back at the wall they produce glare. Fluorescent tubes and halogen lamps are best for this because their low profile makes it easier to shield the eyes from direct light.

In framed cabinets, the face frame helps shield the eyes from under-cabinet lights. But frameless cabinets have no such protecting shield, so a 2" (5 cm) bar has to be added along the front of the cabinet. Some frameless cabinets have recesses built into the cabinet bottoms where lights can be recessed. Some halogen under-cabinet lights plug into a track attached to the cabinet bottom and that shields the eyes.

When fluorescent tubes are used, they should be at least long enough to extend 2/3 of the length of the counter, which might require more than one fixture end to end. A 30W tube is 36" (91 cm) long. A 40W tube is 48" (122 cm) long. As a rule of thumb, figure on 8W for every 12" (30 cm) of counter length.

Some customers might prefer a luminous ceiling or luminous panels in a suspended ceiling. The designer should warn them that these would not give sufficient light for work at counter level. In areas where there are no wall cabinets, down lights in the ceiling or an extended soffit would have to be placed for sufficient overlap of the light fields at counter level. Otherwise both the head and hands of the cook would produce shadows on the work surface. In this case, you can hang pendants 24"-27" (61-69 cm) above the counter with 60W-75W for every 20" (51 cm) of counter. For recessed or surface units at the ceiling, use 75W reflector lamps, 16"-24" (41-61 cm) apart.

For a separate eating area in the kitchen, use a pendant or swag centered 30" (76 cm) above a table, or multiple pendants over a counter 48" (122 cm) wide or more. Use a 100W bulb, or two 60W or three 40W.

(Lighting recommendations and cost comparisons by the American Home Lighting Institute and the General Electric Lighting Institute, Nela Park, Cleveland OH.)

Ventilating the kitchen

Of all the things homeowners don't know about kitchens, the importance of good ventilation probably is the most misunderstood and unappreciated. Every day a working kitchen pours pollutants into the home air--smoke, odor, grease, humidity, toxicity in the case of gas ranges--and without ventilation they all stay in the home.

The problem has been exacerbated in the last two decades by the trend toward more and better insulation and tighter construction. Homes don't "breathe" like houses of old. That means that even if a house has enough fan power for good ventilation it can't work because the airtight house does not provide make-up air, and the fans are, in effect, spinning their wheels.

But whole-house ventilation goes beyond the basics we are covering here. We are interested in the residential kitchen that has residential (not commercial) cooking equipment, and if we vent it properly we at least get most pollutants at their source.

In venting the kitchen we have four basic choices:

• A conventional ventilating hood over the cooktop, vented to the outside;

• A ductless hood with a fan that filters and recirculates air back into the room;

• A downdraft range with a built-in or adjacent countertop vent system that draws the contaminated air into connected ductwork down, then outside simply because it is so close to it.

• A wall fan that exhausts to the outside.

Of these, the ductless hood and the wall fan are least effective. The ductless hood does not remove heat, can clog quickly and spread grease and other pollutants aroundthe room. The wall fan can not be effective until it accomplishes a complete air change in the room, and by that time cooking pollutants are everywhere. But if a wall fan is used, it should be directly over the range.

The downdraft system is effective except in the case of high pots and pans. Its effectiveness

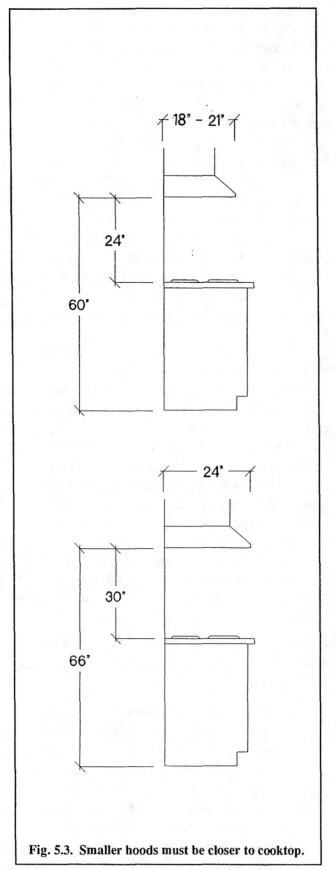

Fig. 5.3. Smaller hoods must be closer to cooktop.

depends on proximity. In addition, the fan is right there and to have enough power it can be quite noisy. For this reason many owners seldom turn it on. An alternative is to specify a downdraft system that places the motor at the end of the ductwork, outside the house. Just be sure the termination point isn't next to the patio table and chairs. The effectiveness of a downdraft system is affected by the number of bends in the pipe run (follow the manufacturer's specs), the length of the run--less than 20' (7 m) for most systems--and the type of wall cap (use the one recommended by the manufacturer).

That leaves the vented hood, a good solution when done right. Doing it right, however, requires a bit more understanding than many kitchen designers have.

The vented hood doesn't just suck up the pollutants from the cooktop. They rise by themselves because they are heated. The hood gathers and holds them momentarily so the fan can then exhaust them.

What we usually see in ads and kitchen photos is a 30" (76 cm) hood over a 30" range. But to do its gathering job properly, the hood should be about 3" (7 cm) wider on each side than the cooktop. A 30" (76 cm) range, therefore, should have a 36" (91 cm) hood.

The depth (front to back) of a hood's holding area determines how high it should be above the cooktop. A hood 18"-21" (46-53 cm) deep should be 24" (61 cm) off the surface. A hood 24" (61 cm) deep can be 30" (76 cm) above the cooktop, which is the maximum for any installation.

There are three considerations for sizing the ventilating fan: The length of its ductwork, the amount of noise it makes and its location. Location is a factor when the cooktop is in a peninsula or island where it is more subject to cross-drafts, requiring a larger hood for more gathering power and therefore more fan power for exhaust.

Duct length is a factor because the duct contains static air which must be moved out be-

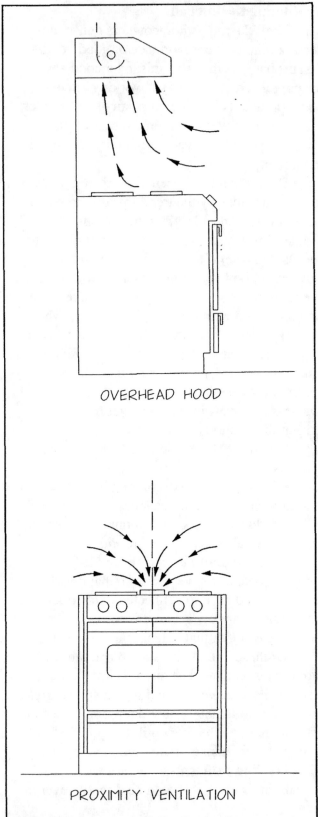

OVERHEAD HOOD

PROXIMITY VENTILATION

Fig. 5.4. Standard ventilating hood exhausts cooking contaminants up and out. Downdraft pulls contaminants down into ductwork.

fore range contaminants can be moved out. The longer the duct, the more power it needs, and if it has a 90-degree elbow that adds, in effect, 10' (3 m) to its length. Each 10' of duct will cost you about 50 CFM (1.4 m³). Generally, designers deduct one third of the CFM rating for a 21' (6.4 M) duct run with one elbow. CFM is for cubic feet (meters) of air moved per minute.

Air movement capacity of fans and their sound levels in "sones" are measured by the Home Ventilating Institute. The HVI recommends minimum standards, but many ventilation specialists consider them too minimum and recommend the following:

• For a hood against a wall, 50 to 70 CFM (1.4-2 m³) x hood area in square feet (m²), but 300 CFM (8.5 m³) minimum;

• For a hood with no back wall, 100 CFM (2.8 m³) x hood area in square feet (m²) but 600 CFM (17 m³) minimum.

• For an open grill or barbecue area with or without wall, 100-150 CFM (2.8-4.2 m³) x hood area in square feet (m²), but 600 CFM (17 m³) minimum.

(Design Guideline 19, page 82, recommends 150 CFM minimum for all surface cooking applieances.)

Sones translate decibels of loudness into how it affects the human ear. Ordinary conversation is 4 sones. A jet plane landing is 256 sones. The pain threshold is 1024 sones. HVI says kitchen vent fans up to 500 CFM (14 m³) should not exceed 9 sones.

We all know homeowners often don't use their vent fans, and we all know why: They consider them too noisy regardless of their sone rating. That suggests the best solution: A centrifugal (squirrel cage) blower exhausting direct to the outside but in a remote location which might be in a basement or attic. One such blower installation can be ducted to serve the bathrooms as well as the kitchen.

In all of this discussion we have ignored one important factor, and that is the big difference between northern and southern states. In cold northern states, when houses are tight and

Fig. 5.5. Ductwork and installation accessories include the following:

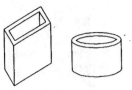

Duct usually is galvanized steel or aluminum, in various sizes and shapes, and in flexible plastic. Popular round sizes are 3" (7.6 cm), 4" (10 cm), 6" (15 cm), 7" (18 cm) and 10" (25 cm); rectangular, 3 1/4" x 10" or 12" (8 cm x 25 or 30 cm).

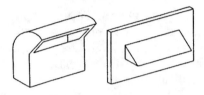

Roof cap or jack is an outside fitting for vertical duct. Pressure-activated damper opens when fan is operating, closes when it stops. Wall cap is an outside fitting for horizontal duct, in slanted shield or flush-mount versions.

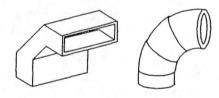

Elbows change direction of air.

Transition duct is for connecting round to rectangular duct, such as when duct must travel inside wall between studs.

Tips from the Pros

For general lighting, I sometimes lay fluorescent fixtures on their sides on top of the wall cabinets and hidden by crown molding. It gives good indirect light and eliminates the soffit.

Conrad E. Muhly III, CKD, Westchester PA

To eliminate shadows caused by pots hanging from a potrack with light above, use PVC pipe to make the potrack and run the wiring down through the pipe to lamps underneath.

Pat Galvin, "Kitchen Remodeling" (Meredith)

For dramatic general light, I open a space between studs to install either fluorescent or incandescent lamps, then cover them with a cultured onyx panel. It is translucent and the light glows through beautifully.

Milton Krieger, Ft. Lauderdale

To show customers the effects of different lighting, we set up two identical light boxes in the showroom with six different light sources inside. We can put a cabinet sample in a box and switch to different lights with toggle switches to show how the light source changes the colors.

Pattie Klassen, CKD, Tucson

I painted the ceiling in a showroom kitchen display a flat black, then stretched white cord across about 6" (15 cm) below to form a perfect grid of 9" (23 cm) squares. Then I lighted the display only with under-counter lights. When customers come in and look up, they swear the ceiling is made of black tile.

Jay Dobbs, CKD, Washington DC

A former customer added a microwave center in a far corner of the kitchen and called to say he needed more light there for a party that same evening. I bought a 6-lamp light bar, drilled a hole up high with a hole saw, mounted the light bar over it, put the cord in the hole and dropped it down between the studs, fished it out at the floor and plugged it into an outlet there. It all took about an hour.

Joe Bahelka, Morrisville PA

well-insulated, an attic can have sub-freezing temperatures for extended periods of time. This means humidity ducted from the range will condense and freeze in the duct and, on melting, drip back into the house. Local codes must be checked because they probably will specify insulation for ductwork in unheated spaces.

Noise control in the kitchen

People generally don't like noise and kitchens tend to be noisy. They are full of mechanical equipment including the dishwasher, refrigerator, disposer, microwave, convection oven fan, vent fan (if you haven't made it remote) and a host of hums and whirs of small appliances. Day and night we have the sounds of running water and clicking solenoids.

In planning a kitchen remodeling project there really is a lot you can do about noise. Here are some examples.

• As already suggested, move the vent fan from the range in the kitchen to an outside wall in the basement, attic or utility room.

• Noise transmits easily to other rooms through heating ducts, electrical outlets and lighting fixtures. Seal these up with insulating material. Use insulating panels under floor underlayment and over the ceiling wallboard.

• Noise transmits easily through a wall because of direct contact with wall studs, even if it is insulated. If you will have walls open you might add a 2x2 (5 cm x 5 cm) to the base plate and to the top header and add a row of wall studs an inch (2.5 cm) from the far wall, and weave insulation between studs the length of the wall.

• Use acoustical tile for the ceiling to help absorb noise.

• Use rubber pads under the dishwasher feet to prevent sound transmission to the floor. If you are installing a disposer, insulate the inside of the sink cabinet. Use a disposer with a rubber grommet where it mounts to the sink drain, and a section of rubber hose between the disposer and the sink U-trap. If the disposer doesn't have a rubber grommet, make a sponge rubber gasket. It won't interfere with installation.

Notes:

6 Construction, Mechanical Basics
Walking our Way through Kitchen Remodeling

A basic knowledge of house construction and residential mechanical systems is essential for a kitchen specialist. You have to know about platform and balloon construction, about studs and joists, windows and doors, plumbing, wiring, heating and cooling.

Any or all of these can be key elements in what you might be trying to do in your design. To attempt to design a kitchen without this kind of knowledge would be akin to driving in a strange city without a road map. The result, if workable, would be uninstallable.

The "skeleton" for this chapter is an actual house in which a new kitchen was installed. As we discuss construction and mechanical systems we'll follow the procedure in our typical house.

Our house is a platform house. That is, the framing members (studs) go from the foundation to the top of the first story where they are interrupted by a platform, and the second story is built on this platform. This platform framing actually was evolved from balloon framing in which the studs go from the foundation all the way to the roof, and intermediate floors are nailed to these long studs. The evolution came because the shorter studs were much easier to handle and were more easily available.

But kitchen designers work in many older homes, and they will find balloon framing in many of these, particularly brick houses and houses in the northeast and Canada. The big difference is that platform framing always is based on stud structures in the corners, but in balloon framing you often will find corners are not defined by studs. You might have to build up the corners before installation. Also, the cavities between studs can go all the way from the foundation to the roof. You may have to drop insulation into this space to protect plumbing. You won't find a lot of these, but you must be aware of them.

Our example house (Fig. 6.0) is a 6-room bilevel frame with full basement, platform construction, fronting on a lake. The house is 15 years old. The kitchen, never remodeled before, is on the lower level. The clients are a professional couple intimately connected with the design field. Only one cooks.

Fig. 6.0. ABOVE is a house under construction. Everything is easily accessible with few installation problems. Our example house, BELOW, that we'll use to illustrate principles and practices in construction, plumbing, wiring and heating is a 6-room frame bilevel, platform construction. It is 15 years old and the kitchen has never before been remodeled. The two windows at bottom right are the kitchen windows. Note the electrical service going to the house at the right. The kitchen designer must be aware of all of these facts by interviewing the customers and surveying the house.

Fig. 6.1. Platform framing, sometimes called western framing, is the most prevalent form of house construction in the U.S. In it, each floor forms a platform on which that story is built. Horizontal framing members are joists, usually are 2" x 8" (5 x 20 cm) for load-bearing floors, 2" x 6" (5 x 15 cm) in the ceiling at the attic if the attic is not finished as living space. Vertical framing members are studs, usually 2" x 4" (5 x 10 cm). Studs are placed 16" (41 cm) apart on center, although sometimes this is increased to 24" (61 cm).

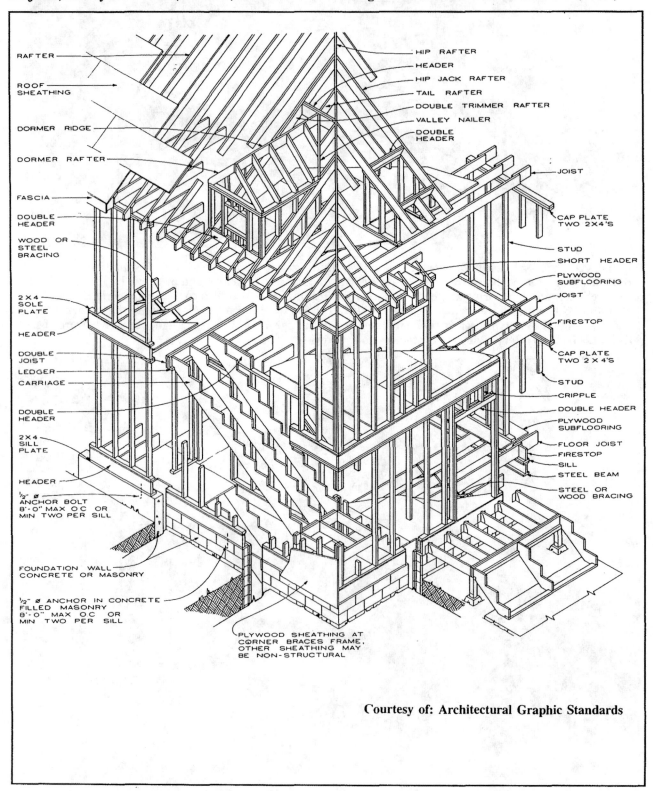

RAFTER
ROOF SHEATHING
DORMER RIDGE
DORMER RAFTER
FASCIA
DOUBLE HEADER
WOOD OR STEEL BRACING
2 X 4 SOLE PLATE
HEADER
DOUBLE JOIST
LEDGER
CARRIAGE
DOUBLE HEADER
2 X 4 SILL PLATE
HEADER
½" Ø ANCHOR BOLT 8'-0" MAX OC OR MIN TWO PER SILL
FOUNDATION WALL CONCRETE OR MASONRY
½" Ø ANCHOR IN CONCRETE FILLED MASONRY 8'-0" MAX OC OR MIN TWO PER SILL
PLYWOOD SHEATHING AT CORNER BRACES FRAME, OTHER SHEATHING MAY BE NON-STRUCTURAL

HIP RAFTER
HEADER
HIP JACK RAFTER
TAIL RAFTER
DOUBLE TRIMMER RAFTER
VALLEY NAILER
DOUBLE HEADER
JOIST
CAP PLATE TWO 2X4'S
STUD
SHORT HEADER
PLYWOOD SUBFLOORING
JOIST
FIRESTOP
CAP PLATE TWO 2 X 4'S
STUD
CRIPPLE
DOUBLE HEADER
PLYWOOD SUBFLOORING
FLOOR JOIST
FIRESTOP
SILL
STEEL BEAM
STEEL OR WOOD BRACING

Courtesy of: Architectural Graphic Standards

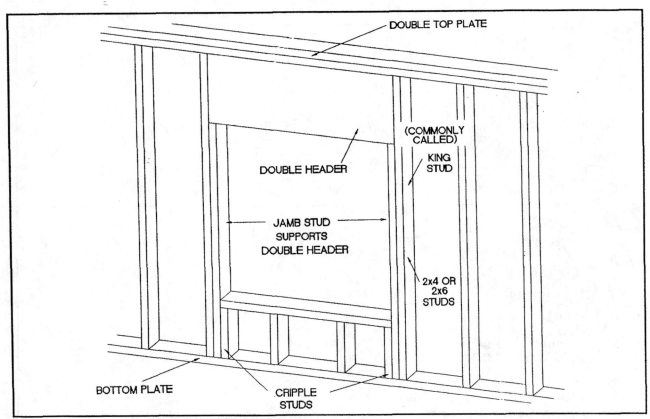

Fig. 6.2. In typical framing, studs are doubled up for extra support at openings, such as doors and windows. A typical wall partition will sit on a wall plate, which is a horizontal 2" x 4" (5 x 10 cm), and will have a double top plate along the top of the studs. Top framing of a door or window will be a double header, which is two horizontal studs, held up by jamb studs. Short lengths of stud will maintain support above the double header. These, called cripple studs, will maintain the 16" (41 cm) stud spacing.

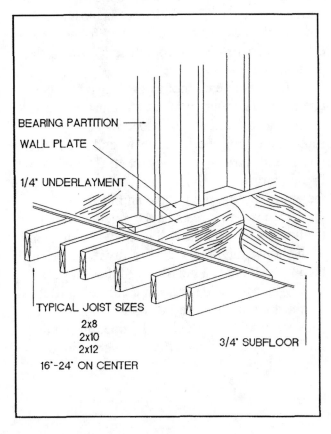

Fig. 6.3 (right). The subfloor is laid directly on floor joists. It serves as a work deck and also adds rigidity to the structure. In older houses this will be 1" x 6" (2.5 x 15 cm) boards laid diagonally across the floor and nailed to the joists. Recently, 4' x 8' (122 x 244 cm) plywood panels have been used for the subfloor. The subfloor normally will be topped by an underlayment of plywood or particleboard, with the finished flooring going on top of the underlayment.

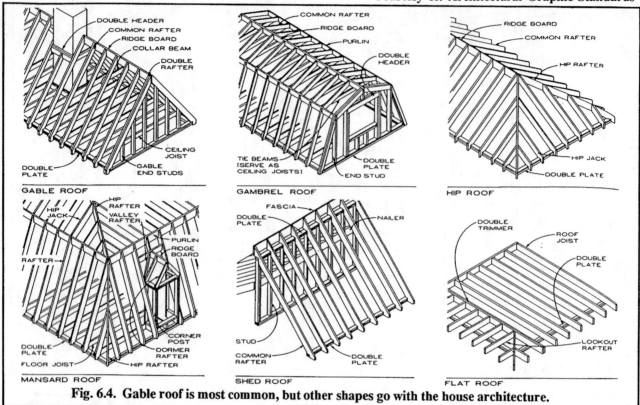

Fig. 6.4. Gable roof is most common, but other shapes go with the house architecture.

Roof forms used in house construction are varied (Fig. 6.4). The gable roof is most common, usually over a flat ceiling and framed with ceiling joists below and roof rafters forming the gable above.

In recent years roof trusses have become common. These are prebuilt structural components made of wood and shaped metal that support the roof over clear spans and that fasten rafters and joists where they meet. Trusses come in many forms, often making it possible to build the entire roof on the ground and then hoist it into place where it rests on the exterior walls of the house. In these cases the entire ceiling area of the house might be clear for any remodeling below. If there is a bearing wall that supports ceiling joists in wide areas, it can be identified by checking in the attic for where the joists meet. Attic ventilation is provided by openings in the soffits or by a roof cap along the gable ridge.

Replacement windows (Fig. 6.5, facing page) are available in several forms and styles. They might come fully assembled or the installer might have to fabricate them on the job. They are designed to fit into existing standard openings. If your opening is not standard you will have to reframe.

A standard double-hung window, as shown in the drawing, has a flat sill on the outside. The inside sill is called the stool and fits on top of an inside apron. The two window panes are the upper sash and lower sash.

If you are replacing a double-hung window, the older model might have weights to counterbalance the separate sashes. Newer windows are spring-loaded along the inner faces of the side jambs, so weights are no longer needed.

Fig. 6.5. Windows come in several styles, might be assembled or installer might have to fabricate them.

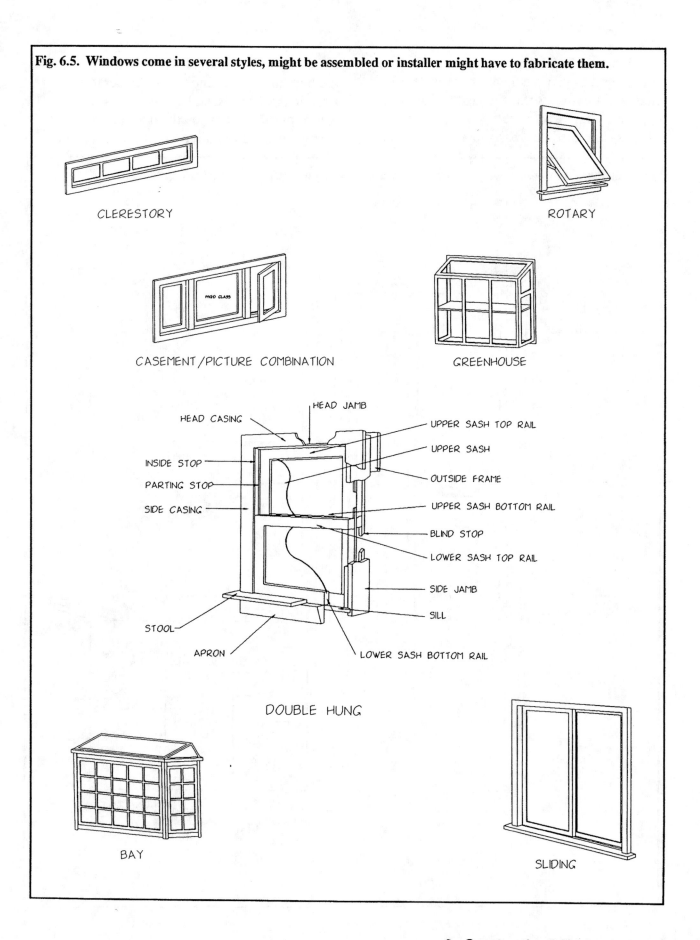

CLERESTORY

ROTARY

CASEMENT/PICTURE COMBINATION

GREENHOUSE

HEAD JAMB

HEAD CASING

UPPER SASH TOP RAIL

UPPER SASH

INSIDE STOP

OUTSIDE FRAME

PARTING STOP

SIDE CASING

UPPER SASH BOTTOM RAIL

BLIND STOP

LOWER SASH TOP RAIL

SIDE JAMB

SILL

STOOL

APRON

LOWER SASH BOTTOM RAIL

DOUBLE HUNG

BAY

SLIDING

Standard interior swing doors are hinged left or right as you see them from inside the kitchen. A casing forms the visible framing, with side jambs and a head jamb for the inner facings, shimmed out for a close fit. The door closes against stop moldings. Hardware includes the butt hinges; the knob, which operates the latch in the latch assembly, and the strike plate that traps the latch when the door closes. It swings in or out, relative to the kitchen itself.

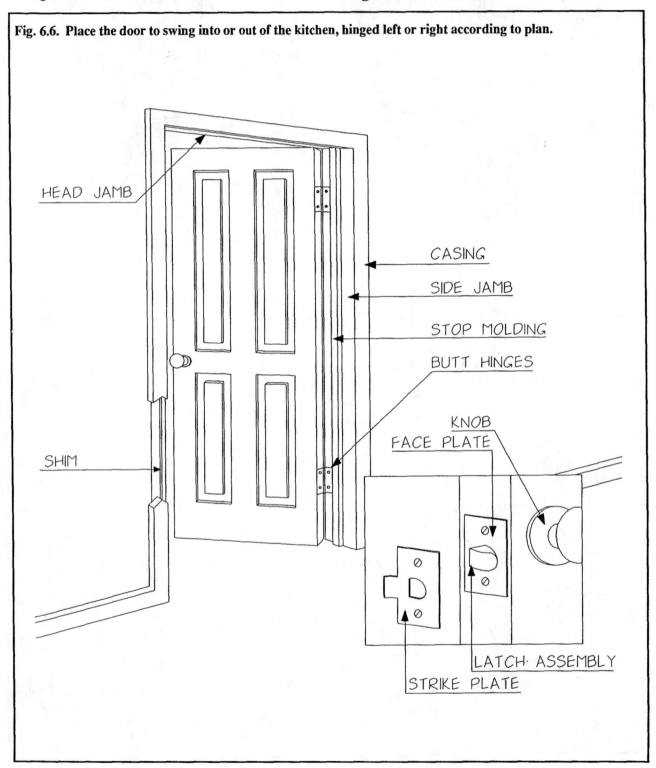

Fig. 6.6. Place the door to swing into or out of the kitchen, hinged left or right according to plan.

HEAD JAMB

CASING

SIDE JAMB

STOP MOLDING

BUTT HINGES

SHIM

KNOB

FACE PLATE

LATCH ASSEMBLY

STRIKE PLATE

Fig. 6.7. In remodeling, note location of mechanical elements such as plumbing, wiring, gas. This is the existing kitchen in our example house.

Fig. 6.8. Remember to check all local codes and get building permits.

On the jobsite you will have to familiarize yourself with all mechanical elements (Fig. 6.7). And, of course, you will have to check local building codes. National codes apply, but will be superseded by local codes. Your building permits must be displayed prominently (Fig. 6.8).

The plumbing system in a house handles water and all water appliances (Fig. 6.9). The water supply system brings fresh water in, under pressure, from the water main or pumped from a well. After the water is used (sinks, dishwasher, tub, toilet) it leaves the house by gravity flow through the drain-waste-vent (DWV) system.

Copper pipe is most used for water supply in remodeling. It can be flexible or rigid. Joints are made with solder or swedge (mechanical) fittings. Building codes often specify copper.

Brass is excellent for pipe, but it is expensive. Joints are made with threaded connections.

Galvanized steel is commonly used for water distribution in the house, so this is what you probably will find in the walls. Joints are threaded or made with malleable fittings. Cast iron is similar to steel in the way it is worked.

Plastic pipe is easiest to work and fastest-growing, although its use sometimes is restricted by code. Plastic pipes include:

• PVC (polyvinyl chloride), good for drains and cold water distribution, not for hot;

• CPVC (Chlorinated PVC), good for hot and cold water distribution. It is self-insulating and cold water lines stay free of condensation.

• PB (polybutylene) is a flexible tubing for hot and cold lines, good for snaking in difficult installations. It was used used in difficult areas and then changed over to PVC or CPVC, but it has been deleted from the code for water supply.

• ABS (acrylonitrile butadiene styrene), used for DWV systems, but subject to excessive expansion and contraction.

The water supply comes in from a city main in 1" or 1 1/4" (2.5 or 3 cm) galvanized pipe or, if it is copper, 3/4" or 1" (1.9 or 2.5 cm).

Fig. 6.9. Home plumbing systems have hot and cold water supply lines. Used water and waste flow out in DWV lines. All traps must be vented to equalize air pressure and prevent siphoning of sewer gases.

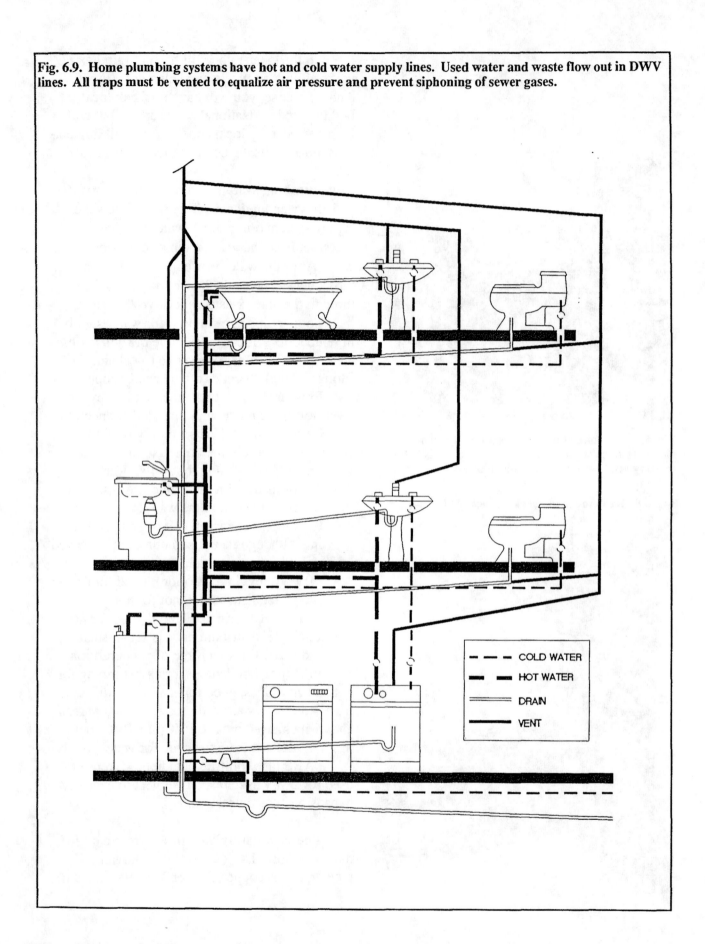

COLD WATER

HOT WATER

DRAIN

VENT

Pressure might be 30-60 psi, preferably nearer to the higher figure.

Water distribution piping should be 3/4" ID (2 cm) (inside diameter) including lines to the water heater and clothes washer. Lines to the kitchen sink and dishwasher should be 1/2" (13 mm), but 1/4" (6.3 mm) tubing is fine for sink risers. For an ice maker, use 1/8" or 3/16" (3 or 9 mm) PB tubing.

The DWV system works by gravity flow, so pipe is larger. It usually is 2" (51 cm). It must slope downward at the rate of 1/4" to 1/2" (6.4 to 13 mm) per foot (30 cm), depending on local code.

Pipes that carry waste water are called waste pipes (Fig. 6.9), except for those that serve toilets which are called soil pipes. All carry waste to a soil pipe, or stack, which is 3" or 4" (76 or 102 cm) and goes to the building drain which extends up through the roof to provide venting. The building drain goes to a sewer which generates dangerous gases, so each fixture protects you with a trap (Fig. 6.10), which is a bend in the pipe that traps water to block gases.

Each fixture also must have a vent pipe (Fig. 6.9) that allows air into the system to equalize atmospheric pressure. Without a vent pipe the rush of water down a drain could cause a siphoning action that would pull the water seal out of the trap and let sewer gases enter the home. The requirement for a vent pipe must be considered when planning a sink in an island. The vent pipe is usually right behind the sink, but the distance between the two can be increased if the drain pipe is enlarged.

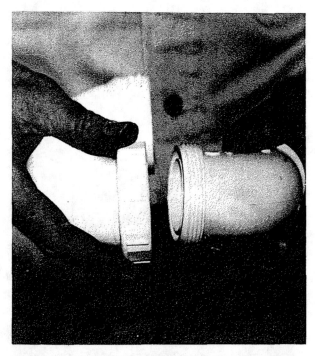

Fig. 6.11. Threaded drain pipe is larger than supply pipe because waste is not under pressure, flows by gravity.

Fig. 6.12. Plumber has to gain access to pipes to get them where they have to go, even if it means cutting into ceilings or walls.

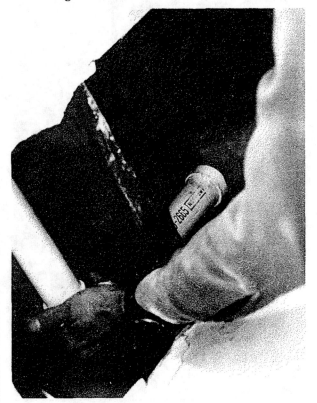

Fig. 6.10. Traps vary in shape according to use.

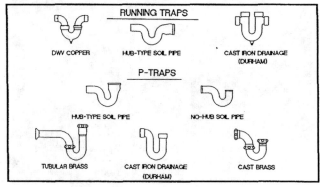

RUNNING TRAPS

DWV COPPER   HUB-TYPE SOIL PIPE   CAST IRON DRAINAGE (DURHAM)

P-TRAPS

HUB-TYPE SOIL PIPE   NO-HUB SOIL PIPE

TUBULAR BRASS   CAST IRON DRAINAGE (DURHAM)   CAST BRASS

Fig. 6.13. To keep pipe hidden from view, plumber sometimes must drill holes in joist and route it through.

Fig. 6.15. Here plumber has to chip out a pipe route in concrete foundation. It means a lot of added time on the plumbing subcontract.

Fig. 6.14. Copper tubing is used for water supply to the sink. Larger plastic pipe is used for drain.

Fig. 6.16. Keeping the jobsite neat can increase client satisfaction. Sweep work areas every day.

The **home electrical system** (Fig. 6.17) brings electricity into the house on *service wires* from the electric utility. They enter the house at a *service entrance*, then go to a meter that measures total use in *kilowatt hours*, then to a *service panel*.

Electrical current goes to the service panel on three wires. Two are 120-volt hot wires. The third is neutral. These provide both 120-volt and 240-volt circuits in the house. Some appliances, such as doorbells, intercoms or special lighting, may operate on *low voltage* current, usually around 10 or 12 volts but possibly ranging from 6 to 24 volts. Their voltage is cut down by a small transformer wired in anywhere between the appliance and the service panel.

Grounding is a safety measure built into every home electrical system. At the service panel and/or at the meter, the main grounding wire is connected to a metal water pipe and grounding rod that is driven at least 8' (244 cm) into the ground. In house wiring, a bare copper or green insulated grounding wire provides an alternate route for any leaking current, protecting the circuit and family members from shock.

The service panel has either fuses or circuit breakers to control the circuits in the house. A single circuit breaker will control a 120V circuit. Any 240V circuit will be controlled by two circuit breakers which might be connected with a plastic cap. Any 240V circuit will serve only one outlet, such as a dryer or electric range. A 120V circuit might serve as many as a dozen outlets, as long as the total amperage of the lights and appliances doesn't exceed the amperage rating of the circuit breaker or fuse. If the customer has a home computer you might need a *dedicated circuit* to protect it against voltage surges that might come when another appliance cycles on or off. This is like any other 120V circuit except that it serves only one outlet.

If you open the door of the service panel you will see all of the circuit breakers or fuses. If you see blank slots with no breakers, they are places where new breakers can be installed to expand the house electrical system with more

Fig. 6.17. Electricity comes to the house in service wires that connect to the service panel. The size of the service conduit and the amperage limitation of the service panel determine how much electrical power is available for the house.

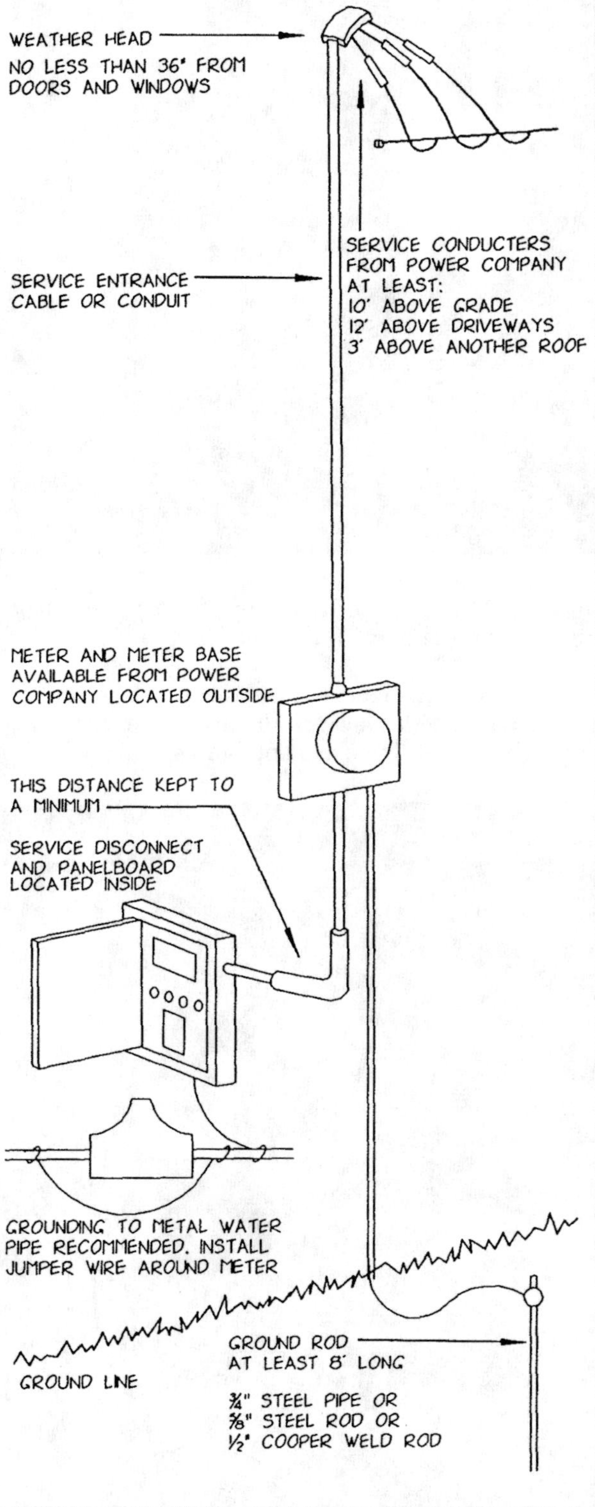

WEATHER HEAD
NO LESS THAN 36" FROM DOORS AND WINDOWS

SERVICE CONDUCTERS FROM POWER COMPANY AT LEAST:
10' ABOVE GRADE
12' ABOVE DRIVEWAYS
3' ABOVE ANOTHER ROOF

SERVICE ENTRANCE CABLE OR CONDUIT

METER AND METER BASE AVAILABLE FROM POWER COMPANY LOCATED OUTSIDE

THIS DISTANCE KEPT TO A MINIMUM

SERVICE DISCONNECT AND PANELBOARD LOCATED INSIDE

GROUNDING TO METAL WATER PIPE RECOMMENDED. INSTALL JUMPER WIRE AROUND METER

GROUND LINE

GROUND ROD AT LEAST 8' LONG
¾" STEEL PIPE OR
⅝" STEEL ROD OR
½" COOPER WELD ROD

Fig. 6.18. The service conduit must be inspected when the project is planned. It must be big enough.

Fig. 6.19. The electrical meter measures consumption as electricity is used.

Fig. 6.20. An old, inadequate service panel simply won't have enough space for all the new wires running from new outlets, lights and appliances.

Fig. 6.21. When a new service panel is needed, make sure the homeowners know the cost. $1,000-$3,000 is not unusual for a new service panel installation.

circuits. In remodeling a kitchen you almost surely will want to add circuits. You might be able to combine some circuits that have light loads (such as for bedrooms) to create an open slot or two for expansion.

Older houses often were rated at only 60A (amperes) for the entire house. Newer houses are rated for 100A. The main breaker on the service panel should show the house rating. It is usually a double breaker in line with all the others, but larger and a different color. This rating might be the number "60" or "100" molded or pressed into the tops of the two breakers. In any kitchen remodeling, consider upgrading to 150A or 200A to provide circuitry for future needs.

If there is no room for expansion, the electrician might add a supplementary panel. But many codes now prohibit these and require that the old service panel be replaced with a new one with more capacity.

The accepted modern standard for wiring in new houses is to put an outlet at least every 12' (366 cm) in every wall and within 6' (183 cm) of every door. These usually are on a 20A circuit with 12-gauge wire, although the slightly smaller 14-gauge is adequate for lighting, radio and television. A dishwasher or clothes washer needs larger 10-gauge wire and a 240V range circuit needs 8-gauge.

The National Electrical Code requires that a kitchen have at least two circuits and must have ground fault circuit interrupts (GFCI) to protect against shocks. A remodeled kitchen will almost certainly require more circuits than that and a lot more outlets. For current or future needs the remodeled kitchen should have a duplex outlet at least every 4' (122 cm) or 5' (152 cm) along the length of the counter. A countertop appliance garage will need one or two strategically placed so they won't interfere with a tambour door.

Fig. 6.22 . Plastic-sheathed wire (Romex) is normally used for circuits not exposed to weather. Any wire that runs outside must have steel jacket, either flexible (center) or rigid.

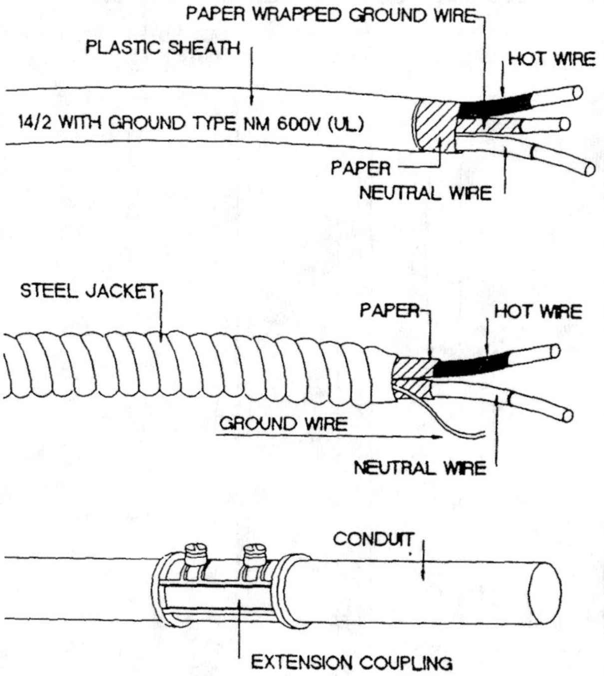

PAPER WRAPPED GROUND WIRE
PLASTIC SHEATH
HOT WIRE
14/2 WITH GROUND TYPE NM 600V (UL)
PAPER
NEUTRAL WIRE

STEEL JACKET
PAPER
HOT WIRE
GROUND WIRE
NEUTRAL WIRE

CONDUIT
EXTENSION COUPLING

Fig. 6.23. Here are actual wires ready to use in a job. Incidentally, putting *anything* on a new countertop should be forbidden by your firm.

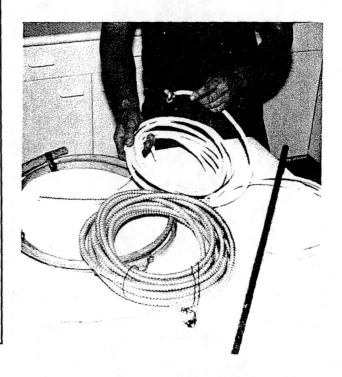

Under the counter, behind the base cabinets, it will need wiring for the range (a separate 240V), dishwasher, disposer, refrigerator, possibly a compactor and ice maker. As a designer, you can do your clients a favor by wiring duplex outlets for all appliances so they can be changed in the future and the new ones be plugged in without going into the wiring.

A duplex outlet is one that has two "receptacles." The receptacle is the place where you plug in a cord. A receptacle with two slots is a 2-wire receptacle. Newer houses have 3-wire receptacles which have two slots and a round hole. The round hole connects to a bonding wire that runs along with house wiring and connects to a ground. Another feature of modern receptacles is *polarization*, in which one slot is larger than the other to accept modern polarized plugs. The larger slot connects to the white neutral

wire, the small slot to the hot wire. This insures that the switch always interrupts the flow of current so no current can flow in when the switch is off. If polarity is reversed, an exposed socket can give a shock even when the switch is off and the light or appliance isn't running.

Wherever there is an outlet or any other place where wires are joined, it must be done in a *junction box*. These metal or plastic boxes come in many sizes and shapes, with knock-out holes so wiring can be brought in from any direction. They usually are nailed to studs, joists or floor plates.

GFCI outlets are required by code in bathrooms, garages, basements and in the kitchen within 6' (183 cm) of the sink. It can be done by installing GFCI circuit breakers in the service panel for those particular circuits, or by install-

Fig. 6.24. Wires have to be snaked through walls and floors of a house. But an outlet can be added wherever there is an electric line when the electrician can open up the wall to get to it. Here a junction box is added in an existing line.

Fig. 6.25. If there is no existing line, a new cable can be "fished" through bottom and top plates, and then a duplex outlet added near the floor.

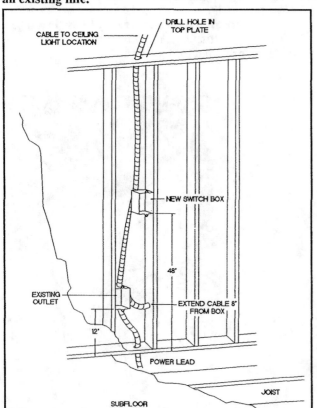

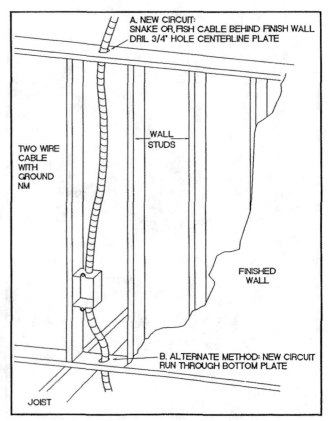

Fig. 6.26. All switches, outlets and fixtures must meet in a junction box so wiring will be safe.

Fig. 6.27. Like the plumber, the electrician must cut holes in walls and fish or snake wires through. Neat cutouts are sign of good workmanship.

Fig. 6.28. Working the wiring to the right places takes added time, which must be charged. Electrician can make it easier by following plumbing lines.

Fig. 6.29. Well-done electrical jobs are neat, with wires clustered and stapled down.

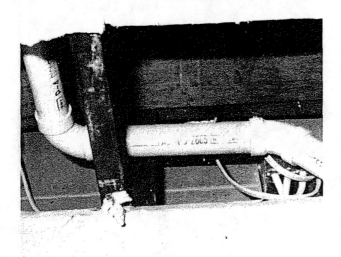

ing GFCI outlets. A GFCI outlet in the first junction box of a circuit will protect all outlets on that circuit.

It works this way. The hot black wire going into an appliance or outlet and the neutral white wire leaving it both carry the same amount of current. A GFCI breaker is so sensitive it will measure a difference as small as .005 amps in the current entering or leaving any device anywhere along the circuit and when it detects the difference it will trip the breaker and shut down the circuit. A GFCI outlet accomplishes the same. On either there will be a test button and a reset button. It should be tested regularly by pushing the test button, then reset by pushing the reset button.

Drywall construction and repair is a necessary step in the late stages of kitchen remodeling. Plumbers and electricians often must make gaping holes in existing wallboard. These holes will disappear totally under thehands of a skilled carpenter with the right materials (Fig. 6.30).

For walls, 1/2"-thick (13 mm) material is used. For ceilings it usually is 5/8" (16 mm). For patching, the hole is evened out to a square or rectangle, and then a piece is cut 2" (6 cm) larger than the hole in each dimension. The top layer of paper is scored the size of the plug and peeled off, leaving the bottom paper layer in place to hold the plug in place with patching compound. A large patch will have to be held in place and secured by bugle-head screws into studs or wood framing that is added behind the hole (Figs. 6.31-34).

Fig. 6.30. Techniques used for installing drywall must be adapted to patching. Nailing to stud must be finished with a slight dimple, later filled with patching compound. Where panels butt, edges must be tapered, filled with joint cement and taped. Metal corners are used, and moldings to finish it off.

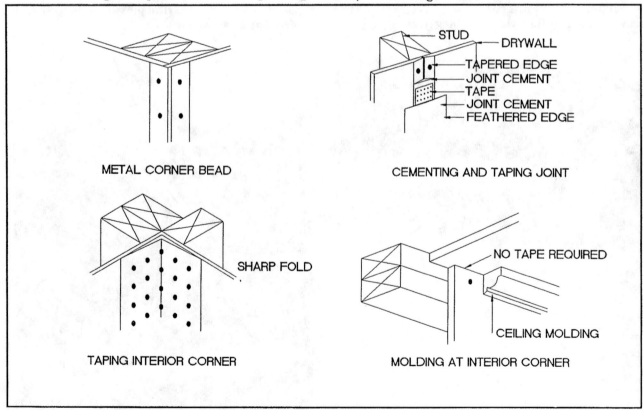

METAL CORNER BEAD

CEMENTING AND TAPING JOINT

STUD — DRYWALL
TAPERED EDGE
JOINT CEMENT
TAPE
JOINT CEMENT
FEATHERED EDGE

TAPING INTERIOR CORNER

SHARP FOLD

MOLDING AT INTERIOR CORNER

NO TAPE REQUIRED

CEILING MOLDING

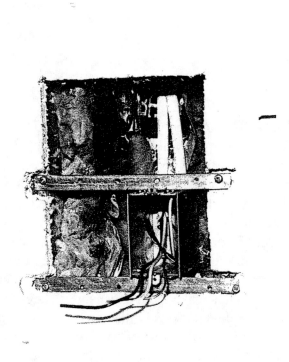

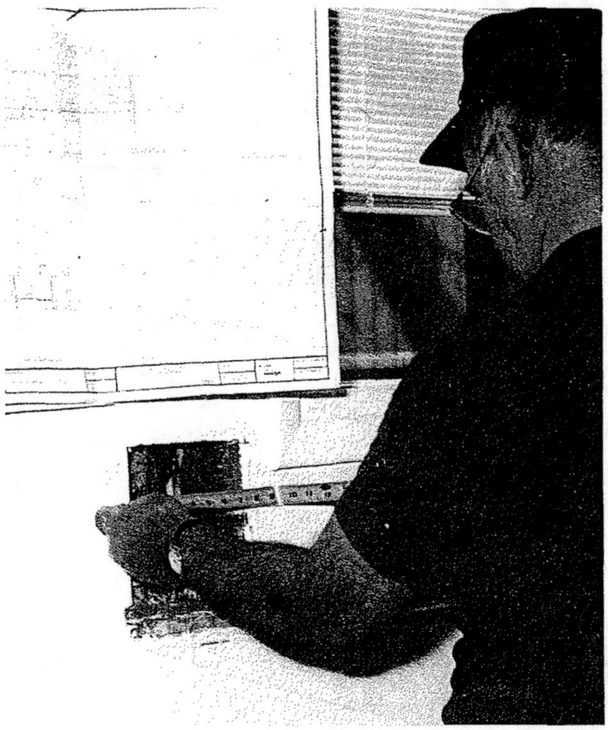

Fig. 6.31. Openings to be patched must be squared, easier with drywall than with lath and plaster.

Fig. 6.32. Carpenter must measure opening and cut drywall patch to fit.

Fig. 6.33. Patch is oversized so layer of paper can hold it in place, but then it must be screwed to wood frame.

Fig. 6.34. Joints then are taped, joint cement is troweled over the tape; edges are feathered for a smooth surface, and patches disappear when done by a good craftsman.

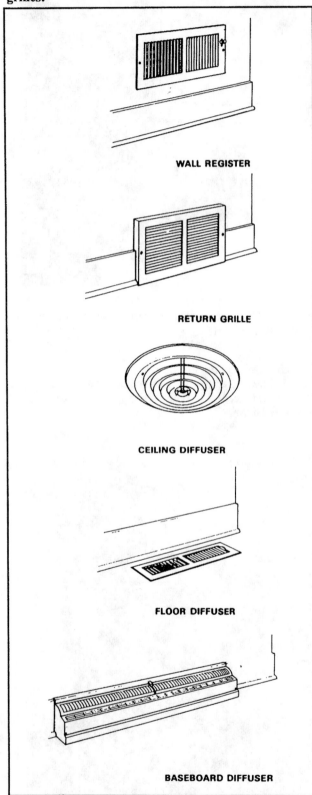

WALL REGISTER

RETURN GRILLE

CEILING DIFFUSER

FLOOR DIFFUSER

BASEBOARD DIFFUSER

Home heating systems can be classified by the fuel they use or by heating medium. Fuels are natural gas, fueloil or electricity. The medium can be warm air, hot water or steam. Water and steam heat the house with radiators piped from a boiler. Warm air is generated by a furnace and is widely favored because it is easy to add a central air conditioning unit and a central humidifier. Electric resistance heaters are easy to install but electric rates make them expensive. They are good for cold pockets in the house.

Warm air is delivered to a room through wall or floor registers or through baseboard or ceiling diffusers. Each room also should have a return grille through which the furnace fan draws air back to the furnace (Fig. 6.35).

If the kitchen being remodeled doesn't have a register, one can be added in a kick space with a duct elbow to route heat into the room through a toekick grille. One company makes heating units specifically for use in the kick space (Fig. 6.36).

Fig. 6.36. Heating unit by Beacon Morris delivers hot air or hot water heat through kitchen kick space.

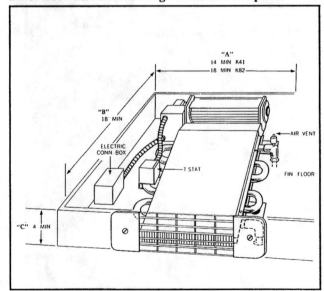

It's installation time after all of the renovation and plumbing and electrical rough-in is completed and all of the repair work is done and resulting refuse is moved out of the way.

When you are ready to install, all of the cabinets, appliances and other equipment and material should be on hand, in protected storage on the premises.

Now let's walk our way through the installation.

Fig. 6.37. Cabinets and other equipment for the new kitchen should be in protected on-premise storage.

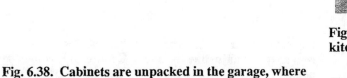

Fig. 6.38. Cabinets are unpacked in the garage, where they are stored, and brought into the kitchen.

Fig. 6.39. Normally, cabinet doors are removed to protect them. Room layout is checked again. Note the 6' ((188 cm) level craftsmen will use.

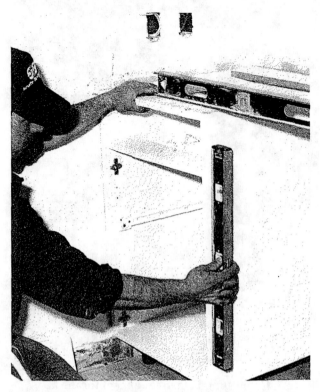

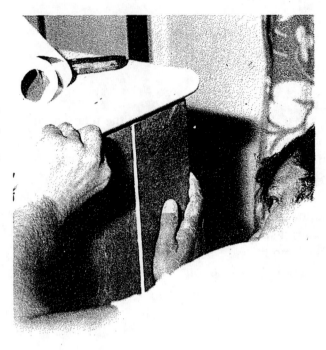

Fig. 6.40. Leveling the cases across the entire run is essential. Also, check that units are plumb vertically. Correct with shims or leveling legs.

Fig. 6.41. After cabinets are installed the doors are replaced and adjustments made. Countertops come next.

Fig. 6.42. Floor is sometimes installed first, then covered while cabinets and tops are installed. More typically, floor goes in last so damage is minimal.

Fig. 6.43. Electrician and plumber return to install and connect sinks, faucets and appliances. The electrician "trims out" the job by installing light fixtures, outlet covers and switches. All should read manufacturers' instructions--and follow them.

Fig. 6.44. After all the planning and work, here's the completed kitchen.

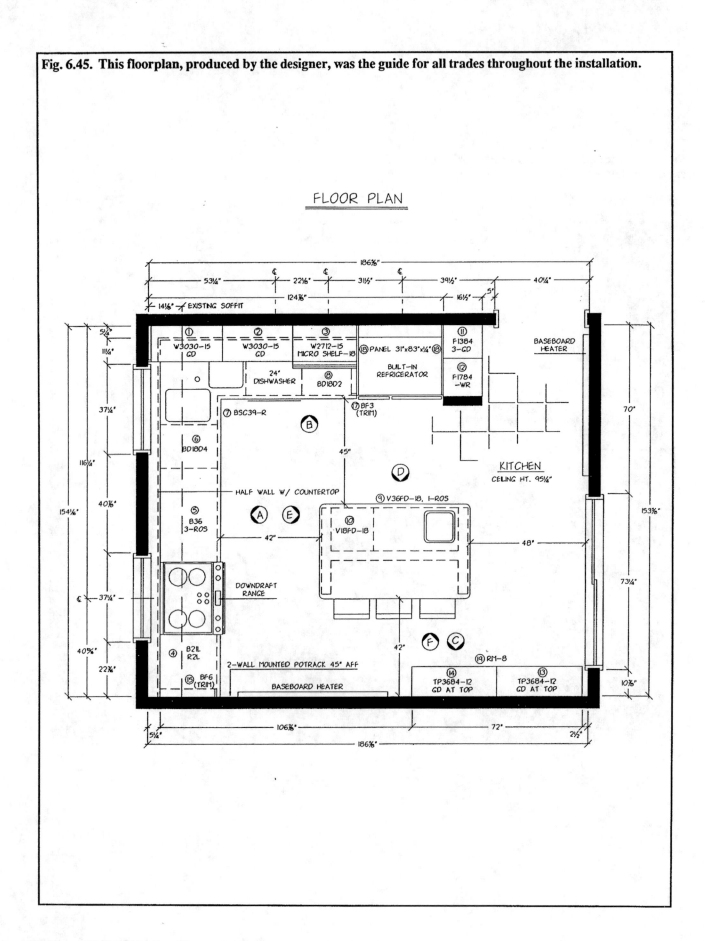

FLOOR PLAN

Fig. 6.46. The floorplan shows where all cabinets and equipment must go, but this mechanical plan also is needed by the tradespeople.

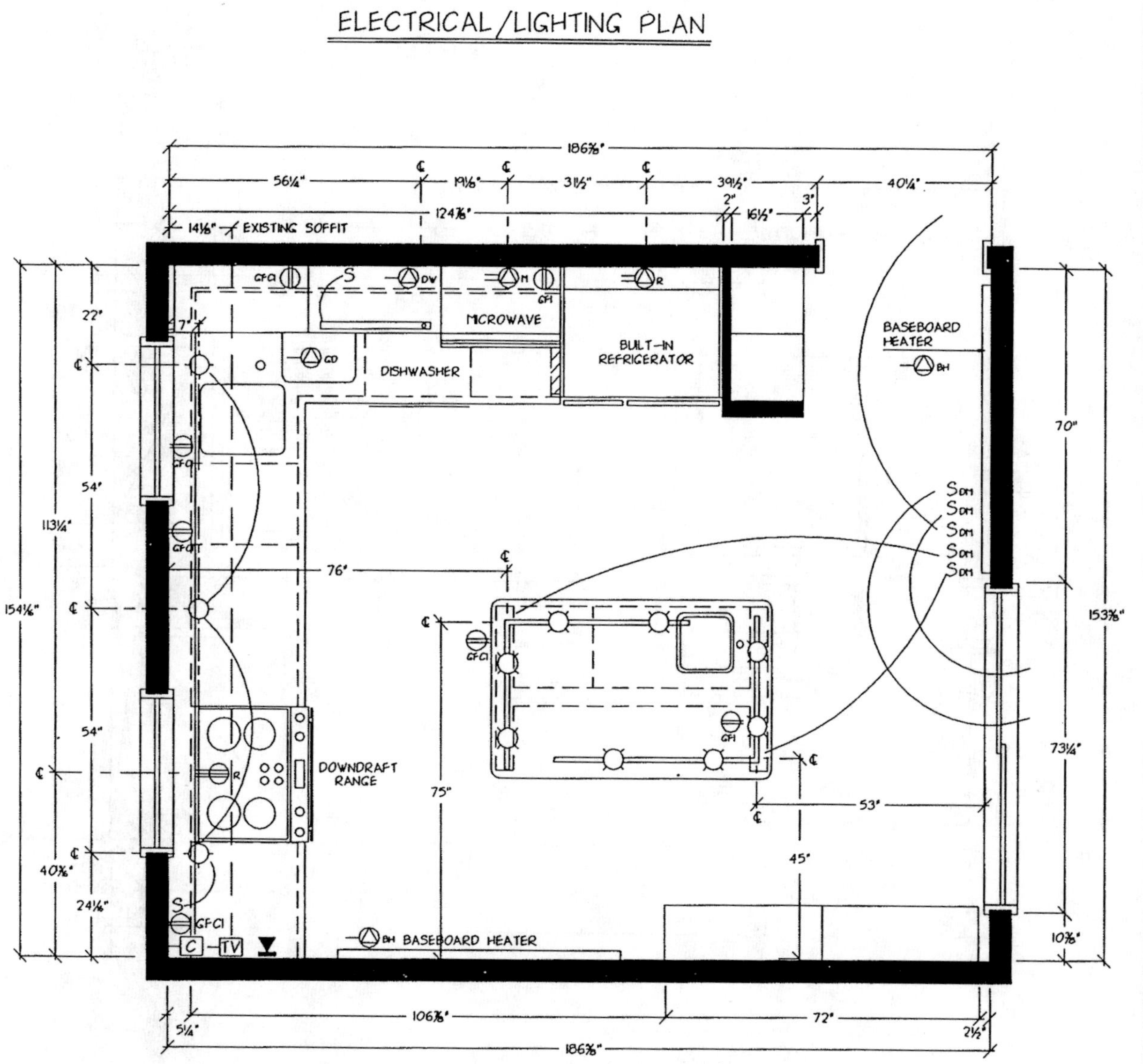

ELECTRICAL/LIGHTING PLAN

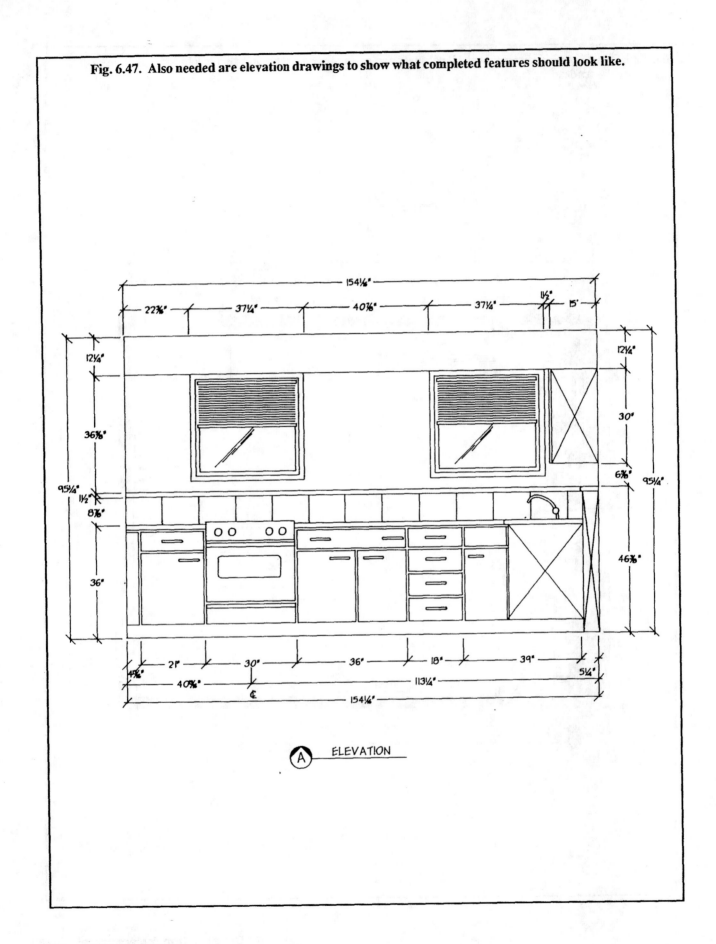

ELEVATION

Fig. 6.48. There should be as many elevation drawings as needed to answer all questions. All of this detail work is required to get the desired results.

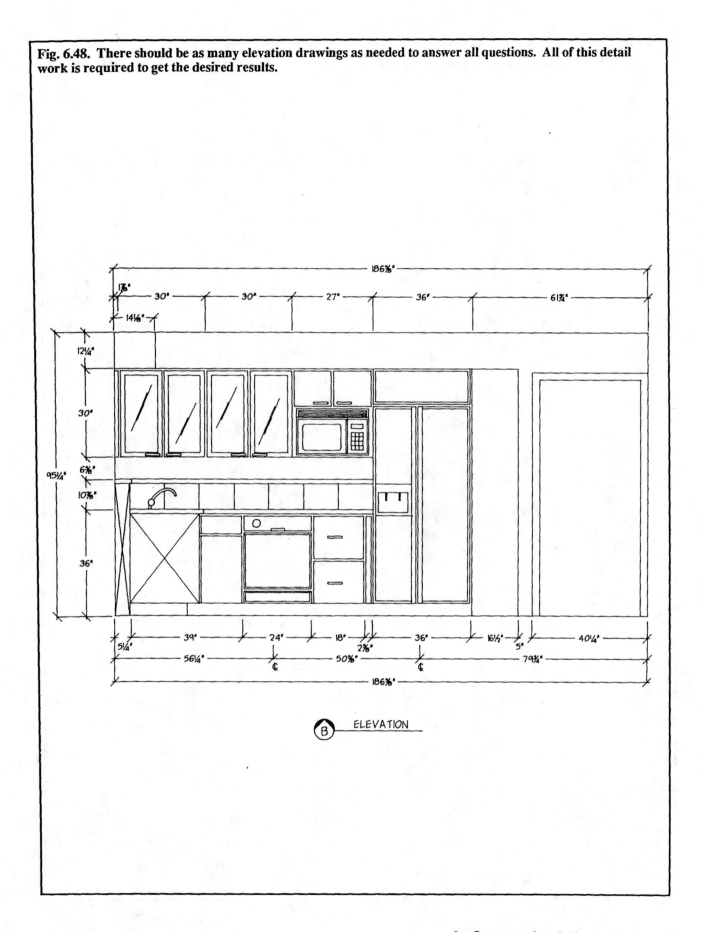

ELEVATION

Fig. 6.49. Finally, the perspective drawing can help bring it alive for both the client and the workers.

7 Presenting & Selling Your Ideas
Focus Your Effort to Close in Three Calls

There are 24 hours in a day, no matter who you are or where you spend the time. But a work day—the time we spend working—is variable. Some of us fit our work day into 8 or 10 hours, and in that span are able to sustain a happy home life, a satisfying personal life and operate a profitable business. Others of us need 12 or 14 hours for that and still find we always are scrambling to catch up.

And when we talk about operating a profitable business we are not talking only about the owner of the firm we work for. We are talking about you and me, because all of us, whether we work for salary or commission, are really operating our own business. Our earnings, our welfare, our happiness and our success depend on how we do it. And the earnings and success of the firm that employs us also depend on how we run our own businesses.

What we all should realize early in this game is that structures exist that enable all of us to do the job right within a reasonable amount of time. We only have to follow established procedures that have been proven in the field, but follow them with commitment and enthusiasm.

Selling starts at first contact

The structures that help you organize the job all the way through completion start in the showroom with your first contact with the customer, who at this time is only a prospect.

Let's follow a typical prospect and a typical designer/salesperson through the procedure, step by step. As we do, remember we are discussing *typical* acts in *typical* situations. There always might be prospects or situations that are atypical, but when such cases arise remember also that these might be prospects that you do not want as customers and that your company can't serve properly and profitably. For all practical purposes in this chapter you are a professional with a full-service professional kitchen firm.

Remember also that you have a goal here, and that is to complete the sale with three customer contacts: A showroom visit, a visit to the home for interview and measuring, and then a visit to the showroom for your presentation, the close and the contract signing.

It won't always work out that way. At times you will have to redo the plans and make a second presentation. But if you remember the goal and focus on it you will be prepared at that first presentation with your best plan and with alternate plans in mind so you can make fast changes and get the contract signed with one presentation. This is one factor that makes the difference between 8-hour days and 12-hour days.

Bright Ideas
on working smarter, not harder

On average I need _____ appointments to make a sale.

I work _____ hours per day, _____ days per week.

I would like to meet with the prospect only _____ times per week.

I would like to work _____ hours per day, _____ days per week.

If I could attain this goal, I will have _____ hours, which translates into _____ days of additional time to do _____ with.

To reduce the number of appointments and the hours it takes to close a sale I will do the following five things consistently when I return to work:

1. _____
   _____ .

2. _____
   _____ .

3. _____
   _____ .

4. _____
   _____ .

5. _____
   _____
   _____ .

Step 1. The meeting.

You see them peering in through the showroom window, a man and woman probably in their 30s, he in a suit (probably worked in the morning, got off in the afternoon), she in slacks and blouse, nice looking. You see them pointing with a lot of smiles and "yes" nods, then they open the door and come in.

(Start sizing them up at the earliest moment. So far this looks good, all positive from the nods to the smiles.)

You let them walk around, looking, feeling the finishes. They are animated and interested, particularly in a peninsula that opens both ways. When you see them starting to slow down, you approach: **"Good afternoon. I'm Marcia Marsh, and I designed that kitchen you're looking at. I designed the peninsula with doors to open both ways so you can get dishes out for a dining area on the other side. Are you thinking about a new kitchen that might have a peninsula in it?"**

That, in essence, is how a showroom should be used. It should show a variety of ideas as well as merchandise. It should have clean, neat displays that stimulate the desires of the prospects who see them, and it should show that you know how to solve kitchen design problems.

That means, obviously, that you should not have taken a sink out of a display to fill an order. That would indicate to the prospects that you sell holes in countertops. Your cabinets should be filled with dishes and things that go in a kitchen, not with literature and the receptionist's purse.

Things I can do to improve the appearance of
1. _____
2. _____
3. _____
4. _____
5. _____

You don't know who these people are yet. Give them a few seconds. If they volunteer their names it is another positive sign. If they are coy about volunteering, ask them. In this case the woman volunteers: **"Hi. I'm Shirley Smith and this is my husband, Bill. We were just driving by and saw your place. This is nice, with the eating bar and all, but I'm afraid it might be too big for our house."**

Step 2. Qualifying the prospect.

Qualifying is a procedure for finding facts without offending. You want to know:

• That the prospect lives in your trading area;

• That the prospect is genuinely interested in buying products that you represent;

• That the prospect can afford to buy;

• That *Now* is the time the prospect wants to buy (critical for clients building a new home);

• That one or more of the people visiting with you will make the buying decision. In this case—and it often is the case—Marcia thinks Shirley will make the decisions except that Bill will want to lay down some specifications on quality and price.

(For business planning reasons, you will also want to ask how they learned about your firm: Referral? Location? Promotion? Advertisement?)

• That you can sell to this prospect and complete the project profitably.

How do you find out these things? You ask, but tactfully.

• **"What part of town do you live in?"** There can be no problem with that question, and you find out quickly if they are local or from far away. Also, it gives you an opportunity to name customers you have served in their area.

• **"Are you planning a new home, or are you thinking of remodeling?"** This is a good ice-breaker question and it will give you timing insights. For example, if they are dreaming about a kitchen for a new home on the drawing board for next year, you can't serve them today as well as you can serve a couple with a new home under construction right now. But take care to be diplomatic. Even if their house is a year away *your selling job has already started.* Be helpful. Tell them they will get information on new kitchen equipment from you over the next year while they are completing their planning. Get their address and stay in touch. But, meanwhile, get on to the other prospects who need a kitchen right now.

• **"Are you interested in a kitchen?"** Too bland. How about **"Are you having some problems with the kitchen you have now?"** That's a leading question, and an emotional response can tip you off to how much they need it or how soon.

Now is the time to start matching the prospect's needs and wants with the products you represent. Structure your showroom presentation around this specific client information. For example, don't spend 20 minutes telling the prospect about the wonderful custom cabinets you have (which take 16 weeks to get) when the prospects just told you they are remodeling their kitchen to be ready for a wedding reception that will be held at home next month. Some firms do develop a set "tour" through the showroom from which they rarely deviate, but many successful selling pros do well tailoring their tour to the clients' specific interests. In our fast-paced world, most clients feel special when they receive special, customized services and attention.

showroom as soon as I return:

_____

_____

_____

_____

_____

And they buy from salespeople who make them feel special.

• **Can they afford it?** It isn't easy to ask that kind of question, so delay it and try to work it in. The companion question to that is **how much are they willing to invest in a kitchen?**

They will be fishing for answers just as you will. They may ask **"How much does this display kitchen cost?"** (Tell them, but point out how the price is affected by the cabinet line, the accessories, the appliances and the unique design features.) Or they may ask how much the "average" kitchen costs. (Without sounding hostile or condescending, answer them with a question: **"How much does the average car cost? How much does the average house cost?"** Or they may ask **"How much are your cabinets per square foot?"** (Refer back to Page 20 for some real answers.)

You can judge their affordability quotient somewhat by the neighborhood they live in, by the car they drive, by what they say about their home, by what they do for a living and how many incomes they have, by their attitude about expensive products in the showroom. (But beware. If they drive a Mercedes it might mean they *can't* afford it rather than that they can.)

• **"How soon would you like to have your new kitchen?"** That's one way to find out if they want to buy now. However, they did come into the showroom now, showing basic interest. For prospects planning a remodeling project, this is a time when your own enthusiasm and creativity can shift the buying decision from later to now.

Speaking about "when," trade magazines have researched how long families live in a house before remodeling it. There seem to be two clear trends: Either they remodel immediately after purchasing, or they wait until they have lived in it 14-17 years.

• **Do you want to sell to them?** Face it. Some customers are impossible. They can be cantankerous. They can be cheap. They can be dishonest. They can be here only to rob you of your ideas before going to the factory outlet. Be aware, but don't be hasty about quitting on them. Always give your customer the benefit of the doubt and never decide to abandon a customer until you first discuss it with your manager.

During this initial showroom visit, the most important thing for you to do is to stimulate conversation, because the more they say the more they will reveal about themselves.

But "conversation" means *they talk, not you.* They talk. You listen.

Questions they can answer with a yes or no tend to close a conversation. Ask questions that open conversation, such as **"what do you like most (or least) about your present kitchen"** or **"how long have you lived with your present kitchen?"**

Step 3. Sell yourself and your firm.

At this first meeting with the prospects in the showroom it is important to let them know that you are creative, innovative and totally helpful, and that your company is dependable, thorough and the best in the business. If your company has been in business for 30 years, this is important to the prospect because there has to be a reason. If your company has been in business for three years, talk of the growth that proves good work and be prepared to offer referrals.

That is not important to people who are out to buy a pound of nails. It can make all the difference when they are going to spend $20,000 for a new kitchen.

If you can get the prospect excited about your talent and your firm's dependability, that prospect can't wait to spend the money.

What's great about my firm?

Why should the prospect buy from me?

Selling to builders is a little different. One successful kitchen specialist shares the following showroom presentation techniques with us.

"I have worked with many contractors who build custom homes. Most of my contacts come when the builder visits our showroom.

"When dealing with contractors, I go through the same showroom visiting steps, but I 'sell harder.' The contractor probably thinks he knows as much as I do and has heard the 'pitch' on cabinets before. So I sell myself, my firm and my products very directly.

"I strive to convince him or her of three things:

*"1. **The quality** of our products is equal to the quality of the new home they are building.*

*"2. **The advantage** of a well-designed kitchen for a home in a competitive real estate market.*

*"3. **The services** that I can provide the builder and the problems I can eliminate for him or her.*

"To establish benefit #1 I praise, praise, praise; the plan, the site, anything I can think of. I then discuss the quality of our product being equal to the quality of the home he or she is building.

"It is sometimes difficult to convince the contractor of the validity of the second benefit he/she will receive: That the house will sell more quickly and for more money with my design and product. But once he sells that first house he is mine for life.

"Point #3 is of the utmost importance to the builder dealing with a homeowner. By the time the contractor gets to the kitchen stage his/her relation with the client might be strained. I tell the contractor that I will take the client 'off his hands.' I will work with them on the design, selections and colors, thus relieving him of this time-consuming, tedious job. This approach is very attractive to the average contractor building a custom home for a homeowner."

To Fee or Not to Fee--Helpful hints about retainer/design fees.

If your firm charges a design retainer, prospects should be made aware of the retainer policy in this first showroom visit, but not until their interest has been heightened as much as possible.

If you are not selling from a showroom the job is more difficult because the showroom provides the best way to demonstrate your ideas, creativity and the products you think will best serve the prospects' needs. But there are answers that can help. One method can be a portfolio of photos and drawings showing solutions to problems, and a knack for quick-draw solutions right in front of the prospect. This can be augmented with trips to dealer or distributor showrooms in the area to show products and how they work.

Step. 4. Sell the appointment.

When everything looks favorable, you want to make an appointment to get into the home to survey these prospects and measure the space.

This is important. If they will make the appointment the job is 90% sold. All you have to do then is be careful not to unsell it. These prospects now become clients.

They know very well that when they commit to an appointment they are almost committing to buying, so they tend to resist even when they really want to buy. Nobody is in a hurry to spend thousands of dollars. You have to sell them

• **on the benefits of doing it right now,**

• **on not depriving themselves needlessly of something they are going to buy anyway,**

• **on getting started before the manufacturers raise prices,**

• **on having their new kitchen before the holidays or before their next party,**

• **on doing it before your busy season,**
• **on buying before Junior uses up all their money on Nintendo games,**
• **or whatever other reasons you can think of.**

When the appointment has been set, tell the clients what to expect. Tell them you will ask a lot of questions and the design will be tailored according to their answers so the new kitchen will be personalized specifically for them, so it will be important that both spouses be present. Advise them to meet with all members of the household and to list their needs, their desires and their kitchen problems, and to rate their relative importance before you arrive.

In the real world, the primary cook alone may meet with you in the survey appointment. If this is the case, be sure all pertinent information gets passed along to any decision-makers (husband, wife, mother-in-law who is paying for the kitchen) in the family. Otherwise you might face unexpected objections in your office presentation.

Step 5. Interviewing and measuring.

There is no way to overstate the importance of the interview in the home. It is critical to identifying design challenges and problems and to creating design solutions. You cannot go back to the office and develop the right design for this particular client without having all of the questions and answers at your fingertips. It can shake their confidence in you if you have to call them to ask additional questions, and without that confidence you will have trouble getting the contract signed.

That is why NKBA developed the Kitchen Design Survey Form (See Appendix E). It is lengthy and detailed because it has to be. It includes general client information; specific kitchen questions on cooks, cooking habits, uses of the kitchen, social habits and kinds of storage needed; design and color data; specs for cabinets, appliances, tops, lighting and other equip-

ment; existing construction details; existing wall elevations and dimensioning.

And through it all you will be selling your company, its reliability and standing in the community, and your own expertise and professionalism. **You have to focus on it every minute, with every word, because you want to close this sale at the next meeting and you can unsell the whole job in seconds.**

During the survey appointment you must accomplish the following to continue the selling process successfully:

1. Reassure the prospects that they have selected the right person and the right firm to handle their project;

2. Identify the prospects' priorities for the project (their "hot button").

3. Establish budget parameters for the project.

4. Complete the product match-up and define the project specification and "who does what."

5. Continue to increase the perceived value of new kitchen in the prospects' mind.

If you can accomplish these five things and measure the room accurately, you will have a very high closing rate and a very healthy referral business to fuel future successes.

To reassure the homeowners that they have selected the right person and the right firm, show up on the right day and be on time. Missed appointments and unexplained tardiness are the most common complaints consumers have about design and building professionals. Set an odd time to meet with the client, such as 9:10 a.m.

As you drive up, notice the neighborhood and the specific house you will visit. If need be, be a little early and stop down the street where you can review your showroom tour notes and get into a frame of mind that can focus totally on the client you are about to meet with.

Use the survey to identify what your prospects *really* want to buy and *how* they want to buy it as you attempt to complete the second challenge of the survey appointment. Do they dream of a hard-working, fuctional kitchen? Or a glamorous room to impress their friends and business associates? Is the room decor more important than its equipment? Is having the room integrated with the adjacent family room much more important than the lineal footage of storage cabinets? Are they more interested in the appliances than they are in the cabinets?

In the real world of kitchen design there is no one "perfect" kitchen. All projects are the result of carefully-made trade-offs based on the family's priorities. Make sure you are totally devoted to planning this kitchen for your clients, not for yourself and not to score 100 on a text-book grading system. You will be happy with your sales numbers if you have such an orientation.

You can conduct the survey at the kitchen table or in the living room. Just make sure that you and the adult family members are away from a blaring television or kids arguing over who gets the computer next.

Remember to reassure the prospective client about the value of the new kitchen when you arrive. And don't overlook how pleasant a few minutes of small talk can be for this couple who might be just a little bit nervous about the whole process of planning, buying and installing a new kitchen.

Use this brief conversation period to adjust your questioning techniques to the style of the prospects. Are they ready to get down to business in a no-nonsense way? Then explain the purpose of the survey and get started. Are they pretty excited about the whole idea of a new kitchen and really enjoying the planning process? Then increase your excitement level to match theirs and make sure you make this

Notes

information-gathering stage of the planning process **fun.**

We have already covered how to answer the question on how much a kitchen costs during the showroom tour. Now you must establish what the budget or investment range is for the specific project. You may think you learned the answer in the showroom tour, but check again by asking "Mrs. Smith, we discussed typical kitchen investment figures in the showroom and seem to agree that a reasonable investment for your project would be between $12,000 and $15,000. Now that I have seen your home, that figure is well justified and would not be considered over-building. Are you still comfortable with that figure?"

Wait for an answer. Don't proceed with a match-up phase of product specifying until you know what the client's budget range is.

The importance of establishing the budget figure before proceding with preliminary product specs and potential design solutions can't be overstated for the novice kitchen planner. Seasoned experts often can talk around the money question, can lead the discussion and establish the figures for the prospect because of their respected position in the community. They also can do a great job guesstimating what this project is going to cost. This is easy to do if the prospect has been referrd by a former client. However, if you are not such a planning professional, don't budge until the number issue has been resolved.

This will save you endless hours of uselessly planning kitchens your client can't or won't pay for and wasting your precious business time redesigning projects that were not well matched to the client's bank account initially. Some firms feel so strongly about this issue that they have developed unit price sheets so that their design staff can accurately estimate the cost of the project while on the survey appointment.

Popular Pricing Formulas
that work for others

The easy part is the "specification match-up" phase of the information gathering process. As you proceed through the survey form you will begin to suggest products that will match up with the client's budget and needs.

To remind the prospects once again how talented you are, don't be afraid to suggest a solution or two to them while you are surveying their needs. For example, you might say: **"Shirley, you just told me about a back problem that you have. We may want to include a tall storage cabinet somewhere in the new kitchen with roll-out shelves below and door-mounted shelves above. This way you will have plenty of storage that won't force you to stoop over to get something out of the cabinet. Does that sound like a good idea to you?"**

(Stop talking. Wait for an answer.)

The proof of how successful this type of personal individualized problem-solving can be for the kitchen specialist was recently reported in a Kitchen & Bath Design News magazine article entitled "We Are Looking for Professionals." Families who had remodeled a kitchen or bath in the last two years were asked **"Why did you choose your source for kitchen/bath remodeling?"** Their reasons all were based on the designer's willingness to listen to them, to incorporate their ideas into the project solution, or to come up with solutions that specifically addressed problems the client had wanted solved.

In this visit to the home you also will have to measure and sketch the existing kitchen space and its features. (See Chap. 2, pps. 13-17). It is necessary that you do the measuring yourself no matter how many times Mr. Smith says he measured it or how many "original blueprints" he shows you. When you measure, DON'T let the clients sit in to talk with you. Tell them you have to concentrate for absolute accuracy and no, you won't touch their cookie jar.

Measuring means a lot more than taking dimensions and checking that the corners are square. The next time you see the Smiths you will give them a price for the design you recommend, so when you measure and sketch you will be looking also for potential job problems. For example, you will be checking in the basement for wiring and plumbing, for ductwork, for a possible old chimney hidden in the walls. That is the mechanical part and you must do it well.

Step 6. Design.

The job after that is to design the kitchen. You have at your fingertips a wealth of information about the clients, their needs and their desires, plus the considerable knowledge you gained just from extensive conversation with them. You know a lot more from having been in their home where you observed the quality, style, color and age of their furnishings and the way they maintain the house. You are ready. So just do it.

Step 7. The Presentation.

Even if you have just designed the perfect kitchen for Bill and Shirley Smith, you still must prepare a presentation that will make them **want** to sign a contract (call it a sales agreement; it's friendlier) at the next meeting, where you will close the sale in the showroom.

Mr. and Mrs. Smith still do not know exactly how much they will invest in their new kitchen, although you have it fairly well bracketed from discussions in the showroom and the interview. You also have acquainted them with the variables of price (see page 20). Now you must present your ideas and solutions to them persuasively.

Many pros believe the best way to do this is to prepare the perfect design as dictated from all you know about the clients, regardless of how it will price out (but within reason). Make a perfectly-drawn floorplan and elevations, plus any perspectives that might be needed to clarify. Some designers even prepare a sample board with swatches of the proposed cabinets, tops, wall and floor coverings, appliance colors, etc. Be prepared to present all of it at a single package price. And be prepared to fight for it (gently), because this plan was produced with a lot of knowledge about what they want and their ability to pay.

But also, be ready for contingencies. Maybe your analysis of their ability to pay was inaccurate. You may have to scale down the price. Be ready for it. Have your own break-down in mind so you can scale down the appliance models, change the cabinet line without changing the appearance dramatically, change the countertop material or take other measures to meet any new or unexpected challenges that the client might present.

Having a second approach to the design solution, apart from the "ultimate" look also is good if you know you are in a bidding competition.

A successful designer shares with us his approach to a client "getting bids:"

"When my clients are getting other bids, I try to be the last figure they receive and I pay extra attention to them. Often other designers will be turned off by the client getting bids. I try to convince them that no other specialist will do as good a job as I will. I present the bidding client with two plans, one very inexpensive and another that offers them the exciting solution that meets all of their requests. I have proven my ability to be competitive, yet have also demonstrated my creative ability to plan the kitchen that is just right for them. Often they will select my better plan because the simple plan was less than the other bids, yet the complex plan was 'just what they wanted.'"

Ways to Work with Prospects Seeking Bids	

Whatever the price, it will cost a lot of money and nobody likes to spend a lot of money. Here, of course, they aren't spending. They are investing. Have you made that clear to them? Have you kept up your enthusiasm about what a great kitchen and what a great deal this is for them?

How the Kitchen Investment Affects Home Value

Whether you have or not, you probably are going to get a series of questions and objections from them during your presentation. Don't worry about it. Expect it. Look forward to these questions.

During any sales presentation the prospect will have objections. Many beginners in the kitchen industry are stopped cold by such questioning. However, objections are, in reality, another way of asking for more information or for clarification. Some successful ways of handling objections are:

1. Anticipate them. Successful salespeople who know their products will learn what the most common objections are. They will learn to pre-handle them by including the information needed to overcome them in a sales presentation.

For example, if the cabinets you represent have an industrial board substrate you need to have in your initial presentation a discussion about the benefits of man-made boards vs. plywood or lumber. This is always an objection within our industry. Answer it before it even comes up.

2. Agree with them. A sales pro agrees with the client's objection, then continues on to present an alternative view for the client to consider. For example, the client might say "this dishwasher seems to be a lot more expensive than the ones I see advertised." The salesperson would agree that it is, but goes on to explain the concept of the life cycle as opposed to purchase price. Life cycle costing is used to determine the actual overall cost of a product based on its initial purchase price, its life expectancy, its cost to operate and its service ratio. In many cases the product that costs more initially will be less expensive in the long run because it uses less energy, needs less servicing and/or lasts longer. Therefore the "fancier" dishwasher my be a better investment for the family.

3. Postpone them. If their objection will be covered later in the presentation, the salesperson should tell the consumer that that question will be answered shortly. However, be forwarned, postponing a question can be dangerous. If the client brings it up again, before the salesperson has reached that point in the presentation, he or she should stop immediately and answer it. Otherwise, it may appear that you are avoiding a particularly important question that the client wants answered.

4. Question them. Sometimes an objection can be best answered after several more questions are asked. Something called the Rule of 3 says that if you ask three questions about a particular objection you probably will get to the real question. The secret to successfully giving the right answer is to make sure you are answering the *real* question. For example, the prospect might say to you that he is going elsewhere because another cabinet line is $3,000 cheaper than yours. At first glance you can be misled into thinking that price is the problem. But another question or two might reveal that he got a quality story on the other firm's intermediate line that he did not get from you on your intermediate line because you were trying to sell him on the top line--because that is what he said he wanted in the beginning.

5. Offset them. Some objections will be minor to the overall sale, yet troublesome to the client. The salesperson should offset this type of objection by offering as many reasons as possible why the individual should proceed with the purchase of the kitchen. It is important that the objection become less important to the client so the sales process can proceed. For example, the client might be most concerned because the cabinet they have selected cannot be delivered in time for the project to be completed before a major family event. The salesperson might try to offset this objection by reminding the client of the life expectancy of a kitchen and how important it is to make the right decision for the long term. To sacrifice product quality and select something immediately available because of a social event can result in the client being disappointed for the next 20 years.

6. Capitalize on them. The salesperson can turn an objection into a benefit. For example, if a builder tells the salesperson he/she realizes that the cabinets are better quality and the kitchen design much more desirable but the price is too high for the house he is building, the designer might explain why the market dictates the use of better cabinetry by saying **"It will give you a better competitive edge, and I am sure the house will sell faster than your competitor's house. This will save costly interest payments for you and well justify the increased investment in the casework for the new home."**

This same objection, "the price is too high," often comes from remodeling clients as well.

Another designer tells us how he handles it when he says: *"When people say it's too much money I try to determine if they mean too much money to spend on **any** kitchen or on **this** kitchen. There is a big difference. If it is too much for this kitchen they probably have other figures and I must backtrack to justify the cost of my project. I remind my clients to compare materials, design and firm, not just price. I suggest cost reduction possibilities for their consideration. However, if it is too much money to spend on **any** kitchen I have failed to qualify the clients in an earlier appointment when the budget should have been determined. Sometimes I have to start all over when this happens."*

Answering objections is one part of the selling process called **"closing the sale."** It is the point where the client has to be ready to commit and pay a first installment that might be as much as 50% of the total project. There is no more posing, no more pretending.

To successfully close the sale, the client must understand what we say, believe what we say and want what we offer.

First, the client must "receive" the material you have presented. In order to close the sale, the client must understand precisely and clearly what you are saying. For example, how many times have you rambled through a floor plan and then had your prospect say to you "is that the window above the sink?" Prospects must understand or they won't buy.

Second, the prospect must believe what you have told them. You must be knowledgeable about your products. You must present yourself in a believable fashion.

Third, you must create a desire in the mind of the clients. They must see themselves in this kitchen which you have designed, enjoying the functionality and the beauty for years to come.

We also must communicate the value and quality of our designs and products so the perceived value of the project we present is equal to or greater than the price we are charging. Facts are not enough. Successful kitchen pros tell us that the facts obtained account for about 15% of the buying decision while 85% of the decision is based on the benefits expected. The most successful feature/benefit approach includes three points—the FAB formula:

1. Feature. Introduce the facts about the product on the design you are discussing.

2. Advantage. Explain to the client why that feature is good in a technical sense.

3. Benefit. Relate that advantage directly to the client. Remember that prospects consistently listen to a radio station in their heads called "WIFM"--What's In it For Me. Relate the benefit to the client.

The FAB Formula Practice Session

Item	Feature	Advantage	Benefit
1.			
2.			
3.			
4.			
5.			

Successful kitchen specialists also do a good job "reading" other people. This too often is described in "hard sell" technique books as a magic formula. Sometimes it is discussed by psychologically-oriented sales trainers. Quite simply, if you can figure out what makes your client happy and modify your presentation so you emphasize that, they probably will be more likely to buy from you. This is basic human nature common sense. It's not stylized sales techniques that you have to practice over and over again in front of a mirror.

For example, if you seem to be dealing with egotists, make sure that you compliment them, consult them on the details and ask their advice. If the individual is specifically interested in the facts around the purchase, the winning closer will appeal to her rational self. People who have a hard time making up their minds often will relate well to someone who pushes just a bit. Someone who wants a "deal" will buy from the salesperson who is smart enough to make sure that the proposal included something that could be given to the consumer for nothing. A client who complains a lot will find a sympathetic ear in the kitchen designer who gets the job. A buyer who seems always to want to argue will buy from someone who translates his irascible attitude into positive statements, calmness and understanding. We all try to get along with people in our daily lives. A successful salesperson pays particular attention to this socializing skill.

Contemporary sales specialists today believe that while asking for the order continues to be a key to high sales volume, the old "tricks of the trade" just don't work any more. For example, trying to confuse the clients so that you can control the sale will be a turn-off to your prospective buyer.

The sale will be made when the clients trust you to solve their problem for a price they perceive to be equal to or less than what the solution is worth. However, several persuasive questions can help you ask for the order if the client is hesitant about "initialing the agreement" that is before them.

For example, you may try one of these three techniques.

1. The "assumptive" close. The salesperson is positive, dogmatic, absolute and confident. These same attitudes will develop in the minds of the client. Their indecision will turn to action. For example, the salesperson never uses the word "if;" the question is only "when!" Or, the salesperson quite simply begins to sign the contract when all questions seem to have been answered.

2. The "pending event" close. The salesperson bases the close on some outside event which hastens the client along in making the buying decision. For example, it might be starting dates, price increases, lead time, factory vacations, holidays or social events.

3. The "what if" close. The salesperson says "If I can do this or that will you accept our proposal today?" This is very effective when it appears that only one obstacle stands in the path of a successful close. The client will feel that he/she is fortunate if the negotiations can be concluded successfully.

One designer sums it up this way: *"As we conclude the presentation appointment, I explain the payment schedule and ask the client to sign the contract. I use statements such as 'to ensure the June 15 starting date all I need now is your signature here at the bottom.' 'As we all seem to agree on the wallcovering, I will need a signature here to get all of the materials ordered.' I turn the contract copy to face them and lay the pen down in front of them or hand it to them, and then I stop talking. I wait for their response. They are not surprised. The contract is not a strange new form. Our contract and specifications are all in one form so they have been handling the document during the in-home survey and this meeting."*

"If I see any hesitation, I then describe the

content of the contract, paraphrasing each part in a positive manner. We need to soften the "fright factor" of legal mumbo-jumbo in most contracts that we are shackled to in today's business environment.

"If my clients hesitate I try to determine the cause. I ask them 'are you unsure of the plan?' 'Are you comfortable with the wallpaper?' 'Would you like to consider an alternate starting date?' Sometimes the client will say, well, they just want to think this over. My response is 'let's think this over together. I'll leave the room for a few minutes so you can discuss any concerns you might have.'

"When I return we will start going through the specs and the plan. The more questions I ask and the more talking they do, the more chance I have of discovering what the problem is.

"Should the clients not sign the contract, I send samples home with them, the plan, a wallpaper book, a door sample, anything so I can arrange another meeting to try once more to conclude the sale.

"When the contract is signed, I always reassure them as to the wisdom of the investment and how much enjoyment they will get from their new kitchen, how honored I am that they selected our firm, and I always say 'thank you.'"

Sales success stories are not built on tricks or gimmicks; just hard work, trying to do more of what worked well and less of what didn't.

Remember, though, all of this energy and all of this talent is wasted if you are not an expert salesperson as well.

By improving your personal communications skills, sizing up your indivudual buyer and having the courage to ask for the order, you will reach the rank of selling super-stars in our kitchen industry.

Tips from the Pros

I try to use friendly words when talking about the kitchen purchase. For example, the "bad" and "good" could be contract price/agreement; cost or price/investment; buy/own; sign/approve; pitch/presentation; deal/opportunity.
  Robert L. Tuthill, Plymouth MA

Use your showroom displays as a showroom tool during the presentation. Take your customer to the room setting and "show them" how quietly the drawer slides are. "Show them" how easy it to reach into a corner susan cabinet.
  Ellen Cheever, CKD, CBD, New Holland PA

While talking about the technical details of the project, keep reminding the customer how much *fun* their new kitchen will be, how *impressed* their friends will be, how much they *deserve* a nice kitchen, how *nice* it will be for the family to gather.
  Joseph Aievoli, CKD, Sacramento CA

Selling is helping. It is not taking advantage of someone. The key is an attitude whereby you give in advance of getting. By definition, selling is helping clients make good decisions.
  Howard Shelov, Los Angeles CA

When you first work with a designer, don't call him or her a decorator. You will make an enemy who will never forget you were offensive.
  Gay Fly, CKD, CBD, Houston TX

Notes:

8 How to Install Kitchen Cabinets
Framed or Frameless, They Must Be Level, Plumb

Good installation is the final step in a kitchen project except for follow-up activities to stimulate referrals. With good, sound installation even inexpensive cabinets can last as long as the most expensive.

Good installation starts with thorough room preparation. It should be clean and ready, with plumbing, wiring and other mechanical rough-in completed, with cabinets, moldings, hardware and other materials on hand and checked to be sure the shipment is complete. If the room will have a new hardwood floor this should be in place if it will extend under the base cabinets. Protect it with cardboard or tarps during the rest of the installation..

How to install framed cabinets

1. Determine whether the floor that will be under the cabinets is level by placing a 4', 6' or 8' (122, 183 or 244 cm) level across the floor. If the floor is not level, mark the high spot. Mark a continuous level line on the wall along the floor (Fig. 8.1).

2. Mark another continuous level line at 34 1/2" (87.6 cm), which is countertop height, and another at 84" (213 cm), 90" (228.6 cm) or 96" (244 cm), according to the finished cabinet height. Mark stud locations on each of these lines (Fig. 8.2). In addition, check squareness of corners using the 3-4-5 rule: Measure 3' (91.4

cm) from a corner on one wall and make a mark; measure 4' (122 cm) along the adjacent wall and make a mark; if the distance between the two marks is precisely 5' (152.4 cm) the corner is square. If the figure is less than that the wall comes in; if it is more, the wall goes out.

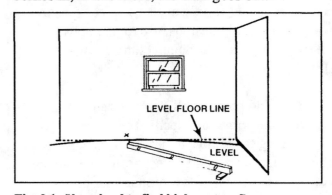

Fig. 8.1 Use a level to find high spot on floor.

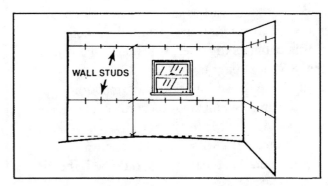

Fig. 8.2. Mark continuous level lines along floor, and at countertop height and tops of cabinets.

3. Lay out the entire cabinet arrangement on the walls and floor. Use a level to plumb (align) all wall and base cabinets so they will be perfectly vertical (Fig. 8.3).

4. Install the wall cabinets. To avoid injury this should be done with two installers. Start by installing the corner wall cabinets. Use a level and shimming materials as necessary to make it plumb, level and square (Fig. 8.4).

5. Mark stud location on the inside back of the cabinet. Drill installation holes at these locations through cabinet back at top and bottom of each cabinet using 1/8" drill bit (3 mm). Fasten cabinet to wall using 2 1/2" (6 cm) wood installation screws into solid wood studs. Each cabinet under 24" wide (61 cm) should receive four screws, two top and two bottom. Cabinets larger than 24" (61 cm) should receive two screws per stud. If only one stud or no studs fall within cabinet dimensions, use toggle bolts following toggle bolt manufacturer's instructions (Fig. 8.5).

6. Blind corner wall cabinets can be pulled out from the corner as specified by the manufacturer. Hang the blind cabinets first, as described above. Normally a filler must be attached to the adjoining cabinet to allow proper door opening and for uniform appearance (Fig. 8.6).

After corner wall cabinets are installed, proceed around wall as indicated on floorplan until all wall cabinets are installed. When joining cabinets together, first clamp the frame (Fig. 8.7, next page). Drill a 1/8" (3 mm) hole through one frame into the other, then join the frames using two installation screws, one near the top and one near the bottom.

(Note: Fig. 8.7 shows this operation with a base cabinet. Wall cabinets should be joined in the same way.)

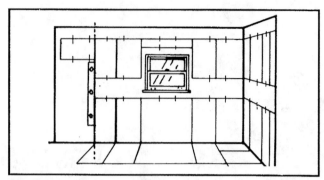

Fig. 8.3. Mark all cabinet locations, plumb all cabinet lines.

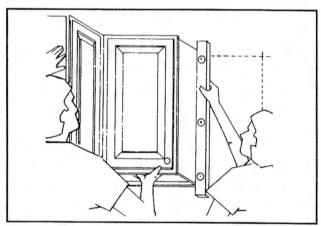

Fig. 8.4. Install corner cabinets; square them with level.

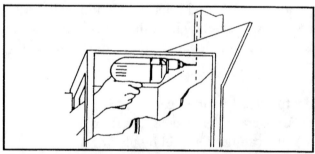

Fig. 8.5. Drill holes in backs, screw into studs.

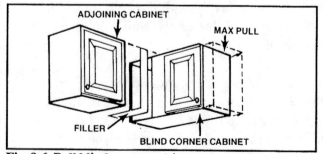

Fig. 8.6. Pull blind corner cabinet out, add filler.

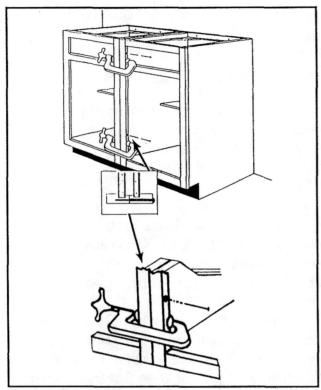

Fig. 8.7. Clamp cabinets and screw them together.

7. Start installing base cabinets the same way you did wall cabinets unless special installation is necessary. All cabinets must be installed perfectly level and plumb, with shimming at floor as needed. If using a void corner, attach the blind corner filler and toekick to both adjoining cabinets (Fig. 8.8, top).

If installing blind corner base cabinets, check floorplan and manufacturer specs to see how far the blind corner is to be pulled from the corner. Position and secure cabinets as was done with wall cabinets. Use a base filler wherever specified on plan (Fig. 8.8, bottom).

Support along back wall must be provided to hold countertop behind cabinets with no support. When installing lazy susan cabinets or voiding out a corner, a wall cleat will be needed for this countertop support. Drill and securely fasten two 36" (91 cm) lengths of cleat material to the wall studs at your predetermined base cabinet height. These cleats must be level with the front rails of a lazy susan, as in Fig. 8.9.

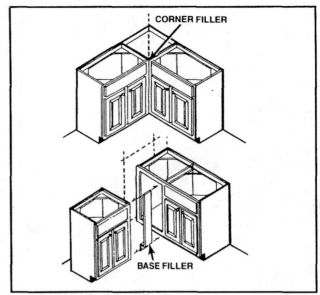

Fig. 8.8. Use corner filler for void corner, base filler for blind base corner.

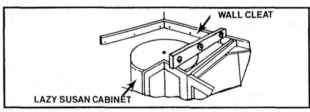

Fig. 8.9. Line wall cleat up with lazy susan front rails.

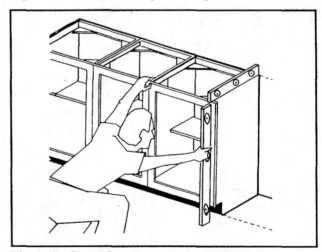

Fig. 8.10. Check for level and plumb as you proceed.

Install adjoining base cabinets by screwing through backs into studs, and attach adjoining front frames as with wall cabinets. Recheck front to back and along front frame for level and check sides for plumb (Figs. 8.10, above, and 8.11, next page). If needed, shim under front (Fig. 8.11) or at back wall (Fig. 8.12, next page).

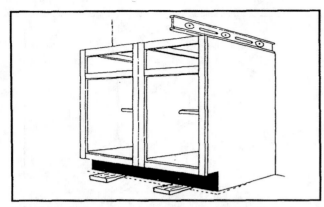

Fig. 8.11. Shim under toekick to level, if needed.

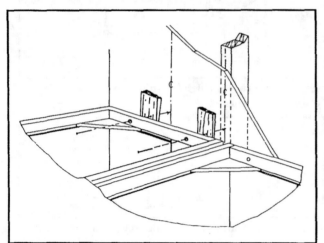

Fig. 8.12. Shims at wall can help level cabinets.

Fillers must be scribed to conform to the shape of the wall (Fig. 8.13). Overlap the filler over the face frame and against the wall, aligned vertically with the frame, and hold it so it can not move.

Adjust the scribing tool to the greatest distance that exists from the wall side of the filler to the wall's greatest concave area (left). Add the dimension that the filler overlaps the cabinet frame (center).

After you have set your scribing tool to the total sum of these two dimensions, place the tool at the top of the filler. Keep the scribing tool at a constant 90-degree angle to the face of the filler and follow the contour of the wall the entire length of the filler piece.

Cut the filler to within 1/8" (3 mm) of this scribe line. Check to see how the filler fits against the wall and finish-sand as necessary. Attach by drilling through the face frame into the filler with flathead wood screws. This procedure is the same for both base and wall cabinets.

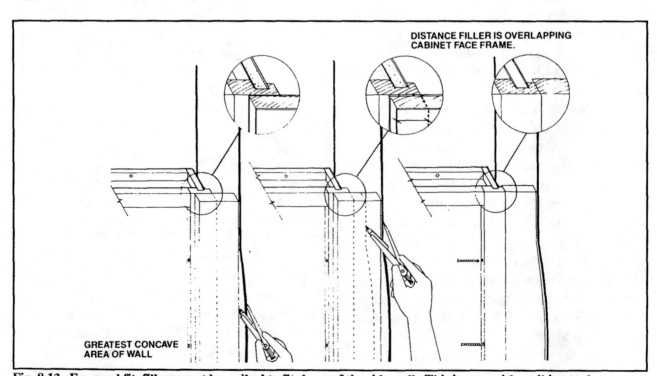

Fig. 8.13. For good fit, fillers must be scribed to fit shape of the side wall. This is easy with scribing tool.

How to install frameless cabinets

Good installation starts with thorough room preparation. It should be clean and ready, with plumbing, wiring and other mechanical rough-in completed, with cabinets, moldings, hardware and other materials on hand and checked to be sure the shipment is complete. If the room will have a new hardwood floor this should be in place if it will extend under the base cabinets. Protect it with boxes from the cabinets.

1. Determine whether the floor that will be under the cabinets is level by placing a 4', 6' or 8' (122, 183 or 244 cm) level across the floor. If the floor is not level, mark the high spot. Mark a continuous level line on the wall along the floor (Fig. 8.14).

2. Mark another continuous level line at 34 1/2" (87.6 cm), which is countertop height, and another at 84" (213 cm), 90" (228.6 cm) or 96" (244 cm), according to the finished cabinet height. Mark stud locations on each of these lines (Fig. 8.15). In addition, check squareness of corners using the 3-4-5 rule: Measure 3' (91.4 cm) from a corner on one wall and make a mark; measure 4' (122 cm) along the adjacent wall and make a mark; if the distance between the two marks is precisely 5' (152.4 cm) the corner is square. If the figure is less than that the wall comes in; if it is more, the wall goes out.

3. Lay out the entire cabinet arrangement on the walls and floor of the kitchen as shown in Fig. 8.16. Plumb (align) all wall and base cabinet lines to insure proper function and appearance. Mark the walls with the cabinet codes as indicated on the floorplan.

The difference between frameless cabinets and framed is that framed cabinets have a face frame attached to the cabinet sides, and the doors are hinged to the frame. With frameless cabinets doors and drawers cover the entire front of the

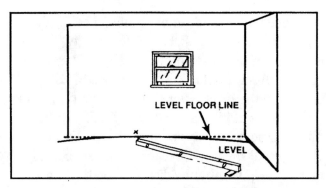

Fig. 8.14. Find high spot, draw level line along floor.

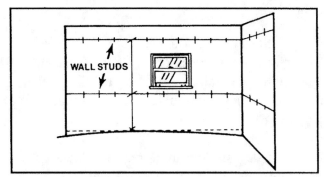

Fig. 8.15. Mark stud locations, draw continuous level lines at countertop height and tops of wall cabinets.

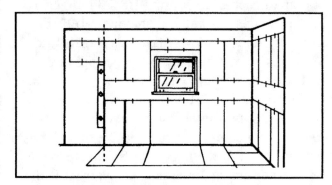

Fig. 8.16. Mark cabinet locations, plumb cabinet lines.

cabinet, and doors are attached directly to the sides of the cabinet, or "box," by means of concealed hinges.

Therefore a scribing filler is needed wherever a cabinet meets a wall to insure proper clearance space. Fillers may also be needed to insure proper functioning of the cabinet when an appliance is adjacent or at right angles to the cabinet, or when the cabinet has roll-out drawers. The door must be able to open a little more than

90 degrees to provide enough clearance for the roll-out shelves (Fig. 8.17). Additionally, frameless cabinet doors are only about 1/8" (3 mm) apart with minimal reveals. Any racking of the cabinet in the installation will mean that drawers and doors will bind and misalign. The slightest misalignment is apparent immediately because of the small reveals. So cabinets must be absolutely level and plumb when installed. Hinges are adjustable for slight adjustment after installation, but not enough to correct an out-of-square condition.

4. Start by installing corner wall cabinets. This requires two installers. Use the level and shimming materials as necessary to align corner cabinets so they are plumb, level and square (Fig. 8.18).

5. Mark stud locations on inside back of cabinets and drill installation holes at these locations through cabinet backs at top and bottom of each cabinet using 1/8" (3 mm) drill. Fasten cabinets to wall by screwing 2 1/2" (64 mm) installation screws into studs (Fig. 8.19). Many installers finish this off by snapping a matching plastic cap over the screw end. Each cabinet under 24" (61 cm) wide should receive four screws, two at the top and two at the bottom. Larger cabinets should receive two screws per wall stud. If there are insufficient studs within the cabinet dimension, supplement with toggle bolts.

6. In using blind corner cabinets, the manufacturer will specify how far the blind corner cabinet can be pulled from the corner. See your cabinet plan for approximate dimensions of pull. Hang the cabinet as described, and attach a filler to the adjoining cabinet to allow proper door opening and uniform appearance (Fig. 8.20). After corner cabinets are in, proceed along wall as indicated on the floorplan until all wall cabinets are installed.

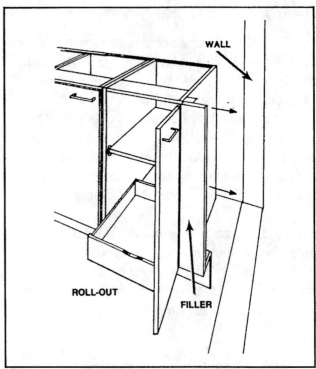

Fig. 8.17. Scribing filler must be used with frameless cabinets to permit proper functioning.

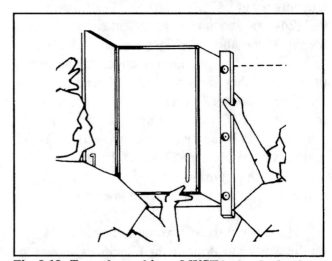

Fig. 8.18. Frameless cabinets MUST be level, plumb.

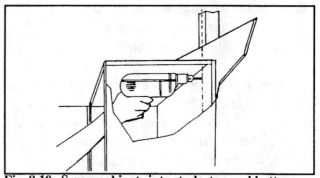

Fig. 8.19. Screw cabinets into studs, top and bottom.

7. Both wall and base cabinets should be attached to adjoining cabinets. When doing so, align and then clamp the cabinets together as in Fig. 8.21., which shows a base cabinet.

8. For screwing adjoining cabinets together, frameless cabinets usually have special screws called "connectors" with one screwing into and through the side of one cabinet and into the connector that goes through the side of the adjoining cabinet (Fig. 8.22). Both ends of these connectors will come with plastic clips that snap in to cover the ends, as this is a very visible area.

9. To install base cabinets, start by installing the leveling leg system to the cabinets. This system (Fig. 8.23) consists of three parts.

The leveling receptacle is the portion of the leveling leg that recesses into the cabinet bottom. It is pressure-positioned and cannot be changed.

The leveling leg itself is the part that allows height adjustability, allowing movement up or down usually by about an inch (2.5 cm), depending on brand, but sometimes much more.

The third part is the toekick clip which fastens to the toekick panel and can be snapped on or off the leveling leg.

Notes

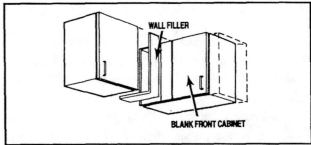

Fig. 8.20. Filler must be used in blind corner cabinet.

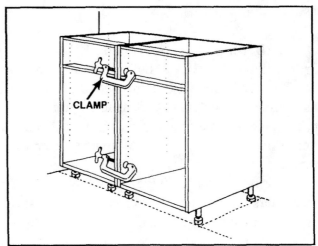

Fig. 8.21. Clamp cabinets to join them with connectors.

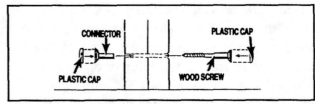

Fig. 8.22. Connectors screw together to join cabinets, are covered with plastic caps.

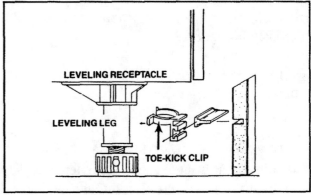

Fig. 8.23. Leveling legs are used with many frameless cabinets for added adjustability.

10. Knock the leveling legs into place in the sockets in the bottom corners of the cabinets (Fig. 8.24). Install the first corner base cabinet, making sure the top is along the level line you have marked on the wall The legs can be adjusted from the outside (Inset). Be sure it is accurate, as it will be the guide for the entire base installation.

11. If using a void corner, attach the corner filler and toekick to both adjoining cabinets (Fig. 8.25, top). If installing blind corner base cabinets, check plan and manufacturer specs to see how far to pull blind corner cabinet from wall. Position and secure cabinets as demonstrated previously. Use a base filler wherever specified in the plan, as in Fig. 8.25, bottom. Base fillers are attached to the base cabinet in the same way demonstrated for fastening cabinets.

12. All cabinets must be installed perfectly plumb and level. Also, support along the back wall must be provided behind cabinets for support of the countertop.When installing lazy susan cabinets or voiding out a corner, a wall cleat will be required to provide this countertop support. Drill and securely fasten two 36"-long (91 cm) pieces of cleat material to the wall studs at your predetermined base cabinet height. These cleats must be level with the front rail of a lazy susan (Fig. 8.26). Install adjoining cabinets as detailed previously in Fig. 8.22.

13. Recheck front to back and along top front for level.

14. Shim at the wall (Fig. 8.28) if cabinets need adjustment front to back. Complete installation by drilling and screwing through cabinet back into studs, and snap plastic caps over screw ends.

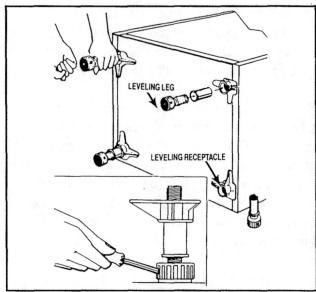

Fig. 8.24. Attach leveling legs to bottom corners of cabinets. They plug into sockets on cabinet.

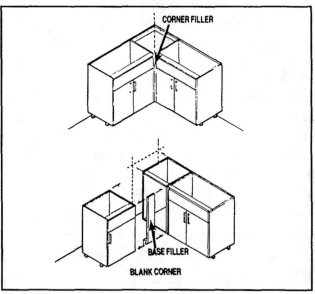

Fig. 8.25. Attach corner or base filler as indicated.

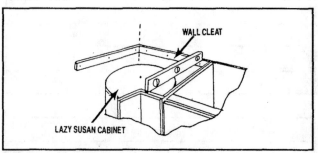

Fig. 8.26. Attach wall cleats to support countertop.

Fig. 8.28. Shim cabinet at wall for front-to-back adjustment.

15. Fillers must be scribed to the wall. To do it, overlap the cabinet filler onto the front of the cabinet, hold firmly to keep it plumb while scribing. Adjust scribing tool for greatest distance from the most concave part of the wall to the closest side of the filler. Add the dimension that the filler overlaps the cabinet frame and set the scribing tool for the total of the two. Pull the scribing tool down, following the contour of the wall, then cut the filler to within 1/8" (3 mm) of the line. Finish-sand as needed for perfect fit. Drill through cabinet side into filler and attach with flathead screws.

16. After installation, slide toekick clips into grooves of toekick panels and clip to legs. Finish edge of toekick with PVC tape.

Fig. 8.29. Scribing fillers must be used where cabinets meet wall.

Fig. 8.30. Slide clips into toekick grooves and clip to leveling legs.

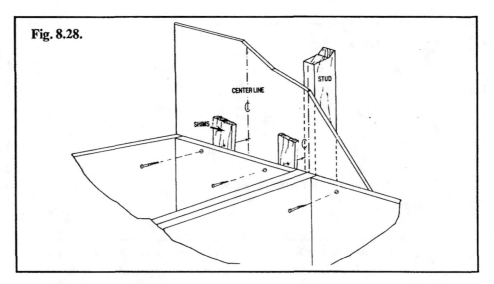

Fig. 8.28.

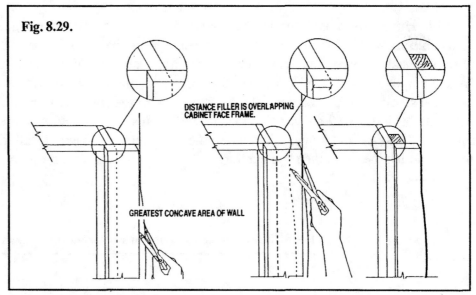

Fig. 8.29.

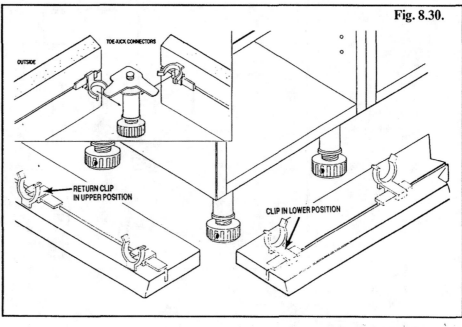

Fig. 8.30.

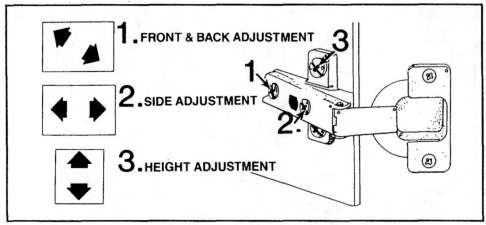

Fig. 8.31. Hinges are adjustable front to back, side to side and up and down.

17. Hinges for most frameless cabinets are adjustable six ways. This is necessary because of tight reveals between doors and drawers. In a typical hinge (Fig. 8.31), a logo plate snaps off to reveal screws. Screw 1 adjusts the door to front and back; screw 2 adjusts side to side, and screw 3 adjusts up and down. You loosen the screws, adjust the door, then tighten the screws.

18. The leveling leg system might not be suitable for some island or peninsula cabinets. Cabinets for these applications may be ordered without leveling legs and a sub-base can be built in the field. Alternatively, blocking can be installed underneath the cabinet after the cabinets have been installed and leveled. Do not use softwood for shimming under cabinets.

Fig. 8.32. Adjust all doors and drawer fronts for perfect alignment.

Appendix A:
Kitchen Appliances,
Fixtures & Fittings

Appendix A--Appliances/Fixtures

Appliances and fixtures for residential kitchens include cooking equipment; refrigeration equipment; water appliances such as the dishwasher, food waste disposer and instant hot water dispenser; the trash compactor, and sinks and faucets.

Cooking equipment.

• a free-standing, slip-in or drop-in range which has surface cooking elements, an oven/broiler or, possibly, an oven and separate broiler. Slip-in models rest on the floor but square up quite tightly with the countertop and cabinet fronts. Drop-ins have flanges on the side that support the range from the countertop, and there might be cabinet framing or a drawer underneath

• a built-in cooktop with two to six cooking elements and a separate built-in oven or ovens that might include convection cooking and/or microwave in one, two or three cavities;

• a separate microwave cooker that is free-standing but can be built in when desired;

• food-warming drawer.

Cooking methods

Most cooking is done with gas or electric fuel. Natural gas cooking appliances can be adapted to LP gas by changing the orifices.

Newer methods include microwave, magnetic induction and halogen. All use electricity, but the equipment and effects are different.

Microwave cooking differs from oven cooking in that an oven surrounds the food with heat and the heat convects inward into the food. Microwaves, on the other hand, penetrate the food and cause oscillation of the molecules. This generates heat within the food, cooking it. This absence of outside heat results in failure of

Fig. A.1. Drop-in range with downdraft ventilation system provides convenient cooking center in 30" (76 cm) space.

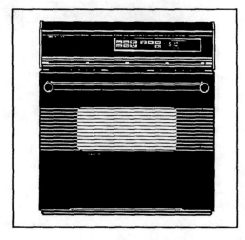

Fig. A.2. Separate built-in wall oven (left) and cooktop (below) provide design flexibility. Oven can be under cooktop or away from it in a wall oven cabinet.

the food to "brown" in the way to which we are accustomed.

Magnetic induction also is "cool" cooking. The burner sets up a magnetic field which causes heat when it encounters a ferrous pot or pan, heating the pot and thus causing the food in it to cook. The cooktop itself remains cool except for minor transmission of heat from the pot or pan.

Halogen burners work somewhat like incandescent light bulbs, heating from electricity passing thorough a tungsten filament in a quartz tube. Halogen gas in the tube combines with evaporated tungsten, but heat from the filament causes the tungsten to redeposit on the filament so it doesn't darken as a light bulb does and it lasts longer.

This is mostly infrared light in wavelengths that pass easily through a glass ceramic cooktop. But about 10% of it is visible light, so it causes the burner to light up immediately with a bright red glow. So the advantage is in that you see the heat, and it heats up much faster than other glasstops. In addition, with a halogen burner you do not need perfect contact between the burner surface and the bottom of the cooking vessel.

Glasstops, incidentally, are much faster and more durable than those of 10 years ago. The black models also are easier to care for because they conceal scratches and do not show fingerprints.

Electric coil elements remain popular, but the newer solid disk elements ("hobs") are becoming more popular because they are fused to the cooktop and thus stay cleaner. They are slower to heat up than conventional coils, but they retain heat better. Flat bottoms are required for the pots and pans with hobs.

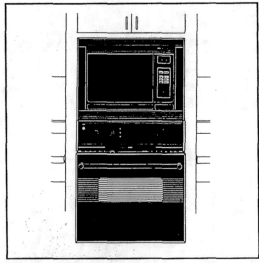

Fig. A.3. Microwave units are always hinged left. Therefore, counter space is needed to the right if the appliance is built into an oven cabinet.

Fig. A.4. The shiny rim around a solid disk electric cooking element will discolor in time. Customer should be advised.

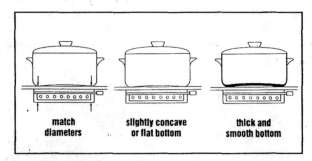

match diameters
slightly concave or flat bottom
thick and smooth bottom

Fig. A.5. Cookware dramatically affects how efficiently a cooktop works. Cookware should be metal, should be heavy, should match the burner in diameter, and should sit flush when hot.

Refrigeration.

• built in or free standing;

• combination 2-door refrigerator/freezer which might be top-mount, which has the freezer on top; bottom-mount, which has the freezer on the bottom; or side-by-side, which has the refrigerator on one side, the freezer on the other;

• two separate appliances. Freezer extras include an ice-maker, which must be plumbed into the freezer compartment, and through-the-door ice and beverage dispensers. Refrigerators, freezers and ice makers also are manufactured for separate under-counter installation.

Dishwashers.

• built in under the counter;

• free standing, or "portable;"

• three basic cycles of wash, rinse and dry, or multiple cycles in more deluxe models;

• built-in heating element in more deluxe models to boost heat of incoming water for better cleaning action when water heater is set to lower temperature;

Food waste disposers.

• batch-fed models are loaded with food waste, then a top cap is turned to lock into place and it starts the disposer;

• continuous-feed models do not have a locking cap and are activated by a switch that might be in the backsplash above the counter.

Batch-fed models are considered safer because the cook can't put a hand down into them when they are working, nor can silverware be dropped in inadvertently.

Disposers are required by law in some communities, banned in others, so check local codes.

Fig. A.6. A dishwasher should have an air gap to prevent any backup. When air gap is connected as shown, any backup would drain into the disposer. Disposer should be emptied before dishwasher is used.

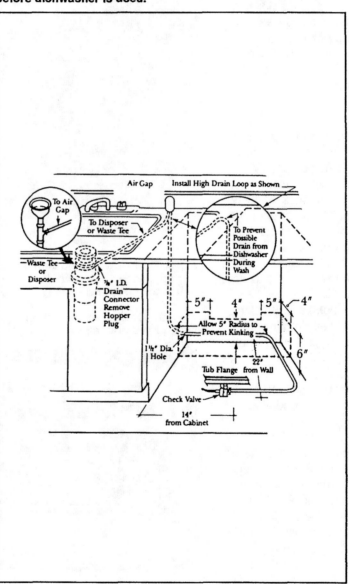

Ventilation.

• fan usually mounted in collection hood over cooktop, ducted to outside;

• downdraft, fan built into range or mounted under counter behind or beside cooktop, draws cooking pollutants down from cooking surface, ducted outside;

• remote fan or blower ducted to hood or to downdraft cooktop, exhausts heat and pollutants to outside, can also serve baths;

• fan in collection hood not ducted to outside, not satisfactory because it recirculates heat and some cooking pollutants;

• fan mounted in wall, exhausts to outside, not efficient venting action.

Sinks.

• might be made of porcelain enamel on steel, the more durable porcelain enameled cast iron, stainless steel, vitreous china or man-made composites such as Corian or quartz compounds;

• some composites can be integral with countertop (all one piece), which adds to design flexibility and avoids the need to install a sink;

• can be installed with clamping rim or be "self-rimming;"

• can be single bowl, double bowl or triple bowl, some with integral drainboard;

• cultured marble with gelcoat surface not recommended for kitchen use.

Stainless steel sinks have been most popular in remodeling. These might be 18- or 20-gauge steel. The 18-gauge is heavier and more satisfactory. They sometimes are designated with two other numbers which refer to the mixture of alloys. For example, 18-8 refers to 18% chrome and 8% nickel content. Chrome enhances the sink's ability to stand up over the years, and nickel helps it withstand corrosion.

Fig. A.7. Microwave and ventilating hood may be combined into one appliance. However, do this only when the cook is tall enough to use the microwave safely and conveniently.

Fig. A.8. Downdraft ventilation eliminates the need for an overhead ventilating hood and fan

A.9. These are typical single sink configurations. The small square

and round sinks are being requested but are too small for

normal kitchen use. At right is a full-sized single bowl kitchen sink.

Fig. A.10. In these typical double sink configurations, the smaller bowl is usually used for food waste

disposer placement and is commonly used for such tasks as salad preparation.. In unit at right

the drainboard can extend over the dishwasher

Fig. A.11. Triple bowl sinks now may be in exotic shapes, but again they feature a small bowl used for

the food waste disposer, plus a medium-sized bowl and a large bowl. They might have three or

four holes for faucet hot and cold water lines and for accessories.

Fig. A.12. The sink, such as this in Dupont Corian, can be an integral part of the countertop. Designer and client can tailor it to family needs.

Fig. A.12. Kitchen faucets have been part of the technological revolution and many now are guaranteed drip-proof for life. While brass still is the main material inside, many have ceramic valve seats that are much more serviceable than in past years. Chrome finish still predominates, but modern faucets come from around the world and might be finished in brass, glass, clear or colored plastic, vitreous china, epoxy, gold or silver.

Fig. A.14. The white-on-white look can be achieved handily with modern appliances and cabinet finishes.

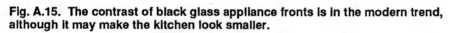

Fig. A.15. The contrast of black glass appliance fronts is in the modern trend, although it may make the kitchen look smaller.

Notes:

Appendix B:
Kitchen Cabinets

Appendix B--Kitchen Cabinets

Kitchen cabinets are made in sophisticated plants that specialize in kitchen cabinets and bathroom vanity cabinets.

Cabinet sizes

Base cabinets, which are set on the floor, are 24" (61 cm) deep (front to back) and 34 1/2" (88 cm) high including a sub-base, or "toekick," that is 4" (10 cm) high. Wall cabinets, which are affixed to the wall with screws, are 12" (30 cm) deep. Standard height for wall cabinets for general storage is 30" (76 cm), but other common heights are 24" (61 cm), 33" (84 cm) and 42" (107 cm). Special heights include 18" (46 cm) to fit over the range and 12"-15" (30-38 cm) to go over the refrigerator. Tall cabinets to be used as pantries or utility cabinets are 84" (213 cm) or 96" (244 cm) high.

Cabinets can be classified by:

1. Type of manufacturer, as stock or custom;
2. Type of construction, as framed or frameless;
3. Construction material, as wood, decorative laminate or steel.

Cabinet types

Stock cabinet manufacturers offer a full range of widths made in 3" (8 cm) modules from 9" (23 cm) to 48" (122 cm). These are made in quantity, in advance, to go into distributor warehouses for quick delivery. Because the cabinets are produced in quantity, the lines can not be stopped for special units.

Custom cabinet manufacturers make cabinets kitchen-by-kitchen after a kitchen has been designed and sold. Generally they are made in the same 3" (8 cm) modules as stock cabinets, but special sizes are made also for a perfect fit in the destination kitchen. Custom producers offer a wide range of wood species, finishes and special units.

Semi-custom cabinets are produced by both stock and custom manufacturers. These usually are produced on a stock basis, but with many more standard interior fittings and accessories than regular stock units, although not as many as are available on custom units.

Cabinet construction

Framed cabinets (Fig. B.1) are made with face frames to which doors are attached. The face frame has horizontal rails and vertical stiles. Some have complete frames to which the top, bottom, sides and back can be attached. In recent years, however, interior frames have been replaced by corner blocks, or gussets, for rigidity.

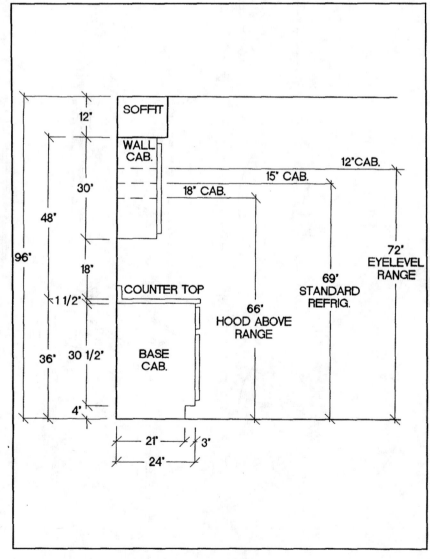

Fig. B.1. Typical Imperial (Inch) cabinet sizes.

Fig. B.2. Framed cabinets are fitted together with various forms of wood joinery and without special hardware fittings. Door hinges attach to face frame and generally do not have multiple adjustments.

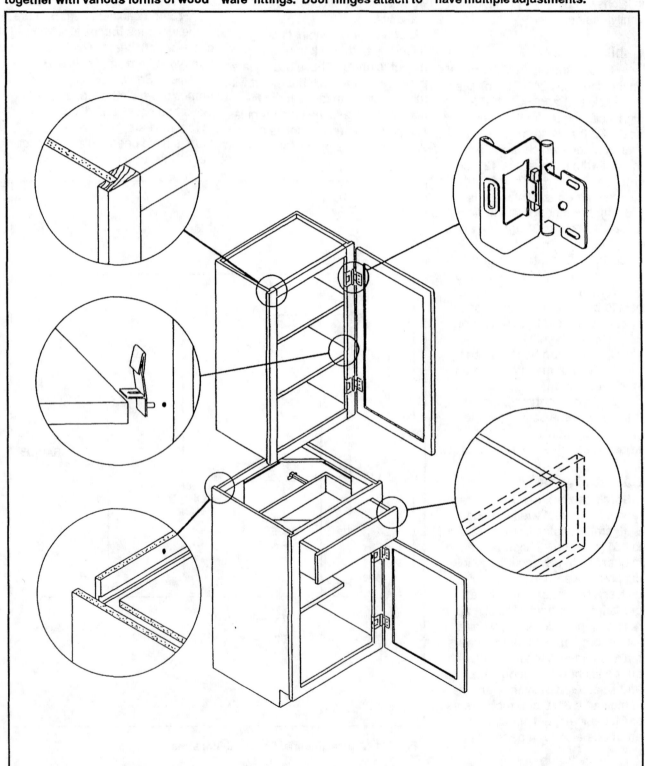

Frameless cabinets (Fig. B.3) have no frames at all. They are simply boxes, made of heavier material for rigidity. Door hinges are mortised into the sides and the doors usually fit over the entire front of the case flush with each other and with drawer fronts. This dictates a very tight reveal, usually 1/8" (3 mm) or less. The slightest misalignment is obvious with such tight tolerances, which is why the doors usually have (and need) 6-way adjustable hinges.

Frameless construction was brought to the U.S. from Europe where it was developed for good reasons. The continent was a bombed-out shambles after World War II. The housing reconstruction job was enormous. At this time particleboard had been developed as a viable substrate, and the German cabinet and furniture industry developed a cabinet construction system based entirely on production and hardware. They developed the 32 mm system in which proper-sized holes would all be predrilled by machines set for all contingencies in particleboard components presurfaced with a melamine laminate. They developed the hardware to fit it, and thus came out with cabinets that could be produced robotically.

Frameless cabinets are not necessarily better than framed. But they can be produced more easily after a heavy investment in tooling. U.S. manufacturers now make frameless cabinets with and without the 32 mm system.

The sleek, contemporary styling resulting from flush doors and drawer fronts produced what we call "the European look."

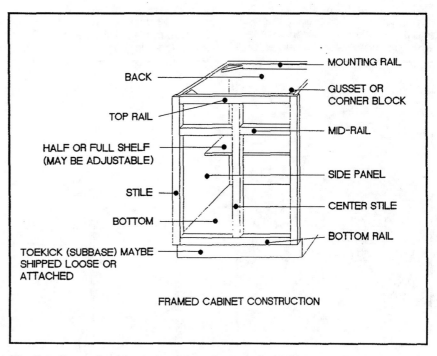

Fig. B.3. Framed cabinets have face frame on which doors are hinged.

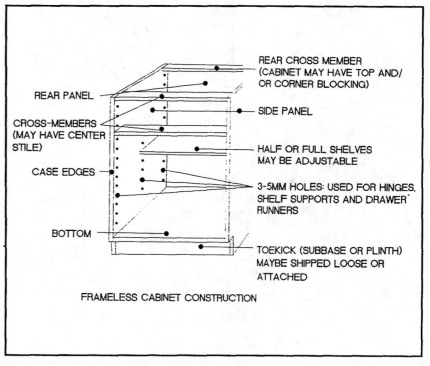

Fig. B.4. Frameless often have predrilled holes for 32mm construction.

Fig. B.4. Typical frameless cabinet construction is oriented to hardware and production. Pins and dowels, which might be wood or metal, are **made to fit specific holes, all of which are drilled when the cabinet is manufactured. Hinges go on the inside. Leveling legs are a feature,** **with a snap-on facia, or plinth, although many U.S. manufacturers prefer the conventional toekick as a sub-base.**

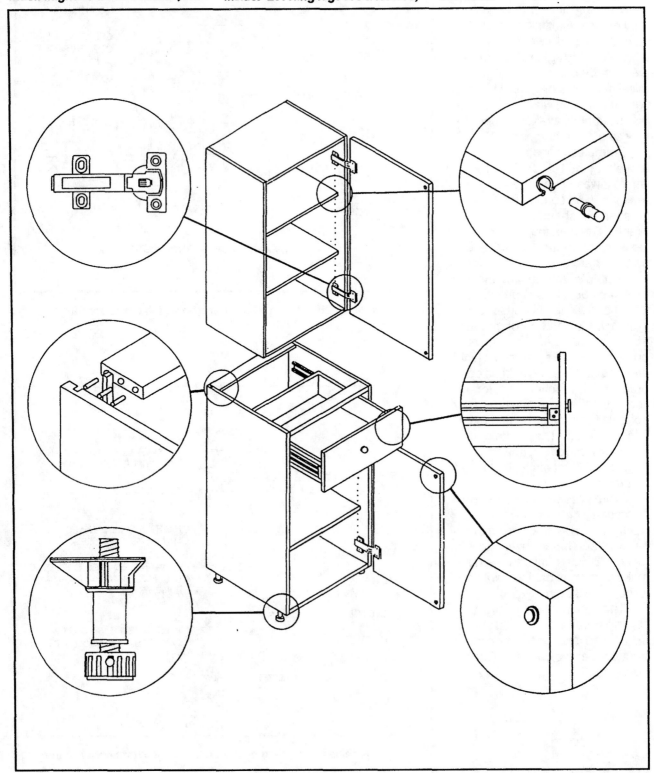

Construction material will be wood in more than 70% of U.S. kitchens. And 75% of that will be oak. Other popular woods are cherry and maple.

Most of the remainder will be surfaced with a decorative laminate, usually on industrial grade particleboard. High pressure laminate is the premium material, but many newer manufacturers (and foreign sources) use a melamine laminated board. This is a low pressure melamine and is not as resistant to impact as high pressure laminate.

It is much easier and less expensive to buy this stock melamine board and cut it up into cabinet components than it is to lay up HP laminate on a substrate and then cut it into components. The result usually is a lower priced product. Both of these, however, are lifetime materials.

Some cabinets have a vinyl surface printed with a woodgrain on the interiors and shelves. Some have a woodgrain printed direct on a wood surface. A newer development is a thermofoil coating laid over a substrate.

Manufacturers, of course, can use similar materials in different ways and get varying results. This means you should study the specifications and the use and care requirements for the lines you represent.

While most consumers prefer wood, it is not as stable dimensionally as industrial grade particleboard or medium density fiberboard, both widely used as cabinet corestock. Wood can warp in humid conditions, and cabinet door construction can contribute to that problem. A raised panel door, for example, will not be stable when the panel is glued in place. If the panel is left floating the door will withstand humidity changes much better. A solid lumber door can

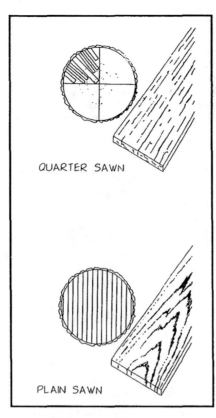

Fig. B.5. Quarter sawn wood, top, has better grain pattern and is usually used on doors. Plain sawn might be used for casework.

have a lot of movement, but a veneered plywood door will overcome the wood's natural shrinking and swelling tendencies.

Finishing is a factor in cabinet quality and price. Some of the fine custom producers have 12 or more steps in the finishing process, with hand-wiping between steps.

The high-gloss finishes we see might be polyester or enamel. To achieve a high-gloss polyester finish is very time-consuming and expensive. High-gloss enamel is easier but is less durable. Glossy HP laminate is often considered quite acceptable at a much more acceptable price. In all cases, however, glossy finishes require more care than matte finishes.

What is Particleboard?

In broad terms, particleboards fall into three general categories: Western board, midwest aspen board and southern pine board. For all-around quality, western board is generally considered the best. It is easy to cut and shape, and does not tend to fuzz up when machined for radius edges.

The name particleboard is based on its composition of particles of wood off-fall bonded together with resin under pressure. The size of the particles in these man-made boards generally is used to identify the stability and screw-holding capacity of different levels of core material.

For example, underlayment is a form of particleboard that has a low density and low resin content. Therefore it is not recommended as a laminate substrate because it has lower dimensional stability, structural strength, moisture resistance and screw-holding ability.

Better particleboards are rated as "45-lb. commercial grade." It weighs 45 lbs. per cubic foot. This is highly recommended for normal laminating. It has smaller particles of wood that increase the surface for the resin to bond to. It therefore has good dimensional stability and provides a smooth surface for laminate bonding.

The finest substrate material is medium density fiberboard (MDF). This is made of even finer fibers than normal particleboard. Its density adds superior screw-holding power, a very tight, clean edge, and an extremely smooth surface. The MDF edge can be shaped to a profile and painted, resulting in an acceptable finished edge for many surfaces.

Today, with the advent of new technology and improved resin and glue methods, the best interior surface for many cabinet applications is some type of a man-made board that has been covered either with a laminated solid-colored surface or a laminated woodgrain surface.

Fig. B.6. Cabinet joinery methods can include all of these. In nearly all cases the joints are held together with staples or brads to allow glue time to cure. It is glue that locks the joints. Rabbet and dado cuts are used in case construction. Dovetail joints and dowels provide more drawer strength.

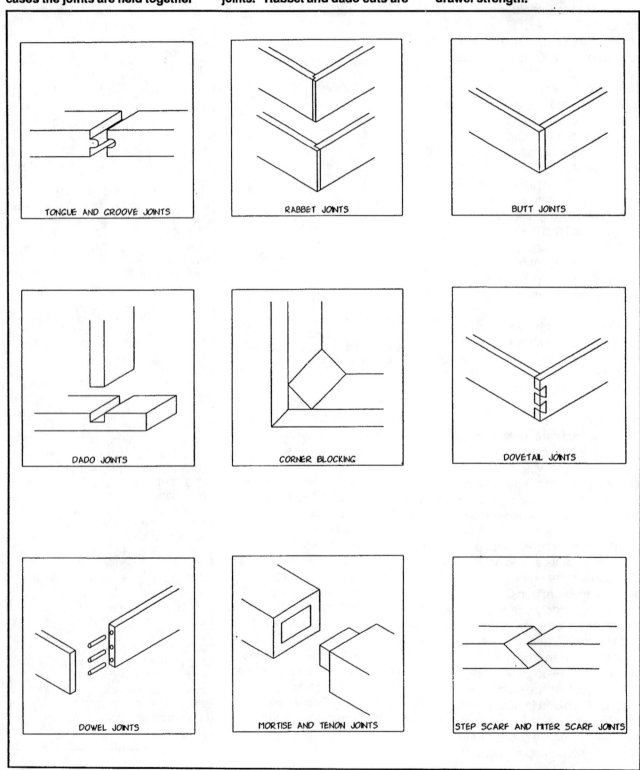

TONGUE AND GROOVE JOINTS

RABBET JOINTS

BUTT JOINTS

DADO JOINTS

CORNER BLOCKING

DOVETAIL JOINTS

DOWEL JOINTS

MORTISE AND TENON JOINTS

STEP SCARF AND MITER SCARF JOINTS

Doors set the style

The doors and drawer fronts are the most visible parts of cabinets, so they determine the style of the cabinets and, indeed, usually of the entire kitchen. While a single maker might have dozens of door styles, the style types are limited.

Flat "slab" doors are simple, flat pieces of lumber or plywood. Some are made up of several vertical pieces covered with a veneer. Sometimes they are routed with a square or provincial groove.

"Raised panel" doors are made with two horizontal rails and two vertical stiles, with a thinner panel floating between. The center panel is machined down at the four edges so the panel is "raised." When this look is done by routing and the door is all one piece, it is a "false raised panel" door. If the panel is flat, it is a "recessed panel" door. These are used in "traditional" styling.

A "cathedral" door usually has a raised or recessed panel, but a cathedral-type arch is formed into the upper rail.

A "board-and-batten" style has vertical boards with chamfered edges, held together by a horizontal batten on the back. Sometimes this look is achieved by routing vertical grooves in the front of a slab door. This is used in "country" or "American" styling. When the boards or grooves are horizontal it is a "lattice" door.

Framed cabinets usually have lipped doors, with the lip fitting over the edge of the face frame. Some manufacturers produce a door that fits into the face frame. This inset dock style is popular in "English country" rooms. Frameless cabinets have flush or flush overlay doors with square edges. This is "contemporary" styling.

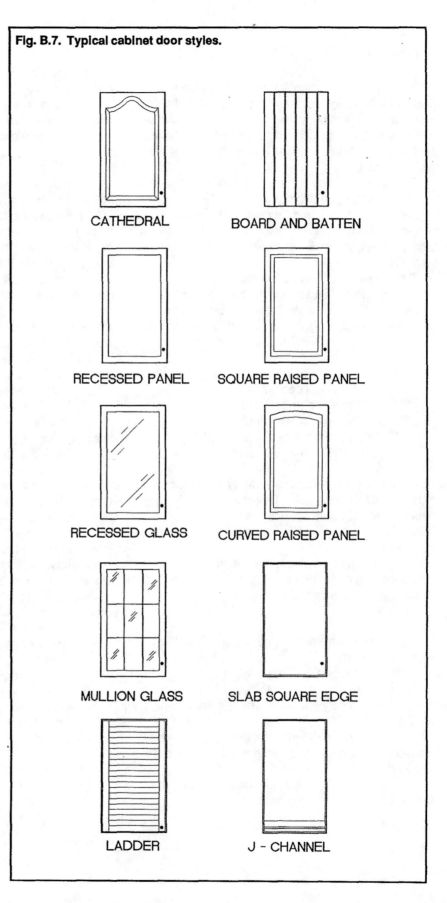

Fig. B.7. Typical cabinet door styles.

CATHEDRAL

BOARD AND BATTEN

RECESSED PANEL

SQUARE RAISED PANEL

RECESSED GLASS

CURVED RAISED PANEL

MULLION GLASS

SLAB SQUARE EDGE

LADDER

J - CHANNEL

Generic Nomenclature

The National Kitchen & Bath Association has modified a generic cabinet coding system that was established originally by the Kitchen Cabinet Manufacturers Assn. This nomenclature provides standardized definitions for sizes and types of cabinets in this workbook.

The system is based on an 11-character code which explains each cabinet category, type of cabinet, width of cabinet, and height (if variable). This system also identifies non-standard cabinet configuration details. The code includes both alpha and numeric symbols.

The code is divided as follows:

1. The first character defines the general type of cabinet. There are six general cabinet categories, one accessory category and one molding/trim category. The six general cabinet categories are:

"W" defines all wall cabinets.
"T" defines all tall cabinets.
"B" defines all base cabinets.
"V" defines all vanity cabinets.
"D" defines all desk cabinets.
"F" defines all furniture cabinets.

(For some manufacturers vanity and desk cabinets are interchangeable. Therefore, the "V" designation is used in both applications. A "D" designation is applied only if sizing between the two casework systems differs.)

Molding and trim pieces are identified by a separate code that describes each piece. There is no major category that sets them apart from the other groupings.

2. The second set of characters identifies the type of cabinet.

For example, a BB is a base blind corner cabinet.

A BC is a base corner cabinet. It may have fixed, adjustable or rotary shelving, which is designated by a letter.

A BD is a base cabinet that features a stack of drawers. A standard B is assumed to have a drawer above the door.

A WO is a wall cabinet that has no doors, therefore it is called an open cabinet.

3. The next two numeric symbols identify the width of the cabinet.

This dimension is always listed because case widths are variable. For most manufacturers these are on 3" (7 cm) modules, from 9" (23 cm) to 48" (122 cm).

4. The next two numeric symbols identify the height of the cabinet.

These two digits are used only if there are varying heights to choose from.

For example, in wall cabinets you can choose from heights of 12" (30 cm), 15" (38 cm), 18" (46 cm), 24" (61 cm) and 30" 76 cm). Some manufacturers also offer heights of 36" (91 cm) and 42" (107 cm).

This is not the case in base cabinets where one standard height is used throughout the kitchen, so no height dimension is part of that code.

Heights assumed for the general categories, are as follows (all plus 1 1/2", or 4 cm, for countertop):

1. Kitchen base cabinets, 34 1'2" (87 cm).
2. Furniture and vanities, 30"-31" (76-79 cm).
3. Tall cabinets, 84" (213 cm) (except as specified).
4. Desk cabinets, 28 1/2"-30" (72-76 cm).

5. The last two characters in the nomenclature system identify any non-standard configurations within that specific cabinet unit.

For example, a D would identify a diagonal corner unit; a GD would identify glass doors; D3 would mean three drawers; TO would mean tilt-out drawer head, R would stand for radius, and so forth.

Accessories to be added to the cabinet are designated following the cabinet code.

Examples are BB, for bread box; CB, for cutting board; HU, for hamper unit; MU, for mixer unit, etc.

Miscellaneous trim and finish pieces with no specific category heading have individual codes.

Thus, VP is a valance panel. VP-C is one in contemporary styling, VP-T is traditional.

A corbel bracket, is CB. OCM is outside corner molding. CM is crown molding.

Cabinet Description		Nomenclature	Tips from the Pros

Cabinet Description

36" High (91 cm)
Blind Corner
Single Door
*2 shelves
*blind panel with 1"
filler (2.5 cm) is typical

36" High 45°
Diagonal Corner
Single Door
* 2 shelves

36" High (91 cm)
90° Corner Pie-cut
* 2 shelves
* 2-piece bifold door is
typical. May have
concave curved door

Wall Cabinet for
Microwave Oven
* trim kit may be avlbl
from cabinet or appli-
ance manufacturer.
* for use with built-in
front-vented micro-
wave units

Wall Cabinet for
microwave oven
* standard cabinet
depth
* fits all free-standing
microwaves

* interior back, sides and top veneered and finished to match shelf and frame is typical.

42" High (107 cm)
Single Door
* 3 shelves

42" High (107 cm)
Double Door
* 3 shelves

Nomenclature

WBC27/3036
WBD36/3936

WC2436D

WC2436PC

WM303618D

WM3036

W1242
W1542
W1842
W2142
W2442

W2742
W3042
W3342
W3642

Tips from the Pros

• When a wall cabinet is planned that is continuous from countertop to soffit or ceiling, (a 48"-
60"-high unit) (122-152 cm), consider special
clearance. Reduce overall cabinet height
slightly. A countertop platform should be
planned beneath the wall cabinet, finished
either to match the cabinet with molding, or the
counter material, so doors willl not rest on the
countertop. Scribing room is built in. A
platform 3/4"-1 1/2" (2-4 cm) is recommended.

• When installing wall cabinets to the ceiling,
make sure there are not recessed lights
designed with the lamp below the edge of the
diffuser (which is flush with the ceiling)., nor
any surface-mounted light closer than the
dimension of the cabinet door when open.
Ideally, the cabinet should be down from the
ceiling an inch or so and trimmed out with
molding to let doors open and close.

Cabinet Description		Nomenclature	Tips from the Pros

42" High (107 cm)
Blind Corner
Single Door
* 3 shelves
* blind panel w/1" filler
(2.5 cm) is typical

WB27/3042
WB36/3942

42" High (107 cm) 45°
Diagonal Corner
Single Door
* 3 shelves

WC2442D

42" High (107 cm) 90°
Corner
* 3 shelves
* 2-piece bifold door is
typical
* may have concave
curved doors

WC2442PC

Wall Cabinet
for Microwave
* trim kit may be avlbl
from cabinet or
appliance manufac-
turer.
* for use with built-in
front-vented micro-
wave units

WM304218D

Wall Cabinet
for Microwave
* standard cabinet
depth
* fits all free-standing
units

WM3042

* interior back, sides and top veneered and
finished to match shelf and frame is typical.

BASE CABINETS

Tray divider cabinet
* full height door
* 2 vertical tray divid-
ers is typical

B9T

• Some cabinet styles (particularly with
heavy molding) can't be built in 9" (23 cm)
width. Check lines you represent.

Single Door
* 1 door
* may have full or
half-depth shelf

B12FD
B15FD
B18FD
B21FD

Single Door
* 1 door
* 1 drawer
* may have full- or
half-depth shelf

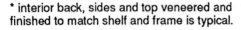

B12
B15
B18
B21
B24

Double Door
* 2 doors
* 2 drawers
* may have full- or
half-depth shelf

B27 to B48
in 3" (7.6 cm) incre-
ments

• In many lines, shallow drawers are
available for B30, B33 and B36 so storage
can be provided directly below a conventional cooktop.

Cabinet Description		Nomenclature	Tips from the Pros

Cabinet Description

Three Drawer
* 2 extra deep lower drawers
* 1 standard drawer

Base Sink
* double door
* false drawer heads

Base Sink
90° corner
* requires 36"-40" (91-102 cm) wall space both directions.
* cabinet size smaller than wall space.
* need end panel for any exposed end
* bottom must be ordered

Base Sink
Diagonal
* single door
* can design to fit flush with adjacent cabinets or be recessed between two cabinets

Base Sink Front
Straight
* double door
* toekick included and shipped is typical

Nomenclature

BD12D3
BD15D3
BD18D3
BD21D3
BD24D3
BD30D3
BD36D3

BS24 to BS48 in 3" (8 cm) increments

BSC36
BSC39
BSC42

*BSCF36 (for front only)

BSC36D
BSC39D
BSC42D

*BSCF36D (for front only)

BSF24
BSF30
BSF33
BSF36

Tips from the Pros

* Designers disagree whether it is better to line up base with wall cabinets or to keep upper cabinet doors even in size. Since base runs are interrupted by drawer banks and appliances, aligning upper doors so all sizes are consistent provides a more uniform design statement.

TALL CABINETS

Oven Cabinet
Universal
* 4 drawer. Remove as needed to accommodate oven.
* in 84", 90", 96" (213, 229. 244 cm) heights.

TOV2784/90/96
TOV3084/90/96
TOV3384/90/96

Utility Cabinet
* Avlbl in 12" or 24" (30 or 61 cm) depths.
* for use with shelf kits w/single or double doors depending on width

TU24/84/90/96
TU27/84/90/96
TU30/84/90/96
TU36/84/90/96

Pantry Cabinet
* in 24" (61 cm) depth only

TP1884/90/96
TP2484/90/96
TP3084/90/96
TP3684/90/96

Linen Cabinet
* Available in 12", 18", 21" depths
* For use with shelf kits w/single or double doors depending on width

TL12/84/90/96
TL18/84/90/96
TL24/84/90/96
TL36/84/90/96

* "Universal" oven cabinets take either single or double ovens by removing drawers. But in some lines you specify single or double. Generally you make the cutout at the jobsite. Standard tall cabinets are generally the same depth as base cabinets. An oven cabinet at the end of a run will be flush, but the countertop will extend out beyond the face of the tall cabinet. The counter edge should be beveled or finished on this slight return, or the tall unit can be pulled out to align with the counter.

* When specifying any tall cabinet, prod clients on how they will use it. You may want to order added shelving when cabinet is ordered.

* Some tall pantry cabinets have swing-out units that require the door to open more than 90°. For these, you might need a filler.
Tall cabinets are usable for more than canned goods and cleaning supplies. Best storage space is 22"-56" (56-142 cm) above floor, so pantry cabinet space can be used for china, silver or serving pieces, small hand appliances and many other things.

Cabinet Description	Nomenclature	Tips from the Pros

**Peninsula
Single Door**
* drawer operates
from one side
* door on each side
hinged at same end is
typical

BP18
BP24

**Peninsula
Double Door**
* 2 doors both sides
* 2 drawers operate
from one side

BP30
BP36
BP42
BP48

Single Drawer
* 2 doors
* 1 wide drawer with
reinforced bottom
* 2 wide roll-out trays
w/ reinforced bottoms
* no center stile for
more efficiency

B36/2ROS

Blind Corner
* blind panel w/3" filler
(8 cm) is typical
* may be reversible for
L or R blind
* cabinet size is
smaller than wall space required. End panel
needed for any exposed end.

BB36/39
BB39/42
BB42/45
BB45/48
BB48/51

• Blind bases of 36", 39" or 42" (91, 99 or
107 cm) have very small doors. For
example, a 36" BB will have only a 9" (23
cm) door opening. It is better to specify
45" or 48" (114 or 122 cm) because door
size will be 18" or 21" (46 or 53 cm) wide.

Lazy Susan
* requires 36" (91 cm)
wall space in both di-
rections.
* cabinet size smaller
than wall space. End panel needed for exposed
end.
* 2 28" (71 cm) diameter pie-cut revolving plastic shelves typical.

BC36LS

• When specifying a lazy susan, corner sink
cabinet or pie-cut corner base with a bifold
door that is hinged right or left, always bifold
the door away from adjacent appliances. If
cabinet hinging is on the same side as appliance, and the appliance extends beyond the
face of the cabinet, the door will not open
completely, limiting access.

Base Corner
* bifold hinged door
* 1 shelf is typical
* requires 36" (91 cm)
wall space both
directions
* cabinet size smaller than wall space. End
panel needed for exposed end.
* may have concave curved door

BC36

• None of these is 24" deep (61 cm). If they
were you could not fit one through a standard
interior door. They usually are 18"-20" (46-51
cm) deep. Make sure installer knows that he
pulls it to 24" (61 cm) deep and doesn't push it
back to the wall.

• When specifying any corner unit with a half-
moon swing-out shelf system, make sure you
know how much of the interior shelf space is
used by the swing-out apparatus. Sometimes
much space is wasted.

Four Drawer
* 1 deep bottom
drawer
* 3 standard drawers

BD12D4
BD15D4
BD18D4
BD21D4
BD24D4

• If placing a drawer unit against a wall with a
window or door opening, use a 1"-1 1/2" (2.5-4
cm) filler between cabinet and wall so drawer
will miss casing. Do the same with a drawer
unit in a corner so drawers at right angles will
miss each other.

Cabinet Description		Nomenclature	Tips from the Pros

VANITY CABINETS

Single Door
* full height door
* 1 shelf

V12FD
V15FD
V18FD
V21FD

• When specifying, find out if the standard shelf is included or if a second one is available. A second shelf is often usable in this cabinet.

Single Door
* 1 door
* 1 drawer
* 1 shelf

V12
V15
V18
V21

Double Door
* full height doors
* 1 shelf

V24FD
V27FD
V33FD
V36FD

Double Door
* 2 doors
* 1 drawer
* 1 shelf

V24
V27
V33
V36
V38

Vanity Bowl Unit
* 3 full height doors

VS42
VS48

Vanity Bowl
Drawer Unit
* 1 full height door
* 2 deep drawers L or
R, top drawer false

VSD24
VSD30
VSD36

Vanity Bowl
Double Drawer Unit
* full height door
* 6 drawers

VSDD42
VSDD48

Vanity Drawer
* 3 drawers

VD12D3
VD15D3
VD18D3

Suspended Drawer
* full width shallow
drawer
* optional desk leg
recesses may be avlbl

VD24SD
VD30SD
VD36SD

Vanity Hamper
* full height door
* detachable wire
basket tilts out w/door
or separate

V18HA

Vanity Storage
48" (122 cm) height
* 2 adjustable shelves

VS2648

Cabinet Description	Nomenclature	Tips from the Pros
INTERIOR FITTINGS		
Roll-Out Shelves * for all base and tall cabinets in place of standard shelves.	ROS	• Make sure the door opens past 90° to allow the shelves to roll out. • In a large pull-out system for multiple waste containers, alert client not to push waste down too strongly. Drawer guide system can be bent.
Swing-Out Pantry Rack * For tall cabinet, swings out for access. * Double-sided, oak with oak adjustable shelves is typical	SPR	
Door Shelf Kit * Mounts on back of door * plastic or wood	PR	
Square Shelf Kit * for tall utility cabinets * 5 shelves is typical	SK	
Revolving Shelf Kit * for tall utility cabinets * revolving plastic shelves w/center rod & brackets typical	RP	
Tilt-Out Sink Tray * fits in sink cabinet * white, almond or stainless steel avlbl	TO	• Some are stainless steel, some plastic. Some go length of sink cabinet. Know your product before presenting it to client. • When specifying, make sure sink cutout is far enough back for space. Some integral sinks don't allow space.
Spice Tray Insert * fits top drawer of base cabinet. * molded plastic, white or almost typical	ST	
Bread Box * fits in lower drawer of BD cabinets * plastic or stainless	BB	
Wine Rack * may be insert for standard cabinet, for bottles to lay in square compartments * may be lattice for special cabinet	WR	• Check length of bottles if installing behind closed doors. Reds will probably fit, some whites. German bottles are longer. • When specifying an inverted glass holder, check size of wine glasses. Some won't fit. Be sure rack won't conceal backsplash outlets.
Cutting Board * pull-out wood above top drawer in BD typical. * may be concealed behind fold-down top drawer front	CB	

Cabinet Description		Nomenclature	Tips from the Pros

Drawer Organizer
* plastic storage unit fits in drawer

DO

• Generally put near dishwasher and sink for immediate access as we load or unload dishwasher or set table. Also useful in desk units.

Mixer Unit
* pull-up hardware for mixer storage

MU

Towel Bar
* pull-out 2-prong or 3-prong is typical

TB

• Don't specify sliding bar under sink if client plans on waste basket directly under it. Know what cleaning supplies will be kept there so you can place everything properly.

Waste Paper Basket
* attached to sink door is typical
* pull-out recycling bin also avaible

WP

Range Hood
* metal liner is typical

RH

Glass Doors

GD

• Glass doors may have mullion, munton designations. This can mean wood strips that divide glass panes, or an applied molding framework that might be fixed or removable. The latter makes cleaning easier.

Appliance Garage
* 15" High (38 cm)
* 18" High (46 cm)
* features roll-up tambour or bifold doors

AG1818
AG2418

• Don't use a continuous wood pull on a tambour door. Fingers won't go under it. Make sure client and electrical contractor understand what it is and install outlets so they won't block tambour door.

Appliance Garage-- Diagonal
* 15" High (38 cm)
* 18" High (46 cm)
* features roll-up tambour or bifold doors
* fits to the backsplash height

AGC2418D

Fillers

WF3
TF3
VF3
BF3

• Be sure to specify whether fillers should flush out with the case, or whether they have an attached flange so they can flush out with the door with the flange continuing back past the case edge.
• For corner wall fillers, don't forget a lower panel that will extend back to the wall. If there is an open soffit you also will need a top return.
• Scribing fillers are used to separate cabinets in corners, provide a surface for a flange to fit against, or to finish a cabinet against a wall and provide clearance for drawer hardware and for interior shelving to work.

Countertop Bracket
* has integral mounting kit
* use for shelf or counter support

CB

• Corbel brackets support extended counters. Generally, an overhang more than 12" (30 cm) needs a support bracket every 36" (91 cm).

Pigeon Hole

PH30
PG36

• May be used vertically or horizontally. Heights will vary according to manufacturer.

Cabinet Description		Nomenclature	Tips from the Pros
Valance, Contemporary * 4 1/4" High (11 cm)		VP-C	
Valance, Traditional * 4 1/4" High (11 cm)		VP-T	
Appliance End Panel		AEP	• With frameless cabinets, include a panel adjacent to any appliances that have a flange that should rest against the cabinet component. In framed cabinets, the frame provides a place for the appliance flange to fit against.
Decorative Appliance Front Panel * may match door detail * generally avlbl for dishwasher, compactor and refrigerator		DWP RP TCP	
Wall Finished Sides		FS	
Decorative Finished Sides * panels with overlay for furniture look		FS-D	• In ordering door style panels for a cabinet side, do you want the panel to finish at the case dimension (12", 30 cm) or the dimension of the case and door (12 3/4", 32 cm). Consider this for a crown molding above, as well.
Outside Corner Molding		OCM	• Outside corner molding is used to seal a joint between two panels at right angles.
Inside Corner Molding		ICM	
Scribe Molding		SM	• Scribe molding is used to finish along an uneven ceiling.
Batten Molding		BM	• Batten molding is used to cover joints between adjacent cabinets.
Crown Molding		CM	• Crown molding is a decorative piece used on top of cabinets.
Galley Rail		GR	• Galley rails are used on top of cabinets to create a display area.
Countertop Molding		TCM	• Countertop edge moldings and backsplash moldings are used to finish the top with solid surface, ceramic tile and laminates. These surfaces should be finished all the way around if used with tile. With solid surface, moldings may be installed unfinished so they can be sanded flush with the top, then finished. Or finished moldings can be installed slightly offset from the solid surface edging.

About The KCMA Certification Program

The Kitchen Cabinet Manufacturers Association Certification Program assures the specifier or user of kitchen cabinets and bath vanities that the cabinet bearing the blue and white seal complies with the rigorous standards set by the American National Standards Institute (ANSI) and sponsored by the Kitchen Cabinet Manufacturers Association (KCMA). Further, the cabinet is an exact duplicate of samples that have been independently tested. The KCMA Certification Program is open to all cabinet manufacturers. Manufacturers may certify one, several, or all of their cabinet lines. Because of this option, only those lines certified are listed.

Compliance with ANSI/KCMA standards is assured by initial cabinet testing, periodic unannounced plant pick-up and testing, and additional testing resulting from complaints. All testing is performed by an experienced independent laboratory.

The kitchen and bath cabinets of certified manufacturers comply with ANSI/KCMA A 161.1-1990, "Recommended Performance and construction Standards for Kitchen Cabinets." The cabinets also comply with the provision of paragraph 611-1.1, "HUD Minimum Property Standards - Housing 4910.1," 9/8/86.

Companies not licensed with the KCMA Program may not claim or imply conformance with these standards for their products. KCMA, as the proprietary sponsor, reserves the right to question any claims of conformance and to test the products of any manufacturer making such claims. Should KCMA discover that a manufacturer is falsely representing that his products meet these standards, KCMA will take appropriate legal action.

If you have questions about the Certification Program or about specific cabinet lines, please write: Director of Certification, Kitchen Cabinet Manufacturers Association, P.O. Box 6830, Falls Church, Virginia 22040, or call (703) 237-7580.

Requirements Cabinets Must Meet To Earn The KCMA Certification Seal

GENERAL CONSTRUCTION REQUIREMENTS

- All cabinets must be fully enclosed with backs, bottoms, sides, and tops on wall cabinets; and backs, bottoms, and sides on base cabinets, with certain specified exceptions on kitchen sink fronts, sink bases, oven cabinets, and refrigerator cabinets.
- All cabinets designed to rest on the floor must be provided with a toe space at least two inches deep and three inches high.
- All utility cabinets must meet the same construction requirements as base and wall cabinets.
- Doors must be properly aligned, have means of closure, and close without excessive binding or looseness.
- All materials must ensure rigidity in compliance with performance standards.

- Face frames, when used, must provide rigid construction.
- For frameless cabinets, the ends, tops/bottoms, and back shall be of thickness necessary to provide rigid construction.

- Corner or lineal bracing must be provided at points where necessary to ensure rigidity and proper joining of various components.
- All wood parts must be dried to a moisture content of 10 percent or less at time of fabrication.

A 10-pound sand bag strikes a cabinet door to measure the ability of the door and connections to withstand impacts.

- All materials used in cabinets must be suitable for use in the kitchen and bath environment where they may be exposed to grease, solvents, water, detergent, steam and other substances usually found in these rooms.
- All exposed plywood and composition board edges must be filled and sanded, edge-banded, or otherwise finished to ensure compliance with the performance standards.
- All exterior exposed parts of cabinets must have nails and staples set and holes filled.
- All exposed construction joints must be fitted in a workmanlike manner consistent with specifications.
- Exposed cabinet hardware must comply with the finishing standards of ANSI/BHMA A 156.9-1988.

The KMCA certification program.

Requirements Cabinets Must Meet
To Earn The KCMA Certification Seal

A door is opened and closed 25,000 times to test its ability to operate under the stress of normal use.

FOUR STRUCTURAL TESTS MEASURE CABINET'S STRUCTURAL INTEGRITY, INSTALLATION

- All shelves and bottoms are loaded at 15 pounds per square foot, and loading is maintained for seven days to ensure that there is no excessive deflection and no visible sign of joint separation or failure of any part of the cabinets or the mounting system.
- Mounted wall cabinets are loaded to ensure that the cabinet will accept a net loading of 500 pounds without any visible sign of failure in the cabinet or the mounting system.
- To test the strength of base-front joints, a load of 250 pounds is applied against the inside of cabinet-front stiles for cabinets with drawer rail, or 200 pounds is applied for cabinets without drawer rail, to ensure reliable front joints that will not open during stress in service or during installation.

- To test the ability of shelves, bottoms, and drawer bottoms to withstand the dropping of cans and other items, a three-pound steel ball is dropped from six inches above the surface. After the test the drawer must not be damaged and must operate as before the test with no visible sign of joint separation or failure of any part of the cabinet or mounting system.
- To test the ability of cabinet doors and connections to withstand impacts, a 10-pound sandbag is used to strike the center of a closed cabinet door and repeated with the door opened to a 45-degree angle. The door must operate as before the test and show no damage or sign of separation or failure in the system.

TWO DOOR OPERATION TESTS MEASURE DURABILITY

- To test the ability of doors, hinges, and means of attachment to withstand loading, 65 pounds of weight is applied on the door. The weighted door is slowly operated for 10 cycles from 90 degrees open to 20 degrees open and returned to the 90 degree position. The door must remain weighted for 10 minutes, after which the door and hinges must show no visible signs of damage, and connections between cabinet-and-hinge and door-and-hinge must show no sign of looseness.
- To test the ability of doors, door-holding devices, hinges, and attachment devices to operate under the stress of normal use, doors are opened and closed through a full 90-degree swing for 25,000 cycles. At the test's conclusion the door must be operable, the door-holding device must hold the door in closed position, hinges must show no visible signs of damage, connections between

cabinet and hinge and door and hinge must show no sign of looseness, and other specifications must be met.

TWO DRAWER TESTS REQUIRED

- To test the ability of drawers and drawer mechanisms to operate with loading during normal use, drawers are loaded at 15 pounds per square foot and operated through 25,000 cycles. The drawers must then remain operable with no failure in any part of the drawer assembly or operating system, and drawer bottoms must not be deflected to interfere with drawer operation.
- To test the ability of the drawer-front assembly to withstand the impact of closing the drawer under normal use, a three-pound weight is dropped 8 inches against loading bars 10 times, after which

A cabinet door is weighted with 65 pounds, then operated 10 times to test the ability of the door and hinges to withstand loading.

The KMCA certification program.

Requirements Cabinets Must Meet
To Earn The KCMA Certification Seal

looseness or structural damage to the drawer-front assembly that impairs operation must not be evident.

FIVE FINISH TESTS CONDUCTED

These tests create, in accelerated form, the cumulative effects of years of normal kitchen conditions on pre-finished cabinets. Cabinet finishes are inspected to ensure that stringent standards of appearance are also met.

• To test the ability of the finish to withstand high heat, a cabinet door is placed in a hotbox at 120 degrees Fahrenheit (plus or minus 2 degrees) and 70 percent relative humidity (plus or minus 2 percent) for 24 hours. After this test the finish must show no appreciable discoloration and no evidence of blistering, checks, or other film failures.

• To test the ability of the finish to withstand hot and cold cycles for prolonged periods, a cabinet door is placed in a hotbox at 120 degrees Fahrenheit (plus or minus 2 degrees) for 1 hour, removed for 1/2 hour, and allowed to return to room temperature and humidity conditions, and then placed in a coldbox for 1 hour at -5 degrees Fahrenheit (plus or minus 2 degrees). The cycle is repeated five times. The finish must then show no appreciable discoloration and no evidence of blistering, cold checking, or other film failure.

• To test the ability of the finish to withstand substances typically found in the kitchen and bath, exterior exposed surfaces of doors, front frames, and drawer fronts are

subjected to vinegar, lemon, orange and grape juices, tomato catsup, coffee, olive oil, and 100-proof alcohol for 24 hours and to mustard for 1 hour. After this test, the finish must show no appreciable discoloration, stain, or whitening that will not disperse with ordinary polishing and no indication of blistering, checks, or other film failure.

• To test the ability of the finish to withstand long periods of exposure to a detergent and water solution, a cabinet door edge is subjected to exposure to a standardized detergent formula for 24 hours. The door edge must then show no delamination or swelling and no appreciable discoloration or evidence of blistering, checking, whitening, or other film failure.

A steel ball drop tests the ability of drawers and shelves to withstand the dropping of cans or other items.

A 24-hour detergent and water solution test checks the door's finish.

The KMCA certification program.

Notes

Appendix C:
Countertops
and Surfaces

Appendix C--Countertops

Countertops for residential kitchens are typically 25" (63.5cm) deep (front to back) to cover base cabinets and under-counter appliances.

They usually are 1 1/2" (4cm) thick, constructed of a 3/4" (2cm) thick top sheet substrate supported by a 3/4" buildup material which usually forms a web support over the cabinets. The top 3/4" material may be surfaced with laminate or tile. Other countertops, such as solid surface or concrete, feature a 3/4" solid finish material as the top sheet.

They have a backsplash which fits against the back wall. It might be 4" or 5" (10 or 13cm) high, or might go all the way up to the wall cabinets. End splashes usually are fitted where tops fit against side walls.

Tops are made of one or more of the following materials:

• **High-pressure (HP) decorative laminate,** which consists of several sheets of Kraft paper sandwiched between and impregnated by a clear sheet of melamine laminate on top and a backer sheet on the bottom, fused under heat and pressure. This is the most popular countertop material, by far.

Laminate sheets are 1/16" (1.59 mm) thick and are adhered to a substrate to form the countertop. The substrate might be 3/4" (19.05

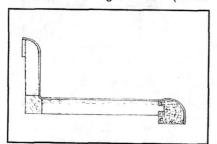

Fig. C.1. A postformed laminate top has one continuous sheet of laminate formed over substrate from front edge to wall over backsplash.

mm) industrial grade particleboard or plywood of at least five plies.

Advantages: Very durable and easy to keep clean; available in hundreds of colors, patterns and simulated woodgrains; widely available in stock lengths as "blanks" which are ready to install, although most are custom-made by local fabricators; inexpensive.

Disadvantages: Subject to cuts and to burns from hot pots (but not as much as people think); not repairable.

• **Solid surface,** a term we apply to several man-made composites that include Dupont Corian, Formica Surell, Nevamar Fountainhead, Avonite, Wilsonart Gibraltar and others. They appear similar but they have differences that affect their stability and workability. In some, the same material is available in colors in paste form for use in routed cuts for dramatic edges or other effects.

These are distinguished from the cultured marbles by the fact that they are homogeneous and can be cut and machined with woodworking tools, whereas the cultured marbles have gelcoat surfaces that are considered too soft for hard, kitchen use and which prevent cutting or drilling.

The solid surfaces are 1/2" to 3/4" thick (13 to 19mm). Some come with integral single, double or triple sinks. Some also are available in thinner form, approximately 1/4" (6mm) for backsplash or other wall applications.

Advantages: Elegant, easy to customize, combine well with other materials, cleanable, repairable.

Disadvantages: High initial cost,

require highly-skilled labor, easy to break when installing, somewhat limited colors and patterns.

Ceramic tile, widely-known and accepted, particularly in the south and western U.S. This material offers tremendous versatility in colors, patterns and for customizing. Technological advances have made it easier to install than in past decades. While conventional or dry-set mortar is preferred, it can be installed on an old top that is sound. Cementaceous boards have been developed to ease tile installation.

Advantages: Versatile; wide choice of colors, patterns; familiar to installers; durable; easy to keep clean; repairable. Won't cut, burn, blister or peel.

Disadvantages: Expensive, more difficult to fabricate, hard, noisy.

• **Marble, granite,** exotic materials that must be cut and worked by professionals. These also are available as man-made composites with high chip content.

Advantages: Fashionable, durable.

Disadvantages: Marble is relatively easy to stain; neither is repairable if broken; expensive.

• **Wood, stainless steel, tempered glass,** commonly used as counter inserts or for short sections for special purposes such as mixing or counter protection.

Good for these purposes. In wood, edge-cut blocks are often favored but thick maple strips also are used.

How to make and install laminated countertops

Laminated tops can be post-formed or square-edge. Post-formed tops are bought as "blanks" in stock sizes or made to order in postforming machines, and cannot be shaped because of the forming. Square-edge tops can be made in the shop or on the job, and are easily shaped into curves.

To make a square-edge top:

1. Measure and plan. Laminate sheets come in widths of 30", 36", 48" and 60" (76, 91, 122 and 152 cm) and lengths of 72", 96", 120" and 144" (183, 244, 305 and 366 cm). Each dimension is 1/2" (13 mm) oversized for trimming.

2. Prepare the substrate surface. It must be clean, dry and smooth. Cut to size.

3. Mark and cut the laminate. Mark dimensions 1/4" (6 mm) larger to allow for trimming after bonding. Place strip of masking tape over the cut line, then mark the line on the tape and cut through tape and laminate with slight pressure on down stroke of the saw. (Masking tape prevents chipping.)

4. Apply edgeband. Coat substrate edge and edgeband with contact adhesive, wait until dry, apply edge with block and hammer. Cut off overhang with router.

5. Apply contact adhesive to laminate sheet and substrate, allow to dry, lay sheet of paper over substrate (it won't stick), then place laminate, index it precisely, then pull paper out a few inches and stick exposed laminate down to substrate. **(Warning: Contact adhesive will grab on contact.)** Pull paper out and stick down remainder of laminate, applying pressure from center outward with a small roller or wood block and hammer. Trim all of the edges with router at 22 1/2-degree angle.

6. Bring top in and place it on counter. Cut out for sink and/or cooktop. Use templates provided to mark top, make straight cuts, then radius corner cuts with router or keyhole saw. (All inside corner cuts MUST be radiused to prevent cracking.)

7. Install sink, appliances according to manufacturer instructions.

8. Apply back and end splashes as needed.

9. To join a mitered corner, Butt sections together, rout recesses on under side and use T-bolts to draw sections tight. (NOTE: If joining corner outside of kitchen, make sure the assembly can be brought in through doorways.)

Special edges with color-through laminates

Color-through laminates have the same color all the way through so routing the edge does not leave the usual dark line. Attractive effects can be achieved with different router bits or by adding wood strips or "stacking" contrasting or harmonizing colors.

In Fig. C.2, from top, a 5/32" rounding-over bit gives a soft, rounded edge. Next, a 45-degree bit makes a colorful bevel edge.

When stacking several colors, cut them slightly oversize, then rout them flush. Then rout with a 45-degree chamfer bit.

Next, a classic curve made with an ogee bit can show three colors.

The bevel edge in the next drawing is achieved by fastening a strip of fine hardwood to the substrate, then applying the edging strip and routing. A somewhat similar treatment in the bottom drawing uses a different bit for the concave effect.

When bonding these laminate sheets together, they must be sanded with a fine 100-grit sand-

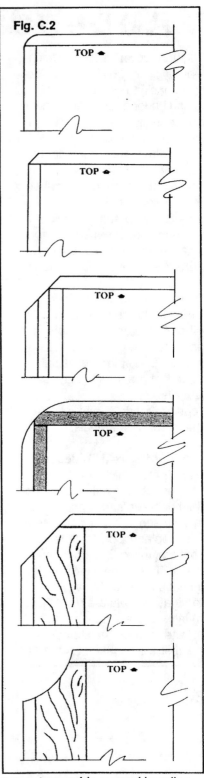

Fig. C.2

paper to provide a good bonding surface, and it is important to use a colorless adhesive such as a solvent-based contact or epoxy. Any color in a glue line will show and can spoil the effect.

Tips for working with solid surfaces

While solid surfaces can be cut and drilled with woodworking tools, it requires fine tools, care and expertise. Some of these materials are sold only to distributors or other qualified firms with trained fabricators on staff.

One slip with a saw or router can ruin a very expensive piece of material. The material is heavy, and in areas such as a sink cutout the small strips of material remaining after the cutout have very little tensile strength and can break easily. All solid surface manufacturers recommend that only factory-trained fabricators install the tops, and you should be familiar with key points and product use restrictions.

Cuts should be made outside the house as much as possible because they result in a veritable "snowstorm." Panels being cut outside must be supported by several sawhorses shimmed to hold the piece level. For a sink or cooktop, only the straight cuts of the cutout should be made before carrying the top inside (Fig. C.3). When it is in place, the corner radius cuts can be made, but with support underneath so the cutout doesn't fall and damage the cabinet below. Also, the cutout can be valuable for trim or other use, so try to avoid damaging it.

Keep unsupported overhangs to a minimum. One firm recommends a maximum of 6" (15 cm) for its 1/2" (13 mm) sheet, or 12" (30 cm) for its 3/4" (19 mm) sheet (Fig. C.5). For more than that, add corbels or other support.

Seams in solid surfaces are butted and welded with a silicone sealant so they are almost imperceptible. In some cases they can be tightened with T-bolts underneath, like a corner miter in a laminated top. One manufacturer

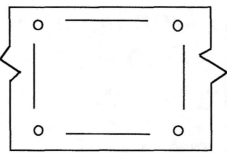

Fig. C.3. This is a pattern suggested for sink cutouts. Solid lines and corner holes are cut in shop. Top is transported to job-site, placed in kitchen, and keyhole saw is used to complete cuts to corner holes which already form radius in each corner.

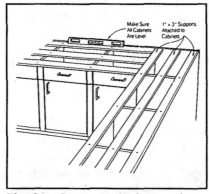

Fig. C.4. Support rails fastened lengthwise along the cabinet run are good means of support for top.

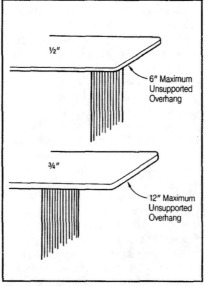

Fig. C.5. Solid surface tops do not have a lot of tensile strength. Maximum overhang for 3/4" (19 mm) material is 12" (30 cm).

also suggests routing out recesses for splines between the two pieces. Another warns that a seam should not come within 3" (8 cm) of an appliance cutout.

For installing the top, a manufacturer suggests attaching three 1"x3" (2.5 x 7.6 cm) wood strips to the cabinets for the length of the run. Install cross-supports (same dimension) to frame each cutout and to support each seam. Dabs of silicone should go on cleaned supports every 18" to 24" (46-61 cm) (Fig. C.4).

A full-height backsplash of solid surface should be installed before the top is installed, and behind it. Silicone dabs will bind it to the wall, but use hotmelt to hold it until the silicone cures. A standard backsplash should sit on top of countertop, affixed with silicone sealant. Backsplash must be sealed to the top, not to the wall. Hotmelt is recommended to hold the backsplash to the wall. If there is movement, the hotmelt bond will break, allowing the backsplash to move with the top.

When installing a cooktop in solid surface, specify a 2"-wide (5 cm) aluminum heat-conductive tape around the cutout.

When installing a solid surface top between walls, allow 1/8" (3 mm) for expansion every 10' (305 cm).

Solid surface edges

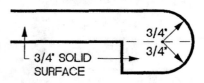

Fig. C.6. For a simple, round edge, add 3/4" (19 mm) build-up strip to 3/4" top, round each with 3/4" radius round-over bit, join with silicone joint adhesive.

(Continued next page.)

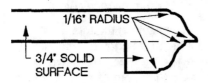

Fig. C.8. Wood edge routed with chamfer bit can be joined to 3/4" sheet with Neoprene panel adhesive.

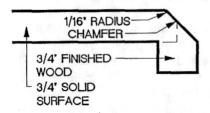

Fig. C.9. Laminate or wood veneer inlays can go in top apron and backsplash. Rout inlay grooves with double fluted bit. Join apron with joint adhesive; backsplash with silicone caulk; strips with acrylic adhesive.

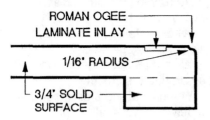

Fig. C.10. A 1/4" (6 mm) colored acrylic sheet can be inserted between layers of Corian. It can be bonded with acrylic adhesive. Rout chamfer edge at top, sand sharp edges to 1/16" (1.6 mm) radius.

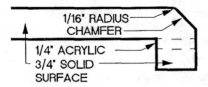

Planning Considerations when Working with Tile

To specify tile properly, designers must be familiar with the broad product classifications.

TYPES OF TILE

Glazed tile: This is made from a mixture of clays that are refined and pressed into a shape. It then receives a coat of metallic oxides and ceramic stains called a "glaze." The tile is fired in kilns as hot as 2,100°F. The firing process can take as long as 14 hours using traditional methods or as little as 1 hour with new "fast fire" technology. Such glazed surfaces can be hazardous to pedestrian traffic if water stands on the surface. Glazed tiles are also available in a matte finish and in an abrasive slip-resistant texture.

A variety of sizes and thicknesses is available. Glazed tiles may wear and scratch over a period of time with continued use. White or light-colored glazed tiles will show wear more rapidly than darker colors. As glazed tiles are different in their susceptibility to scratching, some types are limited in their use.

Decorative tile: Within the glazed family of ceramic tiles, there is a subcategory called "Decos." These attractive accent pieces may include a raised or recessed relief pattern or a painted design. Generally, these decorative pieces are designed for vertical use only. The 3-dimensional tiles may be difficult to clean on a counter surface or floor area. The hand-painted tiles may be so delicate that even general cleaning of countertops or floors will destroy the pattern.

Mosaic tile: In this variety, different types of clays and color pigments are mixed, refined and pressed into shapes. The color goes all the way through the clay or porcelain material rather than being an applied surface finish. Porcelain mosaic tiles are baked at higher temperatures than most other tiles and, therefore, have a harder, denser body. Ceramic mosaics are often small in size and usually sold in mesh-backed 12" x 12" or 12" x 24" sheets. Larger mosaics are also available. The mesh-backed sheets facilitate installation of these small tiles. The small sizes allow contour design applications. They are impervious to water, stain-proof, dent-proof and frost-proof. They are suitable for interior and exterior walls, floors, countertops and vanity tops. Creative graphics, murals and geometric designs can be planned with this product.

Quarry tile: A material made from a mixture of shale, clays or earth which is extruded to produce an unglazed product which has color throughout the tile body.

There is a great variety of quality levels under the broad "quarry tile" heading. The earthen clay tiles may be very soft and irregular in shape so that breakage and installation time is increased. Other types of quarry tiles are so porous that they require a penetrating sealer to protect the surface.

Quarry tiles are suitable for interior residential and commercial floors, walls and fireplace facings. They may be used on exterior surfaces if the area is not subject to freezing.

Tile Trim: The availability of trim pieces is also an important consideration. While the floor can be installed with nothing more than a plain or field tile (tile without any finished or shaped edges), the countertop backsplash calls for specially-designed edging pieces to complete the installation.

Trim pieces are available with a 3/4" radius for conventional mortar installations and a 1/4" radius for organic adhesive installations. These trims are generally more expensive than field tile. The color and texture match is generally good between field tile and trim pieces, but there may be a slight or pronounced color and/or texture difference in some selections. When designers use a tile for the first time, they should visually compare a field tile and trim piece before the order is placed. If there is any discrepancy, the client should approve the difference before the order is placed.

TILE GROUT

Grouts are selected according to the intended use of the space, the type of tile, the method of installation and the width of the grout joint.

Epoxy grout: Made up of epoxy resin and hardener, the major advantage of epoxy grouts is their chemical resistance. They are not stain-resistant. Epoxy grouts provide high bond strength and impact resistance, but they involve extra costs and careful installation. New colors are currently being introduced.

Non-sanded grout: Small joints (not to exceed 1/8") usually use non-sanded grouts. The non-sanded products also should be used in conjunction with soft glazed tiles that could be scratched by abrasive sand. These grouts have a smooth appearance. They are available in many colors.

Sanded grout: Wide joints (up to 1/4") use sanded grouts which have a rougher appearance. A latex additive, used in place of water, improves stain resistance and bonding ability of the grout. The latex additive also eliminates the necessity of damp-curing in some installations. They are available in many colors.

Silicone rubber grout: They feature an elastomeric system employing silicone rubber. After curing they are resistant to staining, moisture, mildew, cracking, crazing and shrinking. They are extremely flexible. Used extensively in pre-grouted tile sheets, they also are appropriate wherever unusual expansion and contraction of adjoining dissimilar surfaces is expected. Colors are very limited.

Ceramic Tile Installation

Two methods of installation are used for ceramic tile projects.

Organic Adhesive: In this method, tile is directly applied to the subfloor, decking or cement, with troweled mastic. When this method is used, the surface will only be raised the thickness of the tile. Manufacturers state that a mastic installation may use any of the following base surfaces: existing tile, gypsum board, fiberglass, wood, paneling, brick, masonry, concrete, plywood and vinyl. The surface must be dry, flat and free of dirt and grease. Any existing structural problems cannot be camouflaged by the installation. If there is a bow in the floor before the tile is installed, it will be there after the tile is installed.

Mortar bed: In this method, the tile is installed on a bed of mortar 3/4" to 1 1/4" thick. Two systems are popular in the United States. In one, the tile is set on a mortar bed while the mortar is still plastic. In the other, tile is set on a cured mortar bed.

A glass mesh concrete underlayment (cementaceous) board may take the place of a conventional mortar bed. It is unaffected by moisture and has one of the lowest coefficients of expansion of all building panels. Additionally, the boards are only half the weight of conventional mortar installations.

With these methods of installation, the floor or countertop height will be raised the thickness of the tile and the mortar bed or concrete board. This height difference may require special floor preparation. In new construction, the subfloor can be recessed to accommodate a tile floor. In renovation projects, a transition method between the new higher tile floor and adjoining floors must be specified. Special toekicks must also be detailed so that the industrial standard of 4"-high kick space is maintained. Standard cabinets with an integral subbase must be raised to accommodate the tile floor butting against the toekick, and extending into openings planned for under-counter or free-standing appliances.

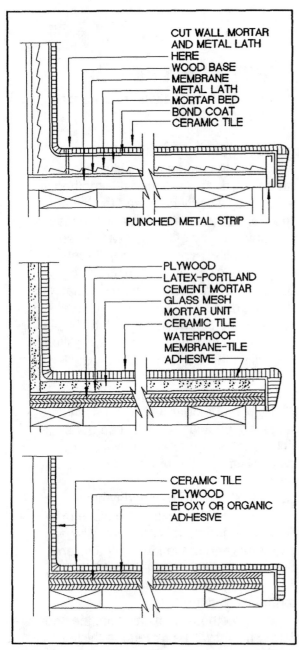

CUT WALL MORTAR
AND METAL LATH
HERE
WOOD BASE
MEMBRANE
METAL LATH
MORTAR BED
BOND COAT
CERAMIC TILE

PUNCHED METAL STRIP

PLYWOOD
LATEX-PORTLAND
CEMENT MORTAR
GLASS MESH
MORTAR UNIT
CERAMIC TILE
WATERPROOF
MEMBRANE-TILE
ADHESIVE

CERAMIC TILE
PLYWOOD
EPOXY OR ORGANIC
ADHESIVE

Fig. C.11. Drawings show sequence of construction materials for installing ceramic tile with conventional mortar on a wood base, on a cementaceous board (Wonder-Board) over plywood, and with adhesive on plywood.

How to lay ceramic tile over an existing laminate countertop

A new ceramic tile surface can be laid over a worn or outdated decorative laminate top as long as the laminate and substrate are sound and smooth. American Olean, which provides a full family of trim pieces, describes the procedure.

If the old top has a metal edging it probably will protrude slightly above the top surface. If this is the case, remove the edge to get a smooth flat surface. Remove the sink and cooktop, if they are present.

1. Lightly sand laminate surface with coarse sandpaper. Sand only enough to roughen the surface. Remove dust.

2. Before spreading adhesive, determine where tile must be cut. Place trim piece on front edge and lay two or three rows front to back, allowing for joints. Mark exact place for cut on the last tile back.

3. Apply an acrylic-based latex adhesive (such as AO 1400) with 3/16" (4.8 mm) V-notched trowel. Use enough for complete contact with each tile, but not so much that it will squeeze up in joints. Use damp sponge to clean up adhesive..

4. Press tiles into adhesive starting with front counter trim. Maintain spacing and straight grout lines. Use damp sponge to clean off adhesive smudges before spreading next area.

5. At sink cutout make corner cut in tile either with tile nippers or a Remington Rod Saw. This is a special carbide grit round blade that fits any standard hack saw. Smooth sharp-cut edges with carborundum stone.

6. Spread adhesive on the backsplash and press tile firmly into place. If cutting is required cut the tiles in the top row. The cuts will be least conspicuous there (assuming a full backsplash) because they will be mostly out of sight, under the wall cabinets.

7. Finish the side edge of the backsplash with bullnose trim. Cut to fit the contour where it meets the countertop trim. Use damp sponge to remove any excess adhesive from adjacent wall surface.

8. Before filling joints between tiles, wait at least one day for adhesive to dry and firm up. Then mix dry wall grout following instructions on the bag. The firm makes a Groutmaster trowel to press grout into joints.

9. Strike all joints with a tongue depressor or similarly shaped tool to make them dense, smooth and uniform. This will make the grout easier to clean for years to come.

10. Use a damp sponge to remove grout film. As tile surface dries, clean off final grout haze with a soft, dry cloth. Be sure surface of each tile is completely clean.

Notes

Notes

Appendix D:
Graphics and
Presentation Standards

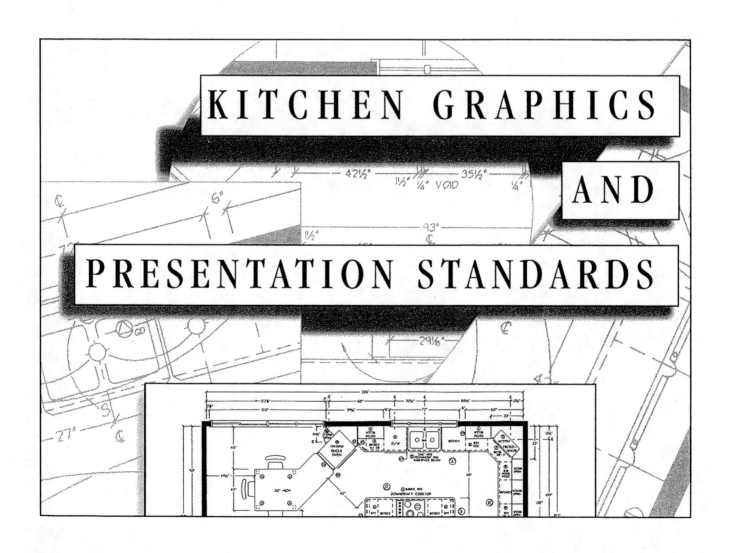

KITCHEN GRAPHICS

AND

PRESENTATION STANDARDS

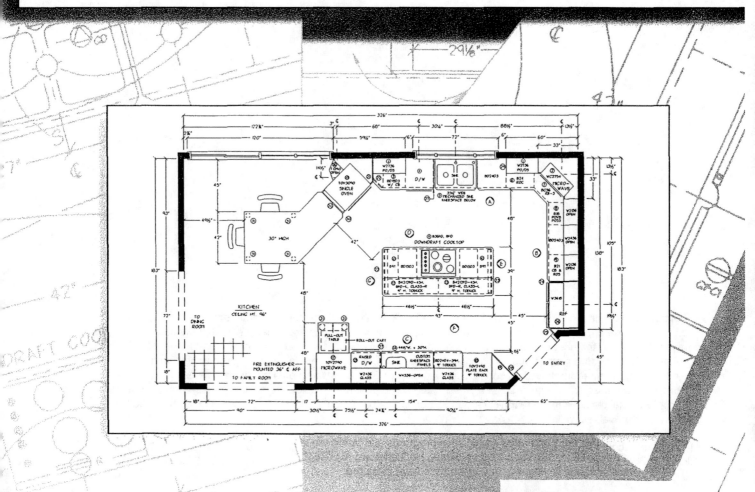

NKBA The Finest Professionals in the Kitchen & Bath Industry

National Kitchen & Bath Association℠

Table of Contents

Purpose

By standardizing floor plans and presentation drawings, Kitchen Designers will:

- Limit errors caused by misinterpreting the floor plans.

- Avoid misreading dimensions, which can result in costly errors.

- Prevent cluttering floor plans and drawings with secondary information, which often make the documents difficult to interpret.

- Create a clear understanding of the scope of the project for all persons involved in the job.

- Present a professional image to the client.

- Permit faster processing of orders.

- Simplify estimating and specification preparation.

- Help in the standardization of uniform nomenclature and symbols.

General Provisions Using Imperial Dimensions

I. Use of Standards

The use of these *National Kitchen & Bath Association Graphics and Presentation Standards* is strongly recommended. They contain a specific set of criteria which when applied by the Kitchen Specialist produce a series of project documents that include the following:

- The Floor Plan

- The Construction Plan

- The Mechanical Plan

- The Interpretive Drawings

    1) Elevations
    2) Perspective Drawings
    3) Oblique, Dimetric, Isometric and Trimetric
    4) Sketches

- Specifications

- Design Statement

- Contracts

Two sample sets of project documents for your review can be found in this publication, one uses imperial dimensions and the other is a metric conversion.

Paper: The acceptable paper for the original drawings of the floor plan, construction plan, mechanical plan, and interpretive drawings is set at a **minimum size of 11" x 17".** Translucent vellum tracing paper, imprinted with a black border and appropriate space available for the insertion of pertinent information is strongly recommended. Copies of original drawings should appear in blue or black ink only on white paper. Ozalid or photocopy prints are acceptable.

The use of lined yellow note paper, typing paper, scored graph paper or scored quadrille paper **is not acceptable.**

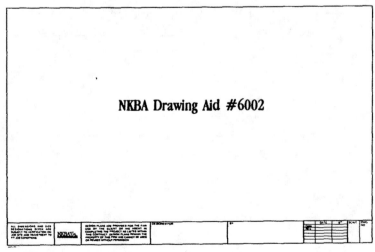

NKBA Drawing Aid #6002

II. The Floor Plan

1) **Size and Scope of Floor Plan Drawings:** Kitchen floor plans should be drawn to a scale of 1/2 inch equals 1 foot (1/2" = 1'0"). * *For metric dimensioning, see Use of Standards using Metric Dimensions beginning on page 34.*

- All base cabinetry should be depicted using a dashed line (- - - -) while countertops are depicted using a solid line.

- The floor plan should depict the entire room when possible. When the entire room cannot be depicted, it must show the area where cabinetry and appliances are permanently installed.

- Floor plans must show all major structural elements such as walls, door swings, door openings, partitions, windows, archways and equipment.

- When the entire room cannot be depicted, the room must be divided by *"break lines"* (—) and must show all major structural elements with adjoining areas indicated and labeled.

- Finished interior dimensions are used on all project documents to denote available space for cabinetry and/or other types of equipment. If the kitchen specialist is responsible for specifying the exact method of wall construction, finish and/or partition placement, the specialist should include partition center lines on the construction plan, as well as the finished interior dimensions.

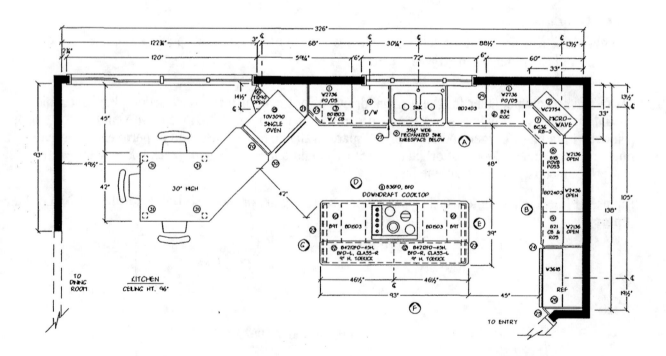

2) Centerline (℄) dimensions: must be given for equipment in two directions when possible.

- Mechanicals requiring centerlines include: cooktops, refrigerators, sinks, wall ovens, microwave ovens, fan units, light fixtures, heating and air conditioning ducts and radiators.

- Dimensions should be pulled from return walls or from the face of cabinets/equipment opposite the mechanical element.

- Centerlines on the mechanical plan will be indicated by the symbol (℄) followed by **a long-short-long broken line** that extends into the floor area.

- When the centerline dimension line is outside the floor area, it is typically shown as the second (and, if required, the third) line following the dimension line which identifies the individual wall segments.

℄ —— - —— - —— - —— - ——

3) Dimensioning of Floor Plan: All drawing dimensions used on kitchen floor plans must be given in **Inches and Fractions of Inches ONLY**, (ie. 124 1/4").

- Combining dimensions listed in feet and inches or the exclusive use of dimensions listed in feet and inches, 10' 4 1/4" **is not acceptable** and should not be used under any circumstances. Again, this would also apply to the metric equivalent, do not combine meters and centimeters.

NOTE:

- Each set of dimensions should be at least 3/16" apart on separate dimension lines which are to intersect with witness lines. These intersecting points should be indicated by dimension arrows, dots, or slashes.

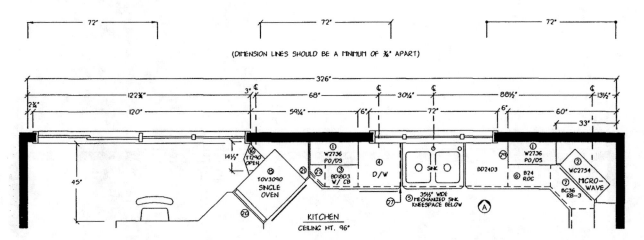

- All dimensions, whenever possible, should be shown **OUTSIDE** the wall lines.

- All lettering should be listed parallel to the title block at the bottom of the vellum paper and break the dimension line near its mid-point. This mechanical drafting technique eliminates errors in reading dimensions.

- An acceptable alternative is to draw all dimensions and lettering so that it is readable from the bottom edge or the right side of the plans with lettering on top of each dimension line.

The following dimensions **MUST** be shown on every floor plan as minimum requirements.

- Overall length of wall areas to receive cabinets, countertops, fixtures, or any equipment occupying floor and/or wall space. This dimension should always be the outside line.

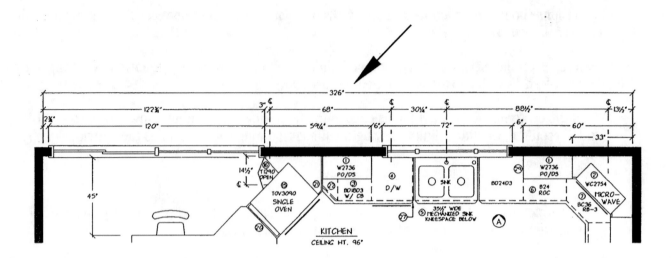

- Each wall opening, (windows, arches, doors and major appliances) and fixed structures (chimneys, wall protrusions and partitions) must be individually dimensioned. Dimensions are shown from outside trim. Trim size must be noted in the specification list. Fixtures such as radiators remaining in place must be outlined on the floor plan. These critical dimensions should be the first dimension line.

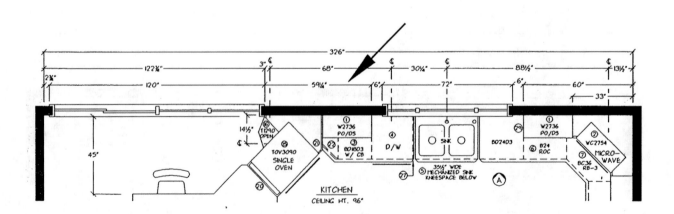

- Ceiling heights should appear on the floor plan. A separate plan for soffits is required when the soffit is a different depth than the wall or tall cabinet below. A separate soffit plan is recommended when the soffit is to be installed **PRIOR** to the wall or tall cabinet installation.

- Additional notes must be included for any deviation from standard height, width and depth. (cabinets, countertops, etc.)

- The exact opening must be given in height, width and depth for areas to be left open to receive equipment, cabinets and appliances at a future date.

- Items such as island and peninsula cabinets, must be shown with the overall dimensions given from countertop edge to opposite countertop edge, tall cabinet or wall. The exact location of the structure must be identified by dimensions which position it from two directions; from return walls or from the face of cabinets/equipment opposite the structure.

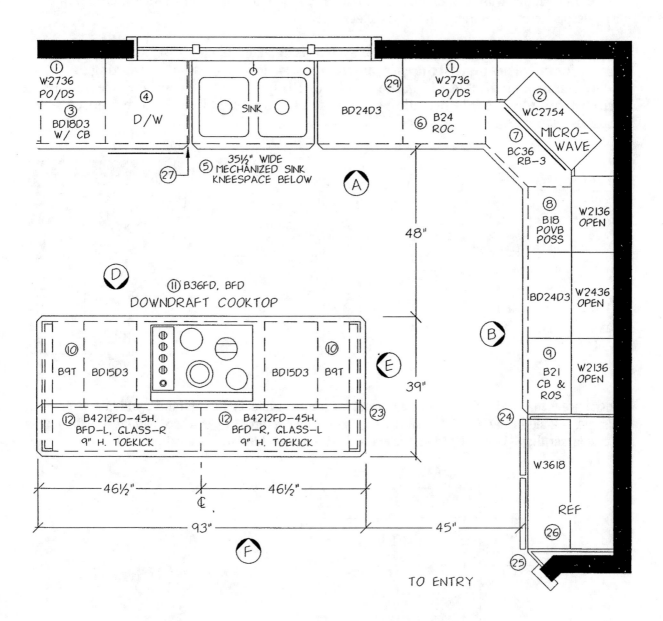

4) Cabinets/Appliances and Equipment Nomenclature and Designation on Floor Plans:

- Cabinets should be designated and identified by manufacturer nomenclature inside the area indicating their position. Cabinet system trim and finish items are designated outside their area, with an arrow clarifying exactly where the trim piece is located.

- To insure clarity, some design firms prefer to number and call out all the cabinet nomenclature in the Floor Plan specification listing.

- Equally acceptable is the use of a circled reference number to designate each cabinet on the Floor Plan and Elevations with the cabinet code listed within the individual unit width on the elevations or in a separate cross-reference list on the elevations.

- **Regardless of which cabinet designation system is selected from above, additional information for supplementary fixtures/equipment and special provisions pertaining to the cabinets must be indicated within the cabinet or equipment area by a reference number in a circle. This additional information should then be registered in a cross-referenced specifications listing on the same sheet.**

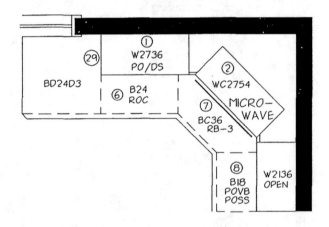

FLOOR PLAN SPECIFICATIONS

① SPECIAL PULL OUT & DOWN SHELVES

② WALL CORNER WITH MICROWAVE BELOW & 1⅞" ANGLED FILLER EACH SIDE

⑥ ROLL-OUT CART

⑦ BASE CORNER WITH 3 RECYCLING BINS

⑧ PULL-OUT VEGGIE BINS & STEP STOOL

㉙ LIGHT VALANCE CREATED ON ALL WALL CABS. WITH 1" RECESSED BOTTOMS

- Special order materials or custom design features, angled cabinets, unusual tops, molding, trim details, etc., should be shown in a section view, (sometimes referred to as a *"cut view"*), a plan view in a scale larger than (1/2" = 1') (a metric equivalent is acceptable), or in elevation view.

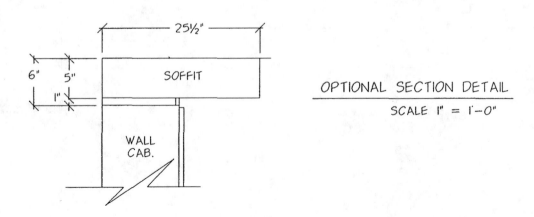

OPTIONAL SECTION DETAIL

SCALE 1" = 1'-0"

Graphics and Presentation Standards for Kitchen Design

III. The Construction Plan

1) The purpose of the construction plan is to show the relationship of the existing space with that of the new design. The construction plan is detailed separately so that it does not clutter the floor plan. However, if construction changes are minimal it is acceptable to combine the construction plan with either the floor plan or mechanical plan.

2) Construction Plan Symbols:

- Existing walls are shown with solid lines or hollowed out lines at their full thickness.

- Wall sections to be removed are shown with an outline of broken lines.

- New walls show the material symbols applicable to the type of construction or use a symbol which is identified in the legend in order to distinguish them from existing partitions.

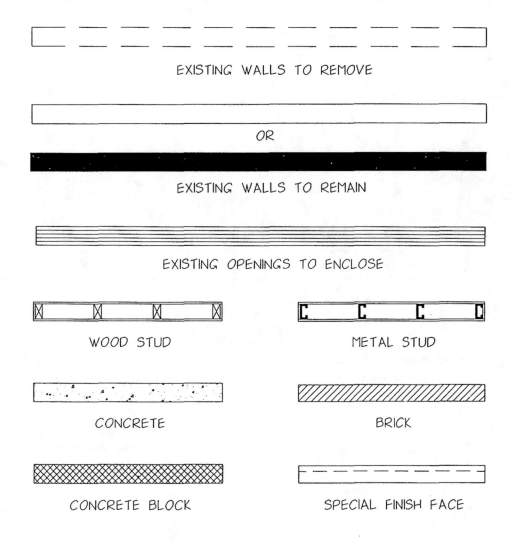

EXISTING WALLS TO REMOVE

OR

EXISTING WALLS TO REMAIN

EXISTING OPENINGS TO ENCLOSE

WOOD STUD   METAL STUD

CONCRETE   BRICK

CONCRETE BLOCK   SPECIAL FINISH FACE

NEW WALLS TO BE CONSTRUCTED

* Symbols taken from Architectural Graphic Standards, 9th Edition

An Example of a Construction Plan:

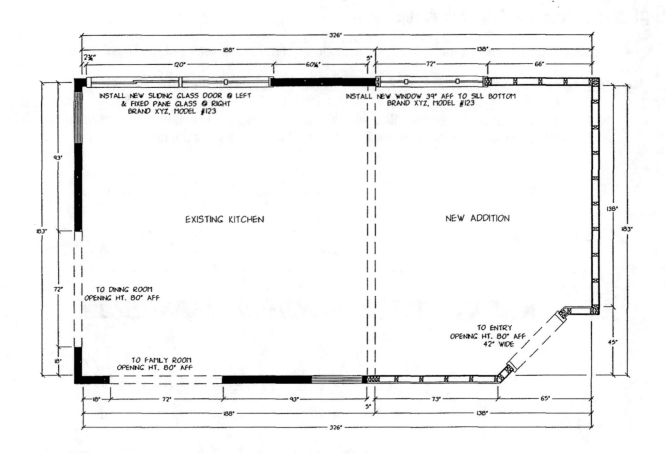

INSTALL NEW SLIDING GLASS DOOR @ LEFT
& FIXED PANE GLASS @ RIGHT
BRAND XYZ, MODEL #123

INSTALL NEW WINDOW 39" AFF TO SILL BOTTOM
BRAND XYZ, MODEL #123

EXISTING KITCHEN

NEW ADDITION

TO DINING ROOM
OPENING HT. 80" AFF

TO ENTRY
OPENING HT. 80" AFF
42" WIDE

TO FAMILY ROOM
OPENING HT. 80" AFF

CONSTRUCTION PLAN LEGEND

EXISTING WALLS TO REMAIN

NEW 16" O.C. WOOD STUD WALLS TO BUILD

EXISTING WALLS TO REMOVE

EXISTING OPENINGS TO ENCLOSE

IV. The Mechanical Plan

- By detailing separate plans for the mechanicals and/or construction, it will help to clearly identify such work without cluttering the kitchen floor plan.

- The mechanical plan should show an outline of the cabinets, countertops and fixtures without nomenclature.

- The mechanicals should be placed in the proper location with the proper symbols.

- All overall room dimensions should be listed.

1) The mechanical plan will consist of the Electrical/Lighting, Plumbing, Heating, Air Conditioning and Ventilation systems. If any minor wall/door construction changes are part of the plan, they should also be detailed on the mechanical plan.

2) A mechanical legend should be prepared on the plan. This legend will be used to describe what each symbol for special purpose outlets, fixtures or equipment means.

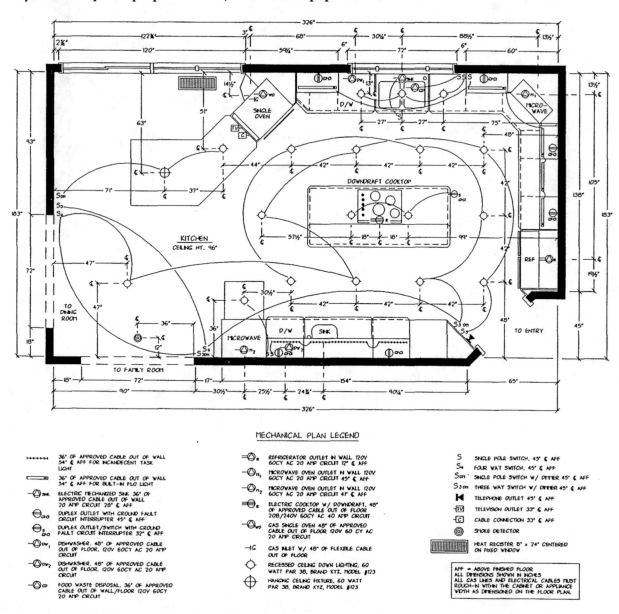

MECHANICAL PLAN LEGEND

3) Centerline (℄) dimensions must be given for all equipment in two directions when possible.

- Mechanicals requiring centerlines include: cooktops, refrigerators, dishwashers, compactors, sinks, wall ovens, microwave ovens, fan units, light fixtures, heating and air conditioning ducts and radiators.

- Centerline dimensions should be pulled from return walls or from the face of cabinets/equipment opposite the mechanical element.

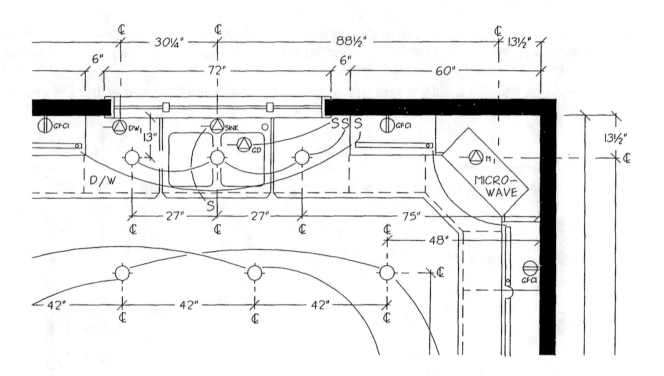

Centerlines on the mechanical plan will be indicated by the symbol (℄) followed by a **long-short-long broken line** that extends into the floor area.

Graphics and Presentation Standards for Kitchen Design

4) Mechanical Plan Symbols:

S	SINGLE POLE SWITCH		—[TV]	TELEVISION OUTLET
S₂	DOUBLE POLE SWITCH		—[C]	CABLE OUTLET
S₃	THREE WAY SWITCH		[T]L	LOW VOLTAGE TRANSFORMER
S₄	FOUR WAY SWITCH		⊗	HANGING CEILING FIXTURE
S_DM	SINGLE POLE SWITCH v/ DIMMER		⊕	HEAT LAMP
S₃DM	THREE WAY SWITCH v/ DIMMER		▬●▬	HEAT/LIGHT UNIT
S_LM	MASTER SWITCH FOR LOW VOLTAGE SWITCHING SYSTEM		▥○▥	HEAT/FAN LIGHT UNIT
S_L	SWITCH FOR LOW VOLTAGE SWITCHING SYSTEM		○	RECESSED CEILING DOWN LIGHTING
S_WP	WEATHERPROOF SWITCH		●	RECESSED CEILING VAPOR LIGHT
S_RC	REMOTE CONTROL SWITCH		⊢—⊣—⊢	BUILT—IN LOW VOLTAGE TASK LIGHT
S_D	AUTOMATIC DOOR SWITCH		▭	BUILT—IN FLUORESCENT LIGHT
S_P	SWITCH AND PILOT LAMP		▭▭	CONTINUOUS ROW FLUORESCENT LIGHTS
S_K	KEY OPERATED SWITCH		▣	SURFACE MOUNTED FLUORESCENT LIGHT
S_F	FUSED SWITCH		▽	WALL SCONCE
S_T	TIME SWITCH		—△_DW	DISHWASHER
Ⓢ	CEILING PULL SWITCH		—△_GD	FOOD WASTE DISPOSAL
⊖	DUPLEX OUTLET		—△_TC	TRASH COMPACTOR
⊖_GFCI	DUPLEX OUTLET WITH GROUND FAULT CIRCUIT INTERRUPTER		—△_R	REFRIGERATOR OUTLET
—⊖_S	SWITCH AND SINGLE RECEPTACLE OUTLET		—△_H	HOOD
⊖_S	SWITCH AND DUPLEX OUTLET		—△_M	MICROWAVE OVEN
—Ⓑ	BLANKED OUTLET		⊜_R	ELECTRIC RANGE/COOKTOP
—Ⓙ	JUNCTION BOX		⊜_WO	ELECTRIC SINGLE/DOUBLE OVEN
—Ⓛ	OUTLET CONTROLLED BY LOW VOLTAGE SWITCHING WHEN RELAY IS INSTALLED IN OUTLET BOX		—⊢_G	GAS SUPPLY
—⊖	SINGLE RECEPTACLE OULET		—△_CT	GAS COOKTOP
⊕	TRIPLEX RECEPTACLE OULET		—△_WO	GAS SINGLE/DOUBLE OVEN
⊕	QUADRUPLEX RECEPTACLE OULET		—△_CW	CLOTHES WASHER
⊜	DUPLEX RECEPTACLE OUTLET—SPLIT WIRED		⊜_CD	CLOTHES DRYER
⊕	TRIPLEX RECEPTACLE OUTLET—SPLIT WIRED		⊜_SA	SAUNA
—Ⓒ	CLOCK HANGER RECEPTACLE		⊜_ST	STEAM
Ⓕ	FAN HANGER RECEPTACLE		—△_WP	WHIRLPOOL
◖	INTERCOM		⊜_TW	TOWEL WARMER
◀	TELEPHONE OUTLET		▥	HEAT REGISTER
Ⓣ	THERMOSTAT			
◎	SMOKE DETECTOR			

ANY STANDARD SYMBOL GIVEN ABOVE W/ THE ADDITION OF LOWERCASE SUBSCRIPT LETTERING MAY BE USED TO DESIGNATE A VARIATION OF STANDARD EQUIPMENT.

WHEN USED THEY MUST BE LISTED IN THE LEGEND OF THE MECHANICAL PLAN.

Symbols taken from Architectural Graphic Standards, 9th Edition

V. Interpretive Drawings

Elevations and perspective renderings are considered interpretive drawings and are used as an explanatory means of understanding the floor plans.

- Under no circumstances should the interpretive drawings be used as a substitute for floor plans.

- In cases of dispute, the floor plans are the legally binding document.

- Because perspective drawings are not dimensioned to scale, many Kitchen Specialists include a disclaimer on their rendering such as this:

> This drawing is an artistic interpretation of the general appearance of the floor plan. It is not meant to be an exact rendition.

1) **Elevation:** Elevations must show a front view of all wall areas receiving cabinets and equipment as shown on the floor plan.

Elevations should dimension all cabinets, counters, fixtures and equipment in the elevation as follows:

- Cabinets with toekick and finished height.

- A portion of the cabinet doors and drawer front should indicate style and, when applicable, placement of handles/pulls.

- Countertops indicate thickness and show back-splash

- All doors, windows or other openings in walls which will receive equipment. The window/door casing or trim will be listed within the overall opening dimensions.

- All permanent fixtures such as radiators, etc.

- All main structural elements and protrusions such as chimneys, partitions, etc.

- Centerlines for all mechanical equipment.

Graphics and Presentation Standards for Kitchen Design

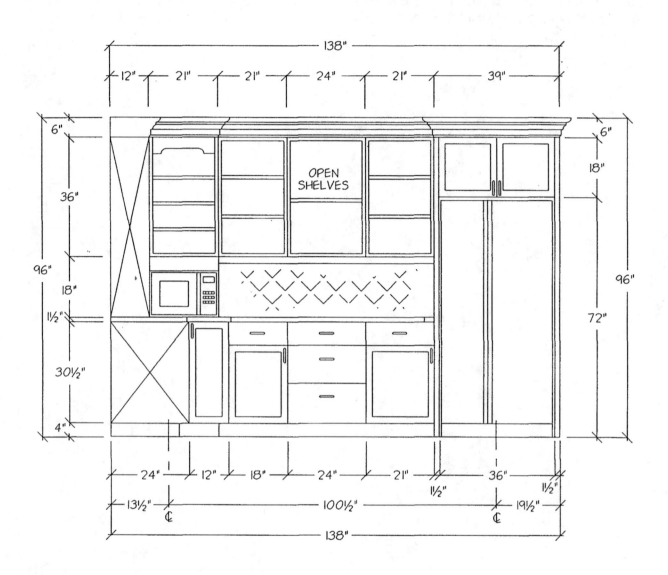

OPEN SHELVES

138"

12" 21" 21" 24" 21" 39"

6" 6"

36" 18"

96" 96"

18" 72"

1½"

30½"

4"

24" 12" 18" 24" 21" 36"

1½" 1½"

13½" 100½" 19½"

138"

ELEVATION
(B)

NOTE:
DIMENSIONS MUST ACCURATELY
REPRESENT PRODUCTS USED.

Graphics and Presentation Standards for Kitchen Design   15

2) **Perspective Drawings:** Perspectives are **not drawn to scale.** Grids, which are available through the **National Kitchen & Bath Association,** can be used as an underlay for tracing paper to accurately portray a perspective rendering. Two such grids are displayed on pages 17 and 18 for your reference.

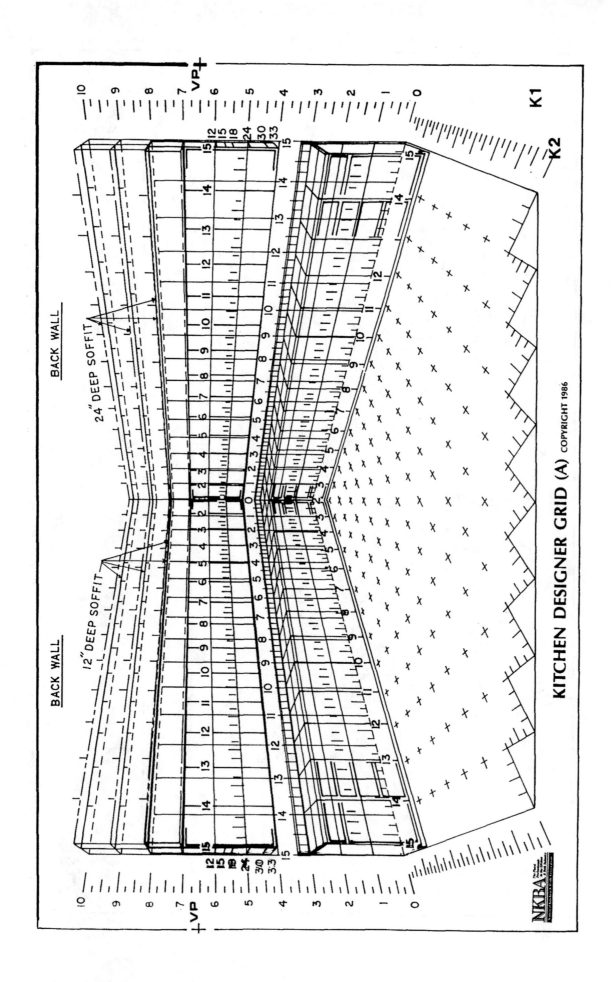

KITCHEN DESIGNER GRID (A) COPYRIGHT 1986

BACK WALL

BACK WALL

24" DEEP SOFFIT

12" DEEP SOFFIT

K1

K2

VP

VP

NKBA

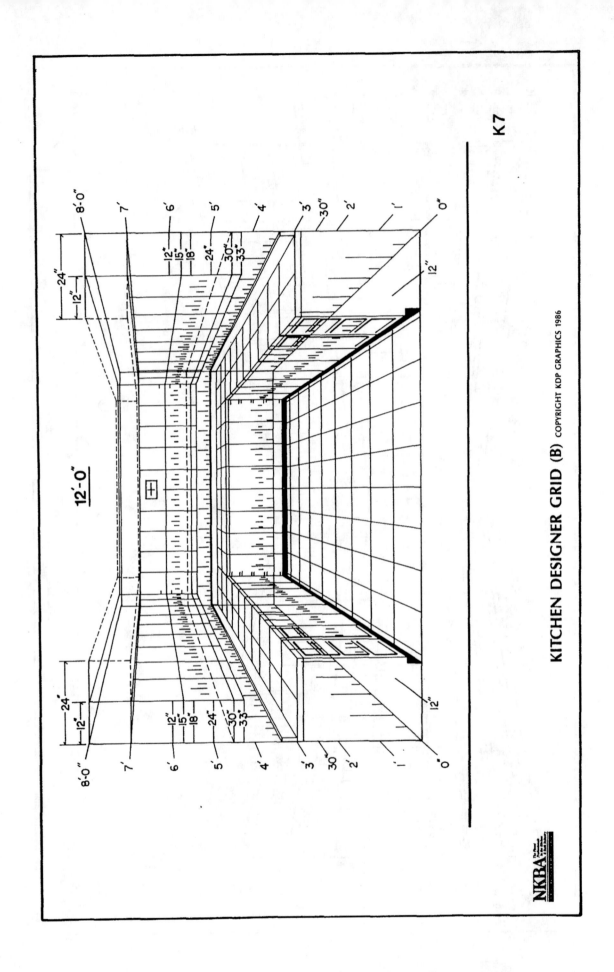

KITCHEN DESIGNER GRID (B) COPYRIGHT KDP GRAPHICS 1986

K7

Designers have the option of preparing a one-point or two-point perspective, with or without the use of a grid.

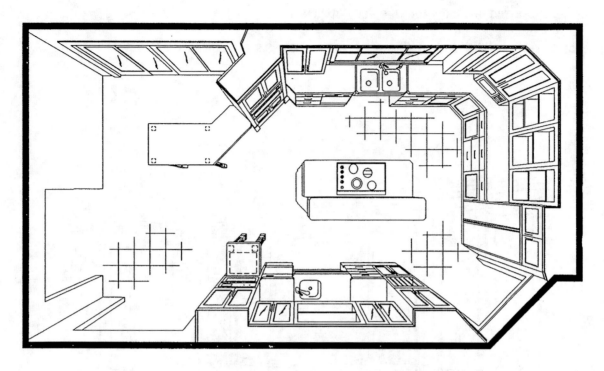

"Birds-Eye View" One Point Perspective

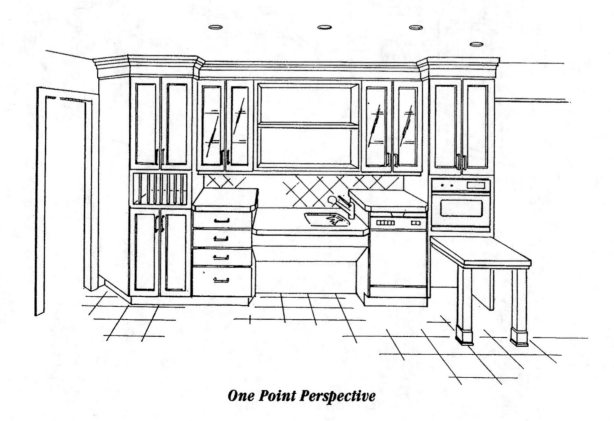

One Point Perspective

- The minimum requirement for perspectives shall be the reasonably correct representation of the longest cabinet or fixture run, or the most important area in terms of usage.

- Perspectives need not show the complete kitchen.

- Separate sectional views of significant areas or features are considered acceptable.

Two Point Perspective

Graphics and Presentation Standards for Kitchen Design

3) **Oblique, Dimetric, Isometric and Trimetric:** Several types of interpretive drawings can be used to illustrate special cabinets and equipment, such as countertops or special order cabinets, where mechanical representation and dimensions are important. These drawings give a simple way to illustrate an object in three-dimensional views.

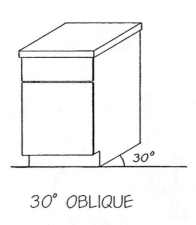

30° OBLIQUE

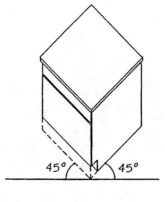

45° DIMETRIC

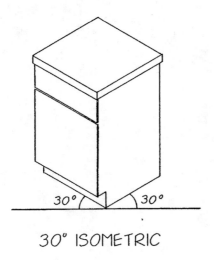

30° ISOMETRIC

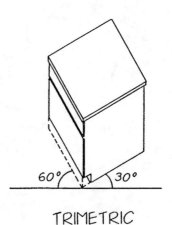

TRIMETRIC

4) **Sketches:** The use of sketches is a quick way to achieve a total picture of the kitchen without exact details in scaled dimensions. This quick freehand sketch can be studied, adjusted and sketched over, as the designer and client attempt to arrive at the most satisfactory layout for the kitchen. The quick sketch then can serve as a guide for drawing an exact plan of the kitchen.

Perspective Sketch

Graphics and Presentation Standards for Kitchen Design

VI. Sample Kitchen Project Drawings

The following set of sample project drawings have been prepared by a Certified Kitchen Designer under the direction of the **National Kitchen & Bath Association.** These sample drawings include:

- Floor Plan

- Construction Plan

- Mechanical Plan

- Countertop Plan *

- Soffit Plan *

- Elevations

- Perspectives

* It is recommended to prepare countertop and soffit plan drawings to further clarify project requirements.

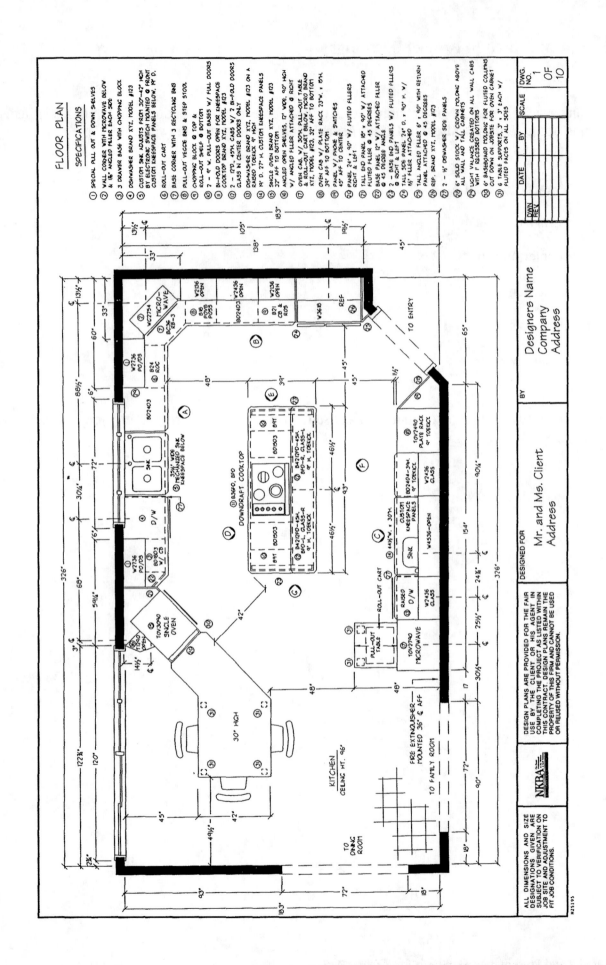

FLOOR PLAN

SPECIFICATIONS

1. SPECIAL PULL OUT & DOWN SHELVES
2. WALL CORNER WITH MICROWAVE BELOW & 16" ANGLED FILLER EACH SIDE
3. 3 DRAWER BASE WITH CHOPPING BLOCK
4. DISHWASHER BRAND XYZ, MODEL #123
5. CUSTOM SINK ADJUSTS FROM 30"-42" HIGH BY ELECTRONIC SWITCH MOUNTED @ FRONT CUSTOM KNEESPACE PANELS BELOW, M'D O.
6. ROLL-OUT CART
7. BASE CORNER WITH 3 RECYCLING BINS
8. PULL-OUT VEGGIE BINS & STEP STOOL
9. CHOPPING BLOCK @ TOP & ROLL-OUT SHELF @ BOTTOM
10. 2 - 4" W. PULL-OUT BASES W/ PULL DOORS
11. BI-FOLD DOORS OPEN FOR KNEESPACE COOKTOP BRAND XYZ, MODEL #123
12. 2 - 17"D, 45H. CABS W/ 2 BI-FOLD DOORS GLASS IN CENTER DOORS ONLY
13. DISHWASHER BRAND XYZ, MODEL #123 ON A RAISED TOEKICK 4" HIGH
14. M' O. 27" H. CUSTOM KNEESPACE PANELS
15. SINGLE OVEN BRAND XYZ, MODEL #123, 27" AFF TO BOTTOM
16. ANGLED OPEN SHELVES, 17" WIDE, 90" HIGH W/ ANGLED FILLER ATTACHED @ RIGHT
17. OVEN CAB. W/ 30"H. PULL-OUT TABLE & ROLL-OUT CART BELOW. MICRO BRAND XYZ, MODEL #123, 32" AFF TO BOTTOM
18. OPEN CAB W/ PLATE RACK 22"W. x 15"H. 39" AFF TO BOTTOM
19. PANEL W/ PHONE, SWITCHES 45" AFF TO CENTER
20. PANEL 24" x 90" W/ FLUTED FILLERS RIGHT & LEFT
21. TALL END PANEL 18" x 90" W/ ATTACHED FLUTED FILLER @ 45 DEGREES
22. BASE PANEL 12" W/ ATTACHED FILLER @ 45 DEGREE ANGLE
23. 2 - BASE-END PANELS W/ FLUTED FILLERS @ RIGHT & LEFT
24. TALL SIDE PANEL 24" D. x 90" H. W/ 16" FILLER ATTACHED
25. TALL ANGLED FILLER 6" x 90" WITH RETURN PANEL ATTACHED @ 45 DEGREES
26. REF. BRAND XYZ, MODEL #123
27. 2 - 14" DISHWASHER SIDE PANELS
28. 6" SOLID STOCK W/ CROWN MOLDING ABOVE ALL WALL AND TALL CABINETS
29. LIGHT VALANCE CREATED ON ALL WALL CABS WITH 1" RECESSED BOTTOMS
30. BASEBOARD MOLDING FOR FLUTED COLUMNS CUT DOWN ON JOBSITE FOR OVEN CABINET
31. 6 TABLE SUPPORTS, 3" x 3" EACH W/ FLUTED FACES ON ALL SIDES

DESIGNED FOR
Mr. and Ms. Client
Address

BY
Designers Name
Company
Address

DWN	DATE	BY	SCALE	DWG. NO.
REV				1 OF 10

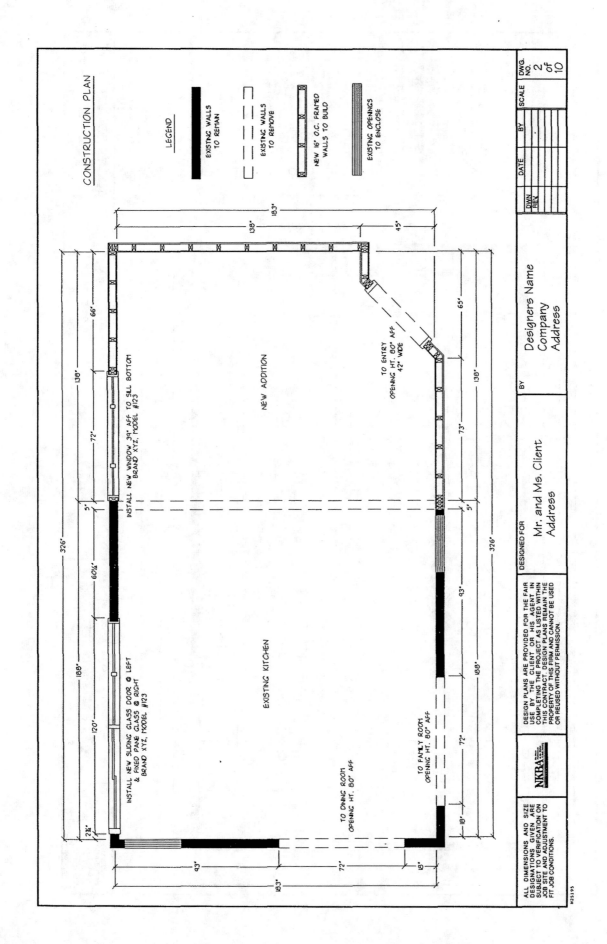

CONSTRUCTION PLAN

LEGEND

EXISTING WALLS TO REMAIN

EXISTING WALLS TO REMOVE

NEW 16" O.C. FRAMED WALLS TO BUILD

EXISTING OPENINGS TO ENCLOSE

NEW ADDITION

EXISTING KITCHEN

INSTALL NEW WINDOW 34" AFF TO SILL BOTTOM
BRAND XYZ, MODEL #123

INSTALL NEW SLIDING GLASS DOOR @ LEFT
& FIXED PANE GLASS @ RIGHT
BRAND XYZ, MODEL #123

TO ENTRY
OPENING HT. 80" AFF
42" WIDE

TO DINING ROOM
OPENING HT. 80" AFF

TO FAMILY ROOM
OPENING HT. 80" AFF

DESIGNED FOR
Mr. and Ms. Client
Address

BY
Designers Name
Company
Address

DESIGN PLANS ARE PROVIDED FOR THE FAIR
USE BY THE CLIENT OR HIS AGENT IN
COMPLETING THE PROJECT AS LISTED WITHIN
THIS CONTRACT. DESIGN PLANS REMAIN THE
PROPERTY OF THIS FIRM AND CANNOT BE USED
OR REUSED WITHOUT PERMISSION.

ALL DIMENSIONS AND SIZE
DESIGNATIONS GIVEN ARE
SUBJECT TO VERIFICATION ON
JOB SITE AND ADJUSTMENT TO
FIT JOB CONDITIONS.

NKBA

DWN
REV
DATE
BY
SCALE
DWG.
NO.
2
of
10

Graphics and Presentation Standards for Kitchen Design

25

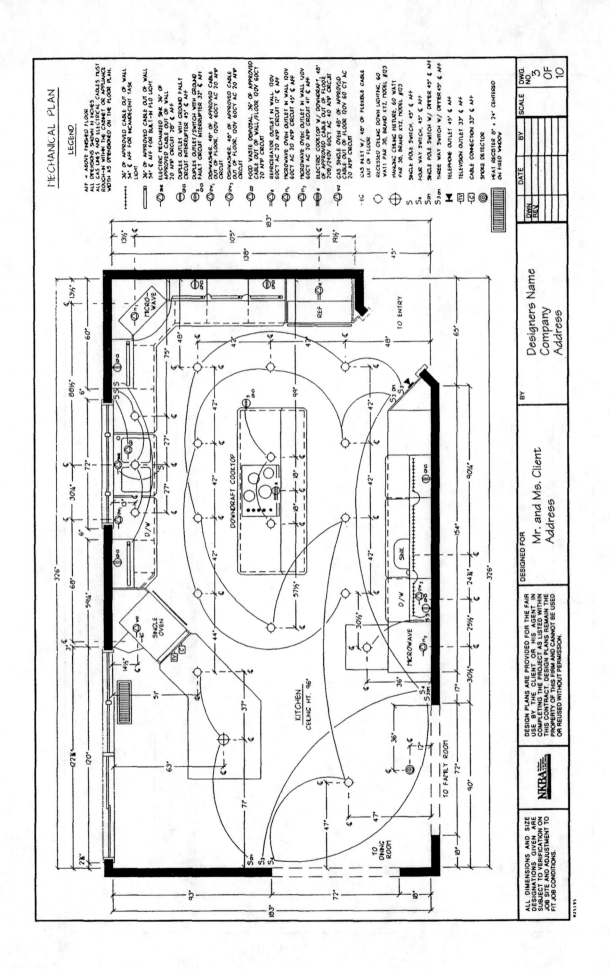

Graphics and Presentation Standards for Kitchen Design

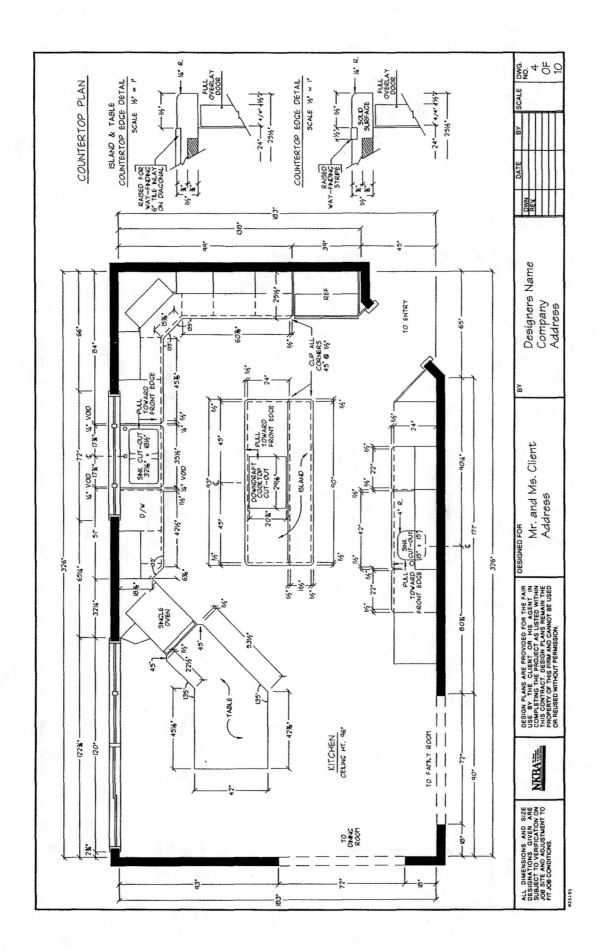

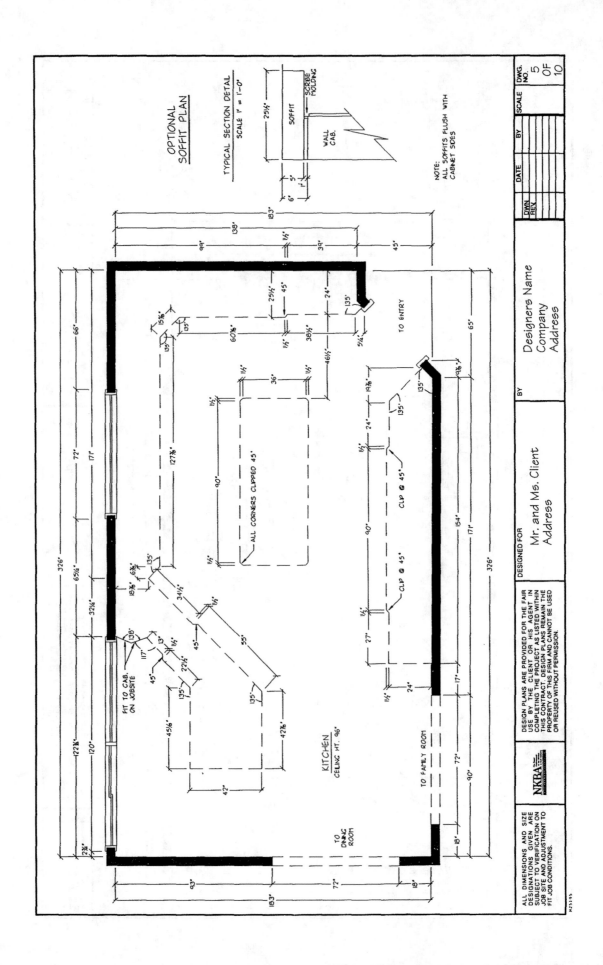

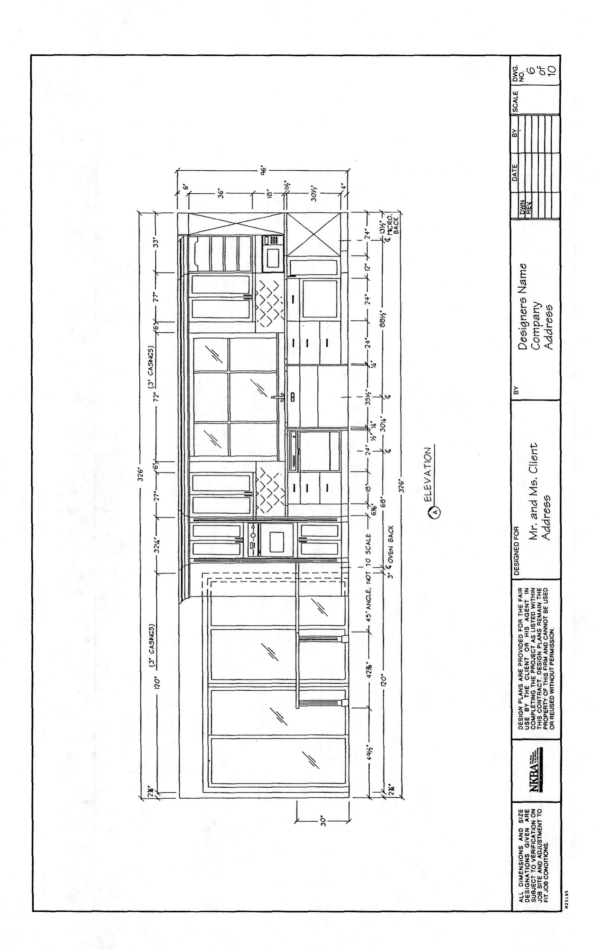

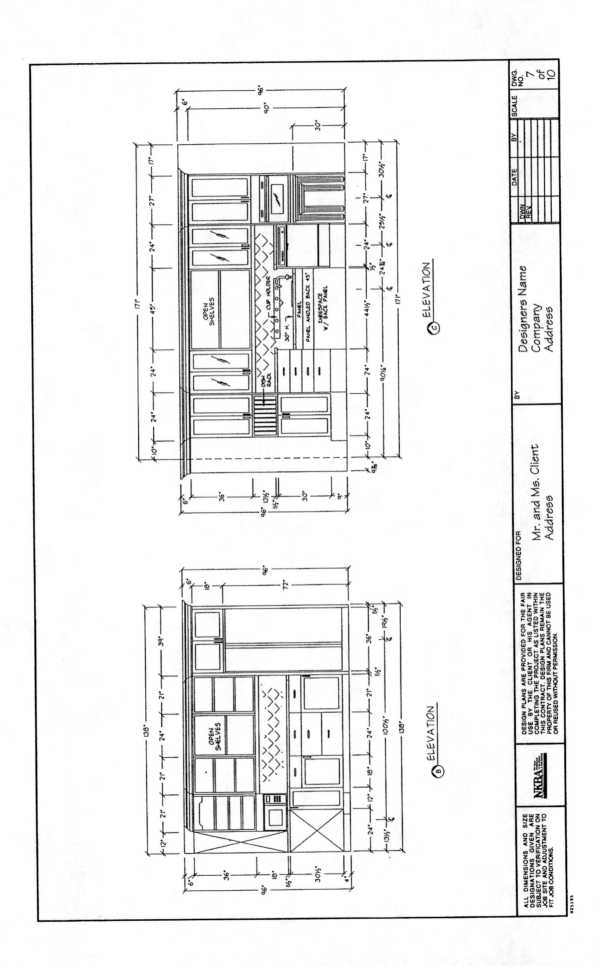

ELEVATION C

ELEVATION B

DESIGNED FOR

Mr. and Ms. Client
Address

BY

Designers Name
Company
Address

DWN
REV

DATE

BY

SCALE

DWG.
NO.
7
of
10

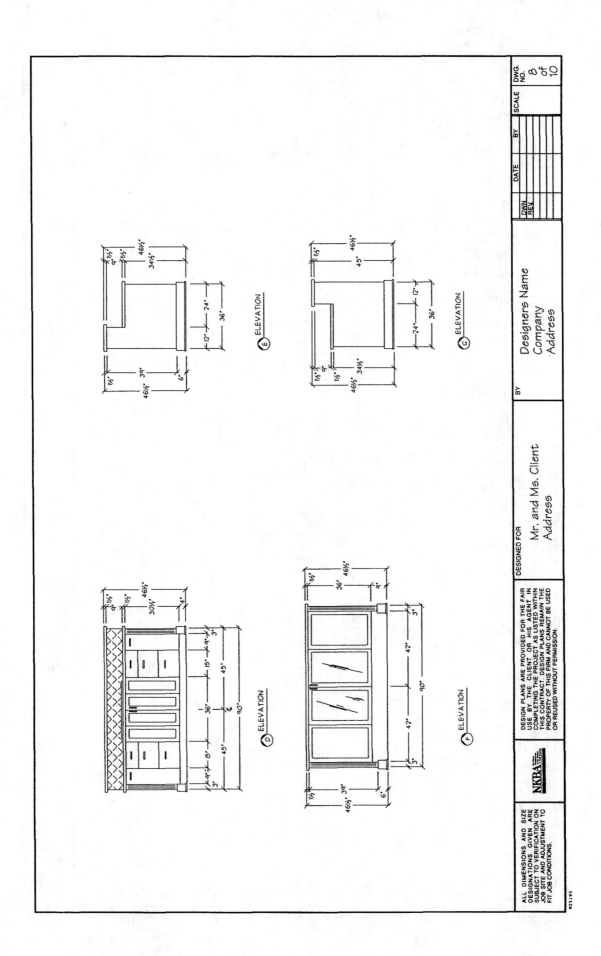

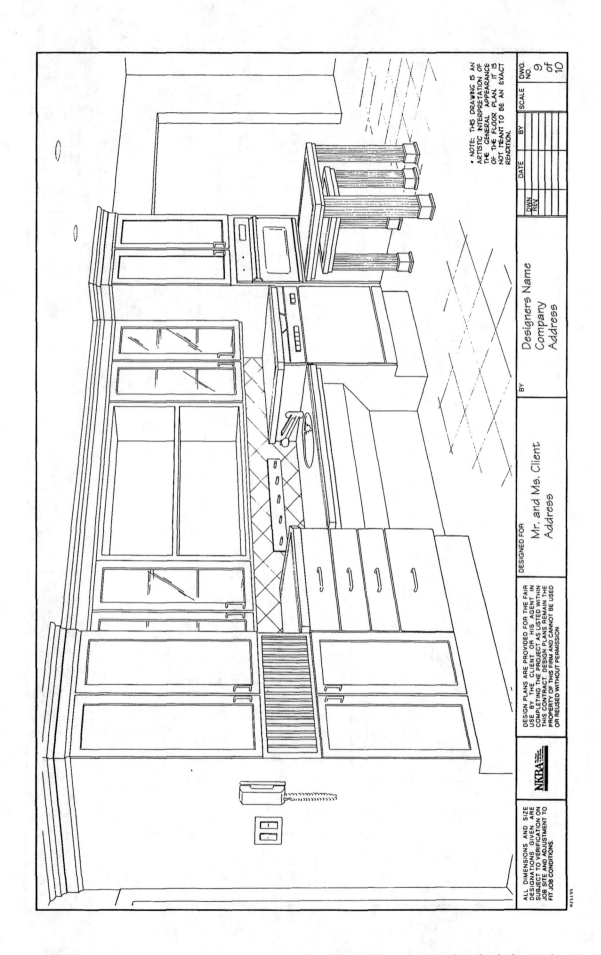

ALL DIMENSIONS AND SIZE DESIGNATIONS GIVEN ARE SUBJECT TO VERIFICATION ON JOB SITE AND ADJUSTMENT TO FIT JOB CONDITIONS.

DESIGN PLANS ARE PROVIDED FOR THE FAIR USE BY THE CLIENT OR HIS AGENT IN COMPLETING THE PROJECT AS LISTED WITHIN THIS CONTRACT. DESIGN PLANS REMAIN THE PROPERTY OF THIS FIRM AND CANNOT BE USED OR REUSED WITHOUT PERMISSION

DESIGNED FOR

Mr. and Ms. Client
Address

BY

Designer's Name
Company
Address

* NOTE: THIS DRAWING IS AN ARTISTIC INTERPRETATION OF THE GENERAL APPEARANCE OF THE FLOOR PLAN. IT IS NOT MEANT TO BE AN EXACT RENDITION.

DATE	SCALE	DWG. NO.
DWN REV		9 of 10

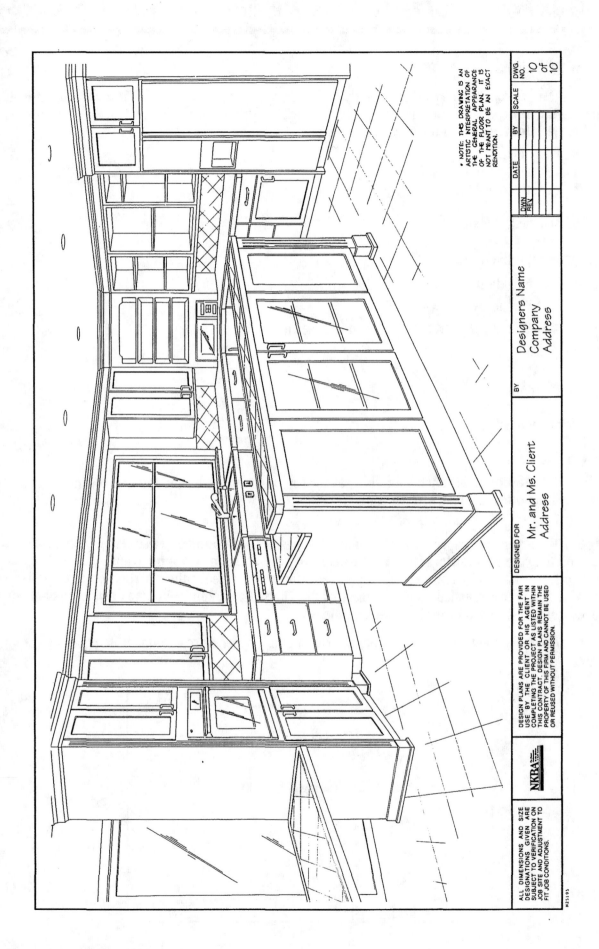

DWG. NO.	10 of 10
SCALE	
BY	
DATE	

DWN
REV

BY   Designers Name
          Company
          Address

DESIGNED FOR   Mr. and Ms. Client
                Address

NKBA

General Provisions Using Metric Dimensions

I. Use of Standards

The use of these *National Kitchen & Bath Association Graphics and Presentation Standards* is strongly recommended. They contain a specific set of criteria which when applied by the Kitchen Specialist produce a series of project documents that include the following:

- The Floor Plan

- The Construction Plan

- The Mechanical Plan

- The Interpretive Drawings

  1) Elevations
  2) Perspective Drawings
  3) Oblique, Dimetric, Isometric and Trimetric
  4) Sketches

- Specifications

- Design Statement

- Contracts

Two sample sets of project documents for your review can be found in this publication, one uses imperial dimensions and the other is a metric conversion..

Paper: The acceptable paper for the original drawings of the floor plan, construction plan, mechanical plan, and interpretive drawings is set at a **minimum size of 28cm x 43cm.** Translucent vellum tracing paper, imprinted with a black border and appropriate space available for the insertion of pertinent information is strongly recommended. Copies of original drawings should appear in blue or black ink only on white paper. Ozalid or photocopy prints are acceptable.

The use of lined yellow note paper, typing paper, scored graph paper or scored quadrille paper **is not acceptable.**

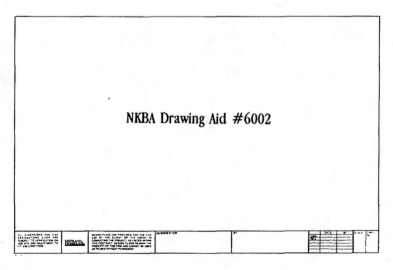

NKBA Drawing Aid #6002

II. The Floor Plan

1) **Size and Scope of Floor Plan Drawings:** Kitchen floor plans should be drawn to a scale of 1 to 20 (ie. 1cm = 20cm). When the designer has a room dimensioned in imperial inches and wants to use a metric based cabinet brand, the industry norm is to use a 1:24 metric ratio as equal to a 1/2 inch scale. *For imperial dimensions, see Use of Standards Using Imperial Dimensions beginning on page 3.*

- All base cabinetry should be depicted using a dashed line (- - - -) while countertops are depicted using a solid line.

- The floor plan should depict the entire room when possible. When the entire room cannot be depicted, it must show the area where cabinetry and appliances are permanently installed.

- Floor plans must show all major structural elements such as walls, door swings, door openings, partitions, windows, archways and equipment.

- When the entire room cannot be depicted, the room must be divided by *"break lines"* (⌁) and must show all major structural elements with adjoining areas indicated and labeled.

Finished interior dimensions are used on all project documents to denote available space for cabinetry and/or other types of equipment. If the kitchen specialist is responsible for specifying the exact method of wall construction, finish and/or partition placement, the specialist should include partition center lines on the construction plan, as well as the finished interior dimensions.

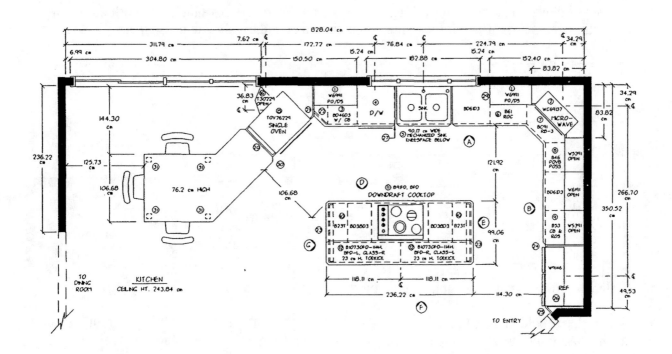

2) **Centerline (₵) dimensions:** must be given for equipment in two directions when possible.

- Mechanicals requiring centerlines include: cooktops, refrigerators, sinks, wall ovens, microwave ovens, fan units, light fixtures, heating and air conditioning ducts and radiators.

- Dimensions should be pulled from return walls or from the face of cabinets/equipment opposite the mechanical element.

- Centerlines on the mechanical plan will be indicated by the symbol (₵) followed by a **long-short-long broken line** that extends into the floor area.

- When the centerline dimension line is outside the floor area, it is typically shown as the second (and, if required, the third) line following the dimension line which identifies the individual wall segments.

3) **Dimensioning of Floor Plan:** When using metric dimensions, some designers also list all wall dimensions in inches. This double sizing helps all parties involved clearly understand the plans.

An example of Time Saving Formulas to convert between metrics would be as follows:

Inches to Centimeters, multiply the total number of inches by 2.54
Centimeters to Inches, multiply the total number of centimeters by .3937

NOTE:
- Each set of dimensions should be at least .5cm apart on separate dimension lines which are to intersect with witness lines. These intersecting points should be indicated by dimension arrows, dots, or slashes.

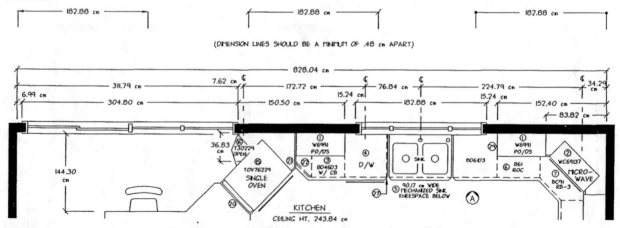

- All dimensions, whenever possible, should be shown **OUTSIDE** the wall lines.

- All lettering should be listed parallel to the title block at the bottom of the vellum paper and break the dimension line near its mid-point. This mechanical drafting technique eliminates errors in reading dimensions.

- An acceptable alternative is to draw all dimensions and lettering so that it is readable from the bottom edge or the right side of the plans with lettering on top of each dimension line.

The following dimensions **MUST** be shown on every floor plan as minimum requirements.

- Overall length of wall areas to receive cabinets, countertops, fixtures, or any equipment occupying floor and/or wall space. This dimension should always be the outside line.

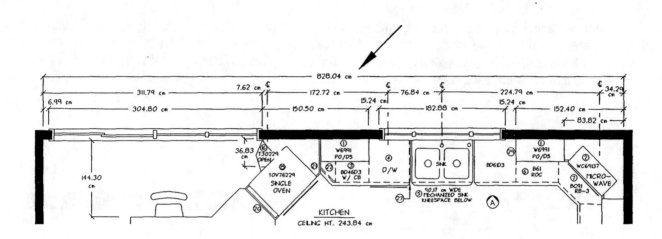

- Each wall opening, (windows, arches, doors and major appliances) and fixed structures (chimneys, wall protrusions and partitions) must be individually dimensioned. Dimensions are shown from outside trim. Trim size must be noted in the specification list. Fixtures such as radiators remaining in place must be outlined on the floor plan. these critical dimensions should be the first dimension line.

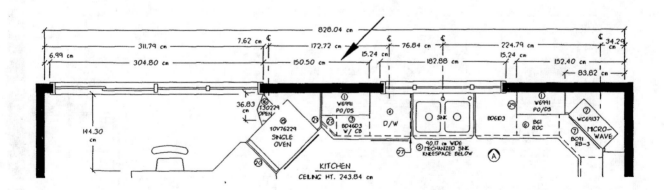

- Ceiling heights should appear on the floor plan. A separate plan for soffits is required when the soffit is a different depth than the wall or tall cabinet below. A separate soffit plan is recommended when the soffit is to be installed **PRIOR** to the wall or tall cabinet installation.

- Additional notes must be included for any deviation from standard height, width and depth. (cabinets, countertops, etc.)

- The exact opening must be given in height, width and depth for areas to be left open to receive cabinets and appliances at a future date.

- Items such as island and peninsula cabinets, must be shown with the overall dimensions given from countertop edge to opposite countertop edge, tall cabinet or wall. The exact location of the structure must be identified by dimensions which position it from two directions; from return walls or from the face of cabinets/equipment opposite the structure.

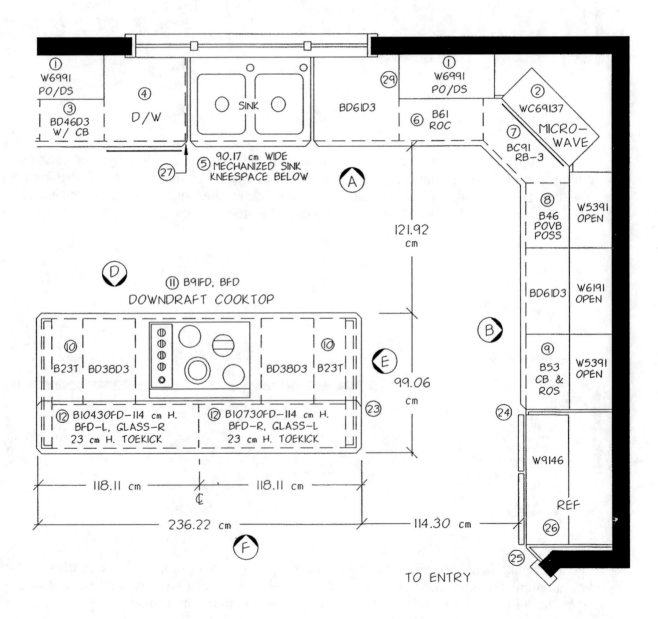

Graphics and Presentation Standards for Kitchen Design

4) Cabinets/Appliances and Equipment Nomenclature and Designation on Floor Plans:

- Cabinets should be designated and identified by manufacturer nomenclature inside the area indicating their position. Cabinet system trim and finish items are designated outside their area, with an arrow clarifying exactly where the trim piece is located.

- To insure clarity, some design firms prefer to number and call out all the cabinet nomenclature in the Floor Plan specification listing.

- Equally acceptable is the use of a circled reference number to designate each cabinet on the Floor Plan and Elevations with the cabinet code listed within the individual unit width on the elevations or in a separate cross-reference list on the elevations.

- **Regardless of which cabinet designation system is selected from above, additional information for supplementary fixtures/equipment and special provisions pertaining to the cabinets must be indicated within the cabinet or equipment area by a reference number in a circle. This additional information should then be registered in a cross-referenced specifications listing on the same sheet.**

FLOOR PLAN SPECIFICATIONS

① SPECIAL PULL OUT & DOWN SHELVES

② WALL CORNER WITH MICROWAVE BELOW & 3.49cm ANGLED FILLER EACH SIDE

⑥ ROLL-OUT CART

⑦ BASE CORNER WITH 3 RECYCLING BINS

⑧ PULL-OUT VEGGIE BINS & STEP STOOL

㉙ LIGHT VALANCE CREATED ON ALL WALL CABS. WITH 2.54 cm RECESSED BOTTOMS

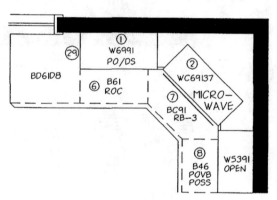

Special order materials or custom design features, angled cabinets, unusual tops, molding, trim details, etc., should be shown in a section view, (sometimes referred to as a *"cut view"*), a plan view in a scale larger than (1cm = 20cm), or in elevation view.

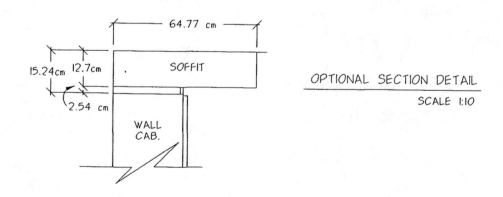

OPTIONAL SECTION DETAIL

SCALE 1:10

III. The Construction Plan

1) The purpose of the construction plan is to show the relationship of the existing space with that of the new design. The construction plan is detailed separately so that it does not clutter the floor plan. However, if construction changes are minimal it is acceptable to combine the construction plan with either the floor plan or mechanical plan.

2) **Construction Plan Symbols:**

- Existing walls are shown with solid lines or hollowed out lines at their full thickness.

- Wall sections to be removed are shown with an outline of broken lines.

- New walls show the material symbols applicable to the type of construction or use a symbol which is identified in the legend in order to distinguish them from existing partitions.

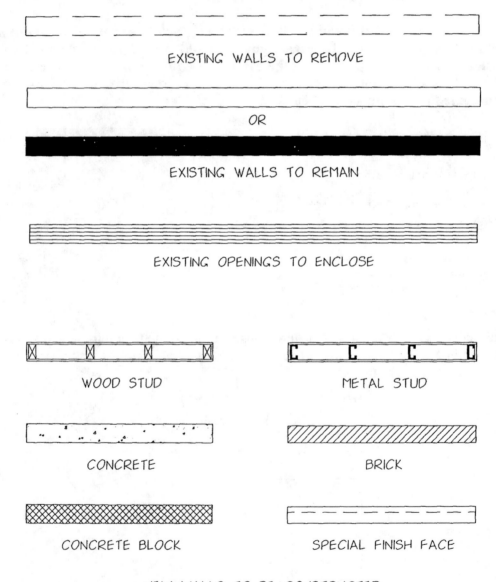

EXISTING WALLS TO REMOVE

OR

EXISTING WALLS TO REMAIN

EXISTING OPENINGS TO ENCLOSE

WOOD STUD · METAL STUD

CONCRETE · BRICK

CONCRETE BLOCK · SPECIAL FINISH FACE

NEW WALLS TO BE CONSTRUCTED

* Symbols taken from Architectural Graphic Standards, 9th Edition

An Example of a Construction Plan:

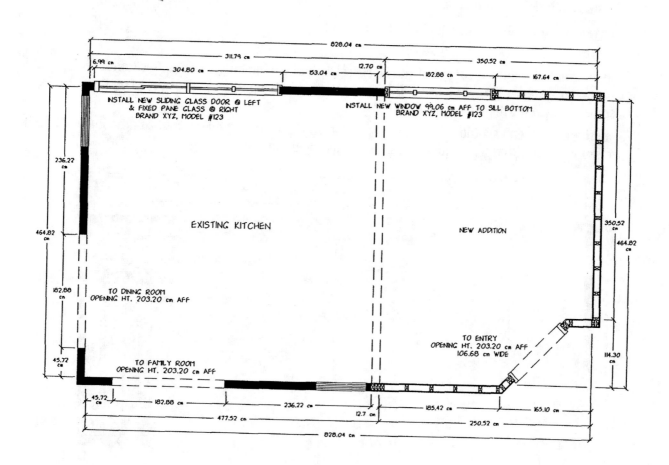

IV. The Mechanical Plan

- By detailing separate plans for the mechanicals and/or construction, it will help to clearly identify such work without cluttering the kitchen floor plan.

- The mechanical plan should show an outline of the cabinets, countertops and fixtures without nomenclature.

- The mechanicals should be placed in the proper location with the proper symbols.

- All overall room dimensions should be listed.

1) The mechanical plan will consist of the Electrical/Lighting, Plumbing, Heating, Air Conditioning and Ventilation systems. If any minor wall/door construction changes are part of the plan, they should also be detailed on the mechanical plan.

2) A mechanical legend should be prepared on the plan. This legend will be used to describe what each symbol for special purpose outlets, fixtures or equipment means.

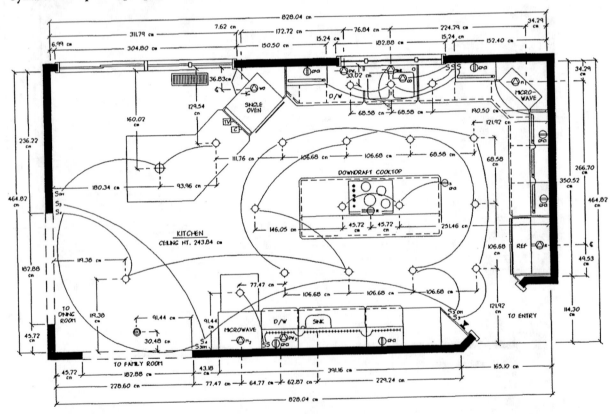

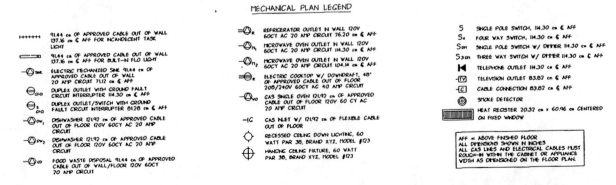

MECHANICAL PLAN LEGEND

Graphics and Presentation Standards for Kitchen Design

3) Centerline (℄) dimensions must be given for all equipment in two directions when possible.

- Mechanicals requiring centerlines include: cooktops, refrigerators, dishwashers, compactors, sinks, wall ovens, microwave ovens, fan units, light fixtures, heating and air conditioning ducts and radiators.

- Centerline dimensions should be pulled from return walls or from the face of cabinets/equipment opposite the mechanical element.

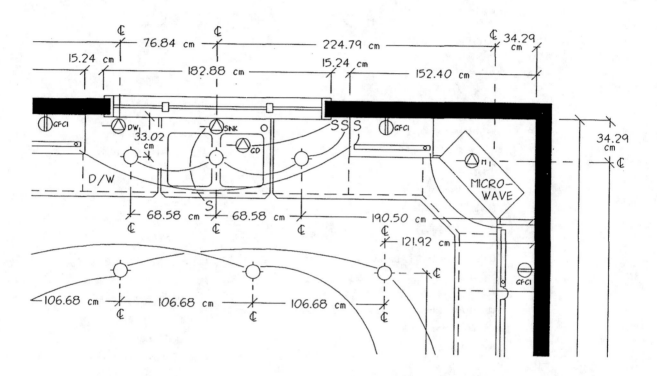

Centerlines on the mechanical plan will be indicated by the symbol (℄) followed by a **long-short-long broken line** that extends into the floor area.

4) Mechanical Plan Symbols:

S	SINGLE POLE SWITCH
S_2	DOUBLE POLE SWITCH
S_3	THREE WAY SWITCH
S_4	FOUR WAY SWITCH
S_{DM}	SINGLE-POLE SWITCH w/ DIMMER
S_{3DM}	THREE WAY SWITCH w/ DIMMER
S_{LM}	MASTER SWITCH FOR LOW VOLTAGE SWITCHING SYSTEM
S_L	SWITCH FOR LOW VOLTAGE SWITCHING SYSTEM
S_{WP}	WEATHERPROOF SWITCH
S_{RC}	REMOTE CONTROL SWITCH
S_D	AUTOMATIC DOOR SWITCH
S_P	SWITCH AND PILOT LAMP
S_K	KEY OPERATED SWITCH
S_F	FUSED SWITCH
S_T	TIME SWITCH
(S)	CEILING PULL SWITCH
	DUPLEX OUTLET
GFCI	DUPLEX OUTLET WITH GROUND FAULT CIRCUIT INTERRUPTER
S	SWITCH AND SINGLE RECEPTACLE OUTLET
S	SWITCH AND DUPLEX OUTLET
(B)	BLANKED OUTLET
(J)	JUNCTION BOX
(L)	OUTLET CONTROLLED BY LOW VOLTAGE SWITCHING WHEN RELAY IS INSTALLED IN OUTLET BOX
	SINGLE RECEPTACLE OULET
	TRIPLEX RECEPTACLE OULET
	QUADRUPLEX RECEPTACLE OULET
	DUPLEX RECEPTACLE OUTLET–SPLIT WIRED
	TRIPLEX RECEPTACLE OUTLET–SPLIT WIRED
(C)	CLOCK HANGER RECEPTACLE
(F)	FAN HANGER RECEPTACLE
	INTERCOM
	TELEPHONE OUTLET
(T)	THERMOSTAT
	SMOKE DETECTOR

TV	TELEVISION OUTLET
C	CABLE OUTLET
T_L	LOW VOLTAGE TRANSFORMER
	HANGING CEILING FIXTURE
	HEAT LAMP
	HEAT/LIGHT UNIT
	HEAT/FAN LIGHT UNIT
	RECESSED CEILING DOWN LIGHTING
	RECESSED CEILING VAPOR LIGHT
	BUILT–IN LOW VOLTAGE TASK LIGHT
	BUILT–IN FLUORESCENT LIGHT
	CONTINUOUS ROW FLUORESCENT LIGHTS
	SURFACE MOUNTED FLUORESCENT LIGHT
	WALL SCONCE
$_{DW}$	DISHWASHER
$_{GD}$	FOOD WASTE DISPOSAL
$_{TC}$	TRASH COMPACTOR
$_R$	REFRIGERATOR OUTLET
$_H$	HOOD
$_M$	MICROWAVE OVEN
$_R$	ELECTRIC RANGE/COOKTOP
$_{WO}$	ELECTRIC SINGLE/DOUBLE OVEN
$_G$	GAS SUPPLY
$_{CT}$	GAS COOKTOP
$_{WO}$	GAS SINGLE/DOUBLE OVEN
$_{CW}$	CLOTHES WASHER
$_{CD}$	CLOTHES DRYER
$_{SA}$	SAUNA
$_{ST}$	STEAM
$_{WP}$	WHIRLPOOL
$_{TW}$	TOWEL WARMER
	HEAT REGISTER

ANY STANDARD SYMBOL GIVEN ABOVE W/ THE ADDITION OF LOWERCASE SUBSCRIPT LETTERING MAY BE USED TO DESIGNATE A VARIATION OF STANDARD EQUIPMENT.

WHEN USED THEY MUST BE LISTED IN THE LEGEND OF THE MECHANICAL PLAN.

Symbols taken from Architectural Graphic Standards, 9th Edition

V. Interpretive Drawings

Elevations and perspective renderings are considered interpretive drawings and are used as an explanatory means of understanding the floor plans.

- Under no circumstances should the interpretive drawings be used as a substitute for floor plans.

- In cases of dispute, the floor plans are the legally binding document.

- Because perspective drawings are not dimensioned to scale, many Kitchen Specialists include a disclaimer on their rendering such as this:

> This drawing is an artistic interpretation of the general appearance of the floor plan. It is not meant to be an exact rendition.

1) **Elevation:** Elevations must show a front view of all wall areas receiving cabinets/equipment as shown on the floor plan.

Elevations should dimension all cabinets, counters, fixtures and equipment in the elevation as follows:

- Cabinets with toekick and finished height.

- A portion of the cabinet doors and drawer front should indicate style and, when applicable, placement of handles/pulls.

- Countertops indicate thickness and show back-splash

- All doors, windows or other openings in walls which will receive equipment. The window/door casing or trim will be listed within the overall opening dimensions.

- All permanent fixtures such as radiators, etc.

- All main structural elements and protrusions such as chimneys, partitions, etc.

- Centerlines for all mechanical equipment.

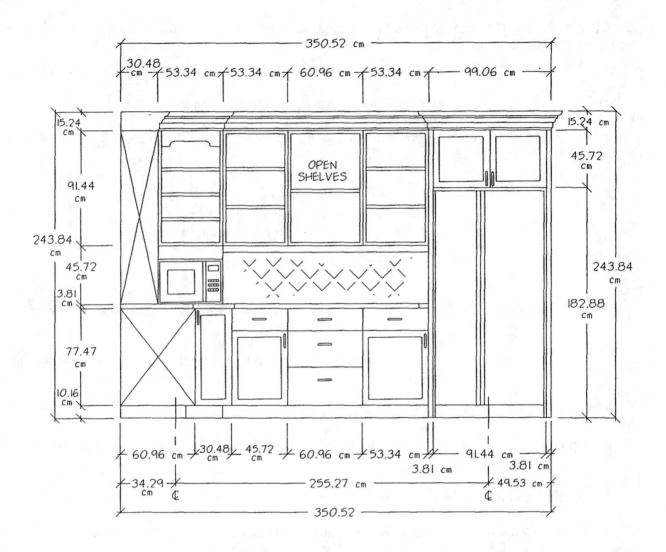

350.52 cm

30.48 cm / 53.34 cm / 53.34 cm / 60.96 cm / 53.34 cm / 99.06 cm

15.24 cm   15.24 cm

OPEN
SHELVES

45.72 cm

91.44 cm

243.84 cm

45.72 cm

243.84 cm

3.81 cm

182.88 cm

77.47 cm

10.16 cm

60.96 cm / 30.48 cm / 45.72 cm / 60.96 cm / 53.34 cm / 91.44 cm

3.81 cm   3.81 cm

34.29 cm   255.27 cm   49.53 cm

350.52

B ELEVATION

NOTE:
DIMENSIONS MUST ACCURATELY
REPRESENT PRODUCTS USED.

2) **Perspective Drawings:** Perspectives are **not drawn to scale.** Grids, which are available through the **National Kitchen & Bath Association,** can be used as an underlay for tracing paper to accurately portray a perspective rendering. Two such grids are displayed on pages 48 and 49 for your reference.

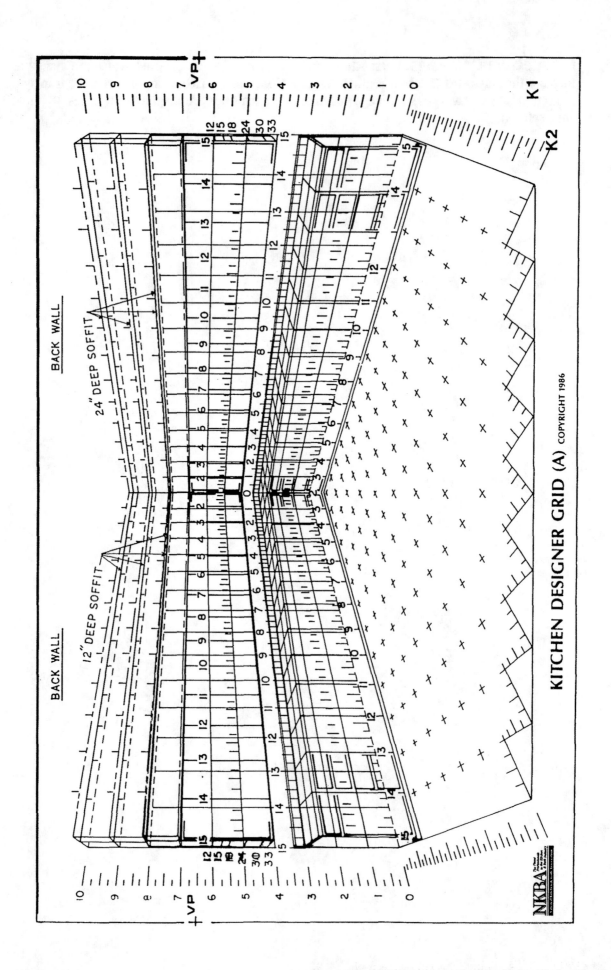

KITCHEN DESIGNER GRID (A) COPYRIGHT 1986

BACK WALL

BACK WALL

24" DEEP SOFFIT

12" DEEP SOFFIT

K1

K2

VP

VP

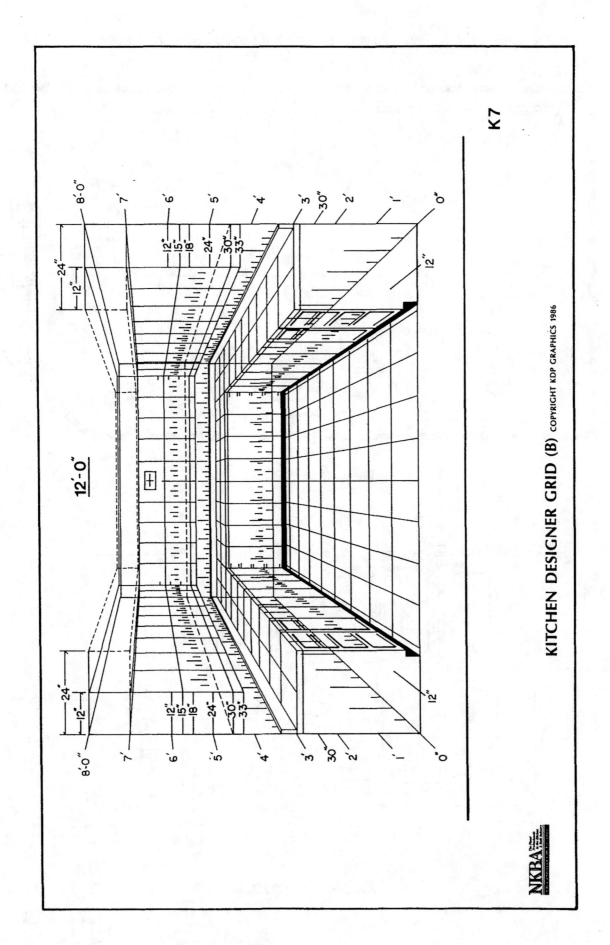

KITCHEN DESIGNER GRID (B) COPYRIGHT KDP GRAPHICS 1986

K7

Graphics and Presentation Standards for Kitchen Design

49

Designers have the option of preparing a one-point or two-point perspective, with or without the use of a grid.

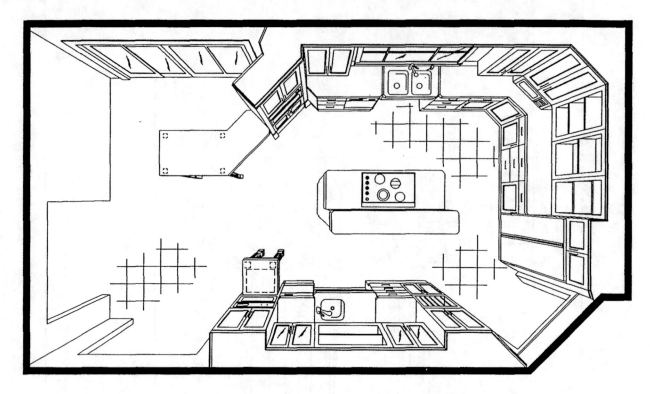

"Birds-Eye View" One Point Perspective

One Point Perspective

Graphics and Presentation Standards for Kitchen Design

- The minimum requirement for perspectives shall be the reasonably correct representation of the longest cabinet or fixture run, or the most important area in terms of usage.

- Perspectives need not show the complete kitchen.

- Separate sectional views of significant areas or features are considered acceptable.

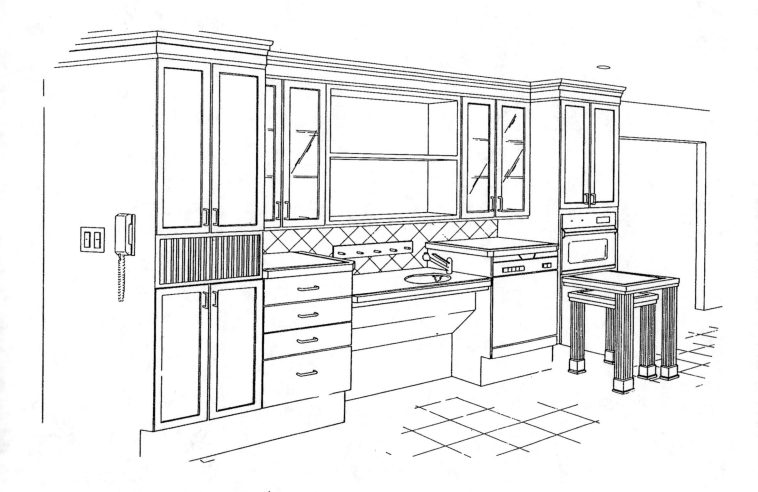

Two Point Perspective

3) **Oblique, Dimetric, Isometric and Trimetric:** Several types of interpretive drawings can be used to illustrate special cabinets and equipment, such as countertops or special order cabinets, where mechanical representation and dimensions are important. These drawings give a simple way to illustrate an object in three-dimensional views.

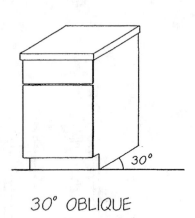

30° OBLIQUE

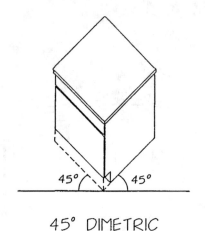

45° DIMETRIC

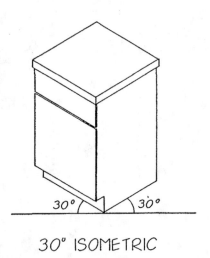

30° ISOMETRIC

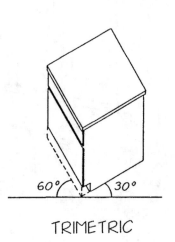

TRIMETRIC

4) **Sketches:** The use of sketches is a quick way to achieve a total picture of the kitchen without exact details in scaled dimensions. This quick freehand sketch can be studied, adjusted and sketched over, as the designer and client attempt to arrive at the most satisfactory layout for the kitchen. The quick sketch then can serve as a guide for drawing an exact plan of the kitchen.

Perspective Sketch

VI. Sample Kitchen Project Drawings

The following set of sample project drawings have been prepared by a Certified Kitchen Designer under the direction of the **National Kitchen & Bath Association.** These sample drawings include:

- Floor Plan

- Construction Plan

- Mechanical Plan

- Countertop Plan *

- Soffit Plan *

- Elevations

- Perspectives

* It is recommended to prepare countertop and soffit plan drawings to further clarify project requirements.

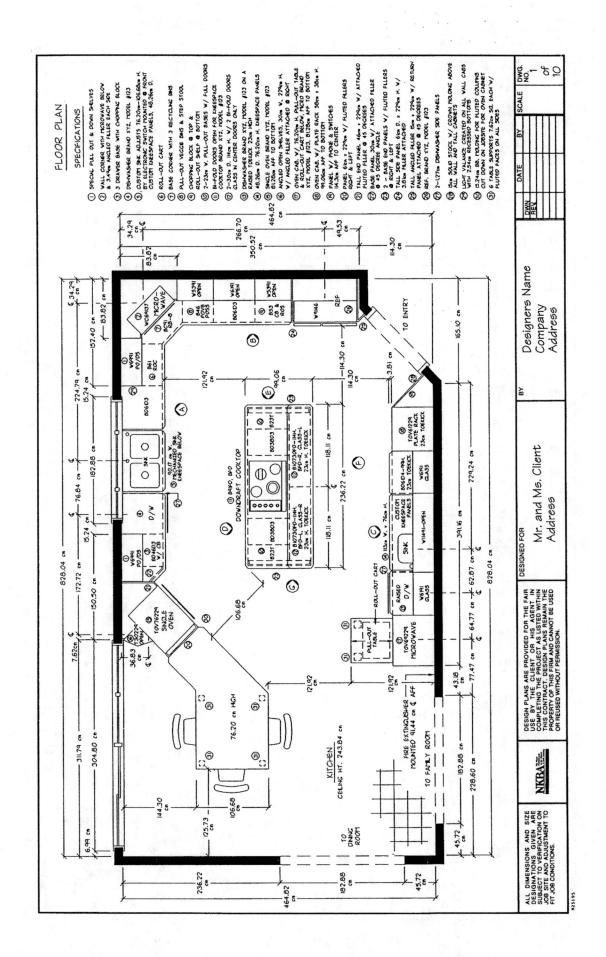

FLOOR PLAN

SPECIFICATIONS

1. SPECIAL PULL OUT & DOWN SHELVES
2. WALL CORNER WITH MICROWAVE BELOW & 3.14cm ANGLED FILLER EACH SIDE
3. 3 DRAWER BASE WITH CHOPPING BLOCK
4. DISHWASHER BRAND XYZ, MODEL #123
5. CUSTOM SNK ADJUSTS 76.20cm-106.68cm H. BY ELECTRONIC SWITCH MOUNTED @ FRONT CUSTOM KNEESPACE PANELS, 43.26cm D.
6. ROLL-OUT CART
7. BASE CORNER WITH 3 RECYCLING BINS
8. PULL-OUT VEGGIE BINS & STEP STOOL
9. CHOPPING BLOCK @ TOP & ROLL-OUT SHELF @ BOTTOM
10. 2-23cm W. PULL-OUT BASES W/ FULL DOORS
11. BI-FOLD DOORS OPEN FOR KNEESPACE COOKTOP BRAND XYZ, MODEL #123
12. 2-30cm D. IH96 H. W/ 2 BI-FOLD DOORS GLASS N CENTER DOORS ONLY
13. DISHWASHER BRAND XYZ, MODEL #123 ON A RAISED TOEKICK 23cm HIGH
14. 48.26cm D. 76.20cm H. KNEESPACE PANELS
15. SINGLE OVEN BRAND XYZ, MODEL #123 81.28cm AFF TO BOTTOM
16. ANGLED OPEN SHELVES, 30cm V., 27cm H. V/ ANGLED FILLER ATTACHED @ RGHT
17. OVEN CAB. W/ 76.20cm H. PULL-OUT TABLE & ROLL-OUT CART BELOW, MICRO BRAND XYZ, MODEL #123, 81.28cm AFF TO BOTTOM
18. OVEN CAB. W/ PLATE RACK 55cm × 30cm H. 90.06cm AFF TO BOTTOM
19. PANEL W/ PHONE & SWITCHES 114.30cm AFF TO CENTER
20. PANEL 61cm × 229cm W/ FLUTED FILLERS
21. TALL END PANEL 46cm × 229cm W/ ATTACHED FLUTED FILLER @ 45 DEGREES
22. BASE PANEL 30cm W/ ATTACHED FILLER @ 45 DEGREE ANGLE
23. 2 — BASE END PANELS W/ FLUTED FILLERS @ RIGHT & LEFT
24. TALL SIDE PANEL 61cm D. × 229cm H. W/ 3.81cm FILLER ATTACHED
25. TALL ANGLED FILLER 55cm × 229cm W/ RETURN PANEL ATTACHED @ 45 DEGREES
26. REF. BRAND XYZ, MODEL #123
27. 7—177cm DISHWASHER SIDE PANELS
28. 15cm SOLID STOCK W/ CROWN MOLDING ABOVE ON ALL TALL CABINETS
29. LIGHT VALANCE CREATED ON ALL WALL CABS WITH 2.54cm RECESSED BOTTOMS
30. 15.24cm BB. MOLDING FOR FLUTED COLUMNS CUT DOWN ON JOBSITE FOR OVEN CABINET
31. 6 TABLE SUPPORTS 7.62cm SQ. EACH W/ FLUTED FACES ON ALL SIDES

KITCHEN
CEILING HT. 243.84 cm

76.20 cm HIGH

DOWNDRAFT COOKTOP

SINGLE OVEN

ROLL-OUT CART

MICROWAVE

PULL-OUT TABLE

FIRE EXTINGUISHER
MOUNTED 91.44 cm @ ¢ AFF

TO FAMILY ROOM

TO ENTRY

REF

TO DINING ROOM

ALL DIMENSIONS AND SIZE DESIGNATIONS GIVEN ARE SUBJECT TO VERIFICATION ON JOB SITE AND ADJUSTMENT TO FIT JOB CONDITIONS.

DESIGNED FOR
Mr. and Ms. Client
Address

BY

Designers Name
Company
Address

	BY	DATE	SCALE	DWG. NO.
DWN				1
REV				of 10

M25195

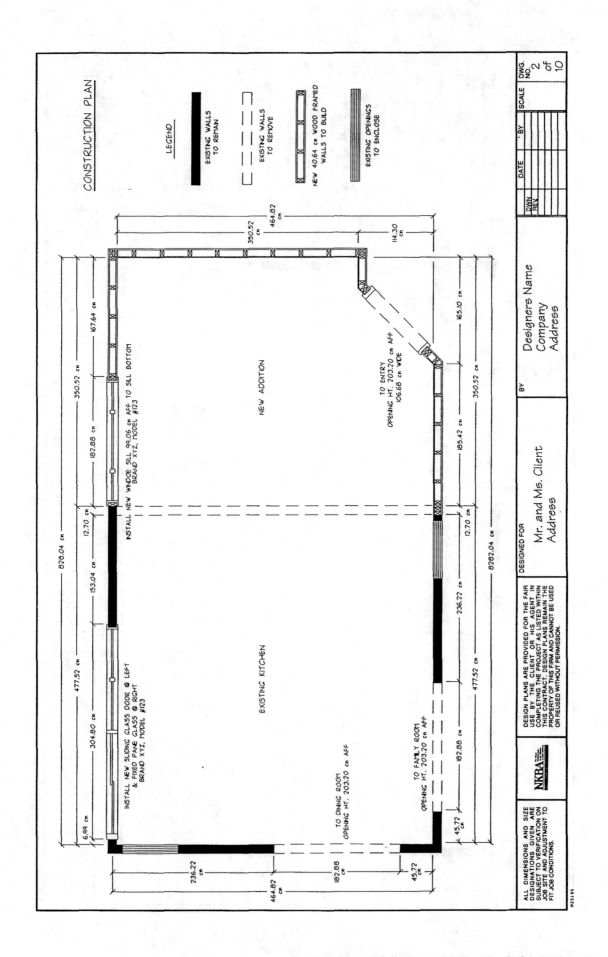

CONSTRUCTION PLAN

LEGEND

EXISTING WALLS TO REMAIN

EXISTING WALLS TO REMOVE

NEW 40.64 cm WOOD FRAMED WALLS TO BUILD

EXISTING OPENINGS TO ENCLOSE

NEW ADDITION

EXISTING KITCHEN

INSTALL NEW WINDOW SILL 99.06 cm AFF TO SILL BOTTOM
BRAND XYZ, MODEL #123

INSTALL NEW SLIDING GLASS DOOR @ LEFT
& FIXED PANE GLASS @ RIGHT
BRAND XYZ, MODEL #123

TO DINING ROOM
OPENING HT. 203.20 cm AFF

TO FAMILY ROOM
OPENING HT. 203.20 cm AFF

TO ENTRY
OPENING HT. 203.20 cm AFF
106.68 cm WIDE

464.82 cm
350.52 cm
114.30
165.10 cm
167.64 cm
350.52 cm
182.88 cm
12.70 cm
153.04 cm
828.04 cm
477.52 cm
304.80 cm
6.99 cm
185.42 cm
12.70 cm
350.52 cm
236.22 cm
182.88 cm
45.72 cm
464.82 cm
236.22 cm
477.52 cm
828.04 cm

NKBA

ALL DIMENSIONS AND SIZE DESIGNATIONS GIVEN ARE SUBJECT TO VERIFICATION ON JOB SITE AND ADJUSTMENT TO FIT JOB CONDITIONS.

DESIGN PLANS ARE PROVIDED FOR THE FAIR USE BY THE CLIENT OR HIS AGENT IN COMPLETING THE PROJECT AS LISTED WITHIN THIS CONTRACT. DESIGN PLANS REMAIN THE PROPERTY OF THIS FIRM AND CANNOT BE USED OR REUSED WITHOUT PERMISSION.

DESIGNED FOR

Mr. and Ms. Client
Address

BY

Designers Name
Company
Address

| DWN | DATE | BY | SCALE | DWG. NO. 2 |
| REV | | | | of 10 |

N25195

Graphics and Presentation Standards for Kitchen Design

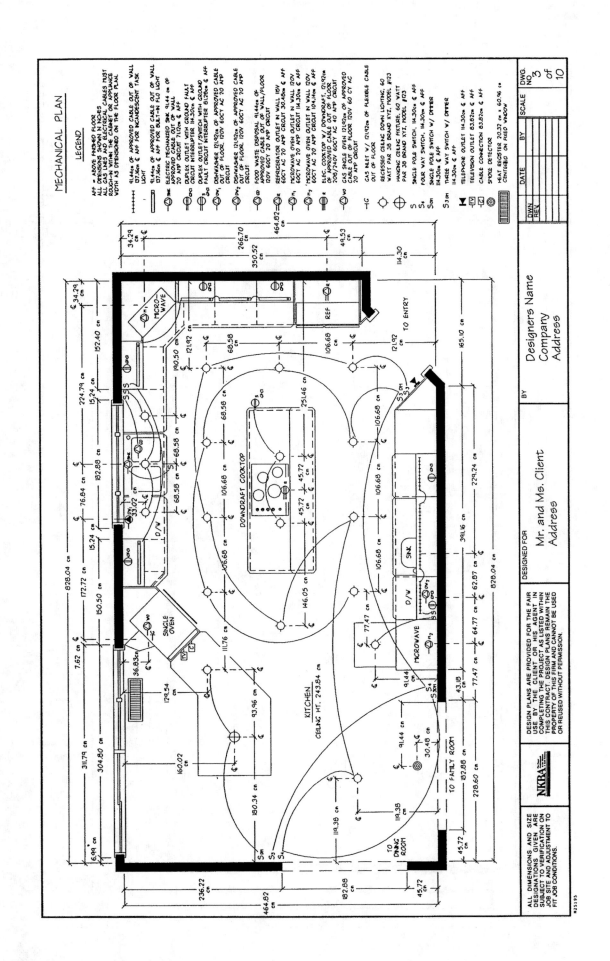

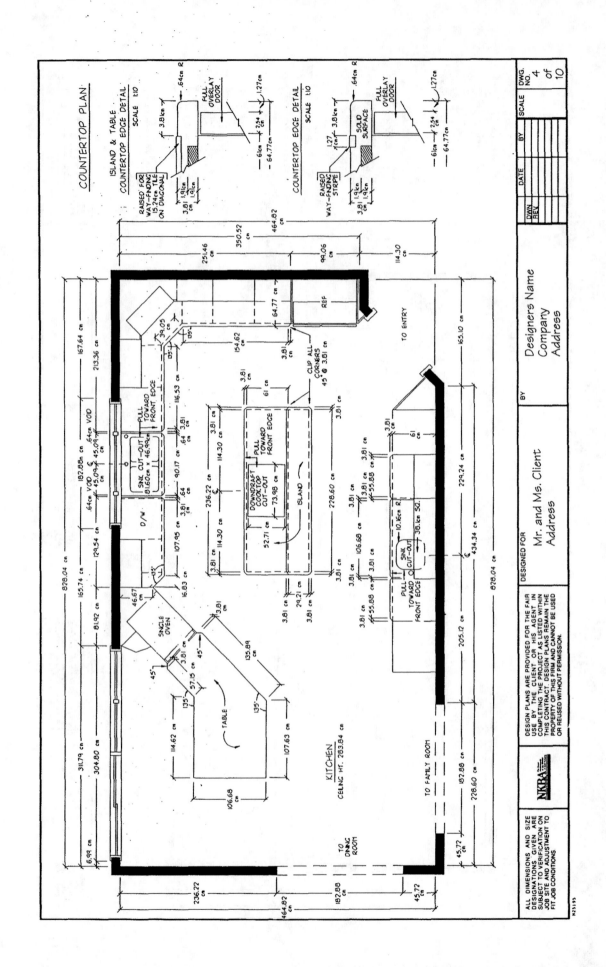

COUNTERTOP PLAN

ISLAND & TABLE
COUNTERTOP EDGE DETAIL
SCALE 1:10

COUNTERTOP EDGE DETAIL
SCALE 1:10

Graphics and Presentation Standards for Kitchen Design

DWG. NO. 4 of 10

Designers Name
Company
Address

DESIGNED FOR
Mr. and Ms. Client
Address

DESIGN PLANS ARE PROVIDED FOR THE FAIR USE BY THE CLIENT OR HIS AGENT IN COMPLETING THE PROJECT AS LISTED WITHIN THIS CONTRACT. DESIGN PLANS REMAIN THE PROPERTY OF THIS FIRM AND CANNOT BE USED OR REUSED WITHOUT PERMISSION.

ALL DIMENSIONS AND SIZE DESIGNATIONS GIVEN ARE SUBJECT TO VERIFICATION ON JOB SITE AND ADJUSTMENT TO FIT JOB CONDITIONS.

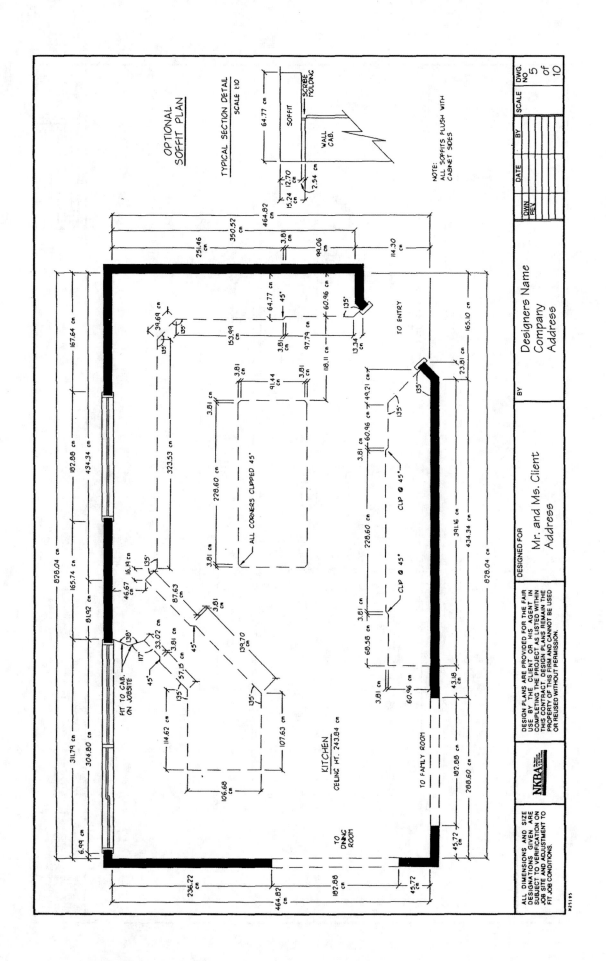

OPTIONAL SOFFIT PLAN

TYPICAL SECTION DETAIL
SCALE 1:10

SOFFIT

SCRIBE MOLDING

WALL CAB.

NOTE:
ALL SOFFITS FLUSH WITH CABINET SIDES

KITCHEN
CEILING HT. 243.84 cm

ALL CORNERS CLIPPED 45°

FIT TO CAB. ON JOBSITE

CLIP @ 45°

CLP @ 45°

TO ENTRY

TO FAMILY ROOM

TO DINING ROOM

DESIGNED FOR
Mr. and Ms. Client
Address

Designers Name
Company
Address

BY

NKBA

DWN
REV

DATE   BY   SCALE   DWG. NO

5 of 10

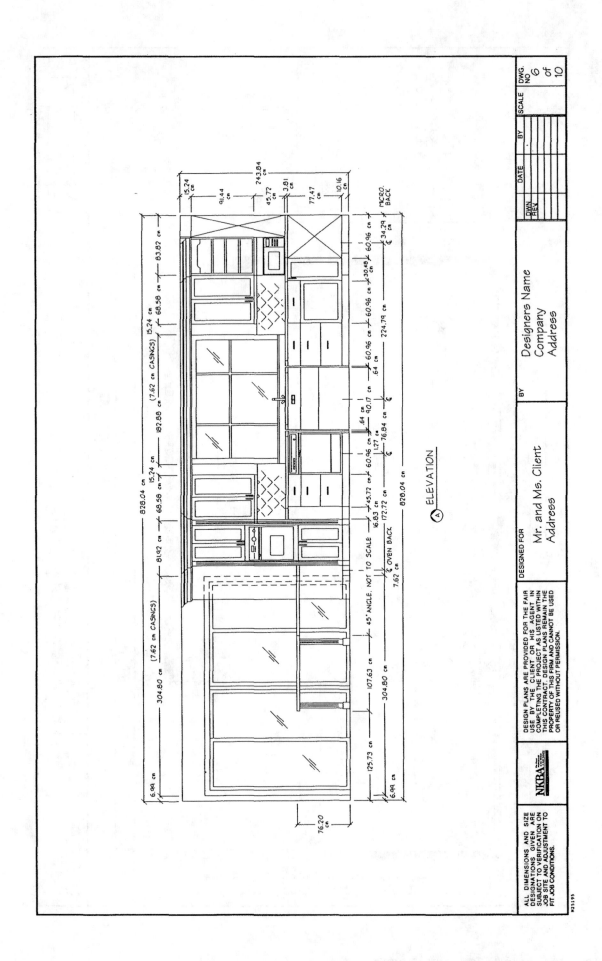

Graphics and Presentation Standards for Kitchen Design

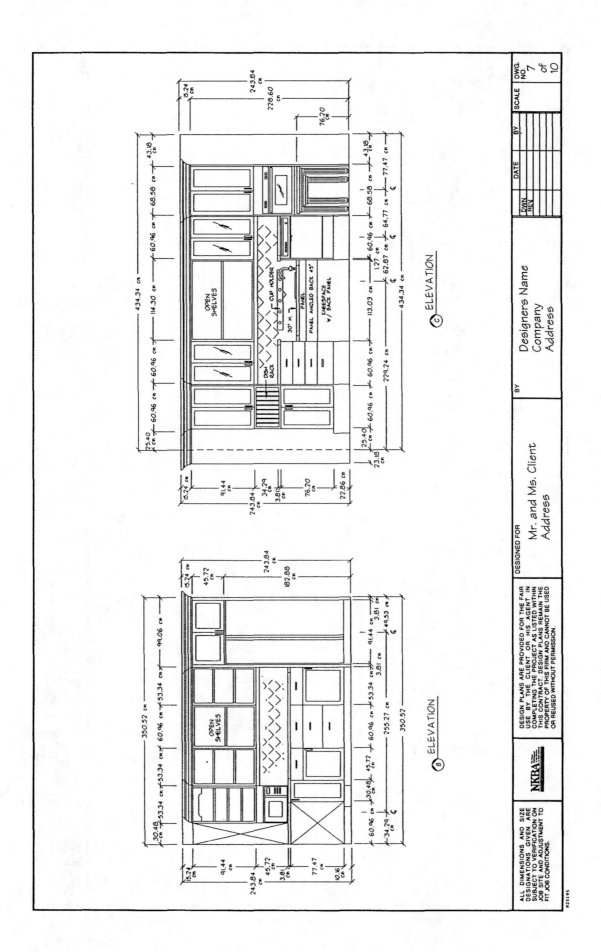

ELEVATION (C)

OPEN SHELVES

CUP HOLDER

30" H.

PANEL

PANEL ANGLED BACK 45°

KNEESPACE w/ BACK PANEL

DISH RACK

ELEVATION (B)

OPEN SHELVES

NKBA

DESIGNED FOR

Mr. and Ms. Client
Address

BY

Designers Name
Company
Address

DATE | BY | SCALE | DWG. NO. 7

DWN
REV

of
10

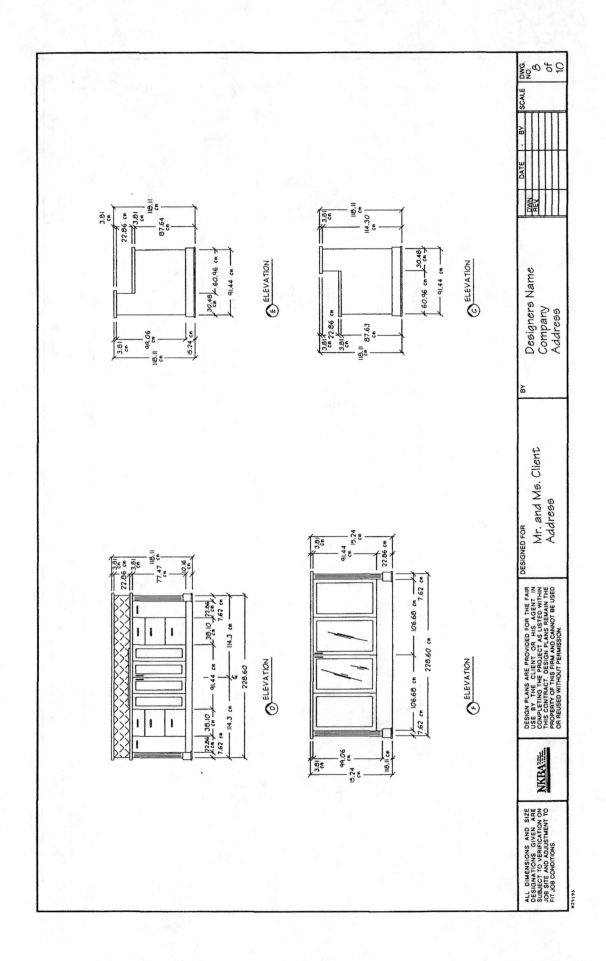

ELEVATION E

ELEVATION G

ELEVATION D

ELEVATION F

DESIGNED FOR
Mr. and Ms. Client
Address

BY

Designers Name
Company
Address

DWN
REV

DATE · BY

SCALE

DWG. NO. 8 of 10

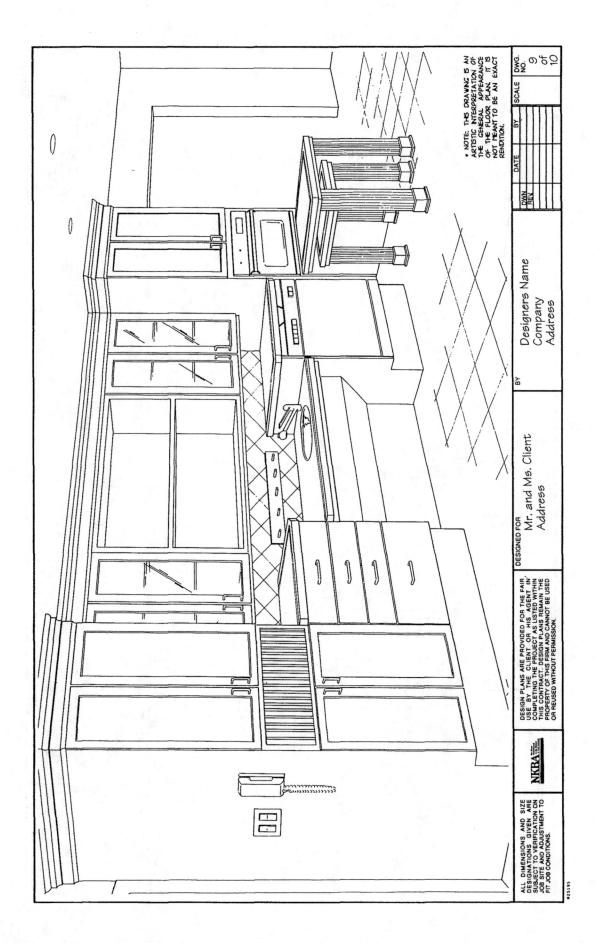

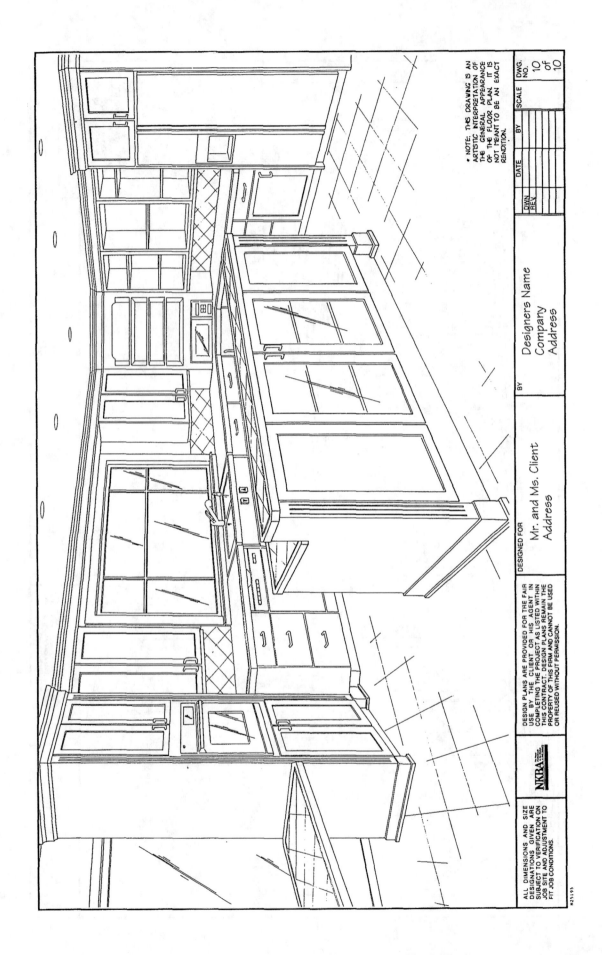

	DWG. NO.	10 of 10
SCALE		
BY		
DATE		
DWN REV		

Designers Name
Company
Address

BY

DESIGNED FOR

Mr. and Ms. Client
Address

NKBA

Graphics and Presentation Standards for Kitchen Design

Specifications

The purpose of the project specifications is to clearly define the details of the products listed and the scope and limits of the job. Specifications may be listed on a separate form, may be part of the working drawings or a combination of both.

- Project specifications define the area of responsibility between the Kitchen Specialist and the purchaser.

- They should clearly define all material and work affected by the job, either directly or indirectly.

- They must clearly indicate which individual has the ultimate responsibility for all or part of the above.

The following Delegation of Responsibilities shall apply: Kitchen Specialists are responsible for the accuracy of the dimensioned floor plans and the selections and designations of all cabinets, appliances and equipment, if made or approved by them.

- Any equipment directly purchased by the Kitchen Specialist for resale, should be the responsibility of the Kitchen Specialist. Further, they must be responsible for supplying product installation instructions to the owner or the owner's agent.

- Any labor furnished by the Kitchen Specialist, whether by their own employees or through sub-contractors paid directly by them and working under their direction, should be the Kitchen Specialist's responsibility. **There should not be a Delegation of Total Responsibility to the Sub-Contractor Working Under these Conditions.**

- Any equipment purchased directly by the owner or the owner's agent from an outside source should be the responsibility of the owner or the owner's agent. The same applies to any sub-contractor, building contractor, or other labor directly hired and/or paid by the owner or the owner's agent.

- Specifications should contain descriptive references to all areas of work.

- All specification categories must be completed. If the job does not cover any given area, the words *"Not Applicable"*, *"N/A"*, or *"None"* should be inserted.

- In each area, the responsibility of either the Kitchen Specialist or the owner or the owner's agent must be assigned.

In all cases, the owner and the owner's agent must receive a completed copy of the project documents PRIOR to the commencement of any work.

STANDARD SPECIFICATIONS FOR KITCHEN DESIGN AND INSTALLATION

Name: _MR & MRS CLIENT_

Home Address: _RENOVATION AVE_

City: _____ State _____ Phone (Home) _(908) 813-6522_

MR. (Office) _(908) 852-0033_

MRS. (Office) _(212) 658-2585_

(Jobsite) _HOME *_

Jobsite Address _(HOME)_

By _DESIGNER'S NAME_

Hereafter called "Kitchen Specialist"

Kitchen Specialist will supply and deliver only such equipment and material as described in these specifications. Labor connected with this kitchen installation will be supplied by the Kitchen Specialist only as herein specified.

Any equipment, material and labor designated here as "Owner's responsibility" must be furnished and completed by the Owner, or the Owner's Agent in accordance with the work schedule established by the Kitchen Specialist.

Equipment, material and labor not included in these specifications can be supplied by the Kitchen Specialist at an additional cost for which authorization must be given in writing by the Owner, or the Owner's Agent.

All dimensions and cabinet designations shown on the floor plan, which are part of these specifications, are subject to adjustments dictated by job conditions.

All surfaces of walls, ceilings, windows and woodwork, except those of factory-made equipment, will be left unpainted or unfinished unless otherwise specified.

If specifications call for re-use of existing equipment, no responsibility on the part of the Kitchen Specialist for appearance. functioning or service shall be implied.

For factory-made equipment, the manufacturer's specifications for quality, design, dimensions, function and installation shall in any case take precedence over any others.

Cabinetry (as per approved drawing)

Manufacturer	ABC

Cabinet Exterior ☒ Wood ☐ Steel ☐ Decorative Laminate ☐ Other

Cabinet Exterior Finish LIGHT OAK STAIN   Cabinet Interior Material MELAMINE Finish WHITE

Door Style FULL OVERLAY, RECESSED PANEL Hardware 4" D-PULL #458N

Special Cabinet Notes

Furnished By ☒ Kitchen Specialist ☐ Owner ☐ Owner's Agent

Installation By ☒ Kitchen Specialist ☐ Owner ☐ Owner's Agent

Countertops (as per approved drawing)

Manufacturer BRAND X / BRAND Y   Material SOLID SURFACE / TILE

Design Details Deck Thickness 3/4" Color WT/NAVY & WT. Edging Thickness 1 1/2" Color WHITE / WOOD

Backsplash Thickness —— Height —— Color ——   End Splash Thickness —— Height —— Color ——

Special Countertop Notes SOLID SURFACE W/ 1/4" radius top & 1/2" RAISED WAY-FINDING STRIP 1 1/2" FROM EDGE / TILE RAISED INLAY W/ WOOD EDGE 1 1/2"

Furnished By ☒ Kitchen Specialist ☐ Owner ☐ Owner's Agent

Installation By ☒ Kitchen Specialist ☐ Owner ☐ Owner's Agent

Fascia & Soffit (as per approved drawing) OPTIONAL

Construction ☐ Flush ☒ Extended ☐ Recessed ☐ N/A (Open)

Finish Material DRYWALL - PAINTED

Special Fascia/Soffit Notes

5" HIGH, 25 1/2" DEEP, 1" SCRIBE SPACE ABOVE CABINETS

Furnished By ☒ Kitchen Specialist ☐ Owner ☐ Owner's Agent

Installation By ☒ Kitchen Specialist ☐ Owner ☐ Owner's Agent

Lighting System

Description	Qty.	Model Number	Finish	Lamp Req.	Furnished By K.S.	Furnished By O/OA	Installed By K.S.	Installed By O/OAS
RECESSED DOWN LIGHTS	18	1234	WHITE	60	X		X	
HANGING PENDANT	1	876	BLACK	60	X		X	
UNDER CAB. INCAND.	3	5647	WHITE	20	X		X	
UNDER CAB. FLUORS.	5	993	WHITE	13	X		X	
Special Lighting System Notes								

UNDER CABINET LIGHTS 54" AFF TO ℄. INCANDESCENT LOW VOLTAGE IS EQUIPPED WITH TRANSFORMER TO RECESS IN CABINET BOTTOM.

HMF12

KEY

K.S. = Kitchen Specialist   O = Owner   OA = Owner's Agent

Appliances

Item	Brand Name	Model	Finish	Fuel	Furnished By		Installed By		Hook Up By	
					K.S.	O/OA	K.S.	O/OA	K.S.	O/OA
Range NA										
Cooktop	XYZ	123	BLACK	ELEC	X		X		X	
Oven	XYZ	123	BLACK	GAS	X		X		X	
Hood NA										
Warming Drawer NA										
Indoor Grill NA										
Microwave 1	XYZ	123	BLACK	ELEC	X		X		X	
Trim Kit	XYZ	89D	BLACK	—	X		X		X	
Refrigerator	XYZ	123	BLACK	ELEC	X		X		X	
Ice Maker	IN DOOR									
Trim Kit NA										
Freezer NA										
Trim Kit NA										
Dishwasher (2)	XYZ	123	BLACK	ELEC	X		X		X	
Trim Kit NA										
Conversion Kit NA										
Food Waste Disposal	XYZ	123	S.S.	ELEC	X		X		X	
Compactor NA										
Trim Kit NA										
Built-in Can Opener NA										
Built-in Toaster NA										
Built-in Mixing Ctr. NA										
Telephone/Intercom	PDQ	5128X	NAVY	—		X		X		X
Television	GENERICA	58T-Y	BLACK	ELEC		X		X		X
Radio NA										
VCR NA										
Washer NA										
Dryer NA										

Special Appliance Notes: TELEPHONE & CABLE OUTLET ROUGH-IN BY OTHERS FINAL PLACEMENT IN FINISH PANELS BY K.S.

Fixtures and Fittings

Item	Brand Name	Model	Finish	Fuel	Furnished By		Installed By		Hook Up By	
					K.S.	O/OA	K.S.	O/OA	K.S.	O/OA
Kitchen Sink #1	XYZ	123	SS	—	X		X		X	
No. of Holes	2									
Faucet	XYZ	123	BLACK	—	X		X		X	
Strainer	XYZ	123	SS	—	X		X		X	
Kitchen Sink #2	XYZ	456	SS	—	X		X		X	
No. of Holes	2									
Faucet	XYZ	123	BLACK	—	X		X		X	
Strainer	XYZ	123	SS	—	X		X		X	
Hot Water Dispenser (2)	XYZ	123	BLACK	—	X		X		X	
Chilled Water Dispenser NA										
Lotion Dispenser NA										
Water Purifier NA										

Special Fixtures and Fittings Notes: UNDERMOUNT SINK #1 & #2 , INSTALL #2 WITH FAUCET AT RIGHT SIDE

Windows and Doors

Item	Brand Name	Model	Finish	Hardware	Furnished By K.S.	Furnished By O/OA	Installed By K.S.	Installed By O/OA
CASEMENT WINDOW	XYZ	123	WHITE	CHROME	X		X	
FIXED WINDOW	XYZ	345	WHITE	CHROME	X		X	
SLIDING GLASS DOOR	XYZ	789	WHITE	CHROME	X		X	

Special Window and Door Notes:

INSTALL FIXED WINDOW & SLIDING DOOR IN SINGLE CASING, PLACE FIXED AT RIGHT, SLIDER AT LEFT

Flooring

		Furnished By K.S.	Furnished By O/OA	Installed By K.S.	Installed By O/OA
Removal of Existing Floor Covering	REMOVE FLOOR & UNDERLAYMENT	X		X	
Preparation of Floor for New Surface	REPAIR & LEVEL AS REQUIRED	X		X	
Installation of Subfloor/Underlayment	NEW 5/8" PLYWOOD	X		X	
New Floor Covering Material Description: VINYL					
Manufacturer ABC Pattern Name GEO-TILE					
Pattern Number 1234 Pattern Repeat 8" SQUARES					
Floor Covering Installation			X		X
Baseboard Material 4" COLONIAL BSBD. LIGHT OAK		X		X	
Transition Treatment			X		X
Remove and Repair Water Damaged Area	AS REQUIRED	X		X	

Special Flooring Notes

FLOOR INSTALLATION BY OWNER'S AGENT WILL BE SCHEDULED WITH K.S. TO FACILITATE A TIMELY COMPLETION

Decorative Surfaces (wall, ceiling, window materials)

Removal Work: Wall _____ Ceiling X Window X   Preparation Work: Wall X Ceiling X Window X

Description	Brand Name	Model	Finish	Material Quantity	Furnished By K.S.	Furnished By O/OA	Installed By K.S.	Installed By O/OA
Remove existing ceiling	—	—	PLASTER	—	X		X	
REMOVE CURTAINS	—	—	—	—		X		X
& RODS/HARDWARE	—	—	—	—		X		X
INSTALL & PAINT CEILING	ABC	—	FLAT	1 GAL	X		X	
PAINT CASINGS	ABC	—	GLOSS	1 PT.	X		X	
PAINT WALLS	ABC	—	EGGSHELL	2 PT.	X		X	
TILE BACKSPLASH								

Special Decorative Surface Notes:

ALL PAINTED SURFACES IN "DESIGNER WHITE" COLOR, TILE BACK SPLASH INSTALLED ON A DIAGONAL, CENTER ROW WHITE, FIELD IN NAVY

BMF12

Electrical Work (except as described above in specific equipment sections)

	Furnished By		Installed By	
	K.S.	O/OA	K.S.	O/OA
Heating System Alteration RELOCATE EXISTING REGISTERS & ADD NEW	X		X	
New Service Panel existing 200 amps sufficient				
Code Update ALL DUPLEX OUTLETS WITH GFCI	X		X	
Details INSTALL ALL APPLIANCES ON DEDICATED	X		X	
CIRCUITS, VENT COOKTOP & OVEN	X		X	
THROUGH FLOOR TO OUTSIDE	X		X	

Plumbing (except as described above in specific equipment sections)

	Furnished By		Installed By	
	K.S.	O/OA	K.S.	O/OA
Heating System Alterations NA				
New Rough-in Requirements per mech. plan (2nd sink, d/w, ref.)	X		X	
Modifications to Existing Lines per Mech. plan (1st sink, d/w)	X		X	
Details				
- SPECIAL FLEXIBLE INSTALLATION REQUIRED	X		X	
FOR PRIMARY SINK THAT ADJUST FROM				
30"-42" AFF				
- 2ND D/W INSTALLED ON 9" HIGH DECK	X		X	
- SET SINK DRAIN BACK FOR KNEESPACE	X		X	

General Carpentry (except as described above in specific equipment sections)

	Furnished By		Installed By	
	K.S.	O/OA	K.S.	O/OA
Demolition Work EXISTING CEILING & WALL	X		X	
Existing Fixture and Equipment Removal DONATED TO CHARITY		X		X
Trash Removal ARRANGE FOR DUMPSTER RT. OF SITE	X		X	
Reconstruction Work (Except as Previously Stated)				
Windows PATCH SIDING, REHANG SHUTTERS	X		X	
Doors PATCH SIDING, REHANG SHUTTERS	X		X	
Interior Walls PATCH AS REQUIRED, NEW SURFACES	X		X	
1/2" DRYWALL PRIMED	X		X	
Exterior Walls ADDITION SIDING TO MATCH EXIST-	X		X	
ING AS CLOSE AS POSSIBLE				
Details				
CUSTOM KNEESPACE PANELS, ANGLED	X		X	
PANELS/FILLERS & MOLDING MITERS				
PERFORMED ON JOBSITE				

Miscellaneous Work

		Responsibility	
		K.S.	O/OA
Trash Removal	EMPTY DUMPSTER ON DEMAND	X	
Jobsite/Room Cleanup	DAILY PICK-UP / SPECIAL POST PROJECT CLEAN	X	
Building Permit(s)	AS REQUIRED	X	
Structural Engineering/Architectural Fees	NA		
Inspection Fees	AS REQUIRED	X	
Jobsite Delivery	STORAGE BY K.S. UNTIL NEEDED	X	
Other			
	SUPERVISE INSTALLATION WORK & SCHEDULE	X	

I have read these specifications and approve:

Accepted: Mrs. Client

Accepted: Mr. Client

Date: 2/23/96

Authorized Company Representative

By: Designer's Signature, CKD

By:

Date: 2-23-96

Design Statement

The purpose of the design statement is to interpret the design problem and solution in order to substantiate the project to the client. Design statements may be verbal or written. Written statements maybe a separate document, may be part of the working drawings or a combination of both.

Design statements should clearly outline:

- design considerations and challenges of the project including, but not limited to: construction and budget requirements, client needs and wants, special requests and lifestyle factors.

- how the designer arrived at their solution and addressed the design considerations and challenges for the project.

- aesthetic considerations such as use of principles and elements of design (ie. pattern repetition, finish/color/surface selections and other details).

It is important that a design statement be clear, concise and interesting to the reader. Written statements may be in either paragraph or bulleted/outline format. As a guideline, a design statement can be written in 250-500 words. Sample design statements follow, showing both acceptable formats.

Sample Design Statement - Paragraph Format

The primary design challenge in the kitchen design for Mr. and Ms. Client was to create a space that is safe and functional for the varying sizes and abilities of the family members. Mr. and Ms. Client are both in their 40's with family members including a 17 year old son, seven year old daughter and a 72 year old grandmother. The grandmother has arthritis, limited eyesight and sometime uses a walker. Since both Mr. and Ms. Client work, the grandmother and the children frequent the kitchen during the day and all family members participate in meal preparation in the evenings and on weekends. The existing kitchen space was insufficient for the families request to work together in the space. The work aisles were narrow, counters had sharp edges and many fixtures and equipment were either out of reach or hard to use by the grandmother and child, posing safety hazards.

The solution began by building a room addition adjacent to the existing kitchen which increased the floor space by approximately 25%. This allowed us to plan generous walkways and work aisles that join multiple work stations within the kitchen. In order to accommodate all the users of the space, the work stations were designed at varied and adjustable heights. The primary sink adjusts from 30" - 42" high allowing flexibility from day to evening and weekends. The secondary work centers are at a stationary 30" height to accommodate the shorter/seated kitchen helpers. All cabinetry was planned with accessibility in mind. Cabinets are equipped with roll-out/pull-out accessories, reduced depths or open shelves. Solid surface counters are heat resistant and designed with special raised and color contrasted "way-finding" edges which aid the grandmother in maneuvering around the space. Additionally, sharp edges were virtually eliminated by clipping all counter corners at 45 degree angles.

A geometric pattern was created with navy blue and white ceramic tile on the floor and backsplash to compliment the light finish on the wood cabinets and achieve repetition/continuity throughout the space. Furthermore, the tile pattern provides contrast which also contributes to the functionality of the space. Finally, all appliances and fixtures were selected based on safety and ease of use, as well as aesthetics. All equipment and fixtures are accented with polished chrome. The faucets have lever handles, appliances have large graphics, high contrast indicators and touch-pad controls.

Sample Design Statement - Outline Format

The primary design challenge was to create a space that was safe and functional for all family members:

- Mr. and Mrs. Client (40's)

- 17 year old son

- Seven year old daughter

- 72 year old grandmother (arthritis, limited eyesight, sometimes uses walker)

The existing space was insufficient:

- work aisles were too narrow

- counters had sharp edges

- many fixtures/equipment out of reach or hard to use by child and grandmother

The solution:

- room addition increased floor space by 25%

- multiple workstations at various heights

- primary sink adjusts from 30"-42"

- cabinetry equipped with roll-out/pull-out accessories

- reduced depth storage and open shelves

- solid surface (heat-resistant) counters

- counter edges were clipped and designed with way-finding inlay stripe

- appliances were selected based on safety and ease of use

Aesthetics:

- tile pattern repeats geometric design

- white and navy color tiles match white counter with navy inlay stripe

- light finished wood cabinets compliment navy

- color contrasts provide safety factor for grandmother's limited eyesight

Graphics and Presentation Standards for Kitchen Design

Contracts

All contract forms used **must** be in strict compliance with Federal, State and Municipal Laws and Ordinances. Reference local codes for compliance standards. Laws do vary, therefore, you should be sure your contracts meet all local requirements.

STANDARD FORM OF AGREEMENT
FOR DESIGN AND INSTALLATION

Approved by the

National Kitchen & Bath Association

Between ....Purchaser

Home Address ....

City ....State ....Zip ....

Phone Number ....

Delivery Address ....

And Seller

1. The Seller agrees to furnish the materials and services set forth in the drawings (numbered................................
and dated ....) and specifications annexed hereto.
The Purchaser agrees to make payment therefore in accordance with the schedule of payment.

Contract Price..	$ ....
Sales Tax (if applicable)	$ ....
....	$ ....
Total Purchase Price....................................	$ ....

Schedule of Payment:

Upon signing of this agreement	$ ....
Upon delivery of cabinets from manufacturer	$ ....
Upon delivery of	$ ....
Upon substantial installation of	$ ....

This contract includes the terms and provisions as set forth herein. Please read and sign where indicated.

2. The standard form of warranty shall apply to the service and equipment furnished (except where other warranties of purchased products apply). The warranty shall become effective when signed by the Seller and delivered to the Purchaser. The warranty is for one year materials and labor.

3. The delivery date, when given, shall be deemed approximate and performance is subject to delays caused by strikes, fires, acts of God or other reasons not under the control of the Seller, as well as the availability of the product at the time of delivery.

4. The Purchaser agrees to accept delivery of the product or products when ready. The risk of loss, as to damage or destruction, shall be upon the Purchaser upon the delivery and receipt of the product.

5. The Purchaser understands that the products described are specially designed and custom built and that the Seller takes immediate steps upon execution of this Agreement to design, order and construct those items set forth herein; therefore, this Agreement is not subject to cancellation by the Purchaser for any reason.

6. No installation, plumbing, electrical, flooring, decorating or other construction work is to be provided unless specifically set forth herein. In the event the Seller is to perform the installation, it is understood that the price agreed upon herein does not include possible expense entailed in coping with hidden or unknown contingencies found at the job site. In the event such contingencies arise and the Seller is required to furnish labor or materials or otherwise perform work not provided for or contemplated by the Seller, the actual costs plus (   )% thereof will be paid for by the Purchaser. Contingencies include but are not limited to: inability to reuse existing water, vent, and waste pipes; air shafts, ducts, grilles, louvres and registers; the relocation of concealed pipes, risers, wiring or conduits, the presence of which cannot be determined until the work has started; or imperfections, rotting or decay in the structure or parts thereof necessitating replacement.

7. Title to the item sold pursuant to this Agreement shall not pass to the Purchaser until the full price as set forth in this Agreement is paid to the Seller.

8. Delays in payment shall be subject to interest charges of (   )% per annum, and in no event higher than the interest rate provided by law. If the Seller is required to engage the services of a collection agency or an attorney, the Purchaser agrees to reimburse the Seller for any reasonable amounts expended in order to collect the unpaid balance.

9. If any provision of this Agreement is declared invalid by any tribunal, the remaining provisions of the Agreement shall not be affected thereby.

10. This Agreement sets forth the entire transaction between the parties; any and all prior Agreements, warranties or representations made by either party are superseded by this Agreement. All changes in this Agreement shall be made by a separate document and executed with the same formalities. No agent of the Seller, unless authorized in writing by the Seller, has any authority to waive, alter, or enlarge this contract, or to make any new or substituted or different contracts, representations, or warranties.

11. The Seller retains the right upon breach of this Agreement by the Purchaser to sell those items in the Seller's possession. In effecting any resale on breach of this Agreement by the Purchaser, the Seller shall be deemed to act in the capacity of agent for the Purchaser. The purchaser shall be liable for any net deficiency on resale.

12. The Seller agrees that it will perform this contract in conformity with customary industry practices. The Purchaser agrees that any claim for adjustment shall not be reason or cause for failure to make payment of the purchase price in full. Any unresolved controversy or claim arising from or under this contract shall be settled by arbitration and judgment upon the award rendered may be entered in any court of competent jurisdiction. The arbitration shall be held under the rules of the American Arbitration Association.

Accepted: ....
                                    Purchaser

Accepted: ....

Accepted: ....
                                    Purchaser

Date: ....

Date: ....

Titling Project Documents

Protecting Yourself

When you design a project for a client, you must protect yourself from liability when referring to the plans and drawings, and you must protect the plans themselves from being copied by your competitors.

When presenting the plans for a kitchen, **NKBA** recommends that you refer to the drawings as *"Kitchen Design Plans"* or *"Cabinet Plans"*. The design plans should have the following statement included on them in an obvious location in large or block letters.

DESIGN PLANS ARE NOT PROVIDED FOR ARCHITECTURAL OR ENGINEERING USE

The individual drawings incorporated in the overall kitchen design presentation must also be carefully labeled. It is suggested that you refer to these other drawings as ***"Floor Plans", "Elevations", "Artist Renderings", and "Mechanical Plans"***.

With respect to the *"Artist Rendering"* , **NKBA** suggests that you include a notation on the drawings which reads:

THIS RENDERING IS AN ARTIST'S INTERPRETATION OF THE GENERAL APPEARANCE OF THE ROOM, IT IS NOT INTENDED TO BE A PRECISE DEPICTION

The entire set of paperwork, which includes your design plans, specifications and contract, can be referred to as the **"Project Documents"**.

You should never refer to the design plan as an *"Architectural Drawing"*, or even as an "architectural-type drawing". **DO NOT USE THE WORDS** *"Architecture"*, *"Architectural Design"*, *"Architectural Phase"*, *"Architectural Background"*, or any other use of the word *"Architectural"* in any of the project documents that you prepare, or in any of your business stationary, promotional information or any presentation materials. Any such reference to the work that you do or documents that you prepare may result in a violation of various state laws. A court may determine that your use of the word *"Architecture/Architectural"*, could reasonably lead a client to believe that you possess a level of expertise that you do not. Worse yet, a court may find you liable for fraud and/or misrepresentation.

Laws do vary per state, therefore, it is important that you consult with your own legal counsel to be sure that you are acting within the applicable statutes in your area. You must clearly understand what drawings you are legally allowed to prepare, and what drawings must be prepared under the auspices of a licensed architect or engineer.

Protecting your "Kitchen Design Plans"

After drafting the design plans for your client, you should insure that they will not be copied or used by a competitor. This may be done by copyrighting the design plan that you prepare.

Copyright is an International form of protection/exclusivity provided by law to authors of original works, despite whether the work is published or not. Original works of authorship include any literary, pictorial, graphic, or sculptured works, such as your design plans, provided they are original works done by you.

Copyright protection exists from the moment the work is created in its final form and will endure fifty years after your death.

Naturally, if two or more persons are authors of an original work, they will be deemed *co-owners* of its copyright. For example; if you as the Kitchen Specialist collaborate with an Interior Designer, you will both be co-owners of the design copyright.

An original work generated by two or more authors is referred to as a *"joint work"*. Generally, a *"joint work"* results if the authors collaborated on the work or if each prepared a segment of it with the knowledge and intent that it would be incorporated with the contributions submitted by other authors. Accordingly, a *"joint work"* will only be found when each co-author intended his respective contribution to be combined into a larger, integrated piece. There is no requirement that each of the co-authors work together or even be acquainted with one another.

A work created by an employee within the scope of his employment is regarded as *"work made for hire"*, and is normally owned by the employer, unless the parties explicitly stipulate in a written agreement, signed by both, that the copyright will be owned by the employee. If you are an independent contractor, the *"works made for hire"* statutes do not include architectural drawings or other design plans, therefore, the copyright in any kitchen design created by you will remain vested with you until you contractually agree to relinquish ownership.

To secure copyright protection for your plans, you are required to give notice of copyright on all publicly distributed copies. The use of the copyright notice is your responsibility as the copyright owner and does not require advance permission from, or registration with, the Copyright Office in Washington, DC.

A proper copyright notice must include the following three items:

- 1. The symbol ©, or the word "Copyright", or the abbreviation "Copy";
  (© is considered as the International symbol for copyright)

- 2. The year of the first publication of the work; and

- 3. The name of the owner of the copyright in the work, or an abbreviation by which the name can be recognized, or a generally known alternative designation of the owner.

An example of a proper copyright notice would be:

Copyright © 1995 Joe Smith

The notice should be affixed to copies of your design plan in such a manner and location as to give reasonable notice of the claim of copyright.

As mentioned previously, you or your firm continue to retain copyright protection of your design plan even if the plan is given to the client after he has paid for it. Although the copyright ownership may be transferred, such transfer must be in writing and signed by you as the owner of the copyright conveyed. Normally, the transfer of a copyright is made by contract. In order to protect your exclusive rights, however, you should include a clause in your contract which reads:

Design plans are provided for the fair use by the client or his agent in completing the project as listed within this contract. Design plans remain the property of (your name)

This clause should also be in any agreement between you and a client who requests that you prepare a design plan for his review. Such a design plan usually serves as the basis for a subsequent contract between you and the client for the actual installation of the kitchen. This type of agreement will prevent the client from obtaining a design plan from you and then taking that plan to a competitor who may simply copy your plan.

So long as you retain the copyright in the design plan, you will be able to sue any party who has copied your design plan for infringement.

Glossary - Graphic Terms

Architects Scale: A measuring tool used to draw at a determined unit of measure ratio accurately; ie. 1/2" = 1', in which each half inch represents one foot.

3/32" = 1'	1/4" = 1'	1" = 1'
3/16" = 1'	3/8" = 1'	1 1/2" = 1'
1/8" = 1'	3/4" = 1'	3" = 1'

It is equally acceptable to use the metric equivalents. (inches x 2.54)

Break Symbol: Indicated by (⤝) and used to end wall lines on a drawing which actually continue or to break off parts of the drawing.

Color: A visual sensation which is a result of light reflecting off objects and creating various wavelengths which when reaching the retina produces the appearance of various hues.

Copyright: Is an International form of protection/exclusivity provided by law to authors of original works, despite whether the work is published or not. Original works of authorship include any literary, pictorial, graphic, or sculptured works such as design plans that are your own original works. The symbol (©) is considered as the International symbol for copyright exclusivity.

Dimension Lines: Solid lines terminating with arrows, dots or slashes which run parallel with the object it represents and includes the actual length of the line written in inches or centimeters inside or on top of the line. Whenever possible, dimension lines should be located outside of the actual walls of the floor plan or elevation.

Dimetric: A dimetric drawing is similar to oblique, with the exception that the object is rotated so that only one of its corners touches the picture plane. The most frequently used angle for the projecting line is an equal division of 45° on either side of the leading edge. A 15° angle is sometimes used when it is less important to show the *"roof view"* of the object.

Elevation: A drawing representing a vertical view of a space taken from a preselected reference plane. There is no depth indicated in an elevation, rather everything appears very flat and is drawn in scale.

Floor Plan: A drawing representing a horizontal view of a space taken from a preselected reference plane (often the ceiling). There is no depth indicated in a floor plan, rather everything appears very flat and is drawn in a reduced scale.

Graphics and Presentation Standards for Kitchen Design

Isometric: The isometric, a special type of dimetric drawing, is the easiest and most popular paraline (three-dimensional) drawing. All axes of the object are simultaneously rotated away from the picture plane and kept at the same angle of projection (30° from the picture plane). All legs are equally distorted in length at a given scale and therefore maintain an exact proportion of 1:1:1.

Kroy Lettering Tape: Translucent sticky backed tape, which after running it through a special typing machine, creates a stick on lettering ideal for labeling drawing title blocks.

Lead: A graphite and clay mixture which is used for drawing and drafting in combination with a lead holder. Similar to a pencil without the wooden outer portion. Available in various degrees of hardness, providing various line weights.

Legend: An explanatory list of the symbols and their descriptions as used on a mechanical plan or other graphic representation.

Matte Board: A by product of wood pulp with a paper surface which has been chemically treated in order to be acid free and fade resistent. The use of matte board will protect drawings from fading, becoming brittle and bending or creasing.

Oblique: In an oblique drawing one face (either plan or elevation) of the object is drawn directly on the picture plane. Projected lines are drawn at a 30° or 45° angle to the picture plane.

Owners Agent: That person or persons responsible for mediating the clients requests with the designer and acting as the interpretor on any area the client is unsure of or in question on.

Ozalid Prints: More commonly referred to as *"Blueprints"*, are a method of duplicating drawings in which special paper coated with light sensitive diazo is used. This paper with drawing on transparent paper, is exposed to ultra violet light creating a negative, then the print is exposed again to the developer which produces the *"blackline"*, *"blueline"* or *"sepia print"* depending upon the paper used.

Perspective: The art of representing a space in a drawing form which appears to have depth by indicating the relationship of various objects as they appear to the human eye or through the lens of a camera.

Photocopy: A method of duplicating drawings in which light causes toner to adhere to paper of various sizes, typically *(8 1/2" x 11")*, *(11" x 14")* or *(11" x 17")*, producing prints in high contrast, which are similar to blackline ozalid prints.

Quadrille Paper: White ledger paper base with blue, non-reproducible ruling lines which all carry the same weight. * **NOTE: This is not an acceptable type of drafting paper for project documentation.**

Section:

Often referred to as *"cut-view"*, these drawings are defined as an imaginary cut made through an object and used to show construction details and materials which are not obvious in standard plan or elevational views.

Technical Rapidograph Pens:

Provides for a smooth flow of ink with stainless steel points or *"Tungsten Carbide"* point of various sizes, again providing various line weights.

Tracing Paper:

Thin semi-transparent paper used for sketching. Also called *"bumwad"* paper.

Transfer Type:

Sometimes referred to as *"Press-Type"* or *"Rub-on-Type"*, is a translucent film with lettering or dot screen images which may be transferred to a drawing by rubbing the image after it is positioned on the drawing paper. When the film is lifted, the image remains on the drawing paper and the film is left blank.

Trimetric:

The trimetric drawing is similar to the dimetric, except that the plan of the object is rotated so that the two exposed sides of the object are not at equal angles to the picture plane. The plan is usually positioned at 30/60° angle to the ground plane. The height of the object is reduced proportionately as illustrated (similar to the 45° dimetric).

Vellum:

Rag stock which has been transparentized with synthetic resin resulting in medium weight transparent paper with a medium-fine grain or *"tooth"* which holds lead to the surface.

Witness Lines:

Solid lines which run perpendicular to the dimension line and cross the dimension line at the exact location of its termination. These lines should begin approximately 1/16" outside of the walls of the floor plan and end approximately 1/16" beyond the dimension line.

Graphics and Presentation Standards for Kitchen Design

Imperial/Metric Comparison Chart

KITCHEN AND BATH FLOOR PLANS SHOULD BE DRAWN TO A SCALE OF 1/2" EQUALS 1' FOOT (1/2" =1'- 0"). AN EQUALLY ACCEPTABLE METRIC SCALE WOULD BE A RATIO OF 1 TO 20 (ie. 1 CM TO 20 CM)

	INCHES	MILLIMETERS	CENTIMETERS
◆ ACTUAL METRIC CONVERSION TO MILLIMETERS IS 1" = 25.4 MM . TO FACILITATE CONVERSIONS BETWEEN IMPERIAL + METRIC DIMENSIONING FOR CALCULATIONS UNDER 1", 24 MM IS USED.	1/8"	3 MM	.32 CM
	1/4"	6	.64
	1/2"	12	1.27
	3/4"	18	1.91
	1"	24	2.54
◆ TO FACILITATE CONVERSIONS BETWEEN IMPERIAL + METRIC FOR CALCULATIONS OVER 1", 25 MM IS TYPICALLY USED.			
	3"	75	7.62
	6"	150	15.24
◆ ACTUAL METRIC CONVERSION TO CENTIMETERS IS 1" = 2.54 CM.	9"	225	22.86
	12"	300	30.48
	15"	375	38.1
	18"	450	45.72
	21"	525	53.34
	24"	600	60.96
	27"	675	68.58
	30"	750	76.2
	33"	825	83.82
	36"	900	91.44
	39"	975	99.06
	42"	1050	106.68
	45"	1125	114.3
	48"	1200	121.92
	51"	1275	129.54
	54"	1350	137.16
	57"	1425	144.78
	60"	1500	152.4
	63"	1575	160.02
	66"	1650	167.64
	69"	1725	175.26
	72"	1800	182.88
	75"	1875	190.5
	78"	1950	198.12
	81"	2025	205.74
	84"	2100	213.36
	87"	2175	220.98
	90"	2250	228.6
	93"	2325	236.22
	96"	2400	243.84
	99"	2475	251.46
	102"	2475	259.08
	105"	2625	266.7
	108"	2700	274.32
	111"	2775	281.94
	114"	2850	289.56
	117"	2925	297.18
	120"	3000	304.8
	123"	3075	312.42
	126"	3150	320.04
	129"	3225	327.66
	132"	3300	335.28
	135"	3375	342.9
	138"	3450	350.52
	141"	3525	358.14
	144"	3600	365.76

Metric Conversion Chart

LENGTH

10 MILLIMETERS = 1 CENTIMETER (CM)
10 CENTIMETERS - 1 DECIMETER
10 DECIMETERS - 1 METER (M)
10 METERS - 1 DEKAMETER
100 METERS - 1 HECTOMETER
1,000 METERS - 1 KILOMETER

AREA

100 SQ. MILLIMETERS = 1 SQ. CENTIMETER
100 SQ. CENTIMETER - 1 SQ. DECIMETER
100 SQ. DECIMETERS - 1 SQ. METER
100 SQ. METERS - 1 ARE
10,000 SQ. METERS - 1 HECTARE
100 HECTARES - 1 SQ. KILOMETER

LINEAR DRAWING MEASUREMENTS

1 MILLIMETER (MM) - .03937"	1" = 25.4 MM	12" - 304.8 MM
1 CENTIMETER (CM) - .3937"	1" = 2.54 CM	12" - 30.48 CM
1 METER (M) - 39.37"	1" - .0254 M	12" - .3048 M

SQUARE MEASURE

1 SQ. INCH - 6.4516 SQ. CENTIMETERS
1 SQ. FOOT - 9.29034 SQ. DECIMETERS
1 SQ. YARD = .836131 SQ. METER
1 ACRE = .40469 HECTARE
1 SQ. MILE = 2.59 SQ. KILOMETERS

DRY MEASURE

1 PINT = .550599 LITER
1 QUART = 1.101197 LITER
1 PECK = 8.80958 LITER
1 BUSHEL - .35238 HECTOLITER

CUBIC MEASURE

1 CU. INCH - 16.3872 CU. CENTIMETERS
1 CU. FOOT - .028317 CU. METERS
1 CU. YARD - .76456 CU. METERS

LIQUID MEASURE

1 PINT - .473167 LITER
1 QUART - .946332 LITER
1 GALLON - 3.785329 LITER

LONG MEASURE

1 INCH = 25.4 MILLIMETERS
1 FOOT = .3 METER
1 YARD = .914401 METER
1 MILE = 1.609347 KILOMETERS

Graphics and Presentation Standards for Kitchen Design

Appendix E:
Business Forms

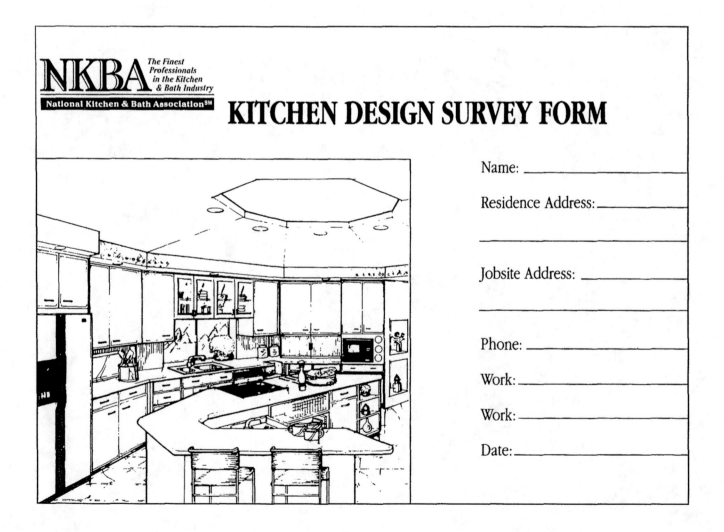

NKBA — *The Finest Professionals in the Kitchen & Bath Industry*
National Kitchen & Bath Association℠

KITCHEN DESIGN SURVEY FORM

Name: _____

Residence Address: _____

_____

Jobsite Address: _____

_____

Phone: _____

Work: _____

Work: _____

Date: _____

 **PRICE QUOTATION**

The **Price Quotation** is composed of two (2) similar forms:
1. Price Quotation, BMF5
2. Price Quotation, w/cost column, BMF5A

The **Price Quotation** will provide:
1. a document to record individual price quotations and cost figures on projects, other than installed remodeling jobs.
2. the client with a written price quotation, and dated price protection.
3. a system to prevent discrepancies between quotations made at different times by different people.

The **Price Quotation**, BMF5 and 5A, should be completed in duplicate. BMF5 will be given to the client for their records and BMF5A should be filed alphabetically by client's name. Whenever the sale is made, form BMF5A can be used for costing purposes. All quotations for material only should only be quoted using the **Price Quotation** forms.

PRICE QUOTATION

For: Client _____

Address _____

_____

Date _____

Based on   Client's Plans ☐   Designers Plans ☐

We are pleased to quote the following:

Sub-total _____

Tax _____

Delivery _____

GRAND TOTAL _____

*Quote valid for _____ days.

Kitchen/Bath Specialist

Note: *Prices are based on costs and conditions existing on date of quotation.

© 1991 NKBA   BMF5-8/91

PRICE QUOTATION

For: Client _____

Address _____

_____

Date _____

Based on   Client's Plans ☐   Designers Plans ☐

Cost

We are pleased to quote the following:

Sub-total* _____

Tax _____

Delivery _____

GRAND TOTAL _____

*Quote valid for _____ days.

_____
Kitchen/Bath Specialist

Note: *Prices are based on costs and conditions existing on date of quotation.

 **SURVEY FORM**

The **Survey Form** is comprised of two (2) separate forms:
1. Kitchen Design Survey Form, BMF6
2. Bath Design Survey Form, BMF7

The **Survey Form** will provide:
1. design information relative to the physical restrictions of the project.
2. design information relative to the personal needs and desires of the client.
3. a thorough reference listing of equipment .
4. a basis of developing a budget for the project.

The **Survey Form** should be completed during the home visit. Care should be exercised to consider all aspects of the project. The information indicated on the Survey Form should be used to set the criteria for the designer.

When the project has been designed, the completed Survey Form should be filed in the job folder of the individual client. The Survey Form should be reviewed with the client during the presentation session.

KITCHEN DESIGN SURVEY FORM

Name: _____

Residence Address: _____

_____

Jobsite Address: _____

_____

Phone: _____

Work: _____

Work: _____

Date: _____

Designer: _____

Appointment:

Scheduled: _____

Call When Ready: _____

Times Available: _____

Directions: _____

Allied Professionals:

Name: _____

Firm: _____

Address: _____

Phone: _____

General Client Information

1. How long have you lived at, or how much time do you spend at the jobsite residence?_____

2. When was the house built?_____ How old is the present kitchen?_____

3. How did you learn about our firm?_____

4. When would you like to start the project?_____

5. When would you like the project to be completed?_____

   _____

6. Has anyone assisted you in preparing a design for the kitchen?_____

   _____

7. Do you plan on retaining an interior designer or architect to assist in the kitchen planning?_____

   _____

8. Do you have a specific builder/contractor or other subcontractor/specialist with whom you would like to work?_____

   _____

9. What portion of the project, if any, will be your responsibility?_____

   _____

10. What budget range have you established for your kitchen project?_____

11. How long do you intend to own the jobsite residence?_____

12. What are your plans regarding this home?_____

    a. Is it a long or short-term investment?_____

    b. Is return on investment a primary concern?_____

    c. Do you plan on renting the jobsite residence in the future?_____

13. What family members will share in the final decision-making process?_____

    _____

14. Would you like our firm to assist you in securing project financing? _____Yes _____No

15. What do you dislike most about your present kitchen?_____

    _____

    _____

16. What do you like about your present kitchen?_____

    _____

Specific Kitchen Questions

1. How many household members? (Ask for approximate ages.)

   _____ Adults   _____ Teens   _____ Children   _____ Other

   _____ Pets   What types: _____

2. Are you planning on enlarging your family while living here? _____
   _____

3. Who is the primary cook? _____

   Is the primary cook left-handed _____ or right-handed _____?

   How tall is the primary cook? _____

   Does the primary cook have any physical limitations? _____

4. How many other household members cook? _____

   Who are they? _____

   Do they have a cooking hobby _____, assist the primary cook with a specific task _____,

   or share a menu item with the primary cook? _____

   Is the secondary cook(s) right-handed _____ left-handed _____?

   How tall is the secondary cook(s)? _____

   Is a specialized cooking center required for the secondary cook(s)? _____

   Do they have physical limitations? _____

5. How does the family use the kitchen? _____

   _____ Daily Heat & Serve Meals   _____ Daily Full-Course, "From Scratch" Meals

   _____ Weekend Quantity Cooking   _____ Weekend Family Meals

   Other _____

6. Is the kitchen a socializing space? _____

7. How would you like the new kitchen to relate to adjacent rooms? _____
   _____
   _____

   _____ Family Room   _____ Dining Room

   _____ Family Home Office   _____ Family TV Viewing

8. What time of day is the kitchen used most frequently? _____

9. What are your kitchen and dining area requests? _____

   _____ Separate Table   _____ 30" Table Height Dining Counter

   _____ New _____ Existing   _____ 36" Counter Height

   _____ Size _____ Leaf Extension   _____ 42" Elevated Bar Height Dining Center

   _____ Number of Seated Diners

10. Do you do any specialty cooking? _____ Gourmet   _____ Canning   _____ Ethnic

11. Do you cook in bulk for freezing _____ and/or leftovers _____?

Specific Kitchen Questions (continued)

12. Do you entertain frequently?_____ Formally _____ Informally

13. Designing the kitchen so that it supports your entertainment style is part of the planning process. Tell me which statement fits you the best:

    _____I like to be the only one in the kitchen with my guests in a separate space that is away from the kitchen

    _____I like to be the only cook in the kitchen, with my guests close by in a family room space that opens onto the kitchen.

    _____I like my guests to be sitting in the kitchen visiting with me while I cook.

    _____I like my guests to help me in the kitchen in meal preparation.

    _____I like my guests to help in the cleanup process after the meal.

    _____I retain caterers who prepare all meals for entertaining.

    _____ The caterers come to the home to serve and cleanup.

    _____ I stop by the caterers and pick up the food.

    _____ I stop at the deli/take-out restaurant to bring part or all of the meal home before entertaining.

    The items that I purchase from outside sources are:

    _____ Appetizers   _____ Salads   _____ Soups

    _____ Entrees   _____ Desserts   _____ Other

14. What secondary activities will take place in your kitchen?

    _____ Computer   _____ Laundry   _____ TV/Radio

    _____ Eating   _____ Planning Desk   _____ Wet Bar

    _____ Growing Plants   _____ Sewing   _____ Other

    _____ Hobbies   _____ Study   _____ Other

15. What is your cycle of shopping for food?

    _____ Weekly   _____ Bi-weekly   _____ Daily

16. What types of products/materials do you purchase at the grocery store?

    Predominantly fresh food purchased for a specific meal. _____

    Predominantly frozen foods purchased for stock. _____

    Traditional pantry boxed/packaged/canned goods purchased for stock. _____

    (1) Types of canned goods:

    _____ Condiments _____ Fruits _____ Soft Drinks _____ Vegetables

    (2) Cleaning products stocked in bulk _____

    (3) Paper products stocked in bulk _____

    (4) Other boxed/packaged food items stocked in bulk _____

    (5) Other _____

Specific Kitchen Questions (continued)

17. Where do you presently store:

_____ Baking Equipment	_____ Non-Refrigerated Fruits/Vegs.	_____ Spices
_____ Boxed Goods		_____ Table/Appointments
_____ Canned Goods	_____ Paper Products	_____ Linens
_____ Cleaning Supplies	_____ Pet Food	_____ Wrapping Materials
_____ Dishes	_____ Pots & Pans	_____ Leftover Containers
_____ Glassware	_____ Recycle Containers	_____ Other
_____ Laundry/Iron Equipment	_____ Serving Trays	_____ Other
	_____ Specialty Cooking Vessels (Wok, Etc.)	_____ Other

Legend: B = Base Cabinet   C = Countertop   L = Laundry Room
          BA = Basement   AG = Appliance Garage   T = Tall Cabinet
          BC = Bookcase   D = Desk   W = Wall Cabinet

18. What type of specialized storage is desired?

_____ Bottle	_____ Dishes	_____ Plastic
_____ Bread Board	_____ Display Items	_____ Soft Drink Cans
_____ Bread Box	_____ Glassware	_____ Spice
_____ Cookbook	_____ Lids	_____ Vegetables
_____ Cutlery	_____ Linen	_____ Wine
_____ Other	_____ Other	_____ Other

19. What type of cabinet interior storage are you interested in?

_____ Lazy Susan	_____ Roll-outs	_____ Drawer Ironing Board
_____ Pantry	_____ Towel Bar	_____ Toe-Kick Step Stool
_____ Vertical Dividers	_____ Tilt-out	_____ Other
_____ Recycling/Waste Bins	_____ Drawer Head	_____ Other

20. What small specialty electrical appliances do you use in your kitchen?

_____ Blender	_____ Elec. Fry Pan	_____ Wok
_____ Can Opener	_____ Food Processor	_____ Other
_____ Crock Pot	_____ Griddle	_____ Other
_____ Coffee Pot	_____ Toaster	_____ Other

21. Have you considered relocating or changing windows or doors in the new plan? _____

_____

22. How do you plan on sorting recyclable trash in your new kitchen?

Sorting into: _____ Plastic   _____ Compact refuse
                  _____ Paper   _____ Trash
                  _____ Glass
                     a. _____ clear
                     b. _____ brown
                     c. _____ green

23. Would you like a sorting station in the:
    _____ kitchen   _____ utility room   _____ garage   _____ basement   _____ outside?

Design Information

1. What type of feeling would you like your new kitchen space to have?

Sleek/Contemporary	_____	Warm & Cozy Country	_____
Traditional	_____	Open & Airy	_____
Strictly Functional	_____	Formal	_____
Family Retreat	_____	Personal Design Statement	_____

2. What colors do you like _____ and dislike _____ ?

3. What colors are you considering for your new kitchen? _____

4. What are color preferences of other family members? _____

5. Have you made a sketch or collected pictures of ideas for your new kitchen? _____

6. Design Notes:

   _____

   _____

   _____

   _____

   _____

   _____

   _____

   _____

   _____

   _____

   _____

   _____

   _____

   _____

   _____

   _____

   _____

Project Specifications

Is this to be a complete kitchen, including:

Category	Source					Description
		Furn By		Install By		
	Use Exist	KS	O/OA	KS	O/OA	Check Appropriate Space(s)
Cabinetry						_____ Wood Species _____ Decorative Lam. _____ Furn. Steel _____ Polyester Other _____ Style _____ Hardware _____ Exterior Color/Finish _____ Interior Color/Finish _____
Countertops						_____ Wood _____ Decorative Lam. _____ Marble _____ Solid Surface _____ Granite Other _____ _____ Tile Size _____ Grout _____ Inserts Edge Treatment _____ Backsplash: Height _____ Backsplash: Material _____ End Splash Sides _____ Decking: _____ Plywood _____ Loose Other _____
Fascia/Soffit						_____ Open _____ Flush _____ Extended _____ Recessed _____ Wallpaper _____ Paint _____ Wood _____ Lighted _____ Gallery Rail _____ Cornice Other _____
Lighting System						Source: _____ Incandescent _____ Fluorescent _____ Halogen Other _____ Location: _____ Cooking _____ Sink _____ Desk _____ Soffit _____ Gen'l Ceiling _____ Table _____ Island/Penn. _____ Under Wall Cab. _____ Mixing Area _____ Window _____ Pantry Other _____ Type: _____ Cove _____ Suspended _____ Recessed _____ Track _____ Surface Mtd. Other _____

KEY

KS = Kitchen Specialist   O = Owner   OA = Owner's Agent

BMF6

Category	Source					Description
	Furn. By		Install By			
	Use Exist	KS	O/OA	KS	O/OA	Check appropriate space(s)
Appliances						
Range						_____ Gas _____ Electric _____ Microwave _____ Convection _____ Drop-In _____ Slide-In _____ Free-Standing _____ Eye Level _____ Self Clean _____ Continuous Clean Size If Retaining Existing _____
Cooktop						_____ Gas _____ Electric _____ Enamel Steel _____ Conven. Coil _____ Ceramic _____ Solid Disk _____ Stainless St. _____ Halogen _____ Induction Color _____ Size If Retaining Existing _____ Accessories _____
Oven						_____ Gas _____ Electric _____ Single _____ Double _____ Self Clean _____ Continuous Clean _____ Microwave _____ Micro/Convection _____ Convection _____ Other Size If Retaining Existing _____
Hood						_____ Decorative _____ Standard _____ Wood _____ Metal Other Material _____ _____ Vented _____ Ductless New Ductwork Need _____ Duct Termination _____ Size If Retaining Existing _____ Ability to Run Ductwork _____
Warming Drawer						_____ Single _____ Double
Indoor Grill						_____ Single _____ Double _____ Combo _____ Gas _____ Electric
Microwave						_____ Built-In _____ Free Standing _____ Trim Kit Other _____ Size If Retaining Existing _____
Refrigerator						_____ Side-By-Side _____ Top Freezer _____ Btm Freezer _____ Rt/Lft Side Hinge _____ Reversible _____ Ice Maker _____ Built-In _____ Under Counter _____ Front Panel _____ Trim Kit Size If Retaining Existing _____
Freezer						_____ Upright _____ Size _____ Chest _____ Size _____ Front Panel _____ Trim Kit

BMF6

Category	Source					Description
		Furn By		Install By		
	Use Exist	KS	O/OA	KS	O/OA	Check Appropriate Space(s)
Appliances (Continued)						
Dishwasher						_____ Front Panel _____ Trim Kit _____ Conv. Kit Existing Plumbing _____
Food Waste Disposal						_____ Batch Feed _____ Continuous Feed
Compactor						_____ Left/Right/Pullout Hinging _____ Front Panel _____ Trim Kit Width If Retaining Existing _____
Built-in Can Opener						_____ Under Cabinet _____ In Wall
Built-in Toaster						_____ Under Cabinet _____ In Wall
Built-in Mixing Center						_____ Under Cabinet _____ In Counter
Telephone/Intercom						
Television						
Radio						
VCR						
Washer						
Dryer						
Fixtures and Fittings						
Sink #1						_____ Single _____ Double _____ Triple _____ Small/Large Bowl _____ St. Steel _____ Porcelain Steel _____ Cast Iron _____ Solid Surface _____ Quartz/Sila. Other _____ Mounting Method _____ No. of Holes _____ Size If Retaining Existing _____ Drain Board: Right _____ Left _____
Sink #2						_____ Single _____ Double _____ Triple _____ Small/Large Bowl _____ St. Steel _____ Porcelain Steel _____ Cast Iron _____ Solid Surface _____ Quartz/Sila. Other _____ Mounting Method _____ No. of Holes _____ Size If Retaining Existing _____ Drain Board: Right _____ Left _____

Category	Source					Description
		Furn By		Install By		
	Use Exist	KS	O/OA	KS	O/OA	Check Appropriate Space(s)
Fixtures (Continued)						
Faucet(s)						_____ 1 Handle _____ 2 Handle _____ With Spray _____ Lotion Disp. _____ Water Purifier Other _____
Instant Hot Water						_____ In Sink _____ In Counter
Chilled Water						_____ In Sink _____ In Counter
Lotion Dispenser						_____ In Sink _____ In Counter
Water Purifier						Located _____
Windows and Doors						

Windows						Casing: _____ Match Existing _____ Finish
						          _____ Replace All _____ Finish
						          _____ Size _____ Profile
						Size _____ Finish _____
						_____ Slider _____ Bow
						_____ Casement _____ Bay
						_____ Double-Hung _____ Support
						_____ Skylight _____ Roof
						Other _____
						Exterior Wall Patch _____
						Sink Vent Relocation _____
						Pass-Thru Surfacing _____
						New Window Sizes: _____
						#1 _____ Screen _____
						#2 _____ Screen _____
						#3 _____ Screen _____
						#4 _____ Screen _____

Doors						Casing: _____ Match Existing _____ Finish
						          _____ Replace All _____ Finish
						          _____ Size _____ Profile
						New Doors:
						_____ Solid Core Size _____
						       Hinge _____ Screen _____
						_____ Steel Size _____
						       Hinge _____ Screen _____
						_____ Hollow Core Size _____ Hinge _____
						_____ Bifold Size _____ Hinge _____
						_____ Pocket Size _____ Hinge _____
						_____ Accordian Size _____ Hinge _____
						Other _____ Size _____ Hinge _____
						Ext. Wall Patch _____
						Int. Wall /Floor Patch _____
						Hardware: Finish _____
						_____ Passage _____ Knob
						_____ Privacy _____ Lever

Category	Source					Description
	Furn By		Install By			
	Use Exist	KS	O/OA	KS	O/OA	Check Appropriate Space(s)
Flooring						
Floor Preparation						Removal _____ Leveling & Shimming _____ Subfloor Material _____ Underlayment: _____ Plywood _____ Particleboard Baseboard _____ Transition Treatment _____
Floor Covering						_____ Wood _____ Carpet _____ Vinyl _____ Natural Stone _____ Tile Size _____ Grout _____
Decorative Surfaces						
Wall Covering						_____ Tile _____ Wood _____ Wallpaper _____ Mirror _____ Paint Other _____
Wall Preparation						_____ New Plaster/ _____ Clean Drywall _____ Patch Exist. _____ Remove Exist. Covering Other _____ Repairs _____
Ceiling Covering						_____ Paint _____ Wallpaper _____ Suspended _____ Vaulted _____ Skylights Other _____
Ceiling Preparation						_____ New Plaster/ _____ Clean Drywall _____ Plywood _____ Stapled/Glued _____ Patch Exist. _____ Remove Exist. Covering Other _____ Repairs _____
Window Treatment						_____ Blinds _____ Fabric _____ Shutters Other _____
Construction						(Describe Required Work)
Electrical						
Plumbing						
General Carpentry						
Demolition						
Trash Removal						
Structural Changes						
Installation						

Miscellaneous Information: _____

BMF6

Existing Construction Details

Construction:

Construction of House: ☐ Single Story ☐ Multi Story   Style of house _____

Room above or below kitchen: _____

Condition and covering of walls: _____

floors: _____

ceilings: _____

soffit/fascia: _____

Squareness of corners _____ Parallel walls to within 3/4" _____

Construction of Floor: ☐ Slab ☐ Frame

Direction of floor joist: ☐ Parallel to longest wall ☐ Perpendicular to longest wall   Joist Height _____

Exterior: ☐ Brick ☐ Aluminum ☐ Stucco ☐ Wood ☐ Other

Interior: ☐ Drywall ☐ Lath & Plaster ☐ Wood ☐ Stone/Brick

Windows can be changed: ☐ Yes ☐ No

Windows: ☐ Sliders ☐ Double-Hung ☐ Skylights ☐ Casement ☐ Greenhouse

Doors can be relocated: ☐ Yes ☐ No

Location of walls can be changed: ☐ Yes ☐ No

Sewage System: ☐ City Service ☐ Septic System   Other _____

Type of roof material _____ Age of roof _____

Household heating/cooling system _____ Age of home _____

Access:

Can equipment fit into room? _____

Basement _____ Crawlspace _____ Attic _____

Material Storage _____ Trash Collection Area _____

Plumbing:

Location of existing vent stack _____ Type of trap_____

Electrical:

GFCI existing: ☐ Yes ☐ No

New wiring access: ☐ Hard ☐ Average ☐ Easy

Existing electrical service capacity _____ The following # of 120V circuits available: _____

The following # of 240V circuits available: _____

Miscellaneous Information: _____

_____

_____

_____

_____

BMF6

Existing Wall Elevation Dimensioning

Windows									
No.	A	B	C	D	E	F	G	H	I
1									
2									

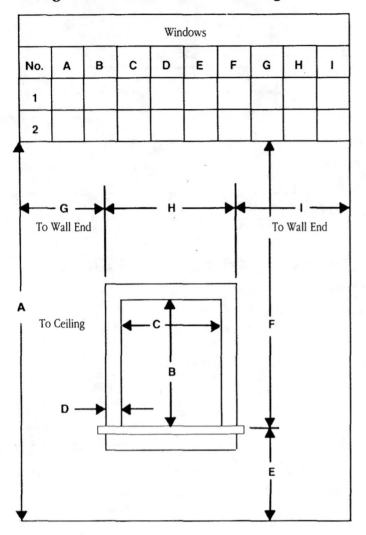

1. Register or Fan							
No.	A	B	C	D	E	F	G
1							
2							

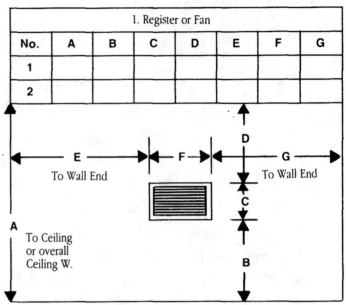

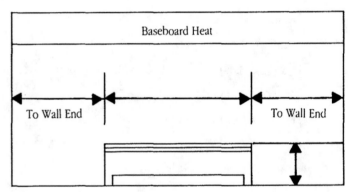

Baseboard Heat

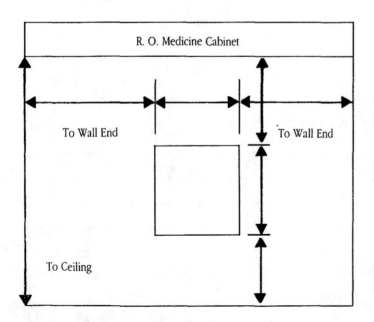

R. O. Medicine Cabinet

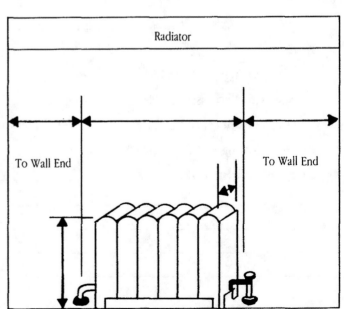

Radiator

Existing Appliance Dimensioning

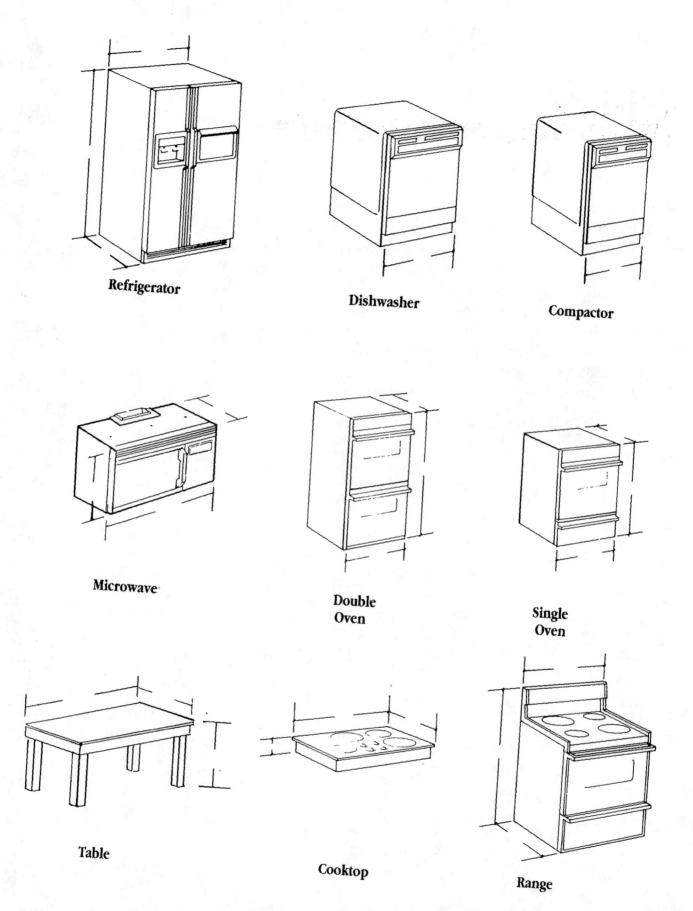

Refrigerator

Dishwasher

Compactor

Microwave

Double Oven

Single Oven

Table

Cooktop

Range

BMF6

SPECIFICATIONS FORM

The **Specifications Form** is comprised of two (2) separate forms:

1. Standard Specifications Form for Kitchen Design and Installation - BMF12
2. Standard Specifications Form for Bathroom Design and Installation - BMF13.

The **Specifications Form** will provide:

1. a standard specification form for all personnel.
2. ample room for a detailed description of the products or details.
3. a deterrent to overlooking any part of the project, including labor.
4. a format similar to the estimate form.

The **Specification Form** should be completed once the design is finished.

STANDARD SPECIFICATIONS FOR KITCHEN DESIGN AND INSTALLATION

Name: _____

Home Address: _____

City: _____ State _____ Phone (Home) _____

(Office) _____

(Office) _____

(Jobsite) _____

Jobsite Address _____

By

Hereafter called "Kitchen Specialist"

Kitchen Specialist will supply and deliver only such equipment and material as described in these specifications. Labor connected with this kitchen installation will be supplied by the Kitchen Specialist only as herein specified.

Any equipment, material and labor designated here as "Owner's responsibility" must be furnished and completed by the Owner, or the Owner's Agent in accordance with the work schedule established by the Kitchen Specialist.

Equipment, material and labor not included in these specifications can be supplied by the Kitchen Specialist at an additional cost for which authorization must be given in writing by the Owner, or the Owner's Agent.

All dimensions and cabinet designations shown on the floor plan, which are part of these specifications, are subject to adjustments dictated by job conditions.

All surfaces of walls, ceilings, windows and woodwork, except those of factory-made equipment, will be left unpainted or unfinished unless otherwise specified.

If specifications call for re-use of existing equipment, no responsibility on the part of the Kitchen Specialist for appearance, functioning or service shall be implied.

For factory-made equipment, the manufacturer's specifications for quality, design, dimensions, function and installation shall in any case take precedence over any others.

(over)

Cabinetry (as per approved drawing)

Manufacturer

Cabinet Exterior   ☐ Wood   ☐ Steel   ☐ Decorative Laminate   ☐ Other

Cabinet Exterior Finish   Cabinet Interior Material   Finish

Door Style   Hardware

Special Cabinet Notes

Furnished By   ☐ Kitchen Specialist   ☐ Owner   ☐ Owner's Agent

Installation By   ☐ Kitchen Specialist   ☐ Owner   ☐ Owner's Agent

Countertops (as per approved drawing)

Manufacturer   Material

Design Details   Deck Thickness _____ Color _____   Edging Thickness _____ Color _____

Backsplash   Thickness _____ Height _____ Color _____   End Splash   Thickness _____ Height _____ Color _____

Special Countertop Notes

Furnished By   ☐ Kitchen Specialist   ☐ Owner   ☐ Owner's Agent

Installation By   ☐ Kitchen Specialist   ☐ Owner   ☐ Owner's Agent

Fascia & Soffit (as per approved drawing)

Construction   ☐ Flush   ☐ Extended   ☐ Recessed   ☐ N/A (Open)

Finish Material

Special Fascia/Soffit Notes

Furnished By   ☐ Kitchen Specialist   ☐ Owner   ☐ Owner's Agent

Installation By   ☐ Kitchen Specialist   ☐ Owner   ☐ Owner's Agent

Lighting System

Description	Qty.	Model Number	Finish	Lamp Req.	Furnished By		Installed By	
					K.S.	O/OA	K.S.	O/OAS

Special Lighting System Notes

KEY

K.S. = Kitchen Specialist   O = Owner   OA = Owner's Agent

Appliances

Item	Brand Name	Model	Finish	Fuel	Furnished By K.S.	Furnished By O/OA	Installed By K.S.	Installed By O/OA	Hook Up By K.S.	Hook Up By O/OA
Range										
Cooktop										
Oven										
Hood										
Warming Drawer										
Indoor Grill										
Microwave										
Trim Kit										
Refrigerator										
Ice Maker										
Trim Kit										
Freezer										
Trim Kit										
Dishwasher										
Trim Kit										
Conversion Kit										
Food Waste Disposal										
Compactor										
Trim Kit										
Built-in Can Opener										
Built-in Toaster										
Built-in Mixing Ctr.										
Telephone/Intercom										
Television										
Radio										
VCR										
Washer										
Dryer										

Special Appliance Notes:

Fixtures and Fittings

Item	Brand Name	Model	Finish	Fuel	Furnished By K.S.	Furnished By O/OA	Installed By K.S.	Installed By O/OA	Hook Up By K.S.	Hook Up By O/OA
Kitchen Sink #1										
No. of Holes										
Faucet										
Strainer										
Kitchen Sink #2										
No. of Holes										
Faucet										
Strainer										
Hot Water Dispenser										
Chilled Water Dispenser										
Lotion Dispenser										
Water Purifier										

Special Fixtures and Fittings Notes:

BMF12

Windows and Doors

Item	Brand Name	Model	Finish	Hardware	Furnished By K.S.	O/OA	Installed By K.S.	O/OA

Special Window and Door Notes:

Flooring

	Furnished By K.S.	O/OA	Installed By K.S.	O/OA
Removal of Existing Floor Covering				
Preparation of Floor for New Surface				
Installation of Subfloor/Underlayment				
New Floor Covering Material Description:				
Manufacturer Pattern Name				
Pattern Number Pattern Repeat				
Floor Covering Installation				
Baseboard Material				
Transition Treatment				
Remove and Repair Water Damaged Area				
Special Flooring Notes				

Decorative Surfaces (wall, ceiling, window materials)

Removal Work: Wall _____ Ceiling _____ Window _____   Preparation Work: Wall _____ Ceiling _____ Window _____

Description	Brand Name	Model	Finish	Material Quantity	Furnished By K.S.	O/OA	Installed By K.S.	O/OA

Special Decorative Surface Notes:

BMF12

Electrical Work (except as described above in specific equipment sections)

	Furnished By		Installed By	
	K.S.	O/OA	K.S.	O/OA
Heating System Alteration				
New Service Panel				
Code Update				
Details				

Plumbing (except as described above in specific equipment sections)

	Furnished By		Installed By	
	K.S.	O/OA	K.S.	O/OA
Heating System Alterations				
New Rough-in Requirements				
Modifications to Existing Lines				
Details				

General Carpentry (except as described above in specific equipment sections)

	Furnished By		Installed By	
	K.S.	O/OA	K.S.	O/OA
Demolition Work				
Existing Fixture and Equipment Removal				
Trash Removal				
Reconstruction Work (Except as Previously Stated)				
Windows				
Doors				
Interior Walls				
Exterior Walls				
Details				

BMF12

Miscellaneous Work

	Responsibility	
	K.S.	O/OA
Trash Removal		
Jobsite/Room Cleanup		
Building Permit(s)		
Structural Engineering/Architectural Fees		
Inspection Fees		
Jobsite Delivery		
Other		

I have read these specifications and approve:

Accepted: _____

Accepted: _____

Date: _____

Authorized Company Representative

By: _____

By: _____

BMF12

Date: _____

THE CONTRACT

The Contract, BMF14 and BMF14A, is the legally binding agreement that clearly defines what products and services will be supplied by the kitchen specialist.

The National Kitchen & Bath Association publishes the attached contract. All legal documents should be reviewed and approved by the firm's legal counsel before implementation.

Approved by the

National Kitchen & Bath Association

Between ....Purchaser

Home Address ....

City .... State .... Zip ....

Phone Number ....

Delivery Address ....

And Seller

1. The Seller agrees to furnish the materials and services set forth in the drawings (numbered.................................
and dated ....) and specifications annexed hereto.
The Purchaser agrees to make payment therefore in accordance with the schedule of payment.

    Contract Price .... $ ....

    Sales Tax (if applicable) .... $ ....

    .... $ ....

    Total Purchase Price .... $ ....

Schedule of Payment:

    Upon signing of this agreement .... $ ....

    Upon delivery of cabinets from manufacturer .... $ ....

    Upon delivery of .... $ ....

    Upon substantial installation of .... $ ....

This contract includes the terms and provisions as set forth herein. Please read and sign where indicated.

2. The standard form of warranty shall apply to the service and equipment furnished (except where other warranties of purchased products apply). The warranty shall become effective when signed by the Seller and delivered to the Purchaser. The warranty is for one year materials and labor.

3. The delivery date, when given, shall be deemed approximate and performance is subject to delays caused by strikes, fires, acts of God or other reasons not under the control of the Seller, as well as the availability of the product at the time of delivery.

4. The Purchaser agrees to accept delivery of the product or products when ready. The risk of loss, as to damage or destruction, shall be upon the Purchaser upon the delivery and receipt of the product.

5. The Purchaser understands that the products described are specially designed and custom built and that the Seller takes immediate steps upon execution of this Agreement to design, order and construct those items set forth herein; therefore, this Agreement is not subject to cancellation by the Purchaser for any reason.

6. No installation, plumbing, electrical, flooring, decorating or other construction work is to be provided unless specifically set forth herein. In the event the Seller is to perform the installation, it is understood that the price agreed upon herein does not include possible expense entailed in coping with hidden or unknown contingencies found at the job site. In the event such contingencies arise and the Seller is required to furnish labor or materials or otherwise perform work not provided for or contemplated by the Seller, the actual costs plus (   )% thereof will be paid for by the Purchaser. Contingencies include but are not limited to: inability to reuse existing water, vent, and waste pipes; air shafts, ducts, grilles, louvres and registers; the relocation of concealed pipes, risers, wiring or conduits, the presence of which cannot be determined until the work has started; or imperfections, rotting or decay in the structure or parts thereof necessitating replacement.

7. Title to the item sold pursuant to this Agreement shall not pass to the Purchaser until the full price as set forth in this Agreement is paid to the Seller.

8. Delays in payment shall be subject to interest charges of (   )% per annum, and in no event higher than the interest rate provided by law. If the Seller is required to engage the services of a collection agency or an attorney, the Purchaser agrees to reimburse the Seller for any reasonable amounts expended in order to collect the unpaid balance.

9. If any provision of this Agreement is declared invalid by any tribunal, the remaining provisions of the Agreement shall not be affected thereby.

10. This Agreement sets forth the entire transaction between the parties; any and all prior Agreements, warranties or representations made by either party are superseded by this Agreement. All changes in this Agreement shall be made by a separate document and executed with the same formalities. No agent of the Seller, unless authorized in writing by the Seller, has any authority to waive, alter, or enlarge this contract, or to make any new or substituted or different contracts, representations, or warranties.

BMF14-A

11.   The Seller retains the right upon breach of this Agreement by the Purchaser to sell those items in the Seller's possession. In effecting any resale on breach of this Agreement by the Purchaser, the Seller shall be deemed to act in the capacity of agent for the Purchaser. The purchaser shall be liable for any net deficiency on resale.

12.   The Seller agrees that it will perform this contract in conformity with customary industry practices. The Purchaser agrees that any claim for adjustment shall not be reason or cause for failure to make payment of the purchase price in full. Any unresolved controversy or claim arising from or under this contract shall be settled by arbitration and judgment upon the award rendered may be entered in any court of competent jurisdiction. The arbitration shall be held under the rules of the American Arbitration Association.

Accepted: ....
                                         Purchaser

Accepted: ....   Accepted: ....
                                                                            Purchaser

Date: ....   Date: ....

BMF14-A

JOB PROGRESS

The **Job Progress** is comprised of one form, BMF16.

The **Job Progress** form will provide:

1. an easy review of the job and the status of each section.
2. a ready instrument for scheduling of the job as it progresses.

The **Job Progress** form should be attached to the inside cover of the job folder, for easy access. The expeditor or individual responsible for ordering labor, product and/or material should complete this form as the information is received or scheduled, generally on a daily basis.

JOB PROGRESS

Name _____ Date Signed _____

Street _____ City/State _____ Zip _____

Home Phone _____ Business Phone _____ Permit # _____

Item	Supplier	PO# and Date Ordered	Due Scheduled	Received Measured	Delivered Installed	Notes
1. Cabinets						
2. Counter Top						
Deck						
Backsplash						
3. Flooring						
4. Decorating						
Material						
Painter						
Paperhanger						
Other						
5. Lighting						
6. Equipment						
Appliances & Fixtures						
7. Plumbing				Rough-in Insp.	Top-out Insp.	Finish Insp.
8. Electrical				Rough-in Insp.	Finish Insp.	
9. Construction & Alteration				Job Insp.	Tear-out	Construction Insp.
				Patch	Set	Trim
10. Inspection						
11. Trash						
12. Extras						

© 1991 NKBA BMF16-8/91

 **CHANGE ORDERS**

The **Change Order System** is comprised of two (2) similar forms:
1. Change in Plans and Specifications, BMF 15
2. Change in Plans and Specifications, BMF 15A

The **Change Order** forms will provide:
1. a legal agreement authorizing and acknowledging any changes made in the contract, plans and/or specifications.
2. cost accounting information for the changes.

The **Change Order** forms should be completed whenever the client requests changes in the contract, specifications and/or plans of the project.

The changes should be explicit and costed in order to indicate any credit or additional charges for the changes.

All parties signing the original contract for the project are required to sign the "Change in Plans and Specifications" form.

CHANGE IN PLANS AND SPECIFICATIONS

Client: _____ Date: _____

Street: _____ Job #: _____

City: _____ Change Order #: _____

Job Address: _____

I hereby authorize _____ to make the following change from the work
originally set forth in the plans and specifications.

Description	Charge	Cost

Additional charge ☐ credit ☐ for above work is $ _____

Payment will be made as follows _____

Authorized signature _____ _____
                              client   client

Authorized signature _____ Date _____
                         kitchen specialist

© 1991 NKBA   BMF15A-8/91

CHANGE IN PLANS AND SPECIFICATIONS

Client: _____ Date: _____

Street: _____ Job #: _____

City: _____ Change Order #: _____

Job Address: _____

I hereby authorize _____ to make the following change from the work
originally set forth in the plans and specifications.

Description	Charge

Additional charge ☐ credit ☐ for above work is $ _____

Payment will be made as follows _____

Authorized signature _____ _____
                              client   client

Authorized signature _____ Date _____
                         kitchen specialist

© 1991 NKBA   BMF15A-8/91

JOB COMPLETION & FOLLOW UP SYSTEM

The **Job Completion and Follow Up System** is comprised of several forms and letters:

1. Completion Report, BMF18
2. NKBA Limited Warranty, BMF19
3. A follow-up letter, BMF20
4. Client Evaluation Form, BMF21

The **Job Completion and Follow Up System** will provide:

1. a signed completion form for your files, indicating your client's satisfaction.
2. an opportunity to supply your client with the warranty form.
3. an opportunity to effect the collection of the final payment.
4. an opportunity to receive additional prospects and a satisfied client.

The **Job Completion and Follow Up System** should be designated as the sales consultant's responsibility, and he/she should visit the job site on the final day of completion. That individual should inspect the job, take care of minor adjustments or complaints, present the warranty, have the Completion Report signed by the client and present the final bill. The client should retain the warranty, sign the Completion Report, and pay the final bill.

The signed copy of the Completion Report should be placed in the job folder for future reference.

The Client Evaluation form should be left with the client to be completed and mailed to your office. When it is received, it should be reviewed by the manager or owner, initialed, and placed in the job folder. Any names, prospects or recommendations should be handled as leads and assigned to the sales consultant that handled the job.

The Finest Professionals in the Kitchen & Bath Industry

National Kitchen & Bath Association℠

The firm (warrantor), whose name, address and phone number appears on the face of this document, warrants and presents to the party in the space designated the following:

Materials covered by this warranty, supplied and installed by the firm, or under its direction and supervision shall be guaranteed for a period of one (1) year from the date given against defects in workmanship and material.

Installation performed by the firm, persons in its direct employ or subcontractors employed specifically by it's warranted to be of good workmanlike quality in accordance with customary industry practices.

All articles supplied by the firm but manufactured by others shall not be covered by the warranty other than to the extent of the warranty given by such manufacturer or his distributor from whom the firm obtained the product.

In the event of defects in workmanship and material and the failure of products supplied by the firm to conform with the agreement or warranty, the firm will repair or replace said product or material; provided, that the defect or malfunction was not due to accidents, alterations by the customer, misuse, abuse or neglect. The firm shall not be responsible for shipment and installation costs as the result of repairing or replacing the item.

In order to obtain performance of any warranty obligation the customer shall immediately contact the firm in writing and cooperate fully in supplying the necessary information, as well as access to the premises, relative to the defect or malfunction.

The item purchased under this agreement shall be used exclusively by the customer and by no other person, and therefore there shall be no third party beneficiary to any of the warranties, express or implied, contained in this agreement.

The implied warranties of fitness and merchantability are to coincide with the duration of this warranty and not extend beyond that date. Some states do not allow limitations on how long an implied warranty lasts, so the above limitation may not apply to you.

The firm shall not be liable for consequential damages or loss caused by the malfunction of equipment not specifically installed by its own employees or subcontractors in it employ. Some states do not allow the exclusion or limitation of incidental or consequential damages, so the above limitation or exclusion may not apply to you.

This warranty gives you specific legal rights, and you may also have other rights which vary from state to state.

The firm warrants the materials identified on the cover of this warranty to be designed and engineered in accordance with the standards advocated and set forth by customary industry practices.

- -

Completion Report

Client _____   Date _____

Street _____   Home Phone _____ _____

City _____ State _____ Zip _____   Work Phone _____

This certifies that all labor and materials specifiec in the plans and specifications dated _____ , have been inspected and accepted as complete and satisfactory.

Client _____

(Please type on your letterhead)

Dear

We have recently completed some work for you and we know that you will be pleased with that investment in your home for a long time.

Knowing that the greatest source of our new business is through the recommendations of satisfied clients, we would greatly appreciate it if you would complete the evaluation letter enclosed and return it to us in the envelope provided.

If for any reason a problem develops, please do not hesitate to call on us. The number to call for service is (type in your service telephone number).

Once again, many thanks for the opportunity of adding your name to the constantly growing list of our satisfied clients.

Sincerely,

(company name)

(Signed by the President or owner)

 **COMPLETION REPORT**

Client _____   Date _____

Street _____   Home Phone _____

City/State _____ Zip _____   Work Phone _____

This certifies that all labor and materials specified in the plans and specifications dated _____ , have been inspected and accepted as complete and satisfactory.

Client _____

Date _____

 **COMPLETION REPORT**

Client _____   Date _____

Street _____   Home Phone _____

City/State _____ Zip _____   Work Phone _____

This certifies that all labor and materials specified in the plans and specifications dated _____ , have been inspected and accepted as complete and satisfactory.

Client _____

Date _____

(Please type on your letterhead)

Dear

Thank you for allowing us to serve you!

If we have failed to live up to your expectations, we hope that you will tell us why so that we can please you in the future.

We are constantly seeking ways and means to improve the quality of our service. Any deficiencies which your comments might reflect will be corrected immediately.

Please answer the following questions and mail in the envelope provided:

	excellent	good	poor
Was the showroom visitation conducted to your satisfaction?	☐	☐	☐
Was the designer/consultant helpful?	☐	☐	☐
Was the designer/consultant available when needed?	☐	☐	☐
Were the workman neat and clean?	☐	☐	☐
Was the job completed in a satisfactory manner?	☐	☐	☐
Were your communications with the company handled satisfactorily?	☐	☐	☐
Would you recommend our company to your friend?	☐	☐	☐

Any other comments: _____
_____
_____
_____

If any of your friends or acquaintances are interested in any of our products or services, may we use your name as a reference? (Please list the name and address of the interested person.)
_____
_____
_____

Thank you very much for the above information. We sincerely hope that we can be of service to you again in the future.

SERVICE CALL SYSTEM

The **Service Call System** is comprised of one "Customer Complaint Form", BMF 17.

The **Customer Complaint Form**, BMF 17, will provide:

1. a record of all customer complaint calls.
2. an instrument to implement corrective action.
3. a permanent record of job deficiencies by product or trade.

The **Customer Complaint Form** is to be completed whenever a client has reason to request service to rectify a complaint. After the call is received, the Customer Complaint Form is filed in a loose-leaf binder (preferably red) as the top page. The binder is placed on the manager's desk (or expeditor). The job folder for the particular job is removed from the file for review by the manager (or expeditor). When it is ascertained that the call is a warranty (no charge) adjustment, the appropriate trade or service agency is notified. If the service required is an out-of-warranty adjustment, the client is notified by telephone that the service will be performed as soon as possible, with proper coordination of the service agency, and explanation of the charges that will be made is given.

After the service agency or tradesman notifies you that the corrective action has been completed, the form is noted with the requirements and what action was completed. The client is contacted to see if the service adjustment has been completed and everything is satisfactory.

Customer Complaint Form, BMF 17, is then filed in the client's job folder for future reference.

CUSTOMER COMPLAINT FORM

Customer's Name: _____ Home Phone: _____ Work Phone: _____

Address: _____ City/State: _____ Zip: _____

Date of Complaint: _____ Date Installed: _____ Job #: _____

Nature of Complaint: (be specific): _____

_____

_____

_____

_____

_____

_____

Complaint Received By: _____

Corrective Action Taken: _____

_____

_____

_____

_____

Corrective Action Taken By: _____ Date: _____

Complaint Corrected: _____ Date: _____

Requirements: _____

_____

_____

_____

_____

Completion Noted By: _____

Verified With Customer By: _____ Date: _____

Remarks: _____

_____

_____

_____

SAMPLE